Y0-BCG-276

THE MARCH
OF DEMOCRACY

THE MARCH
OF DEMOCRACY

THE RISE OF THE UNION

By
James Truslow Adams

ILLUSTRATED

CHARLES SCRIBNER'S SONS
NEW YORK · · LONDON
1934

PREFACE

PREFACE

THE history of America as contrasted with that of Europe is as yet brief but by no means simple. Beginning with conditions in the Old World which resulted in the discovery and peopling of the New, we have to trace the rise of thirteen distinct commonwealths, the formation of a new nation welded out of them, the hostile alignment of great sections in that nation, one of the greatest military struggles of modern times, and the emergence of a united country with the development of one of the greatest of modern democratic and industrial civilizations.

Both in the earlier and latest periods of our history, we have been entangled in the politics and wars of Europe. We have never really been isolated, and not only streams of immigrants but streams of cultural influence have steadily come to us from across the sea. These, as well as the political and military entanglements, require frequent digressions from our own domestic story to enable us to understand it by reference to European currents. Moreover, the simplicity of the older writing of history, dealing almost wholly with wars and politics, has long since passed. The story of how thirteen small agricultural dependencies became the Federal nation of today, independent, highly industrialized, with a culture and an outlook becoming daily more and more "American," is a story which must be woven of many strands, strands somewhat difficult to gather owing to the vastness of our territorial extent and the differences in our several sections.

In dealing with the United States in a single volume or two, one must to a great extent choose between a narrative of events and a philosophical interpretation. I have at various times and in different ways tried to do what I could to interpret both our past and present. But it is impossible either to interpret for ourselves or properly to appraise the interpretations of others, unless we have a clear understanding of the course of events in the past. Generalizing and philosophizing are delightful and fascinating tasks, but likely to be of little worth without a more prosaic basis of correct factual knowledge.

In the history now offered, to be completed to the present day in two volumes, I have therefore undertaken to lay such a foundation for the reader, and to tell as accurately and impartially as possible the story of the rise of our nation, touching on as many aspects in as much detail as space permits. The old type of history of a generation or two ago had its faults of omission. There is some danger, however, that in correcting these, we may have run somewhat into another fault, that of stressing too much one or another of the factors, such as the economic one, which are rightly considered to be of great influence. History, like human nature, is vastly complex. There is no one key,—economics, religion, politics or what-not,—to an understanding of the whole. Here again I have tried to hold the balance even, and not to substitute for the old "drum and trumpet" merely the voices and motives of the market place, or a picturesque account of manners and arts and thought.

I realize fully the difficulties of such a task, and gladly acknowledge my obligation for many valuable suggestions and corrections made by Professor Allan Nevins and Doctor Will D. Howe.

JAMES TRUSLOW ADAMS.

WASHINGTON, D. C.,
  April 19, 1932.

CONTENTS

CONTENTS

ILLUSTRATIONS

HALF-TONES

ILLUSTRATIONS

ILLUSTRATIONS

ILLUSTRATIONS

ILLUSTRATIONS

TEXT CUTS AND MAPS

ILLUSTRATIONS

ILLUSTRATIONS

ILLUSTRATIONS

THE MARCH
OF DEMOCRACY

CHAPTER I

DISCOVERY AND SETTLEMENT

NOTHING is known with any certainty as to the origin of human life on the American continent. The history of the race which has been called "Indian," owing to the mistake of Columbus which we shall note presently, is shrouded in the mist of inference. The earliest ancestors of the barbarians whom the white men found inhabiting the more temperate and tropical regions of the New World may have come from Asia by way of the islands in Behring Strait or even across a land bridge which may have existed in earlier geologic ages.

Nothing, however, can be determined with the evidence yet at hand, and in any case these primitive "Americans" have little to do with the America of today. Unlike the original Britons, whose blood became intermingled with that of the successive invading hordes of Saxons, Danes, and Normans, the Indians never mixed their blood with that of the English settlers who were to become dominant in North America. The history and present culture of Mexico cannot be understood without ample consideration of Indian influence, but those of the present United States need take little heed of the aborigines. They have, indeed, left their traces. A good many words of Indian origin are embedded in our vocabulary and we owe to the savages a large number of our most beautiful and interesting place-names. The earliest white settlers were greatly helped by the Indian's knowledge of woodcraft, by the use of important foods, notably Indian corn or maize, known to the natives, and by other items in the Indian culture. But such influences were comparatively slight as compared with those of races elsewhere who have really fused their blood, language and culture with those of the conquering race.

The white man himself, for the most part, regarded the Indian merely as forming the same sort of obstacle to his own advance and success as was offered by the wild animals or the hindrances of

I

climate and topography. Indeed, until very recently, we have treated them as we have treated all other forces opposing our steady advance across the continent and our subduing of it as quickly as possible to our own wants. The record of our dealings with the first owners of our soil is one in which, except for isolated instances, we can take no pride, and which has left a bloody stain on the pages recording almost every decade of our history.

That history, unlike the records of the great powers of the Old World, begins with marked abruptness. In Europe, race gives place to race, and civilization to civilization, and in tracing them back the authentic record merges into myth and legend. It is true that our roots lie deep in the past of the European nations from which came the multitudes of immigrants who, with their descendants, have peopled the United States. Nevertheless, the passage overseas combined with our later breaking of all political ties and our failure to assimilate and mingle with any native population has served to delimit our history within a comparatively short period of recorded time.

Many of our institutions, like our language, come to us from England, and we must take account of influences from the many ancestral lands whence our people are descended, but as generally understood and accepted by us, our history begins with the first discoveries and settlements along our coasts, little more than four centuries ago at most.

Nearly five hundred years before that beginning, Europeans may indeed have landed on our shores. Almost as little is definitely known, however, of the possible explorations of the Norsemen within the present limits of the United States as of the origin of the Indians whom they may have encountered. About 982 Erik Thorwaldson, sailing from Norway, discovered Greenland, and a colony was later planted there. His son, Leif Erikson, and others discovered lands farther west, and efforts have been made to locate their landings all the way from Labrador to Long Island Sound but nothing can be ascertained with certainty as to the localities suggested by the very uncertain data given in the old Sagas.

Some remains, formerly believed to have dated from their time, such as the old mill at Newport, have long since been proved to belong to later periods, and learned discussions over such inscriptions as those on the Dighton Rock have proved nothing. One of the most interesting of these relics, and one which seems to have some real claim to authenticity, is the "Kensington Stone" found in the roots of a tree at Kensington, Douglas County, Minnesota, in 1898. The runic inscription on it indicates that the point where it was found marks the southern limit of an expedition of Norsemen who came overland from Hudson's Bay in 1362; and the summing up of the evidence in 1932 would seem to give this record the best claim, which, however, is only a claim, to being the earliest monument by white men within our limits. These Norse voyages and explorations, wherever they may have been made, were without further influence on history and apparently had nothing to do with the later and authentic discoveries.

These latter were occasioned by reasons quite dissimilar to the more or less adventurous spirit which led Leif and possibly others to voyage westward from the little colony in Greenland.

The European world of the fifteenth century, descended from Greece and Rome, was hemmed in on all sides by impassable barriers of sea and desert or by the barbarian hordes which were beginning to press in on it from the East. This outer Barbarian world was practically as little known geographically as it had been in the days of the Roman Empire. It was a world, however, with which Europe, as always, had commercial relations, the greatest and most lucrative trade being with the mysterious "East." From China, the Spice Islands, India and many lands, the spices, pearls, jewels, rugs, silks, and other commodities of which Europe had need found their way by trade routes hidden from the knowledge of European merchants. These routes had their western termini in ports of the Mediterranean, encircling its eastern end from Constantinople to Alexandria.

In the fourteenth, fifteenth, and early sixteenth centuries, the warlike hordes of the Ottoman Turks spread out from their centre in Asia Minor. Steadily pursuing their conquests, they passed the Bosphorus and captured Constantinople in 1453, and had overrun Egypt by 1522. All the termini of Europe's greatest trade routes thus fell into their hands. The process had been gradual, and the Turks did not prohibit all trade, but in the long period of conquest, the disturbances of violence and war, new taxes, and other hindrances to the old established commerce gravely affected the trading life of Europe.

This threatened throttling of the business of the European peoples came at just the period when, after ten centuries of readjustments, they were beginning to feel a great rebound of energies within the new forms of institutional and intellectual life which they had slowly evolved. Moreover, due to the steady northwestward thrust of the Turks, this superabundant energy, greater even than that of the Roman Empire, was compressed within a comparatively small area. To the south, the Sahara Desert and the hordes of Islam set an impassable barrier. To the west and north were unknown or frozen seas, mysterious and terrifying. European energy was rapidly rising but walls seemed to be closing in on it. It was as though a liquid were being brought to the boiling point in a container which was contracting. Vent or explosion was inevitable. Thanks to ocean exploration a vent was found, and within four centuries European civilization was to spread over the whole globe.

In the fifteenth century, sensitive to the increasing difficulties of the Oriental trade by the old routes, and ignorant of the great downward protuberance of the African continent, Portuguese explorers sought to find a way to the Orient by sailing eastward south of the Sahara. If successful they hoped to tap the trade at its source and to eliminate the land routes and the Turks. Finally after two generations of advance, Bartholomew Diaz rounded the Cape of Good Hope. He had proceeded far enough, before being forced to turn back by a mutinous crew, to make him sure that the goal lay just beyond. In 1498 Vasco da Gama, following the track of Diaz, reached India and saw the welcome domes of Calicut. After a voyage of 18,000 miles he returned to Portugal with a rich cargo and yet more precious knowledge. Even his predecessor, Diaz, had discovered, however, a dozen years before, that this route to the Indies would be portentously long.

Certain that the East could be reached by sea, and believing in the theory, thought by many to be incredible, that the world was round, Columbus had conceived the idea of reaching the Indies by sailing West. He hoped thus to save the long and useless journey around Africa, and had the globe been as small as he thought and had the then unknown American continents not blocked the way,

THE KENSINGTON STONE

Courtesy of the Minnesota Historical Society, St. Paul, Minnesota.

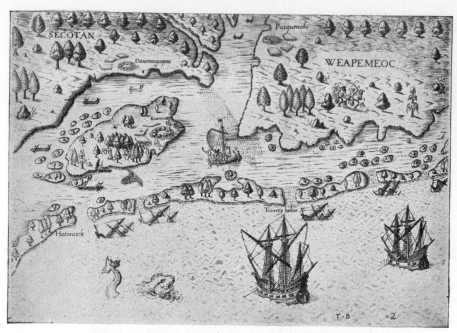

THE ARRIVAL OF THE ENGLISHMEN IN VIRGINIA

*From a drawing by John White of Raleigh's First Colony, 1585, in De Bry's
"Grand Voyages," Frankfort, 1590.*

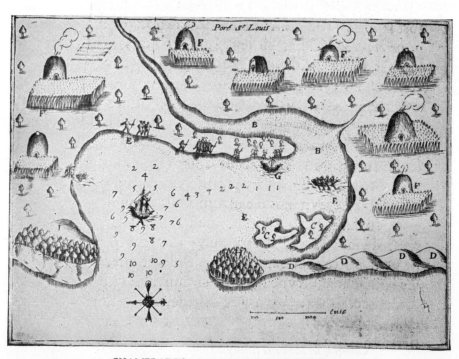

CHAMPLAIN'S MAP OF PLYMOUTH HARBOR

From Champlain's "Voyages," 1613, in the Lenox Collection, New York Public Library.

he would have outflanked the Portuguese, as they had outflanked the Turk. At last, helped by the Spanish monarchs, Ferdinand and Isabella, he set sail from Palos August 3, 1492, with his crew of eighty-nine in three tiny vessels, of which only one had a deck.

With the days passing into weeks, and the weeks into months, he and his companions voyaged westward until on the evening of October 11 a flaring light was seen as though on a shore. The next morning the explorers landed on the beach of some small island in the Bahamas which we cannot accurately identify. The story has been told so often that in the efforts to make a "fresh presentation" of American history a number of recent historians have gone so far as not to mention Columbus at all! He belongs forever, nevertheless, with the small and select band of men who by novel vision and indomitable will have influenced the entire subsequent course of history. Even to his death, after subsequent voyages, Columbus continued to believe that he had attained Cathay or "The Indies" as the Orient was called, which error accounts for the name Indians given to the inhabitants of the lands which he explored. In reality he had found a New World in which Europeans could live and which would absorb their surplus energies for centuries.

Once it was demonstrated that land could be reached by sailing west and, quite as important, that a return was possible, the original discoverer had many successors. In 1497 John Cabot, an Italian like Columbus, sailed from Bristol in the employ of the English King Henry VII, and landed either on the Newfoundland, Canadian or Labrador coasts. In 1524 Verrazano, under the flag of France, explored our shore possibly from Carolina to Newfoundland. The Spaniard Gomez was somewhere within the same limits the year following, and the maps of the time show the rapidly increasing geographical knowledge gained.

It is not necessary to chronicle the many explorations, along the coasts or in the interior, which were made in the ensuing century, for, with Verrazano, the chief three contestants to claims on America had appeared,—Spanish, English, and French. Nor is it necessary to relate the diplomatic struggles of the claimants or the first abortive attempts at settlement by the English under such dreamers of empire as Sir Humphrey Gilbert or Sir Walter Raleigh. We may pass on to the opening of the seventeenth century by which time the claims to what was at last realized to be a new continent and not the Indies had taken somewhat definite shape.

With the exception of Portuguese Brazil, Spain, with a well-established empire in Peru and Mexico, claimed—and in part possessed by colonization,—all of South and Central America, our present Gulf coast, our Southwest, and the land between the Rockies and the Pacific. France claimed all of Canada and the Mississippi Valley, while England considered as hers the whole of the North American continent from Florida to Canada and from the Atlantic to the Pacific. The conflicting character of these claims is evident, and was more than once to plunge the world into war.

The new land which had been found by Columbus and his followers was no gorgeous East with silk-clad princes, teeming millions, spices, and precious jewels. For the most part it was a forbidding wilderness inhabited by naked savages. Only where the Spaniards, encountering the barbaric cultures of the Aztecs and the Incas, had discovered treasure of silver and gold, mines, and an ample labor supply, was there easy wealth to be reaped. Quickly a transplanted Spanish culture was established based on the riches and populousness of the older barbaric kingdoms. The 160,000 Spaniards who it has been estimated were in New Spain by 1574 had libraries, printing presses, scholars, and universities long before a single Englishman had been able to establish a foothold in the North.

The French, after trying colonization in Florida, whence they were driven out by the Spaniards, established a fortified post at Quebec under the indomitable Champlain, who had explored and mapped our New England coast. From that year, 1608, they continued to hold Canada until 1763, although always with a sparse population. The French empire in America was to be ever far-flung, a sort of combined trading post and missionary enterprise gilded by imperial dreams. Since Canada apparently lacked mineral or agricultural wealth, the Indian fur trade became the dominant interest, and French traders and explorers roamed west to the Great Lakes and down the valley of the Mississippi, establishing forts and trading centres in the vast hinterland behind the Appalachians.

The influence of the French on the destinies of the continent, however, was to prove out of all proportion to the numbers and strength of the colonies. Had France not established New France and had she not been despoiled of it by the English in 1763, she would probably have had no motive to abet the English colonies in their revolt of 1776, and that revolt instead of being successful would have been merely one more of the innumerable suppressed rebellions in the history of the British Empire.

The year before Champlain built his fort at Quebec and faced the first terrible winter from which only eight of the twenty-eight settlers were to emerge alive, a handful of Englishmen had planted the first successful English colony far south in Virginia. To them the future belonged, but before picking up the thread of our own history, which will thenceforth be continuous, we must turn to observe the England of the seventeenth century, which with a population half that of London today was to send out the swarms which were destined to found a new English nation overseas.

In some respects that little, bustling, fast-changing England of 1600 was in the lead of the European nations. France was dissipating her energy in continental wars and entanglements. Spain, which in spite of the huge annual supply of gold derived from her American possessions had been steadily sinking in power and prestige, had received a staggering blow when the English defeated her Armada in 1588. Even before that the English sea-dogs—Drake, Hawkins, and the rest—had been yelping on her trail like wolves, and bringing down galleon after galleon laden with treasure. When the entire "invincible" Armada had been sunk or scattered to the winds, the daring and pretensions of English seamen rose to new heights. Spain was no longer a deterrent to any New World venture.

England was also the first of the great nations to pass from the stage of feudalism to more modern conditions, and, though both government and society were aristocratic, her plain citizens were the freest in the world. Under the Tudors, who were English to the core in all their aspirations, there had been a great outburst of conscious nationalism and patriotism. Henry the Eighth had declared the English Church independent of the Pope, and to the hatred of the French and Spanish as competitors and foreigners had been added that of Protestant for Catholic in an age when religion was a passion. Robust individualism was rampant and took many forms, whether in men of action like Drake, Raleigh, Frobisher, and

7

others, or in the brilliant band of men of letters, with Shakespeare at the head, who are still the glory of English literature. This individualism extended to more ordinary folk, business men intent on extending trade, or independent-thinking citizens deciding for themselves the problems of their spiritual life.

Puritanism was one of the forces of the period. The word has been used in many meanings but we may here consider it as applied to the movement against what were considered errors, abuses or evils in the ecclesiastical or moral life of the time. Protestantism, when it had denied the authority of the single Catholic Church, had opened the way to an anarchic individualism in the interpretation of the Bible as the Word of God; and in an era of increasing intellectual energy and personal liberty it was impossible that any organization should say to all individuals "thus far and no farther" in schism.

The Puritans were made up of all sorts of minds, from those of great noblemen, like the Earl of Warwick, or thinkers, like Milton, to illiterate cobblers or farmhands. Their protests against tenets or ceremonies of the English Church and against the manners and morals of non-Puritans were of all degrees of intensity. Some wished to reform Church or society from within, others, the Separatists, felt they must withdraw entirely. In those days, religious heresy aroused passions similar to those aroused today by economic heresies, and too radical religious beliefs were held to be as inimical to the safety of the State as are Socialism or Communism in the America of our own century. The extremer Puritans therefore suffered some persecution and feared worse. Moreover, among Protestants themselves, the demand to the right of individual interpretation of the Bible did not lead, as might have been expected, to tolerance. The individual, having found for himself what he believed to be the Truth, and convinced of its universal validity and importance, all too often felt compelled to force it on other men, and to found sects or societies in which it alone should be recognized.

About the beginning of the seventeenth century profound economic changes were also in progress. Among other things, the steady and vast flow of gold from New Spain had thrown the old price structure of goods and labor into confusion. Some classes were rising and others were falling in the economic scale. This, added to the changes from feudalism to capitalism and from agriculture to an incipient industrialism, was rapidly upsetting long-established conditions in the nation. There was much unrest and unemployment among the laboring and lower middle-classes. In the upper middle-class of "gentlemen" those who could not adjust themselves to the new order were slipping down, while others, making use of the rather abundant capital due to the great increase in Europe's gold supply, were making ventures in new trades overseas and growing rich.

Many "companies" were being formed to permit groups of these men to join in trading to Muscovy, the Levant, India, Guinea, and elsewhere, such companies being typical of a new form of economic adventure not only in England but in France, Holland, and other countries. In some cases they were formed to buy land and to colonize it, as in Ireland. In others they were primarily trading companies, but on account of the conditions of commerce this meant also control of the depot or trading station and its inhabitants established at the end of a trade route in a foreign and frequently uncivilized land.

Thus, at the time we have reached, all the conditions were ripe for England to begin the attempted exploitation of some part of the New World. Briefly, there was an enormous reservoir of energy seeking an outlet. There were many people, only a part of whom were being drained off by the colonizing projects in Ireland, who were discontented with the religious, social or economic situation in which they found themselves at home. Much unemployment on the one hand was offset by accumulations of new capital on the other in possession of energetic and adventurous merchants seeking profitable investment and accustomed to take large risks for corresponding gains.

Spanish profits from America had been colossal but that nation was no longer powerful enough to act as the growling dog in the manger of such parts of the New World as she did not actually occupy. France, although she had explored our Atlantic seaboard, had chosen to concern herself with Canada and the fur trade of the interior. The Portuguese had been excluded from North America by the Papal Bull of 1493, and the enterprising Dutch had as yet shown no interest in Western schemes or exploration. With the formation of the East India Company in 1600 the great English chartered companies had covered practically all quarters of the globe open to exploitation by English capitalists except the New World.

VIRGINIA
CHARTERS.

NUMBER I.

King JAMES I.'s Letters Patent to Sir Thomas Gates, Sir George Somers, and others, for two several Colonies and Plantations, to be made in VIRGINIA, and other Parts and Territories of AMERICA. Dated April 10, 1606.

I. JAMES, by the grace of God, King of England, Scotland, France, and Ireland, Defender of the Faith, &c. Whereas our loving and well disposed subjects, Sir Thomas Gates, and Sir George Somers, Knights, Richard Hackluit, Clerk, Prebendary of Westminster, and Edward-Maria Wingfield, Thomas Hanham, and Ralegh Gilbert, Esqrs. William Parker and George Popham, Gentlemen, and divers others of our loving subjects, have been humble suitors unto us, that We would vouchsafe unto them and may in time bring the infidels and savages, living in those parts, to human civility, and to a settled and quiet government; Do, by these our letters patents, graciously accept of, and agree to, their humble and well intended desires.

IV. And do therefore, for Us, our heirs and successors, Grant and agree, that the said Sir Thomas Gates, Sir George Somers, Richard Hackluit, and Edward-Maria Wingfield, adventurers of and for our city of London, and all such others, as are, or

KING JAMES CHARTER

As the opening of it appears in *The Charters—A Narrative of the Proceedings of the North American Colonies in Consequence of the Late Stamp Act*. Printed in London in 1766.

From the Bancroft Collection, New York Public Library.

Consequently the next step in commercial expansion inevitably pointed to North America.

On April 10, 1606, King James I granted a charter to two groups of capitalists, one group being mostly resident in London and the other in and around Plymouth. In this document, usually called the first Virginia Charter, England definitely claimed the right to that part of North America between the 34th and 45th parallels of latitude, or from about Cape Fear River to Passamaquoddy Bay. Each chartered group, or "company," was given the right to a hundred miles of coast, stretching a hundred miles inland, for colonization, the London Company having the exclusive right to plant south of latitude 38 and the Plymouth Company north of 41. The intervening strip was open to either of them, but neither was allowed to plant within a hundred miles of the other.

In spite of an ineffective protest from Spain, the London Company, under the chief patronage of Sir Robert Cecil, at once proceeded to make use of its privileges. The main hopes for profit lay in the possible discovery of precious metals and of a water passage through what was thought to be a narrow continental barrier to the markets of the East. A colony, however, was desirable for several reasons, and in December, 1606, 120 persons were sent out in three ships which did not reach the shore of Chesapeake Bay until the 6th of the following May.

About thirty years earlier Raleigh had made two unsuccessful attempts to plant a settlement in Virginia, one of them being notable for the birth of the first English child in America, a little girl who was christened Virginia Dare, and whose fate is shrouded in the mystery which surrounds the entire colony of 1587, no trace of which could be discovered when help was sent out to it four years later. They may have perished of starvation or been massacred by the Indians. When the attempt was again made to plant a colony in 1607, it is possible that the savages recalled the previous intrusion. In any case they at once attacked the first landing party of new settlers. The site chosen for what was to prove the cradle of the American people was at Jamestown, then called James Fort, and was marshy and malarial. What with sickness, the savages, an ill-devised form of government, and inexperience with pioneering needs, the first few years were stark with tragedy.

The tragedy is certain though the details are largely shrouded in mystery. One of the chief actors, the famous Captain John Smith, has left us an account of them but in the long and crowded career of that adventurous person it is difficult to pick out truth from fiction as told with great gusto by himself. We know, at any rate, that when the supply ships sailed for England the second time in April, 1608, 144 out of a total of 197 immigrants had died.

Renewed efforts were made by the London promoters, who grossly misrepresented conditions to intending emigrants, and in June, 1609, nine more vessels were despatched with about 500 persons of both sexes and all ages. One vessel sank. One ran ashore on Bermuda. Plague and fever stalked the decks, and when the survivors reached

Jamestown they found there only a hundred whites, some encamped about twenty miles away and some living with the savages. There was no food on shore and hardly any on the ships. Disease and hunger worked on the immigrants like scythes on wheat. In their madness for food, men dug up dead and putrid Indians, and sat by their dying comrades waiting to seize on their flesh.

It was more than humanity could stand and the decision was made to abandon the colony. There was in store, however, a sudden and dramatic turn in events. At the very moment when the 150 survivors of the 900 adventurers were sailing for home down the James, a ship was sighted bringing Lord de la Warr with food and help. All decided to make one more effort, and the frightful "starving time" of 1609–10 was a turning point in the settlement of the United States. A severe military government was instituted and order came to the colony. With the expiration of the seven years during which property was to be held in common stock, private ownership was instituted and did much to stimulate hope and ambition. Peace was bought with the Indians. Sir Thomas Gates, Sir Thomas Dale, and George Yeardley, all soldiers of a "hard-boiled" type, succeeded as governors in bringing the colony through its trials. Dreams of gold and silver or the Northwest Passage evaporated and the colony settled down to the cultivation of tobacco as its staple.

It has been estimated that by 1625, when at last the colony had become firmly established, 1095 persons were living in Virginia, but to secure this result and to establish what was to be the American nation, over 4500 had perished from starvation, massacre or disease. The 5649 immigrants who may be called the first Virginians, were of all types,—a few gentlemen with servants, a few genuine criminals, some soldiers and professional men, more or less riff-raff and much excellent material in the way of artisans, mechanics and so on. When stability and private ownership came after the first few horrible years, the types of newcomers most in evidence were men with capital to build plantations and those known as indentured servants. The latter, who were of considerable importance in our history, were of all grades. Some came from jails but that means little as in that day men were imprisoned in England for very minor offences and even trifling debts. Under an indenture, men, women, and children were sold or sold themselves into service in the colony for a term of years,—two or three up to seven or more,—to pay for their passage. Their term of service completed they could claim land and start life afresh in the New World. Under the strain of the mal-adjustments in the economic condition of England, many of good standing at home took advantage of this way of making a new beginning, and the word servant, which covered schoolmasters, younger sons of good families, and others, is misleading. It meant merely in many cases those who sold themselves into service in exchange for the costly voyage to America which they could not otherwise pay for. As the trade became organized, wicked ships' captains began to kidnap boys and girls on the streets and sell their time in America.

The original charter granted by King James in 1606 was followed by others in 1609 and 1612, the last being revoked completely in 1624, when Virginia became a Royal Colony. There ensued, however, no disturbance to property rights or popular liberties. The first charter, happily, in words which the Americans were always to cherish and remember, had provided that the colonists and their descendants "shall have and enjoy all liberties, franchises, and immunities within any of our other dominions, to all intents and purposes as if they had been abiding and born within this our Realm of England or any other of our said dominions." That promise of liberty had been the original basis on which Englishmen had first been induced to settle in America.

For the first decade, however, the colonists had had little or no voice in managing their own political affairs. In April, 1619, Sir George Yeardley arrived from London with new instructions as governor, the most important of which was that thereafter the people were to have a share in their own government and that twenty-two burgesses were to be elected from nine "plantations" and three "cities" to form the lower house of the new legislature. Actually at first, there were eleven little local organizations, variously called "city," "borough," "hundred" or "plantation," each represented by two burgesses in the lower legislative house. This with the council of six as an upper house, and the governor, brought the governmental machinery to a type that was to be familiar in its broad outlines, though with local variations, throughout colonial America.

On July 30, 1619, the legislature met and political self-government was formally inaugurated on the American continent. The following year it was likewise instituted in the colony of Bermuda. A significant but less happy event in the same year that the Burgesses thus started at Jamestown on their colonial Parliamentary career was the arrival of a Dutch ship whose captain sold twenty negro slaves to the planters.

Although the stability and prosperity of Virginia were now in striking contrast to the early years, disease continued to take an appalling toll, and in 1622 there was an unexpected attack by the savages, the result of both these factors being that after the massacre there were fewer than 900 settlers left in the colony. Nevertheless, emigrants continued to pour out from England, but the mismanagement and scandals connected with the London Company finally brought about the voiding of its charter, as we have stated, in 1624. However, in spite of all vicissitudes the colony grew, as did its confidence in governing itself, so that in 1635 the House of Burgesses dared even to depose a royal governor. The English character as well as race had indeed established itself in the New World.

Meanwhile efforts by the Plymouth Company to found a colony in New England had not succeeded, one experiment of wintering in Maine with inadequate resources having signally failed. Every year, however, French, Spanish, Dutch or English ships were to be found along our shores for fishing, fur trading or exploring, and the New England coast had become well known. In 1609, Henry Hudson, often miscalled "Hendrik," an Englishman in Dutch employ, had discovered the river that bears his name; and in 1614 Captain John Smith was exploring and mapping the Massachusetts coast and acquiring unlimited faith in the possibilities of the region. Virginia, however, was thirteen years old before the first band of settlers were to effect a permanent lodgment in the North, and then by accident.

In 1606, the year when the first emigrants embarked on their ships for Chesapeake Bay, another small group made up of the Separatists we have mentioned above, fearful of being able to continue peaceably their religious life in England, had emigrated to Holland, settling in Leyden. Being English, they were not happy living among foreigners; they feared demoralization for their children; and found it hard to make comfortable livings. For these and other reasons, they determined, as an endless stream of emigrants of all races has since, to try their fortune in the New World.

The Virginia colony having proved successful, they decided to settle near that. Having secured the needed financial backing of capitalists in London, 102 passengers crowded into the *Mayflower*

[The Mayflower Compact — handwritten manuscript facsimile]

THE MAYFLOWER COMPACT

The first part, from the original Bradford manuscript.

In the Massachusetts State Library.

and set sail from Southampton in the summer of 1620. Only a third of these, under the lead of William Brewster, were "Pilgrims" from Leyden, the rest being a nondescript lot of settlers picked up in London or elsewhere and shipped by the capitalists. It may be pointed out that a "Mayflower descendant" may thus have had a far from desirable ancestor!

It was November before they sighted Cape Cod and, after running into dangerous shoals in an effort to make southward for Virginia, they decided to disembark at some favorable spot near at hand. It was thus by chance that the famous landing at Plymouth was made. Finding themselves outside the limits of the Virginia Government, with no charter of their own, and with a very mixed lot of persons to control, the more substantial passengers decided before landing to draw up a covenant to be signed by all the men providing for a simple form of self-government under which officers were to be elected and laws enacted.

During the first few years of this second American settlement many of the troubles which the Virginians had encountered were met again,—heavy sickness, occasional attacks from the savages, and economic difficulties until private ownership replaced the partly communal form of economic life forced on them by their capitalist backers. Neither the disorders nor the trials were so severe, however, as they had been in the Southern adventure, and the little democracy governed itself with notable success.

Chief among the leaders which it developed was William Bradford, a Puritan at once determined and lovable, a man of strong will, high courage, sound sense, and, although a farmer's son, of scholarly tastes. His *History of Plymouth Plantation* is the earliest contribution of importance to American historical writing, and still has a charm that few other American books could claim until nearly two centuries later. The peppery tempered but loyal little soldier, Captain Myles Standish, was the sword of the colony.

Meanwhile other English settlers, some worthy and others distinctly not so, began to settle singly or in small groups along the New England coast. Colonies of English were also going out to the West India islands,—St. Kitts in 1623, Barbadoes and St. Croix in 1625, Nevis and Barbuda in 1628. These and other islands were to become of great value to the Empire later, and we cannot understand some points in our own subsequent relations to England if we do not bear that fact in mind. It is also important at this stage of our story to think of the movement of colonization, now setting out from England in every direction, as a whole. By 1640 probably over 65,000 English people had left their homes for the New World, without counting the large numbers who went to Ireland. Many different motives animated them, these often being combined in the same individual. Religion was only one of the moving impulses, but it was to be especially notable in the next, and by far the largest, colony yet to be planted in America, just as it had been the chief motive with the minority Pilgrim band on the *Mayflower*.

In the eastern section of England Puritanism was particularly strong among a group of influential families and clergy, and in that same section economic distress among the lower middle and labor-

> Of plimoth plantation
>
> And first of y̅ occasion, and Jnduṡments ther vnto; the which that y̅ may truly vnfould, y̅ must begine at y̅ very roote & rise of y̅ same. The which y̅ shall endeuor to manefest in a plaine stile; with singuler regard vnto y̅ simple trueth in all things, at least as near as my slender Judgmente can attaine the same.
>
> 1. Chapter.
>
> It is well knowne vnto y̅ godly, and judicious; how euer since y̅ first breaking out of y̅ lighte of y̅ gospell, in our Honourable nation of England (which was y̅ first of nations, whom y̅ Lord adorned therwith, after y̅ grosse darknes of popery which had couered, & ouerspred y̅ Christian world) what warrs, & oppositions euer since satan hath raised, maintained, and continued against the

FACSIMILE OF PART OF THE FIRST PAGE OF THE MANUSCRIPT OF BRADFORD'S HISTORY OF PLYMOUTH PLANTATION

From the original in the Massachusetts State Library.

ing class was unusually acute. In 1628 a group of men of that district, some of whom had already been interested in a fishing company at Cape Ann, secured a patent for land running from 3 miles north of the Merrimac River to 3 miles south of the Charles, a strip about 60 miles wide and 3000 long, as it ran to the Pacific Ocean!

They at once despatched John Endicott with about 60 persons to take possession and prepare for a colony. There was already a little settlement at Salem and there Endicott wintered. The next year 400 people were sent out, and a Royal charter was secured for a Massachusetts Bay Company, much on the lines of the other company charters. This provided, in part, that the members of the company, known as "freemen," should constitute the "General Court" which was to meet quarterly and once a year elect a governor, deputy-governor, and board of assistants. The "Court" was also given power to make such rules, or laws and ordinances, as should not be repugnant to the laws of England.

Events in that country were moving rapidly, and the future was becoming dark. The King dissolved Parliament in anger and was to rule for the next eleven years without one. Nine of the popular leaders had been imprisoned in the Tower. Important Puritan, and what we might call today "Liberal," families were deeply anxious, and were considering the New World as a possible asylum.

Probably on account of this situation, the influential men in control of the Massachusetts Bay Company decided upon taking an unprecedented and what was to be a unique step in the history of English company colonization. They determined to send the actual charter to the colony itself. By doing so they, in practice, transformed what was intended to be a mere trading company charter into what they came, without legal justification, to consider the constitution for an almost self-governing State. The step was to prove of great importance in the subsequent relations of Massachusetts to the British Government, and to the development of colonial political thought.

The first governor elected, in England, was John Winthrop, a gentleman of good family and position who, like so many others, had found himself unable to keep up his accustomed scale of living under the altered economic conditions of the time. He had been used to living well, with seven or eight servants, and the future for himself and his children had already seemed black to him when a final blow fell with the loss of a government office which he held. He was also a Puritan, and the outlook seemed as unpromising from the standpoint of enjoying his religious beliefs as it did from that of maintaining his inherited social position in his county. In his case, as in most, various motives thus reinforced one another in urging him to the experiment of going out to the American wilderness. The letters of himself, his wife and children reveal a singularly affectionate and cultured family life, and it must have been with heavy hearts that they left their old Suffolk home.

However, in 1630, Winthrop sailed for Massachusetts with a band of nearly a thousand colonists, who settled what later became the towns of Charlestown, Boston, Medford, Watertown, Roxbury, Lynn, and Dorchester. By 1634 he estimated the total population at four thousand, and Massachusetts had become the most powerful settlement on the entire North American coast.

The new colony was as strong in convictions as in numbers. There was a marked Puritan tinge in all the colonies, as in England itself, and the laws passed by the settlers in Virginia with regard to manners, morals, dress, and church-going differed but little from those to be passed in Massachusetts, though Virginia established the Church of England and New England became Non-Conformist. The Massachusetts leaders, however, both lay and clerical, were of the strictest sect of the Puritans and gave the tone to the whole community. They attempted to make their State a theocracy with themselves as the sole interpreters of the Word of God in civil and ecclesiastical affairs, which they considered practically as one, and in 1631 the General Court declared that only church members could be admitted as freemen, that is have a vote in the government. It was hoped by the leaders that by this device they could maintain strict political as well as religious control. They had come to the New World to worship as they chose and had no intention of being interfered with by those of different belief whether in England or within their own newly established settlements. John Endicott exemplified best the dogmatic, harsh, unyielding, and intolerant type which the movement evolved, but even gentler and sweeter characters, like those of Winthrop or the Reverend John Cotton, grew less broadly humane under the conditions of life in the Theocracy.

The hard years of first settlement, the sectarian's belief in his own monopoly of Truth, the subtle infection of suddenly acquired power both as civil rulers and religious prophets, all tended to emphasize what we have come to regard as Puritanism in its most exaggerated and least charitable form. The leaders disliked and distrusted democracy or even permitting the ordinary citizen a voice in government, and did their best to stave off civil as well as religious dissent. But if too often they seemed intent on making the wilderness blossom like the thistle instead of like the rose, they developed around the core of "the New England conscience" a character which, with all its ugly excrescences, was to form an invaluable strain in the nation of the future. It is only just to point out, however, that this same strain accounts for much of the fanaticism and intolerance which have too often marked our national life and opinion.

Colonizing had by this time passed beyond the stage of doubtful success, and in 1632 the foundations for yet another colony were laid next to Virginia. Lord Baltimore, a Catholic peer, received a charter from King Charles which permitted him to found a settlement where Catholics would be tolerated, named in honor of the Queen, Mary-land. Although this charter was not that of a trading company like the others, but created a Palatinate like the Bishopric of Durham, it was notable that, whereas in England the Bishop had practically uncontrolled power of legislation, Baltimore could make laws only "with the advice, assent, and approbation of the freemen or the greater part of them or their representatives." Unlike the French and Spanish colonies, the seed of liberty and self-government was thus dropped into the ground of every English town, plantation, and colony at their very beginning. From their inception, the English colonies throughout the New World were the freest communities then in the world, a fact which, combined with other conditions, immensely favored their progress on democratic lines.

Our main concern has been thus far with the genesis of the United States, but we must recall that during all the period we have covered there was amazing activity all over the globe,—England, France, and Holland, for example, contending with one another for commerce and empire out in India and the Islands of the Far East. The dispelling of the mystery and terror of the earth's open seas had afforded the needed vent to Europe, and the danger of explosion had been replaced by a furious burst of energy as the possibilities of world exploitation dawned on the European mind. The rise of the United States is but one, though for us the most important, of the results of Europe having found a way to break through the fifteenth-century encirclement of barbarous races, forbidding deserts and innavigable waters.

CHAPTER II

THE COLONIAL SYSTEM TAKES FORM

THE period covered by this chapter, roughly from 1634 to 1690, was notable for the gradual evolution of a colonial system out of the scattered beginnings made at haphazard by the commercial ambitions of a few groups of capitalists or needy courtiers, partly assisted in the process of colonization by the religious hopes or fears of particular groups. The evolution proceeded in two directions—first, the actual peopling of the American coast and the Caribbean islands in a vast semicircle extending from Maine to Barbadoes, and, secondly, in the attempt to develop in England a theory of imperial needs, obligations and government. We shall speak of the second point later, and with regard to the first our attention must be almost wholly directed to the continental half of the semicircle. We may note, however, to get the proper perspective from the imperial point of view,—that in addition to the greater importance of her natural products, the island of Barbadoes alone in 1642 had a larger English population than all the New England colonies combined.

The New England population, however, had increased rapidly from the Puritan settlement until about 1640, when the prospects for Puritans in England altered completely, and for the better, with the Puritan revolution there. After that, the stream of emigration to New England dried up almost entirely for well on to two centuries. Within eight years after the arrival of Winthrop the number of settlers in the section had increased to perhaps seventeen thousand, and besides the colonies of Plymouth and Massachusetts four new ones had been founded—Rhode Island and Connecticut in 1636, New Haven in 1638, while there had been settlements in a New Hampshire since 1622, and a number in Maine. The date of "founding" of many of the colonies is somewhat vague for in many of them there were occasional stray single settlers or even small groups who had squatted on lands or more lawfully preceded larger bodies sent out after legal possession had been secured by charter or otherwise. There is no advantage in waxing too hot over what is often a verbal quibble. The settlement of a solitary, like the interesting Blackstone, for example, removing to live in Rhode Island, can scarcely be called the founding of a new colony, the term being better applied to the establishment of a permanent and fairly strong body of citizens with established forms of local government.

We may note that the establishment of New Hampshire, Rhode Island, and Connecticut was owing in each case to the opposition aroused in the minds of many by the narrow and tyrannical ruling Puritan oligarchy in control of Massachusetts. Just as the leaders of that colony had fled or been forced from England, so now many were fleeing or being forced from their colony in the New World to seek for greater liberty, as well as for new and well-located lands. As we have pointed out, resistance to intellectual or religious authority and insistence upon private judgment do not, unfortunately, necessarily result in tolerance. Indeed, the exaggerated importance given to his own views by the protesting individual seems rather to be likely to result in an aggressive *in*tolerance. Moreover, there is no intolerance more overbearing than that springing from the belief by persons of rather narrow experience in their own superior morality or brand of religious truth. The local Massachusetts leaders had been people of no importance whatever in England when they suddenly found themselves ruling a commonwealth. They had also taken heavy risks to find a place where they not only could worship as they chose but could raise themselves in the social and economic scales. Having found it, they had no intention of allowing affairs to slip from their grasp. This was all quite human but militated strongly in some ways against the best interests of Massachusetts.

For many generations there were to be two strands in the history of that commonwealth,— resistance by the colony as a whole to any encroachments by England, and resistance by the more liberal elements among the colonists themselves to the ruling oligarchy, who believed not that the people should rule but that they should *be* ruled by the specially elect of God.

For a while, the leaders refused to allow the people even to see

THE OLD SHIP CHURCH, HINGHAM, MASSACHUSETTS, BEGUN IN 1681

An example of the earliest type of town meeting-house which was a rectangular building
with hipped roof surmounted by a belfry containing a bell.

From a later print, courtesy of the State Street Trust Company, Boston.

OLD MEETING–HOUSE, SANDOWN, NEW HAMPSHIRE, BUILT IN 1774

Prior to the Revolution, the smaller meeting-houses outside of the towns were usually
without a steeple.

By courtesy of the Society for the Preservation of New England Antiquities.

AN OLD PRINT OF THE COLLEGE OF WILLIAM AND MARY IN VIRGINIA
SHOWING IT AS IT WAS ABOUT 1732

This print was taken from the so-called "Copper Plate" recently found in the Bodleian Library at Oxford by research workers on the staff of the Williamsburg Holding Corporation which is engaged in restoring a part of Williamsburg to its eighteenth-century appearance. The building in the centre is the Wren Building.

THE WREN BUILDING AS IT IS TODAY

the charter, and carried matters with a high hand. In 1631 the men of Watertown protested against paying a tax levied on them, rightly claiming that only the freemen could tax themselves. It was in that year the oligarchy ruled that only church members could be free-men. In 1634 two representatives elected from each town were finally granted a sight of the charter, when they found that they had been deprived of their rights under it. It was then decided, after a mild uprising against Winthrop and the other leaders, that the General Court, made up of delegates from the towns, should meet four times a year, and that it alone should have power to pass laws, elect and remove officials, lay taxes and grant lands.

Almost from the beginning, the Congregational form of church had been adopted in Massachusetts. By this system each church was independent of all others, chose its own pastor, and was composed only of such persons as could satisfy the rest of the congregation of their regenerate state. They were bound together by a covenant, and this church group and the political organization of the town became the two cells from which the New England social organism was built up. Adding the village or town school, soon introduced, the three ideas are to be found throughout our history wherever New England influence has penetrated. The tendency of all three was profoundly democratic, but this in no way altered the attempt of the leaders, such as even Winthrop and Cotton, who were opposed to democracy, to prevent its application to civil government.

Many complaints had been made about affairs in the colony in London when its peace in America was disturbed in 1635 by the ideas of Roger Williams. Williams had a gentle and winning per-sonality, and soon fell foul of the bigotry of the Massachusetts lay and clerical leaders. Unfortunately, besides preaching religious tol-eration he added certain dangerous doctrines, claiming, for example, that title to American soil was vested in the Indians and not in the King. After a trial, in which both religious and political motives bore their part, he was sentenced by the Massachusetts authorities to be banished the following spring. Escaping from home in mid-winter, after having heard he was to be shipped to England, he made his way through the snows and bitter cold of a New England January to Narragansett Bay where he founded the new colony of Rhode Island, for which he obtained a charter in 1644.

Meanwhile others wished, voluntarily, to emigrate from Massachusetts, and the beautiful valley of the Connecticut attracted some of these. In 1635 a law was enacted that no one could leave Massachusetts without consent of the authorities, but it was finally decreed that the Reverend Thomas Hooker and a band of settlers might go. By the end of the following year there were probably 800 people at Hartford and neighboring places, and thus our endless western migration from the "settled East" had begun.

Chriſtenings

make not

CHRISTIANS,

OR

A Briefe Diſcourſe concerning that name *Heathen*, commonly given to the INDIANS.

As alſo concerning that great point of their CONVERSION.

Publiſhed according to Order.

London, Printed by *Iane Coe*, for I. H. 1645.

A FACSIMILE OF A REPRINT OF THE ORIGINAL TRACT WRITTEN BY ROGER WILLIAMS IN 1643
Contained in "Rhode Island Historical Tracts," 1st Series, No. 14.

The government of Massachusetts, as we have said, as much as the rich Connecticut meadows, was probably the cause of the exodus. When the form of government of the new settlements was under consideration in 1638, the settlers having no charter, Hooker preached his famous sermon, arguing for fixed laws and popular control of the government and magistrates. Those who have the power to elect, he claimed, have the power to control, and "the foundation of authority is laid, firstly, in the free consent of the people." When the "Fundamental Orders" were accepted as the basis of government, they contained no reference to the King, and, probably as a reaction against conditions in Massachusetts, provided that the governor should not be eligible for re-election and that there should be no religious qualification for the franchise.

In the same year, 1638, in which Hooker was preaching his liberalism at Hartford, New Hampshire received its most important early accession to population in a group of refugees from Massachusetts. This emigration was consequent upon the trial of Ann Hutchinson, followed by her banishment, and the fining or disfranchisement of many of her followers. Just when this affair was at its height an important body of intending settlers arrived in Boston from England headed by the Reverend John Davenport and several wealthy laymen. Resisting entreaties to remain in Massachusetts, they decided on New Haven as the site for their rather rigid theocracy, and settled there in 1638. Like Hooker and his followers they had no charter, but unlike them they entered into a reactionary covenant, making church membership essential for freemen and entrusting all government to an elected body and governor who for many years were restricted in authority only by the laws of Moses. For various reasons the colony, although it grew, never prospered, and in 1661 was absorbed by Connecticut.

New England was thus rapidly expanding, and it was able to do so in comparative safety as a result of the terrible Pequot War in 1637. It was the story of white aggression and racial hatred which was unhappily to be repeated on almost all of our frontiers for two and a half centuries. The chief incident of this first New England war was the surprise by the Puritans, under the lead of Captain John Mason, of the main village of the savages. In the dark, with a strong wind blowing, the two entrances to the stockade were guarded to prevent any escape, and then a torch was applied. Five hundred Indian men, women, and children were burned to death, the Puritan leader merely remarking that by the Providence of God there were 150 more than usual at home that awful night.

The fear of a general Indian uprising in 1642 led to a league among the four colonies of Massachusetts, Plymouth, New Haven, and Connecticut. Under the name of the New England Confederation this league functioned rather feebly for forty years, and was of slight importance. Its chief significance is in showing how easily these colonies, which were beginning to plant themselves without charters or thought of King or Parliament, were slipping toward a belief in entire political independence in managing all their own affairs.

A step toward intellectual independence also was taken by Massachusetts in 1636 when Harvard College was established to train up a godly ministry. Much used to be made of this event, but when we contrast the courses of study and the scholarship produced in our first "college" with what the Spaniards had achieved long before at such universities as those in Mexico City or Lima, perhaps a more modest estimate of this event in our educational history may be preferable. It tended, moreover, to increase the provincialism of New England by encouraging it to keep students at home for an inferior training instead of sending them, as the other colonies later did, to enjoy the better opportunities in the universities of Europe.

By the mid-century, Massachusetts was hardening into the most cruel and narrow period of its long, and in many ways glorious history. Winthrop died in 1649, and Cotton in 1652. Such mild restraining influences as there had been of gentleness, charity, and toleration appear for a while to have lost their power. Civil and ecclesiastical control passed to men of the type of Endicott. New England may well be proud of four such founders of her States as Bradford, Winthrop, Williams, and Hooker, but by 1657 only Williams remained, and his colony of Rhode Island was alone to play a noble part in refraining from the persecutions of the Quakers which blotted New England history between 1656 and 1663.

In the earlier of these years, a few weeks after the Massachusetts government had hung Ann Hibbens as a witch, two Quaker women, from England by way of Barbadoes, arrived in Boston. At once persecution began, and as others came it was increased in severity. The penalties, which included besides the selling of Quaker children into slavery in the West Indies, the imprisonment, beating, and torturing of their elders, culminated in the hanging of three men and one woman. At the request of Massachusetts all the other New England colonies, with the exception of Rhode Island, passed severe laws against the sect, though none tortured or killed them as did the leading Puritan State, then largely under the influence of Endicott and the Reverend John Norton.

Williams replied to the request of Massachusetts (though his colony was threatened with dangerous reprisals if it did not comply), that the Rhode Islanders had no laws against any one declaring by words only their religious beliefs, whatever they might be, and that although he conceived the doctrines of the Quakers tended to the subversion of civil government, nevertheless it would be found always that if Quakers were allowed to preach in peace and were not persecuted, they would gain fewer adherents by their sayings than they would by suffering and martyrdom. The General Assembly of Rhode Island added that the colony prized freedom of

The Wages of Sin;

OR,

Robbery juftly Rewarded:

A

POEM;

Occafioned by the untimely Death of

Richard Wilfon,

Who was Executed on *Bofton* Neck, for Burglary,

On *Thurfday* the 19th of *October*, 1732.

THis Day from Goal muft *Wilfon* be conveyed in a Cart, By Guards unto the Gallows-Tree, to die as his Defert.

Here we may fee what Men for Stealth and Robbing muft endure; And what the Gain of ill got Wealth will in the End procure.

NEW ENGLAND PUNISHMENT

A facsimile of a broadside in the Library of Congress.

conscience "as the greatest happiness that men can possess in this world."

In the forty years since the passengers on the *Mayflower* had unexpectedly been landed on the shores of Massachusetts instead of Virginia, New England must have seemed to its old inhabitants to have made astounding progress. In spite of the terrible conflict with the savages yet in store,—King Philip's War of 1676,—the older settlements were now as safe as shire towns in England, though the frontier, that ever-present factor in American life, was open and liable to sudden attack and massacre. It would be a mistake to think even of Massachusetts as a land only of dour countenances, and hangings of witches or Quakers. Our first woman poet, Anne Bradstreet, had penned her love verses there, students ragged each other at Harvard, children played around school doors. Literature had begun in New England, and though much of it is musty theology that no one reads today, Bradford and Winthrop had written valuable histories, and Williams in Rhode Island and Hooker in Connecticut had wrought out the ideals of the rule of the people, and of intellectual toleration.

The ordinary citizen, living on his farm owned in fee simple, untroubled by any relics of feudalism, untaxed save by himself, saying his say to all the world in town-meeting, had gained a new self-reliance. Wrestling with his soul and plough on week days, and the innumerable points of the minister's sermon on Sundays and Meeting days, he was coming to be a tough nut for any imperial system to crack. All were not farmers, though most were, and a merchant class of larger or smaller traders was springing up in the seaports and in villages along navigable rivers, carrying on a commerce with the mother country, the Wine Islands, Africa for slaves, the West Indies, and their own fellow continental colonists to the south. For part of the century, however, between the English of New England and those of Maryland and Virginia lay colonies of Dutch and Swedes.

THE

TENTH MUSE

Lately fprung up in AMERICA.

OR

Severall Poems, compiled

with great variety of VVit

and Learning, full of delight.

Wherein efpecially is contained a compleat difcourfe and defcription of '

The Four { Elements,
Conftitutions,
Ages of Man,
Seafons of the Year.

Together with an Exact Epitomie of the Four Monarchies, viz.

The { Affyrian,
Perfian,
Grecian,
Roman.

Alfo a Dialogue between Old England and New, concerning the late troubles.

With divers other pleafant and ferious Poems.

By a Gentlewoman in thofe parts.

Printed at London for Stephen Bowtell at the figne of the Bible in Popes Head-Alley. 1650.

TITLE-PAGE (REDUCED) OF THE FIRST EDITION OF ANNE BRADSTREET'S POEMS

From the New York Public Library.

HARVARD COLLEGE, CAMBRIDGE

From left to right the buildings are: Holden Chapel, 1737; Hollis Hall, 1762; Harvard Hall, built in 1766 upon the site of the original building which had been destroyed by fire; Stoughton Hall, the gift of William Stoughton, presiding judge at Salem witch trials, which was torn down and replaced in 1805; Massachusetts Hall, 1720.

From the engraving by Paul Revere, in the Essex Institute, Salem, Massachusetts.

BOWEN'S VIEW OF YALE COLLEGE, 1786

Left: the Athenæum erected in 1761.   Right: Connecticut Hall, 1750.

By courtesy of Yale University Library.

Wm Penns, old Meeting House at Chester Pennsylvania.

WILLIAM PENN'S MEETING-HOUSE AT CHESTER AND A LETTER FROM PENN TO THE INDIANS

This letter, reproduced in part, was addressed by Penn, and sent in care of three commissioners to the Indians living on the land for which Charles II had given him his grant. In it he expresses his hope for an amicable purchase of the land and a life of peace and accord for all.

From the Library of Congress.

From 1610, the year following Hudson's discovery of the river named for him, Dutch traders had frequented its mouth to traffic with the Indians, and in 1614 had founded a fort and small trading post on the site of what is now Albany. In 1623 the Dutch West India Company, a trading company such as we have become familiar with, planted a small settlement on Manhattan Island, where a few huts had been built some years before. The Dutch claim to New Netherland, with its principal town of New Amsterdam, was more or less indeterminate but included New York and Long Island, New Jersey, and Delaware. Of course it was not recognized by the English.

The Dutch were in fact rather late claimants, though their brief history in America was picturesque enough, and many prominent New York families like to trace their ancestry back to them. Their stay was a troubled one for they were in almost constant dispute not only with the advancing New Englanders in Connecticut and eastern Long Island, and the Virginians in Delaware, but also with colonies of Swedes which had been planted at Wilmington and surrounding points. The latter were finally conquered by the Dutch in 1655, but nine years later an English fleet arrived at the mouth of the Hudson and forced the Dutch governor, the redoubtable Peter Stuyvesant, to surrender. In honor of the Duke of York, the King's brother, to whom the territory had been granted, the colony and town were renamed New York, and the Dutch sway within the present United States came to an end. The two favorites to whom the Duke of York granted the land between New York and Delaware Bay founded East and West, now New, Jersey, the two colonies soon coming largely under the control of the Quakers, Berkeley, who had received West Jersey, selling out his rights to them almost immediately.

The Dutch had not believed in self-government by their colonists, and the history of New Amsterdam had been turbulent. The small town early acquired its modern cosmopolitan aspect, and it is said that eighteen languages were spoken on its streets in the Dutch period. Except for a few words adopted into our language, some social customs locally, and many romantic legends, the Dutch influence, however, has been almost negligible in the development of our institutions and culture in spite of much written to the contrary.

Charles II, who had returned to the English throne in 1660, after the Cromwellian interregnum, was only too willing to use the vast lands of America as grants to noblemen for his own or their benefit, and just as he granted the Dutch territories to his brother, so he also granted to a group of eight nobles the lands south of Virginia which are now included in North and South Carolina. Colonization was rather slow, but Charleston was settled in 1670, and grew fairly rapidly, a large accession of French Huguenots arriving ten years later. Rice growing, which was introduced in 1693, resulted in a great increase in slavery, rapid fortunes, and a basis of wealth and leisure which was to make South Carolina, within a few generations, perhaps the leading American colony in æsthetic culture and social charm.

The last colony founded in the period of this chapter was Pennsylvania, a charter for which was granted to the Quaker William Penn in 1681. Planting his chief town of Philadelphia on the bank of the Delaware, he expressed the wish that each house should always be surrounded by a garden so that the city might remain "a green country town," and "always be wholesome," an ideal of city planning which, until too late, we have most unhappily forgotten. Notable also in Pennsylvania under the leadership of Penn, alone among all the colonies, was the benevolent and honorable attitude adopted and maintained toward the Indians. Treaties were not only made but kept, and the relation of Penn to the savages forms one of the few episodes in the long annals of our treatment of the native which honest Americans would not wish to have blotted out.

Although, as we shall see in the next chapter, there was soon to be a large influx of Germans into Pennsylvania, the colony had been founded mainly as a retreat for Quakers, and thus one more sect found refuge among us, adding to the fast growing complexity of our life even in this early period. In the neighboring colony of Maryland, in order to protect the Catholics, a law had been passed in 1649 by the colonial assembly (in which Catholics were in the majority at the time), providing that no person professing to believe in Jesus Christ should in any way be troubled or molested. Maryland and Rhode Island thus led the way toward complete toleration, at least for professing Christians.

Before proceeding to consider the second point of which we spoke

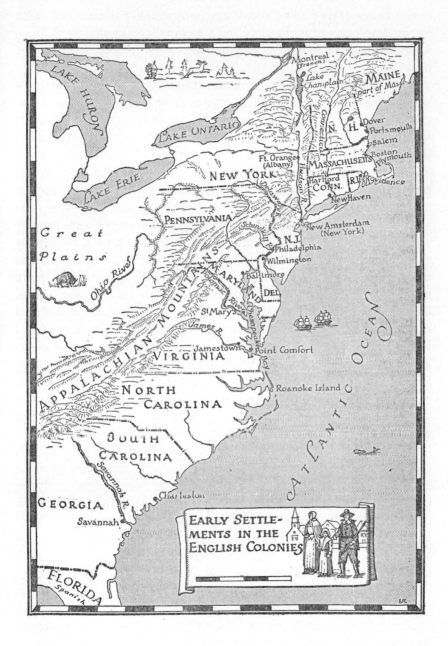

Lake Huron

Lake Ontario

Lake Erie

Great
Plains

Ohio River

Montreal
(French)

Lake
Champlain

MAINE
(part of Mass.)

N. H.

Dover
Portsmouth
Salem

Ft. Orange
(Albany)

MASSACHUSETTS

Boston
Plymouth

NEW YORK

Hartford
CONN.

R.I.
Providence

New Haven

PENNSYLVANIA

New Amsterdam
(New York)

N.J.

Philadelphia

Wilmington

MARYLAND

Baltimore

DEL.

St Mary's

James R.

APPALACHIAN MOUNTAINS

Jamestown

Point Comfort

VIRGINIA

NORTH
CAROLINA

Roanoke Island

SOUTH
CAROLINA

GEORGIA

Savannah R.

Charleston

Savannah

ATLANTIC OCEAN

FLORIDA
Spanish

EARLY SETTLE-
MENTS IN THE
ENGLISH COLONIES

31

at the beginning of this chapter as characterizing the period,—that is, the development in England of a colonial theory and practice,—we may note briefly one or two aspects of American development thus far.

First of all, in the colonies, as contrasted with England itself or with the French and Spanish empires in America, there was the great diversity in both race and religion. Within two generations from the gaining of a permanent foothold by the dominant English, we have already found large groups of Dutch, Germans, Swedes, and Huguenot French coming to make homes here for the purpose either of bettering themselves socially and economically, or to escape from persecution.

This diversity was greatly to increase in the future, but at its very inception the United States became both a hope and a refuge for those of many races, and not merely of a single one. There was also the marked variety in religion. Although all the colonies were under English rule, Catholics, Congregationalists, Lutherans, Church of England adherents, Quakers, and others, could all find rapidly growing and prosperous communities in which they could make their homes, and be unmolested. The intolerance of individual colonies, notably the Puritan ones, should not obscure the remarkable religious freedom that had come to exist within a group of colonies of a single European power. It could have been found at that time under neither French nor Spanish rule, but only under English.

Owing chiefly to soil, topography, and climate, there had also come about a rapid but clearly marked differentiation in the social and economic life of the various colonies. In New England all the physical factors in agriculture tended toward small farms which could most profitably be tilled by the head of a family with little help other than that of sons or a hired man. The system of small holdings tended to emphasize that compact type of settlement which naturally developed from the New England form of migration, which was that of a group closely knit together by being members of the church which was their chief concern. The small holding, the church, and the town meeting in New England all militated in that section against a loosely scattered mode of settlement.

New York had been started purely as a trading post. For more than a century, the policy of huge land grants adopted by both Dutch and English rulers; the importance of the fur trade for the only colony which (by the Hudson-Mohawk Valley route) had easy access to the interior of the continent; and the magnificent harbor the colony possessed, were all to determine its character as mainly commercial in a group of colonies that were otherwise dominated by agriculture.

Passing southward to Maryland, Virginia, and the Carolinas, we find agriculture again holding sway. In them the staple and exhausting crop of tobacco (except for rice to the far South) demanded larger landholdings than in New England, and brought about a more scattered way of living, as well, eventually, as a seemingly imperative demand for that black slave labor which was economically unprofitable on the much broken and stony surface of the Puritan colonies. These effects were not all felt in the South during its earlier and economically struggling period, but were to be of great importance after 1700.

Another characteristic of the English colonies as contrasted with those of any other nation at that time was the extraordinary amount of liberty granted to the individual colonist. Looking back from the vantage ground of a different era, we are too apt to think that the colonists were naturally entitled to this, and that in their constant struggles for ever greater liberty they were fighting against a tyrannical government. This was far from the case. As well as we can, we have to judge each age by the ideas dominant in it and not in our own. Neither France, Spain, nor even liberty-loving little Holland, dreamed of giving their colonists when they left the mother country anything like the freedom which England granted to hers.

Charles II was assuredly no lover of democracy or the liberty of the common man, yet although the charters which he granted for the colonies of New York, the Jerseys, Pennsylvania, and Carolina were of the type known as proprietary, and were based on the model of the Bishopric of Durham, they all contained, like that granted by the first Charles on the same model for Maryland, the clause we have noted that the proprietor, unlike the Bishop, could make laws only "by and with the consent of the freemen."

All Americans under the proprietary charters were thus given much more liberty in self-government than was enjoyed by their fellows in England in the Durham Bishopric. The circumstances of distance and the inability to be properly represented in Parliament were to raise special and difficult problems for our ancestors in America, as well as for the government in England. Nevertheless, in studying the story of our incessant struggle against the English government it is only fair to bear in mind that ours were the freest colonies in the world during all of our colonial period.

Charles II, as we have said, was no lover of a too-great liberty of the subject, and the restoration of the Stuarts in his person in 1660 brought troublous times for the Americans in many colonies. According to the generally accepted theory of that day, which seemed not at all tyrannical but only natural to all statesmen in Europe, colonies existed chiefly for the benefit of the mother country. Following the breakdown of the unified world of the Roman Empire and the long incubation period of the Middle Ages, the modern theory and emotions of nationality were fast emerging. Politics, religion and commerce, which had been decentralized, were beginning to be considered as essentially clustering around each national State for its own inhabitants. According to the economic theory of the time, real wealth was believed to consist in a store of the precious metals. That State was thought to be best off which accumulated the largest store, either by mining or favorable trade balances. Thus developed the "Mercantile Theory,"—by no means dead today,—which demanded that a country should always have a balance in its favor to be settled by imports of gold.

When Europe broke its barriers and the period of over-seas empires was inaugurated, the theory of empire was naturally based on this theory of wealth. In order that an empire should owe others as little as possible, each sought to be as nearly self-contained as might be, in both the supplies of its needed raw materials and the markets for its finished products, so as to absorb as much as might be of the profits throughout all the economic scale and be as independent as possible of others. Speaking generally, the colonies, plantations and trading posts of the British Empire were supposed to supply the raw materials for British manufactures and such other materials, for food or other needs, as could not be produced in the British Isles. Thus, for example, England had its fisheries on the Newfoundland coast,

34

the tobacco and rice colonies of our South, the sugar islands of the West Indies (to which the valuable island of Jamaica had been added in 1655), its fort in Guinea protecting its slave trade, and its settlements in India, Sumatra, Java, and the Celebes for the products of the Far East. On the other hand, the colonists were supposed to increase the market for British manufactured goods, and to buy these with the money which they received from the sale of their raw materials. The increase of colonial population, beyond what was necessary merely for producing and shipping home the lumber, sugar, tobacco and other raw materials, was considered of value solely from the standpoint of increasing the number of consumers of British goods.

According to this elaborate scheme, England was to remain the centre of manufactures, banking, and military resources, while the colonies were to confine themselves to the rôles of producers of raw materials and consumers of English manufactures. In a world of empires competing for over-sea territories, the duty of protecting colonies against, so to say, being kidnapped by another empire, and also to guard the trade routes, fell to the navies of the home countries in Europe. When in 1650 and 1651, under Cromwell, and in 1660 and 1663, under the returned Stuarts, England passed Navigation Acts placing certain restrictions on the freedom of colonial trade with the outside world, this was not deemed tyranny but only reasonable regulation in exchange for protection and the smooth working of the imperial trade machinery. This theory of empire was not simply English. It was universal at the time, and on the whole England applied it with a far more enlightened and generous spirit than did either France, Spain, or Holland.

This far-flung empire, which had come into existence almost haphazard, and in scarcely more than fifty years when Charles II came to the throne, had no co-ordinated system of government. Especially during the troubled years of the Cromwellian Commonwealth, the American colonies in particular had been left much to themselves, and had got in the habit, even more than usual, of going their own way with little or no thought of the governing power at the centre of empire. Massachusetts had even dropped the King's name from its legal writs. The years between the restoration of the Stuarts in 1660 and their fall in 1688 were marked in America by constant efforts to reassert royal authority and increase royal control over the colonists.

Some of the efforts were logical and reasonable in theory but all proved irritating in practice. Many of the royal governors were incompetent or venal, and in 1676 the people of Virginia finally broke into revolt against Governor Berkeley under a leader named Nathaniel Bacon. Tobacco was not only the staple crop of Maryland and Virginia but also served as currency in the absence of coin, and frequent trouble arose from fluctuations in value. Before 1675 there had been for some time much distress in the colony owing to the low prices of what was at once crop and currency. This was due in part to over-production and in part to the fact that the navigation laws cut the settlers off from all markets save that of England, and it was said that the planters were merely the slaves of the English merchants.

In all times of economic maladjustment the poor and weak are the worst sufferers, so there was a good deal of grumbling against the bad government of the colony and the richer classes allied to the governor's set.

Matters finally came to a head when the governor and the tidewater gentry declined to make any move to protect the frontier settlements against serious attacks by the Indians, and the poor people found a leader for armed revolt in Bacon. Although the rebellion collapsed in a few months with Bacon's death from fever, it was not unsuccessful. The King recalled Berkeley in disgrace, appointed one of the "'rebels" governor, and remedied some of the grievances. The uprising has a special interest as indicative of the many minor cleavages beginning to appear between rich and poor, old settlement and frontier, in the several colonies.

New England never fitted into the scheme of empire based on the Mercantile theory. With the exception of some timber she produced no raw material needed by England. Her fishing fleets competed with those of the home country. Having no staple crop and always driven to find means of paying for her imports from the mother country, she tended to encroach on English manufacturing to supply her own needs, and to trade not only with the West Indies within the empire but illegally with islands and countries outside it. Many complaints reached the King that the New

Englanders were disobeying the laws of trade, that they were persecuting the Quakers and others, and that they were beginning to consider themselves as practically independent. These charges were mainly true.

At first it had seemed as though Charles II might prove liberal. In 1660 he had despatched a special messenger to Massachusetts to restrain that colony from further persecution, and the next year he granted charters to both Rhode Island and Connecticut which were so satisfactory to the people that they continued to be used as State constitutions until well into the nineteenth century. In 1676, however, he sent as Collector of Customs at the port of Boston and special investigator to Massachusetts a certain Edward Randolph to report on conditions. From the standpoint of efficient imperial administration, these were bad enough but Randolph was also almost insanely prejudiced against the colonies, particularly the Puritan ones, and his reports for many years painted the colonists in the blackest colors to the home authorities. By 1684 he had succeeded in having the Massachusetts charter forfeited in England and the commonwealth transformed into a royal colony. Writs were also issued against the charters of Connecticut, Rhode Island, the Jerseys, and Delaware. Pennsylvania narrowly escaped, but although Stuart rule was nearing its end and these cases were never determined against the colonies, another scheme was put into execution.

From the standpoint of administration there was much to be said in favor of uniting at least certain groups of colonies into larger units. Local character, pride, and jealousies were already so strong however that the thought sprang from bureaucracy rather than from practical statesmanship. As intercolonial jealousies and the impossibility of getting united colonial action on any common Indian or fiscal policy were among the causes which were to precipitate the Revolution in 1776, it is interesting to speculate on what might have happened, had the colonies, almost a century earlier, been united. It is futile, nevertheless, to do so, for they would not have consented to become so. Charles tried the plan in part, and in 1686 Sir Edmund Andros arrived in Boston with a commission to rule over all of New England, New York being added two years later to the consolidated province, as were also the two Jerseys.

The new Administrator was honest but without tact, and in any case occupied an impossible position. He greatly increased his difficulties by unnecessary stirring up of trouble over such matters as censorship of the press, Episcopal rights, land titles, registry fees, and the enclosure of the common lands, but he was no tyrant though his term is usually spoken of as the "tyranny of Andros." The powers granted him in his commission were so broad that he might have been a veritable tyrant had he so desired. In truth he had no such wish and in his term as governor of New York previously he had shown popular tendencies by supporting the colonists' demand for the re-establishment of an Assembly.

AT THE TOWN-HOUSE in

BOSTON:

April 18th. 1689.

Sir,

OUr Selves as well as many others the Inhabitants of this Town and Place adjacent, being surprized with the Peoples sudden taking to Arms in the first motion whereof we were wholly ignorant, are driven by the present Exigence and Necessity to acquaint your *Excellency*, that for the Quieting and Securing of the People Inhabiting this Countrey from the imminent Dangers they many wayes lie open, and are exposed unto, and for Your own safety; We judge it necessary that You forthwith Surrender, and Deliver up the Government and Fortifications to be preserved, to be Disposed according to Order and Direction from the Crown of *England*, which is suddenly expected may Arrive, promising all Security from Violence to Your Self, or any other of Your Gentlemen and Souldiers in Person or Estate or else we are assured they will endeavour the taking of the Fortifications by Storm, if any opposition be made.

To Sr. Edmond Androß Knight,

Wait Winthrop	*Elisha Cook.*
Simon Bradstreat.	*Isaac Addington.*
William Stoughton	*John Nelson.*
Samuel Shrimton	*Adam Winthrop.*
Barthol. Gidney	*Peter Sergeant.*
William Brown	*John Foster.*
Thomas Danforth	*David Waterhouse*
John Richards.	

Boston Printed by *S Green.* 1689.

FACSIMILE OF A BROADSIDE OF 1689 CALLING UPON
ANDROS TO SURRENDER HIS POWERS AND PERSON
From the original in the Library of Congress.

Under the plan for a "Dominion of New England," however, all popular assemblies had been done away with and the governor was to rule and tax only with the advice and consent of the council. After the Colonists' long experience in self-government any such effort to rule them from above was insane folly, but the end was near.

In March, 1689, young John Winslow arrived in Massachusetts from Nevis with authentic news that the Stuarts had been overthrown in England and that William of Orange and his wife Mary had been proclaimed Sovereigns of Great Britain. The information also reached the other colonies and was received with popular rejoicing. In Boston, Andros, Randolph, and other royal officials were thrown into jail to await the new King's command. In New York, Francis Nicholson, who had been serving as Andros's deputy, fled to England and the populace rose under an impetuous German leader, Jacob Leisler, who continued to rule that province almost as a dictator for two tumultuous years. In Maryland also there was an armed revolution, colored by the religious animosity between Catholics and Protestants. Apart, however, from these three ripples that lapped our shores from the great storm overseas, the colonists waited in peace to learn what the sudden change in English rule might hold in store for them.

A

LETTER

From A

Gentleman

OF THE

City of New - York

To Another,

Concerning the Troubles which happen'd in That Province in the Time of the late Happy REVOLUTION.

Printed and Sold by *William Bradford* at the Sign of the Bible in *New - York,* 1698.

FACSIMILE OF THE TITLE-PAGE OF A LETTER DENOUNCING LEISLER AND HIS FOLLOWERS

From the original printed by Bradford in the New York Public Library.

CHAPTER III

THE DUEL WITH FRANCE

WHEN James II dropped the Great Seal of England into the Thames as he fled to France the Stuart dynasty and tyranny were ended. The new monarchs, William and Mary, were not absolute, and from the nature of the Revolution which had brought them to the throne the influence of Parliament and of the merchant class in England were both increased. The colonies gained much by the change but not as much as they had expected.

The Stuarts had contemplated a colonial system in which the supreme power would reside in themselves and which would be administered locally in the provinces by governors and councils appointed by them with no bothersome popular assemblies. That dream was dropped in the Thames with the Great Seal, but on the other hand the eighteenth century was dawning, the age of reason, of logic and legality. The colonial charters which had been threatened by James were safe under William, but the new one granted to Massachusetts in 1691 indicated a new trend. Under it the province became a royal colony, with a governor appointed by the King, an assembly elected by property owners, and a council elected by the assembly with the governor holding a veto power over nominations and legislation. Freedom of conscience, however, was provided for all Protestants, and the old Puritan theocracy was denied further control, a property and not a religious qualification being provided for the franchise.

The eighteenth-century policy of colonial administration was to be marked by the desire to reduce all the colonial governments to a more or less uniform status of royal provinces; the royal officials, from governor down, were to be expected to maintain the prerogative; and Parliament was to take a more active part in passing laws designed to regulate trade and other imperial concerns within colonial borders.

A TRUE COPY

OF THE

OATHS

That are appointed by Act of Parliament, made in the
First Year of Their present Majesties Reign; to be
Taken instead of the Oaths of Supremacy and Allegiance, and the Declaration appointed to be made,
Repeated and Subscribed

I *A. B.* do sincerely Promise and Swear, That I will be Faithful, and bear true Allegiance to Their Majesties, King *WILLIAM* and Queen *MARY.*
So help me God, &c.

I *A. B.* do Swear, That I do from my Heart Abhor, Detest, and Abjure, as Impious and Heretical, that Damnable Doctrine and Position, *That Princes Excommunicated or Deprived by the Pope, or any Authority of the See of Rome, may be Deposed or Murthered by their Subjects, or any other whatsoever.*

And I do Declare, That no Foreign Prince, Person, Prelate, State, or Potentate, hath, or ought to have any Jurisdiction, Power, Superiority, Preeminence, or Authority Ecclesiastical or Spiritual within this Realm.

So help me God, &c.

I *A. B.* do solemnly and sincerely in the presence of God, profess, testifie and declare, that I do believe that in the Sacrament of the Lords Supper, there is not any Transubstantiation of the Elements of Bread and Wine into the Body and Blood of Christ, at or after the Consecration thereof, by any person whatsoever, and that the Invocation or adoration of the Virgin Mary or any other Saint, and the sacrifice of the Mass as they are now used in the Church of Rome, are Superstitious and Idolatrous. And I do solemnly in the presence of God, profess, testifie and declare, that I do make this Declaration and every part thereof in the plain and ordinary sence of the words read unto me, as they are commonly understood by English Protestants, without any Evasion, Equivocation or mental Reservation whatsoever, and without any Dispensation already granted me for this purpose by the Pope, or any Authority or Person whatsoever, or without any hope of any such Dispensation from any Person or Authority whatsoever, or without thinking that I am or can be acquitted, before God or Man, or absolved of this Declaration or any part thereof, although the Pope or any other Person or Persons or Power whatsoever should dispence with, or annul the same or declare that it was null and void from the beginning.

FACSIMILE OF THE OATH OF ALLEGIANCE TO KING WILLIAM AND
QUEEN MARY
From the Library of Congress.

The period from 1690 to 1763 was to be notable for three main currents of events. First, in America itself, there was to be a shift from the mere planting of new colonies to the consolidation and expansion of those already planted, with much increase of population and new racial admixtures. Secondly, in England, there was to be a logical and understandable, if unwise, effort to consolidate the colonial administration and to bring a uniformity consonant with the eighteenth-century mind out of the extreme variety left by the less logical and legalistic seventeenth. Thirdly, on both sides of the water, there was to be the long duel with France, which was to result, in 1763, in the ejection of that nation from Canada and the West.

During her history America has enjoyed exactly one century, from 1814 to 1914, of more or less isolation from the struggles which have almost incessantly torn Europe. Both before and after that century we have always perforce taken an active part in international affairs. Until the peace of 1814 we were caught in almost every eddy of European policy, and although the hundred years of isolation was in many ways of inestimable advantage to us in our formative period, that has now passed forever, whether we would wish it so or not. Even in that period of comparative isolation, however, there was constant interchange of cultural and other influences between Europe and ourselves, and to understand both our past and the problems of our future it is better to think in terms of that constant inter-relationship rather than of our merely partial and temporary isolation.

The fall of the Stuarts in England at once precipitated war between England and France, which automatically involved the colonies of both empires in America. To the south of the English colonies, there was Florida,—then a province much more widely extended geographically than the modern State,—where were the hostile Spaniards. North of Maine, and everywhere to the west of the Allegheny Mountain chain, were the French. English America occupied merely a narrow strip of coast, a thousand miles long and only two or three hundred miles wide,—much in shape like Chili today. To the east was the sea, and to the west the wooded heights of the mountain frontier. Between these two, in the narrow thousand-mile strip, were our towns or scattered farms and plantations.

In 1690 there were about 215,000 English as against possibly only about 12,000 French. The French, however, were a unit and could carry out a single, highly centralized policy. The English were

FRENCH
SETTLEMENTS
in North America

◉ French Forts

under twelve different local governments, of varying efficiency, developing different policies, and all so extremely jealous of one another as to make united action practically impossible. In addition, there was the Indian.

Racial pride or prejudice had prevented any fraternization between the English settlers and the savages. Moreover, in most of the colonies the fur trade was of very minor importance. The English were fundamentally farmers and home-builders. With the exception of the Iroquois in central New York, the native for the English was neither a business partner nor a military ally. He was, for the most part, a dangerous animal, like the panthers, wolves, and wild-cats, or a nuisance like the stones and tree stumps, to be cleared away before advancing settlements.

The French, on the other hand, had no racial antipathy. They became brothers of the savages, lived with them and took Indian mistresses or wives. They were traders, adventurers, explorers, not settlers, and roamed thousands of miles in the interior of the continent, making friends of all the Indian tribes, and erecting forts and trading posts. By about 1700 they had established these as far west as Minnesota, and up and down the Mississippi River and its tributaries, although New Orleans was not founded until 1718. If the French had no objections to taking squaws for wives, neither had they any scruples about using the savage braves as allies in war and turning them loose to scalp, torture, and murder our ancestors along our whole frontier. This was what made the mere 12,000 French so formidable to the English.

The war begun in Europe in 1689 between two civilized nations was almost immediately echoed back from the American forests by the warwhoop of the savages. With much cruelty, parties of French and Indians fell on our settlements at such far separated points as Portland, then called Falmouth, Salmon Falls, and Schenectady. The New England colonies and New York, burning with desire for revenge, called a joint meeting to plan a common campaign against the enemy, but, as was almost always to prove the case, they were unable to co-operate efficiently. An expedition sent out by Massachusetts under Governor Phips got as far as attacking Quebec unsuccessfully, but the French and Indians continued to harry the New England frontier unmercifully, and when peace was declared in Europe in 1697, "King William's War," as it was called in America, had been entirely indecisive on our side of the water.

Peace was of short duration, and in 1701 began the struggle which European historians call "the War of the Spanish Succession" and which we call "Queen Anne's War." Lasting until the Peace of Utrecht in 1713 it was of much the same character as the preceding one, save for the not unimportant fact that England tried to assist the colonists by sending out naval expeditions to work in concert with them for the conquest of Canada. The Spanish, being allied with the French, also raided our Carolina settlements from Florida. New England suffered most, however, and the attack on Deerfield in 1704, when fifty French, with a couple of hundred Indians, killed fifty-three of its inhabitants and carried off more than a hundred captive, was merely one of the best-known of many episodes in our border wars.

Unfortunately the attempted co-operation between the British fleet and the New Englanders in several successive years brought only losses and irritation to the colonists, owing mainly to the incapacity of the British commanders. Nevertheless, when peace was signed England had made several notable gains in America. Besides the Hudson Bay region, Acadia, which became the province of Nova Scotia (New Scotland), and Newfoundland were ceded to her by France, with a beneficial effect on the American fisheries. Spain granted her special privileges in the slave trade, which greatly increased that traffic and was not unimportant as a factor in fastening slavery on our later South.

The eighteenth century was one of favoritism, patronage, and venality in politics. England was no worse, and rather better, in the tone of her public life than most countries, but the evil system made for confusion, lack of efficiency, careless and incompetent statesmanship. In spite of constant squabbling between the popularly elected American assemblies and the royally appointed governors, America was a loyal part of the empire.

Unhappily, whenever the Americans and English tried to work together, as in the several abortive Canadian expeditions in Queen Anne's War, the only result had been mutual exasperation. Thus in the war with Spain which began in 1739 under the odd name of "the war of Jenkins's ear," the colonists made a notable display of loyalty. American volunteers were asked for by the British for a joint expedition against the Spanish West Indies. Over 3700 Americans, mostly from New England, volunteered and went, of whom over two thirds died, chiefly as a result of the total inefficiency of the British naval and military officers. The disgraceful conditions in the British Navy at that time, the darkest period in its glorious history, were, perhaps, no worse than those in our own army department at the time of the Spanish War, but whereas in the latter case we were all Americans in the mess together, in the first case the colonials naturally contrasted their own willingness to help with the incapacity of the government over-seas.

Co-operation was much more successful in the War of the Austrian Succession, 1744–1748, when in 1745 a joint attack was made on the strong fortress of Louisbourg by the British fleet under Commodore Warren and an American force, largely made up of men from Maine, under command of William Pepperell of Kittery. The colonials and English, as well as both branches of the service, worked together in harmony for once and captured the French stronghold. Unfortunately the favorable effect of this on American sentiment was largely destroyed by the fact that in the treaty of peace England returned to the enemy the fortress stronghold, so important to America and in the capture of which all the colonies had taken great pride. Under the conditions of the moment, England, which was always thinking of the empire as a whole, and herself as centre, could do nothing else. The Americans, however, naturally felt that their efforts had been thrown away and their interests sacrificed, although England made a heavy payment in cash to Massachusetts to reimburse her for a large part of the cost of the expedition.

A much more important struggle was now imminent. The various treaties between England and France had never settled the questions between them. The desires of the two empires were clashing in many parts of the world, but our own story is confined to America. There also the two contestants were closing in on each other.

The English government was beginning to look westward across the mountains to the fertile lands beyond, where also a group of Virginians, including two brothers of George Washington, had obtained a grant to 200,000 acres of land south of the Ohio River, and another large land company, likewise west of the mountains, had been organized. On the other hand, the French, whose posts and settlements extended up and down the whole Mississippi Valley from New Orleans to Lake Superior, had been working eastward. They also coveted the Ohio Valley and the country between the mountains and river.

In 1753 the two currents met. After some preliminary parleys, an expedition was sent out by Governor Dinwiddie of Virginia under command of George Washington, then a lad of twenty-one, as lieutenant-colonel. The French were too strong for him, and he had to surrender to the enemy at Fort Necessity on the 4th of July, 1754. The question was now clearly posed. Was the whole of the country west of the mountains to remain in the possession of the French with their savage allies, or was it to be open to settlement and development by the English colonists? That was the *American* problem.

The *imperial* one was far wider, and ranged from the Mississippi to the Ganges. England realized the desperate nature of the struggle upon which she was now to enter. The world was at stake,— not simply the American continental colonies but the rich West Indies, the balance of power in Europe, the African trade, India, the wealth of the Orient, the life of empires. Every resource would be needed and have to be strained. How far could the Americans handle alone their own end of the affair? United they had great potential strength, but could they, jealous as they were, unite?

England suggested that we call an intercolonial conference to consider the question from the standpoint of a joint Indian policy, for it was the Indian allies of the French rather than the French themselves that counted. Twenty-five delegates from seven colonies met in the old City Hall at Albany in 1754, the most distinguished gathering of native American ability that had yet been seen. Among others, there were Thomas Hutchinson of Massachusetts, later to be bitterly hated as a Tory but at this time regarded as one of the best and greatest of Americans; James De Lancey, like Hutchinson a man of great wealth and Lieutenant-Governor of New York; Benjamin Franklin from Pennsylvania; Stephen Hopkins of Rhode Island; and others, all notable in their colonies. The Indians were also there, "King Hendrick" of the Mohawks, representing the Six Nations. He complained bitterly that whereas the French were men and building forts everywhere, the English were "like women, bare and open, without fortifications anywhere."

A treaty was made with the savages, but the larger problem of a Plan of Union, advanced by Governor Shirley of Massachusetts, failed of success. A plan proposed by Franklin was, indeed, agreed upon by the convention but did not meet acceptance generally when referred back to the several colonies for approval. Jealousies and provincialism of outlook are characteristic of all colonies at a certain stage of their growth, as the later histories of Canada and Australia witness, but it is only fair to keep our failure of 1754 in mind when we shall come to consider the later policy of England.

The following year England sent over two regiments of regulars under command of General Braddock to strike at the French by capturing Fort Duquesne at the junction of the Alleghany and Monongahela Rivers. The story of his defeat and death in the wilderness and the saving of the remnant of his army by Washington is well known. Braddock was a brave officer but obstinate, lacking in tact, and, with his long experience in European warfare, disdainful of advice by the Americans. A regular army officer is rarely an easy person for civilians or militia to get along with, and there was much ill-feeling between the English regulars and our colonials who had had experience in Indian raids but did not suffer discipline gladly.

The English General Loudon, in New York and New England, also did nothing to raise the Americans' respect for British official efficiency or tact. Nevertheless, these facts should not make us forget that as the war went on it was waged more and more by the forces sent over by England and less by the militia of the colonies. The years 1756 and 1757 were full of disasters, but after the great William Pitt swept away the lesser politicians in England and became Prime Minister, the trend of events changed swiftly.

In 1758, 41 British warships and 11,000 troops, with only a few Americans, recaptured Louisbourg. Colonel Bradstreet captured Fort Frontenac on Lake Ontario. General Forbes with 1200 Highlanders and four times that number of colonials marched against Fort Duquesne, to find it abandoned by the French, and the place was renamed Pittsburgh. In his attempt to attack Canada by the Lake Champlain route, General Abercrombie made a bad failure, but the following year, 1759, Fort Niagara, Ticonderoga, Crown Point, and Quebec were all taken from the enemy by British forces in which there was but a sprinkling of colonials, the capture of Quebec being effected under the immortal Wolfe. More than twice as many New Englanders took part in the attack on Havana in 1762 as were included in the capture of the French city. Although Spain had come to the aid of France, England was victorious in all quarters by 1763. France's naval power was temporarily destroyed; she had lost India; and in the Treaty of Paris she ceded all of her possessions in North America east of the Mississippi to England except the small island at the mouth of that river. By a secret treaty she also ceded all of "Louisiana" west of the river to Spain. Her North American Empire had crumbled to dust.

It is well that it did so, for had England, fighting with Prussia against France, Spain, and Austria, lost instead of won, the effect on our history would have been almost incalculable. Even if a defeated England had not been forced to turn over her American colonies to the rule of France, those colonies at best would have been encircled for an indefinite period by the successful Catholic powers, without the English ideas of liberty, and in control of perhaps a hundred thousand savages to unleash on our borders. There could have been no expansion for us westward across the mountains. There would have been in the next generation no American Revolution and no United States. It was the strength of England and not that of the colonies which had achieved the world victory, a point on which we shall have to dwell later. Deferring the larger aspects of the end of the war, we must return to consider local American affairs.

Although the duel for empire, lasting for seventy years, had been fought in many quarters of the world as well as in America, it was naturally the part that the Americans had taken which interested them most and seemed to them all-important. We minimized our constant inability to unite, and on the other hand magnified all our own local successes and examples of bravery in border war. We had been in close co-operation with the British regulars on many occasions and almost without exception had gained a poor impression of them, both for inefficiency and bad manners.

Just as the city man is inclined to think himself superior to the countryman, so the citizen of any home country is likely to adopt a somewhat superior attitude toward the colonial, always and everywhere. We could not have ousted the French without the power of England but the general picture remaining in our minds was well exemplified in the popular contrast between the brave but overbearing and pig-headed Braddock and the quiet young Washington who knew so much better the needs of our frontier form of war. The sum total of irritation between British subjects on the two sides of the water had thus been notably increased by a couple of generations of joint undertakings.

In civil government there had also been a constant cause for irritation in all the colonies, except Connecticut and Rhode Island, neither of which had a Royal Governor. That official occupied everywhere a very difficult position. As the representative of the King and of the central authority in the empire, he was expected to maintain the royal prerogatives. On the other hand, he was dependent for his salary not on England but on the votes of the colonial assemblies. Every governor, as Benjamin Franklin said, "has two Masters; one who gives him his Commission, and one who gives him his Pay."

Owing to the excessive space usually given to New England in our earlier histories, the struggles in Massachusetts between the assemblies and such governors as Shute or Burnet have tended to make it appear that the fight for liberty was peculiarly a New England product. In fact, such contests were waged everywhere, in the Proprietary and Royal Colonies alike, nowhere more constantly and openly, for example, than in New Jersey and Pennsylvania. Some of the governors sent out were excellent men, such as Spotswood or Burnet, but England had not then developed that civil service for colonial administration which has become the finest in the world. Many colonial governors in the eighteenth century were mere needy adventurers, but, good or bad, they were bound to be storm centres of bitter political controversy.

Control of the purse has always been the strongest bulwark of freedom, and it was fortunate that England left this control to the colonists. They, on their side, naturally employed it to the fullest extent, and the whole history of this period is the story of constant use of financial pressure by the assemblies to secure the approval of the governors to popular measures and even to force them to disobey their instructions and the terms of their commissions. Under the circumstances of distance, lack of direct representation in Parliament, and other matters incidental to the colonial status, such contests between the popularly elected assemblies in America and the governors from over-seas, generation after generation, came to appear like a contest not merely between the subject and the Crown as it would have in England, but as a struggle by the Americans for their rights as Americans against the power of the mother country.

Against local opposition of one sort or another it was almost im-

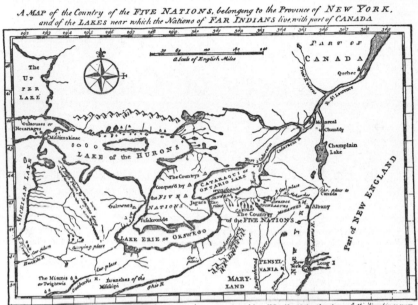

A MAP of the Country of the FIVE NATIONS, belonging to the Province of NEW YORK, and of the LAKES near which the Nations of FAR INDIANS live, with part of CANADA

FACSIMILE OF A MAP IN COLDEN'S *HISTORY OF THE FIVE NATIONS,*
PRINTED IN LONDON IN 1747
From the Lenox Collection, New York Public Library.

possible even for a good governor to adopt a wise policy. Governor Burnet's experience in New York before he was transferred to Massachusetts well illustrates the difficulties of the whole colonial situation. One of the greatest, if not the greatest danger, to the American colonies was the French; and the power of the French was their control of the Indians by means of the fur trade. In 1726 Burnet, having consulted with the expert on Indian affairs, Cadwallader Colden, author of the *History of the Five Indian Nations,* sought to check the French influence by establishing an American trading post at Oswego and also by stopping the sale of Indian trading goods to the French at Montreal by the Albany merchants. The English trading goods were better and cheaper than the French, but selling them to the French to use with the Indians was almost like selling firearms to an enemy.

New York, of all the colonies, was the best situated, on account

July 14th. 1703.
Prices of Goods

Supplyed to the

Eastern Indians,

By the several Truckmasters ; and of the Peltry received by the Truckmasters of the said *Indians*.

ONe yard Broad Cloth, *three* Beaver skins, *in season*.
One yard & half Gingerline, *one* Beaver skin, *in season*
One yard Red or Blew Kerley, *two* Beaver skins, *in season*.
One yard good Duffels, *one* Beaver skin, *in season*.
One yard & half broad fine Cotton, *one* Beaver skin, *in season*
Two yards of Cotton, *one* Beaver skin, *in season*.

What shall be accounted in Value equal One Beaver in season : Viz.

ONe Otter skin in season, is one Beaver
One Bear skin in season, is one Beaver,

INDIAN TRADE—A FACSIMILE OF A BROADSIDE
In the Library of Congress.

of its easy entry to the interior of the continent by the Hudson-Mohawk Valleys, to engage in the fur trade on a large scale. By a shrewd use of its superior goods and location, the colony could have done much to alienate the Indians from the French in the very heart of their central empire. This would have been of great advantage not only to New York but to other colonies whose frontiers were constantly ravaged. The New Yorkers, however, cared nothing about the other colonies, and the merchants of Manhattan and Albany, who were getting rich from selling goods to Montreal, thought little of the frontier. They took care therefore, after the manner of "big business" always, to block sound social policy for the sake of profits. They not only wrecked the governor's plan but his own career.

Throughout this period there was constant effort to resist imperial control and to demand larger rights; and almost invariably the colonists won. Sometimes this was accomplished peacefully, as in Pennsylvania, where the proprietor Penn agreed to a new Charter of Privileges in 1701, enlarging the rights of self-government; or was the result of tumultuous revolution as in North Carolina, where for seven years before "Cary's Rebellion" in 1711 the poorer people had been carrying on armed resistance against the authorities and wealthier elements.

England, as we have said, thought of the American colonies, when she thought of them in statesmanlike fashion at all, as merely one part of an interdependent and nicely balanced economic empire. Our ancestors naturally thought of them as their own, with which they could do as they liked and whose natural resources and trade opportunities were to be exploited to the limit, primarily for their own benefit. Just as capital and labor rarely look at economic problems from the same point of view, so the metropolis of any empire and one of its colonies often clash in their views without either of them suspecting that they may be narrow-minded or selfish. The point of view evolves unconsciously from all the surrounding conditions of each.

Such a clash of views and interests left a landmark in this period in the "Molasses Act" passed by Parliament in 1733. The colonies had always tacitly acknowledged the right of that body, becoming more active in imperial legislation as the century advanced, to pass laws designed to regulate the trade of the empire as a whole. It was part of the price paid for being a member of a strong empire instead of a waif outside in days when such a waif was sure to be pounced on by some imperialistically minded nation. The expanding commerce of the colonies, however, was beginning to be hampered by the restrictions of the Navigation Acts, and there was much smuggling and clandestine trading with countries outside the imperial system.

New England, as we have noted, had always fitted least easily into the mercantile scheme from the nature of her products. She had gradually built up a trade which rested to a considerable extent on rum. Selling horses, timber, and other products to the sugar planters in the West Indies, she got in exchange molasses from which she distilled rum which she used in the slave trade and for heavy domestic consumption, lay and clerical. By 1730 the British Sugar Islands were fast running down, and the French islands were far richer and more fertile. As New England trade was being diverted to them, the British West Indian planters brought the matter up in Parliament and asked for a bill prohibiting the Americans from trading with the French.

Clearly the interests of two integral parts of the empire were in conflict. As a member of Parliament wrote, "our Northern Colonies tell us, 'If we pass the Bill, we destroy their Trade,' and our Southern Colonies say, 'If we do not pass the Bill, they are undone.'" There was also a larger question. The whole period was dominated by the contest between England and France. Was it wise for Parliament to allow the New Englanders to build up French commercial power in the West Indies at the expense of the British? It was decided to sacrifice New England's local interest to the larger ones of the empire as a whole, and a bill was passed laying a prohibitive duty on the import of rum or molasses from the French islands.

Had the law been obeyed by the New Englanders their trade would have been ruined and their whole economic structure, none too strong, would have toppled. They naturally felt that Parliament had completely sacrificed them. The tremendous danger of Parliamentary interference with American affairs had become evident. On the other hand, England made no serious effort to enforce the law, and the French trade went on as before, only thenceforward as illegal smuggling. The lessons, however, of the latent danger from the power over-seas, and the ease with which it could apparently be flouted, were not lost on our ancestors. To the just wrath of Pitt they continued to do a highly lucrative business with the French Islands even during the French and Indian War, when such trading was having a serious ill effect on their own struggle with the enemy.

The growing self-confidence and self-consciousness of Americans in this period was due not only to contacts with English officers, constant and successful struggles to control governors, and easy nullification of Royal orders and Acts of Parliament. Between 1690 and 1763 the population increased from 215,000 to about 1,800,000. Only one new colony had been founded, that of Georgia in 1732, and most of the increase thus occurred in the older ones. The Georgia colony had been started by General James Oglethorpe, an English philanthropist, who secured a charter with the sole idea of making a retreat in the New World where poor people from the debtors' prisons might start life afresh. Being granted the land between South Carolina and the Spaniards in Florida, he set to work but the colony grew slowly. Comparatively few debtors emigrated, but on the other hand Scotch Highlanders and Germans both settled in considerable numbers.

What happened in Georgia was symptomatic of what was occurring in all of the colonies. There was little English immigration during the eighteenth century, the marvellous growth in population being mostly due to native births and to large influxes of Scotch, Irish, Germans, and to a lesser extent, Swiss. All these facts tended to make the American of 1760 feel himself more of an American and less of an Englishman than his ancestors had done some generations before.

In the early part of the century there was great distress both in Ireland and Germany. In the former, drought, sheep-rot and disease seemed destined to complete the ruin wrought by the political and economic policy of the British. Those who suffered most were the Scotch Presbyterians in the north of the island, whose standard of living had been higher than that of the Catholic Irish in the south. In the second decade of the century long term leases for farms fell in in great numbers and stony-hearted landlords demanded double and treble rents to renew them. A vast exodus of these people began to America, where they arrived chiefly in Philadelphia and from thence poured out into the frontier counties of Pennsylvania and down into the Shenandoah Valley.

Though they came to all of the colonies, notably the Carolinas, they always went out to the frontier, where land was cheap, and made the finest frontiersmen we have known. Of the social effects of this great movement of a people we shall speak in the next chapter, and are here concerned only with what we may call its imperial aspect. It is impossible to calculate accurately the number who came, but historians have estimated them as high as 500,000, and I think we may conservatively place it at 300,000 to 400,000, counting the immediate descendants of the immigrants. When it is recalled that great numbers of these came to us with hatred for England as one of their strongest passions, it becomes evident that something very momentous had happened in the relations between the mother country and the American colonies.

Germany had not recovered from the terrific slaughter and dev-

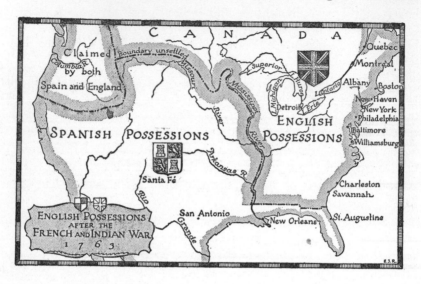

astation of the Thirty Years' War, and in the Palatinate and other provinces, as in the German cantons of Switzerland, there were intense poverty, suffering, and religious persecution in the early eighteenth century. From this mass of human misery came another great movement of population to our shores, the Germans settling largely in Pennsylvania, Maryland, and Virginia, the Swiss going mostly to Carolina. For these Germans also there are no statistics in the modern sense, but I think it safe to say that by 1763 there were at least 100,000 of them in the colonies, and quite possibly many more. This stock had no hatred of England, but on the other hand, no knowledge of her or loyalty to her. They knew only their new homes in America and their struggles to win them.

By 1763 England had won her duel with France. She owned North America from the Atlantic to the Mississippi, and from

Spanish Florida to the Arctic Sea. But in this vast territory were the irreconciled French in Canada, possibly 300,000 savages who were hostile to English rule, several hundred thousand Scotch-Irish with a tradition of hatred for English oppression, 100,000 Germans who cared nothing about England, perhaps 400,000 black slaves who knew nothing of her, and a sturdy population of possibly 600,-000 of her own sons and their descendants who were loyal but who were chips of the old block in their love of liberty and who had been used to a greater degree of self-government in all their daily concerns than even Englishmen enjoyed at home. Here was a problem that would call for the wisest possible statesmanship. Before we consider it further, and the failure to solve it, we must pause to get a better idea of what sort of life our ancestors had built up by the time that they were forced into a bloody civil war with the nation from which a majority of them had sprung.

CHAPTER IV

AMERICAN LIFE IN 1763

ALTHOUGH by the period now reached by our story there was much diversity among all of the thirteen colonies, they also fall easily into three quite clearly differentiated groups,— the Southern, Middle, and New England. It was in the tidewater and older sections of these that the differences between colonies and groups were most noticeable. Back of all of them, from Maine to Georgia, ran the frontier where conditions were comparatively uniform, as were also the attitudes of the frontiersmen toward the wealthier residents of the old settlements. We shall come to this important point later in the chapter, and must consider here the broad differences between the groups named.

The Southern one, which included the oldest colony, Virginia, extended from Georgia to Maryland. It was not a region solely of big plantations. There were many small planters who tilled the land themselves without slaves or with only two or three. But as we shall see, life had been getting harder for these poorer people, many of whom had gone to the frontier; and the wealth which the rich had gained had come from securing in one way and another large estates in land and ample slave power with which to work them.

Slavery was recognized by law and practiced in every one of the colonies, but it was economically profitable on a large scale only in the South, with its milder climate and its simple and undiversified agriculture. In Maryland, great landowners like the Carrolls, who had one grant of 60,000 acres, and the Dulanys, also with large grants, had made fortunes by settling German immigrants on their properties as tenant farmers. But for the most part through the South the important families, socially and economically, were the owners of large plantations, for tobacco or rice, who lived on them in a sort of patriarchal life with their troops of blacks. The only town larger than a village was Charleston, which may have had a population of 9000, and the type of life of the southern gentleman was much like that of well-to-do squires in the counties of old England, modified by climate and slavery. His ties with the old country were

---

March 10, 1752.

R AN away from the Subfcriber, living in *Prince George* County, about a Fortnight ago, a lufty well-fet *Virginia*-born Negroe Man Slave, named *Vallen*; he is a fmooth-tongued cunning Fellow, and it's probable will endeavour to impofe on People, by pretending to be what he is not; and it's not unlikely will change his Name; he is between 30 and 40 Years of Age, about 5 Feet 10 Inches high, and had on when he went away, an Oznabrigs Shirt, a Cotton Waiftcoat and Breeches, dy'd Yellow, and a Pair of Breeches not dy'd. Whoever will take up and fecure him, fo that I may have him again, fhall have Two Piftoles if taken up on the South Side of *James* River, if in *Carolina*, or the North Side of *James* River, Three Piftoles Reward, befides what the Law allows, paid by

William Broadnax.

AN ADVERTISEMENT FOR A RUNAWAY SLAVE
The reward offered for capture varies according to the location.
From "The Virginia Gazette" of 1752.

close. London merchants bought his staple crop once a year, looked after his money or debts, and shipped over on order his clothes, silver, books, and mahogany. His sons frequently went to England to study at the universities or master law in the Temple, and to get

Cleared Outwards.

March 26. The Warren, of Whitehaven, Robert Lerham, for Whitehaven, with 238 Hhds. of Tobacco.

April 4. Sloop Molly, of Virginia, Solomon Ewell, for Barbados, with 416 lbs. of Tobacco, & 1950 Bufhch of Corn.

ADVERTISEMENT OF CARGOES IN VESSELS OUT OF VIRGINIA
From "The Virginia Gazette" of August 7, 1752.

their social training in London or in Tunbridge Wells and other fashionable English spas, as depicted by Thackeray in *The Virginians.*

In the Middle Colonies of Pennsylvania, New Jersey, and New York, we find quite different ways and occupations. In the first, the mixed population of Quaker English, Germans, Welsh, and Scotch had modest farms or were acquiring wealth in manufacturing, such as breweries and iron works, or in trade. Philadelphia was the largest city on the continent and a bustling place of over 20,000 people of whom so many were Germans that the street signs were painted in the two languages. Money and social position there belonged rather to the city merchant or manufacturer than to the planter, as in the South.

New York was the second largest city, having just outdistanced Boston, and was a cosmopolitan town chiefly interested in commerce. Thanks largely to having had a succession of peculiarly unscrupulous governors early in the century, such as Fletcher and Cornbury, many New York families had acquired huge grants of land up the Hudson and elsewhere, and there was a social distinction in the possession of such spoils. They had developed, however, no such plantation life as in Virginia southward, and had been too grasping as landlords to succeed in planting tenant farmers as had, in such a business-like way, Carroll and Dulany in Maryland. The great manorial families in New York, nevertheless, were extremely influential in the government and in controlling the distribution of offices. Seven townships belonged to the Livingstones; the Beekmans and Schuylers owned most of Dutchess County; the Phillipses and Heathcotes, six manors in Westchester; and the van Rensselaers nearly 700 square miles near Albany. Lord Cornbury, as governor, had made one single grant of 2,000,000 acres, and it was chiefly out of such favoritism or bribed gifts, that had come the old New York "aristocracy." Besides the landed proprietors, including the old Dutch "patroons" along the river, there was also growing up a class of rich merchants, whose power and influence increased with their wealth. These were especially numerous and rich, of course, in the city of New York itself, whose commerce vied with that of its greater competitor, Philadelphia.

Crossing into the Puritan colonies we would at once have sensed a great difference, as all travellers of the day did. Boston was a town of 15,000 and Newport about half as large, but for the most part New England was a land of small farms closely grouped in villages about the church. There were a neatness and a thriftiness lacking farther south, and the village greens and the landscape with its elms and meadows and hedgerows could almost be mistaken for a bit of old England. As in the Middle Colonies, wealth came chiefly from manufacturing or shipping, but the sturdy farmer, of pure English descent, having his say in town meeting or as church member,

THE GIBBS HOUSE, CHARLESTON, SOUTH CAROLINA. BUILT IN 1752

IN THE VIEUX CARRÉ, THE OLD FRENCH AND SPANISH PART OF
NEW ORLEANS

Photographs by Edward Larocque Tinker.

JOSEPH CABOT HOUSE, SALEM. BUILT IN 1748

VAN COURTLANDT MANSION, NEW YORK. BUILT IN 1748
From the Essex Institute, Salem.

counted for more in the scene than he did in plutocratic New York or in polyglot Pennsylvania. As each New England town had been settled, its inhabitants had been allotted lands in fee simple, and with no fresh immigration for many generations and no alien stocks, a native yeomanry had grown up with a remarkable degree of tenacity and independence.

In a hundred and forty years, the stony ground, a cruel climate, and a profound preoccupation with religious problems according to Calvin, had "set" the New England character. Since 1692, when a hundred and fifty persons were imprisoned for witchcraft in Massachusetts and twenty were killed, the devil had not been thus fought there with carnal weapons of the law, but there was still a certain strength of beliefs and a grim determination in New England that was not to be found in money-making New York, or among the Quakers or German Pietists of Pennsylvania, or the easy-going Southerners. New England was a land apart, and desired to remain so, its inhabitants having always been taught by their clergy to consider themselves as peculiarly the people of God in a wicked world. It was in a sense the Scotland of America.

The original immigrants who settled all the colonies were from much the same social grades in England whether they had settled North or South. Everywhere there had been a sprinkling of "gentlemen," as the term was then understood, among the great mass of farmers, artisans, and others, but practically without exception the whole of the colonial population had sprung from the laboring and the middle classes, upper and lower, scarcely a single titled aristocrat and only a comparatively few "younger sons" having made their homes over here. The origin, for example, of such Virginia families as the Beverleys, Byrds, and Carters had been merely good middle class in Europe, as had been that of the French families in South Carolina or Dutch in New York which were to become notable. Both virtues and vices vary in different classes, and those in America were almost wholly untinged by the aristocratic. This does not mean that there were not social distinctions, clearly made and sharply insisted upon, in colonial days. There most assuredly were. But America generally, then as always, was based on the middle-class outlook, using the phrase in no invidious sense, rather than upon the aristocratic.

On the other hand, men are moulded by different forms of social and economic life, and as these came to vary in the different sections, the ideals of each became different from the others. The aristocrat has been the product of generations who have been in a position to rule others, and who have learned the habits and responsibilities of such rule; who from wealth and leisure have developed the art of manners and social life; and who from possessing an assured social position, buttressed by visible emblems, have acquired independence of public opinion. The man who has a notable

---

To be SOLD, by the Subscriber, near the Capitol, in Williamsburg,

GENUINE French Claret, at 40 s. per Dozen, Samples whereof may be had at 4 s. a Bottle, net Barbadoes Rum at 5 s. per Gallon ; also fine Madeira Wine, English Beer, and Hughes's Cyder, at the common Rates ; also a Cask of fine Hogs-Lard, of about 230 lb. Weight, with several Pots of Capers and Anchovies.

2   Daniel Fisher.

AN ADVERTISEMENT OF A SALE OF A SHIPMENT OF LIQUOR, CAPERS, AND ANCHOVIES

From "The Virginia Gazette" of 1752.

estate on which his family has been living for generations, who devotes his time to hunting, social life, and governing, develops a different set of qualities and ideals from one who may be just as wealthy and educated, but who lives a town life and is constantly preoccupied with the making of money from trade in severe competition with others.

By the middle of the eighteenth century, the ideals of the South with its great plantation economy and of the North with its rising mercantile interests, had begun to draw apart. The rich southerner, like the second William Byrd of Westover, for example, with his 180,000 acres, living on his large and well-known estate, with a public recognition that came quite as much from his family and place as from his own efforts, having little to do with trade and not understanding it very well, responsible for ruling and looking after his numerous slaves, regarding himself from boyhood as belonging to a superior race, devoting himself to sport and cultivating a social life of great charm, often too heedless as to expenditure and his scale of easy living, began to develop the aristocratic qualities. The entailing of the larger estates upon the oldest son also helped to build up the types and ideals of an aristocratic life.

On the other hand, in New England, without such estates, without entail, and with fortunes made or lost in trade, there was little or no tendency to modify middle-class ideals of the best and also sometimes of the narrowest sort. Business dynasties are usually brief. The richest man in New England, for example, John Hancock, inherited a fortune made by his uncle and lost it himself. Both in the Northern and Middle Colonies, the period was notable for the constant rise of new men to financial eminence. The money of the upper social class of New England was based on trade, and as ever in history, there was a vast difference in outlook between the agrarian and commercial groups. The New Englander handled his business affairs

ADVERTISEMENT OF THE BRIGANTINE *JANE*
CARRYING PASSENGERS AND FREIGHT

From "The Pennsylvania Gazette," October 27, 1748.

shrewdly and well, far better than the southerner. He took both his intellectual and religious life more seriously, and just as his class in England disliked the aristocracy there, so the New Englanders disliked the very mild aristocracy which had begun to develop in the South. On the other hand, the southerner looked down upon and disliked the New Englander. He regarded him much as an old Tory, hunting county squire in the old country would have regarded a tradesman or a London merchant. The beginnings had already been made for one of the most disastrous sectional cleavages in our history, to be steadily widened for nearly a century following.

Although the first American guide book had been published in 1732, travel between the colonies was difficult, and this helped to maintain the differences between them and to foster local peculiarities. In 1754 a combined stage and boat line was advertised to run twice a week between Philadelphia and New York, and a few other lines were started in the next decade, but the roads were bad, as were most inns, and the traveller had to rely almost solely on his own private carriage or even more, on riding horseback. New England merchants carried on some commerce by boat with the Southern colonies, but there was extremely little social intercourse between the sections. A Carroll of Maryland might go to old England, but it was as unthinkable that he would go to New England for pleasure as it was that a John Adams should tour Virginia or the Carolinas. If each had done so, they would have discovered that as compared with their fathers' times, wealth had greatly increased and the scale of living.

In all the colonies they would have found their richer friends living in beautifully designed houses of the Georgian type. The earlier architecture of the first few generations had derived rather from the mediæval in Europe, and there had been much variety in the styles introduced by English, Dutch, Swedes, Welsh, Germans, and others, but these pleasant differences tended to disappear after about 1720. Foreign strains in America have always been quickly absorbed into the prevailing English, and the new mansion of a rich German, Dutch, or Welshman came to be built uniformly in the Georgian which spread up and down the whole coast.

The change of style from the earlier period correctly interpreted a change in colonial conditions. The frontier had come to be far off from the older settlements. Life in the latter was as safe, stable, and almost as conventional as in any county of England. Wealth had accumulated and its possessors desired a dignified setting in which to display it and to conduct their social life. For this, both the architecture of the Georgian house and its furnishing were admirably adapted. They were at once dignified and homelike. The two interiors preserved in the Boston Museum of Fine Arts, one of 1690 and the other of 1750, mark vividly the change that two generations had brought. The beamed ceiling had given place to plaster (often in the larger houses of exquisite design in decoration); the rough boarding of the wall had become beautiful panelling, painted white or covered with paper imported from England; the bare floor had been covered with oriental rugs; the oak chairs with wooden or rush seats had been replaced by mahogany upholstered in satin or

Room from West Boxford, Massachusetts. *Circa* 1675-1704.

Room from the Jaffrey House, Portsmouth, New Hampshire. *Circa* 1750.

TWO INTERIORS PRESERVED IN THE BOSTON MUSEUM OF FINE ARTS

SANTA BARBARA MISSION, CALIFORNIA, 1787–1800

Left: ST. MICHAEL'S CHURCH, CHARLESTON, SOUTH CAROLINA, BUILT IN 1742

Right: SAN XAVIER DEL BAC, TUCSON, ARIZONA, BUILT BY THE FRANCISCANS
ON THE SITE OF FATHER KINO'S MISSION, FOUNDED ABOUT 1700

brocade. As we study the furniture or the rooms of this period, happily preserved in many places beside the Boston and Metropolitan Museums, we are struck by their perfect taste, their dignity, and sense of peace.

In New England, although the mansions were often as spacious as in the South, there was a certain compactness about them which befitted the long hard winters, and the town dwelling. In the South they were often in three sections, a large central portion and two smaller ones on either side, sometimes connected with the main portion and sometimes not. None of them would have been "great houses" in the English sense, but all, North and South, would have been roomy, comfortable, and often of exquisite proportions and of daintier craftsmanship in their decorative carving than those contemporary with them in England.

One Marylander, Doctor Alexander Hamilton, who did venture North, found in Rhode Island "the largest and most magnificent dwelling house" he had seen in America, that of Captain Godfrey Malbone in Newport. Wealth in New England being concentrated in the towns, the finest domestic architecture of the period has to be looked for in such places as Boston, Marblehead, Salem, and Portsmouth. Mostly of wood in the North, the larger houses were of stone in the Middle Colonies and of brick in the South. Innumerable examples might be cited of these beautiful and dignified dwellings in every colony of the period, but we may suggest as examples the McPhaedris house in Portsmouth, the Vassall in Cambridge, the Jumel in New York, Cliveden in Germantown, Westover and Mount Airy on the James in Virginia. In South Carolina, plantation wealth was being expended also in town life, and such houses as that of Miles Brewton were being built to provide a luxurious setting for a social scene as brilliant as any on the continent.

For the rich who lived in these houses, English culture, so roughly transplanted more than a century before, had come to perfect flowering. The long narrow strip of the English colonies had been settled. The rough work of pioneering seemed about over. Life was much what it was in English provincial towns and counties, only a little freer, a little less hemmed in by old conventions, customs, and class restrictions. Within a few years the storm of war was to overwhelm this old English-American life, the West was to be opened, and for more than a century a wild scramble was to ensue for untold riches, while the frontier leaped from the Appalachians to the Mississippi, from the Mississippi to the Rockies, from the Rockies to the Pacific. In the vast turmoil of it all, modern America was to be born, and the life of these old Georgian house dwellers was to come to seem as remote and un-American as that of English squires. But just before all this was to burst upon us it seemed as though America had come of age and settled down to maturity as a fully developed English provincial civilization.

Life had been hard in the early days and in the work of pioneer-

WHEREAS some ill-difpos'd Perfons have reported, that the Subfcriber hath not fufficient Entertainment : This is to give Notice, That all Gentlemen who will favour me with their Company, may depend on good Entertainment, at the *Crown* Tavern, oppofite to the *Printing-Office,* in *Williamfburg,* by

Their humble Servant,

William Dunn.

A RIVALRY BETWEEN TAVERN KEEPERS APPARENTLY INSPIRED THIS ADVERTISEMENT
From "The Virginia Gazette," 1752.

ing there had been little chance to cultivate the arts. Something had perforce to be given up in the struggle to plant a civilization where there was nothing but wilderness and savage foe. The farmer or artisan who in the settled life of the Old World had satisfied his craving for self-expression by carving the beams of his house, making chests and other pieces of furniture, carving or painting them in the winter evenings, found his time and strength occupied by sterner tasks. The man who in England might have sat by the fire and read his book, found his time and hands more than occupied in wresting a farm or plantation from forest or stony upland. Folk art and the cultivation of the mind tended to disappear, and products and activities to become wholly utilitarian. Perhaps 1700 marked the lowest artistic and mental period of the colonies. But with wealth accumulated and the wilderness conquered, an indigenous American culture, though on English models, sprang up, and while folk art did not return, there came to be a ready market for the professional artist or craftsman.

In the middle of the century B. Roberts, Alexander Gordon, and

Jeremiah Theuss were all painting portraits in South Carolina of the leading families there—the Ravenels, Porches, Manigaults, Izards, and others. In Virginia Charles Bridges was painting the wealthy planters with their wives and daughters. Hesselius in Maryland, Robert Feke in Newport, and John Smibert in Boston were among the other portrait painters, of whom each colony had its favorite. Copley was perhaps the most fashionable, and Benjamin West, who was to become President of the Royal Academy in London, was beginning his career. Landscape painting was also becoming popular, and in 1757 there was an exhibition in New York of work which was entirely that of Americans.

Music was cultivated and in the larger towns there were frequent concerts of the best compositions of the time rendered by orchestras

An Addrefs from the Society called *Quakers*, was prefented to the Houfe and read, *Pefl Meriaiem* fetting forth, that they have, with real Concern, heard that a Company of Stage Players are preparing to erect a Theatre, and exhibit Plays to the Inhabitants of this City, which they conceive, if permitted, will be fubverfive of the good Order and Morals, which they defire may be preferved in this Government, and therefore pray the Houfe to frame and prefent to the Governor, for his Affent, a Bill to prohibit fuch enfnaring and irreligious Entertainments.   *Ordered to lie on the Table*

A PROTEST OF THE QUAKERS OF PHILADELPHIA AGAINST THE APPEARANCE OF DAVID DOUGLASS AND HIS PLAYERS IN 1759

From the original Journal of the General Assembly, in the Genealogical Society, Philadelphia.

capable of playing operatic overtures and symphonies. In 1759 the first musical society, the "Orpheus Club," was organized in Philadelphia, and in 1762 was founded the well-known "Saint Cecelia Society" in Charleston after a less formal existence during the preceding quarter of a century. Both musicians and actors from Europe usually went first to the rich and luxury-loving West Indies, and thence to America by way of the South Carolina capital, where there was probably more and better drama and music to be heard than anywhere else in the colonies. New England still forbade "stage plays" as being of the devil, but from New York south there was ample opportunity to hear the works of Shakespeare, Addison, Congreve, and others, among the best or most popular dramatists of the day. This was especially the fact after the arrival of the noted English actors, Mr. and Mrs. Lewis Hallam, who came in 1750 and found so much encouragement that they remained for twenty years, playing not only in the large cities but in such small towns as Port Tobacco, Petersburg, Fredericksburg, and others in the South. The minor arts, such as silver-smithing, glass blowing, furniture making, and others, were also developing craftsmen whose work is eagerly sought after by collectors of today.

By the end of this period, eight of the colonies had their own

THE EARLIEST BUILDING OF THE BOSTON LATIN SCHOOL, ABOUT 1645

For the first ten years of its existence, school was held in the house of the head master. In the picture is shown also the rear of King's Chapel.

colleges, Harvard in Massachusetts (1636), William and Mary in Virginia (1693), Yale in Connecticut (1701), Princeton in New Jersey (1746), University of Pennsylvania (1751), Dartmouth in New Hampshire (1754), Columbia in New York (1754), and Brown in Rhode Island (1764). Some of these institutions were, it is true, but the germs of the later ones, of which even the names have been changed, but the beginnings are noteworthy of what was to be a continuous growth. Probably New England led in the matter of education, although her excellent school laws were far from being generally observed. In that section as elsewhere the statute books give very unreliable evidence as to real conditions, and Massachusetts tax-payers were not seldom as averse as those elsewhere to spending money on schools. These were not compulsory and the so-called "free" village and town schools of New England were so only for

ISAAC ROYALL, FOUNDER OF THE ROYALL PROFESSORSHIP IN THE
HARVARD LAW SCHOOL, AND HIS FAMILY

From the painting by Feke in Harvard University.

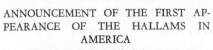

By PERMISSION of the Hon.ᵇˡᵉ *ROBERT DINWIDDIE*,
Efq; His Majefty's Lieutenant-Governor, and Commander in
Chief of the Colony and Dominion of *Virginia*.

By *a Company* of COMEDIANS, *from* LONDON,
At the THEATRE *in* WILLIAMSBURG,
On *Friday* next, being the 15th of *September*, will be prefented,
A PLAY, Call'd,
THE
MERCHANT of *VENICE*.
(Written by *Shakefpear*.)
The Part of *ANTONIO* (the MERCHANT) to be perform'd by
Mr. CLARKSON.
GRATIANO, by Mr. SINGLETON,
Lorenzo, (with Songs in Character) by Mr. ADCOCK.
The Part of *BASSANIO* to be perform'd by
Mr. RIGBY.
Duke, by Mr. Wynell.
Salanio, by Mr. Herbert.
The Part of *LAUNCELOT*, by Mr. HALLAM.
And the Part of *SHYLOCK*, (the JEW) to be perform'd by
Mr. MALONE.
The Part of *NERISSA*, by Mrs. ADCOCK,
Jeffica, by Mrs. Rigby.
And the Part of *PORTIA*, to be perform'd by
Mrs. HALLAM.
With a new occafional PROLOGUE.
To which will be added, a FARCE, call'd,
The ANATOMIST:
OR,
SHAM DOCTOR.
The Part of *Monficur le Medecin*, by
Mr. RIGBY.
And the Part of *BEATRICE*, by Mrs. ADCOCK.
⁎⁎⁎ No Perfon, whatfoever, to be admitted behind the Scenes.
BOXES, 7s. 6d. PIT and BALCONIES, 5s. 9d. GALLERY, 3s. 9d.
To begin at Six o'Clock.
Vivat Rex.

ANNOUNCEMENT OF THE FIRST AP-
PEARANCE OF THE HALLAMS IN
AMERICA

From "The Virginia Gazette" of August 28, 1752.

MRS. HALLAM AS "MARIANNE" IN
"THE DRAMATIST"

*From the Theatre Collection of the Harvard College
Library.*

NASSAU HALL AND THE PRESIDENT'S HOUSE, PRINCETON, 1764

From an engraving in Princeton University Library, after the painting by James Parker.

GEORGE WHITEFIELD PREACHING

From the portrait by John Woollaston in the National Portrait Gallery.

those children whose parents could not afford to pay. The New England system theoretically, however, was the best of all colonial ones, and the Boston Latin School possibly the finest in the country, though there were excellent private schools elsewhere, notably in Philadelphia.

New York was strikingly backward in educational, and to a considerable extent, in intellectual interests. In the South it is rather difficult to judge of conditions, although clearly they were not as inferior to New England as used to be thought from a mere study of the laws. Southern children of the richer classes usually had tutors, and when this training was followed by a few years at an English university they got a better education than fell to the lot of the New Englanders of the same social grade. The scattered mode

---

NOTICE is hereby given, That *Symes's* Free School, in *Elizabeth-City* County, will be vacant on the 25th of *March* Inst. a Tutor of a good Character, and properly qualified, may meet with good Encouragement, by applying to the Trustees of the said School.

N. B. The Land Rent of the said School is 31 *l. per Ann.* besides Perquisites.

AN OPENING FOR A "TUTOR OF GOOD CHARACTER" IN THE SYMES'S
FREE SCHOOL IN ELIZABETH CITY COUNTY
From "The Virginia Gazette" of March 12, 1752.

of settlement in the South made the problem of educating the poorer children more difficult than in the compact New England villages, but there were a good many schools in existence, and the southern apprenticeship laws provided that the apprentice must be taught at least to read and write.

The original object aimed at in American education had been to make good Christians rather than good citizens. William and Mary College in Virginia, like Harvard and Yale in New England, had been founded to train up a godly ministry. The New Englanders had made their schools town schools at a time when the suffrage was limited to church members, but when that restriction was withdrawn in the new charter of 1691, they found that the school system had been secularized. Nowhere was there a realization of the value of education merely for citizenship. The general secularization of thought however, proceeded apace in the colonies and in this,

America as usual reflected the dominant current of thought in Europe.

By 1763 our religious life was very different from what it had been a couple of generations earlier. Even in New England the first fervor of the original refugees had been cooling and the theology petrifying. Everywhere in the colonies, the people were deprived of much that in the customs and surroundings of the Old World, rich in human experience and accomplishment, had afforded color and emotional outlets. The great mass of Colonists had become emotionally starved in their narrow, dull and hardworking lives. Over these, whether in the Anglican South or Puritan New England, the extraordinary years of revivalist meetings known as "the Great Awakening" swept like a forest fire.

A number of preachers, such as Gilbert Tennent and the great Jonathan Edwards, had been preaching in a way deeply to stir the religious emotions of their hearers, and there had been minor revivals in the colonies before George Whitefield came over from England in 1738. As he and lesser preachers toured the colonies, the repressed emotions of their hearers wrought congregations to frenzy. Under the lead of the evangelicals, churches were split into what were called "Old Lights" and "New Lights," and for the first time all of the colonies were caught up in the wave of a common movement. There was intense bitterness mixed with the emotions which broke congregations in twain, but when the excitement subsided about 1744, American religious life had undergone a profound change.

The complete domination of the ministers of the old sects of whatever sort had been broken, and the influence of the conservatives who had opposed the movement, much weakened. It was in a sense a popular uprising, and the new evangelicals of all denominations felt themselves bound closer to one another than to the conservatives of their own sect. Whitefield, like John Wesley who came over in 1735, was almost more interested in pure humanitarianism than in religion, and after the first reaction of indifference following the surges of emotion, the whole movement left Americans with a greater interest in education and humanitarian reforms, in what may be called the secular aspect of religion, and with greater independence toward the individual clergyman, against whom they had asserted their own views. This was notably true even throughout Puritan New England. In that section the old ideal of the theocratic State had passed, and everywhere the field of secular interests had widened as religion had become more personal.

This drift in the spiritual life of the colonies is exemplified both in the character of the literature produced in them as the century advanced and in the shift of the intellectual centre from New England to Pennsylvania and the South. In 1705 Robert Beverley in Virginia had published his *History and Present State of Virginia* and three years later an unknown author in Maryland produced a satiric poem of genuine interest and power called *The Sot-Weed Factor*. Although both of these are more living today than most of the printed matter turned out in Boston, that town unquestionably held the primacy in intellectual matters in the period. For sheer bulk of writing probably no American author has ever equalled Cotton Mather, then the leading clergyman in the New England metropolis, who is credited with over four hundred titles. His *Diary* and his most celebrated work, the *Magnalia Christi Americana,* have much historical and antiquarian value but it is doubtful if any one outside of local New England enthusiasts ever reads him for pleasure today. This is not true of a much greater *Diary* of another Bostonian of the period, Judge Samuel Sewall, which is not only a mine of information for the life of the time but affords a very living picture of a man who is much nearer to us in character and outlook than the warped and self-torturing Mather and was also, perhaps, more typical of the upper-class Massachusetts of the day in which he carried on his profession, wrestled with his daily problems, and carried on his amusing wooings.

Jonathan Edwards, pastor of the church at Northampton, and a far greater man than Mather, was to prove in the mid-century the greatest theologian New England or possibly America has produced, but it is noteworthy that unlike Mather he neither sought nor possessed any influence on political life. As a clergyman of such dominating power he could not have escaped, a century or half century earlier, being one of the chosen leaders of the theocratic State. No one has ever carried out with more impeccable logic the Calvinistic theology, and his great treatise on the *Freedom of the Will* is one of the books of world importance published in America. His theory, however, of the utter depravity of the human soul did not suit the growing optimism and comfort of the times. Dismissed by his congregation and made president of Princeton he well illustrates the passing of the old theology from popular to mere academic interest.

PART II.

WHEREIN IT IS CONSIDERED, WHETHER THERE IS OR CAN BE ANY SUCH SORT OF FREEDOM OF WILL AS THAT WHEREIN ARMINIANS PLACE THE ESSENCE OF THE LIBERTY OF ALL MORAL AGENTS; AND WHETHER ANY SUCH THING EVER WAS OR CAN BE CONCEIVED OF.

SECTION I.

SHEWING THE MANIFEST INCONSISTENCE OFT HE ARMINIAN'NO-TION OF LIBERTY OF WILL CONSISTING IN THE WILL'S SELF-DETERMINING POWER.

HAVING taken notice of those things which may be necessary to be observed concerning the meaning of the principal terms and phrases made use of in controversies concerning human liberty, and particularly observed what *liberty* is according to the common language and general apprehension of mankind, and what it is as understood and maintained by Arminians; I proceed to consider the Arminian notion of the *freedom of the will*, and the supposed necessity of it in order to moral agency, or in order to any one's being capable of virtue or vice, and properly the subject of command or counsel, praise or blame, promises or threatenings, rewards or punishments; or whether that which has been described as the thing meant by liberty in common speech be not sufficient, and the only liberty which makes, or can make, any one a moral agent; and so properly the subject of these things.   In *this* Part

A PAGE FROM JONATHAN EDWARDS'S "FREE-DOM OF THE WILL"
From a reprint in the New York Public Library.

The man who both in his writings and his life best exemplifies the new preoccupations of the colonists was Benjamin Franklin, who abandoned Boston in his boyhood, was thereafter identified with Philadelphia. In the aphorisms that he scattered through his enormously popular *Poor Richard's Almanac,* such as "God helps them that help themselves," he struck a chord to which the people responded as they no longer would to the divines, and in his *Autobiography,* not published until after the Revolution, he not only gave for the first time the story of the rise from poverty to riches and power of a typical American career, but did so in words that went home to the simplest understanding. Not only was the most influential American writer no longer a New Englander, but more books of all sorts now came to be published outside that section than in it.

Just as the æsthetic life of the other colonies, notably in music and the drama, had become richer than that of New England, so also was the lead in scientific research passing to them. Franklin of course was to be our most noted scientific philosopher of his day, but even before the middle of the century Colden in New York, James Logan and John Bartram in Philadelphia, all had European reputations for their botanical studies. In Virginia, John Mitchell was writing the first American treatise on the principles of science, and throughout the South Mark Catesby had been carrying on his researches in natural history. In Charleston, Doctors John Lining and Lionel Chalmers were studying problems of weather and the only man in America, Doctor William Bull, who had a genuine degree as Doctor of Medicine (from Leyden) was established in that town.

The public library movement, which has been one of our notable contributions to civilization, got under way in this period, and of the seventeen subscription libraries started between 1745 and 1763 not only was the most important one that founded by Franklin, in Philadelphia, but one third of the whole number were in Pennsylvania. Massachusetts had led the way in journalism with the publication of our first newspaper, the *Boston News-Letter* in 1704, but by 1763 the best papers were all published south of New York. The most influential was *The Pennsylvania Gazette,* but the literary interest of the *South Carolina Gazette,* which published the best original verse in America, and of the various *Virginia Gazettes,* whose prose articles, in the one published by William Hunter, were quoted all over the colonies, exceeded those of any of the other score or so of colonial journals. New York was notable not only for *The New York Gazette* published in that city by William Bradford, but also for the important struggle carried on there for the freedom of the press by Peter Zenger. It was a little early yet for magazines, but a dozen, all short-lived, had been started of which four had met their deaths in Boston and eight in the Middle Colonies.

By 1763 there was thus in the colonies a well-established cultural life conforming to the eighteenth-century English pattern. So shrewd a man as Franklin considered that the country was completely settled, and the richer classes had become conservative in their outlook on what they considered to be a properly organized and well stratified society. As we shall see, the "lower classes" gave them plenty of anxiety but the magnates hoped to keep these in hand. The task, however, was not to be easy, for especially in such centres as New York, Boston, and the other larger towns, the mechanic and artisan classes were advancing rapidly in both self-consciousness and demands for political power. Under astute leaders, notably Samuel Adams, they were a few years later to form one of the most important elements in bringing the legal disputes with England into the fires of social and class passion. Another group, of different sort, which quickly increased in prestige and influence from the mid-years of the century was that of the lawyers, often despised in some communities and even legislated against a generation or two earlier, but who, in their own way, were also, like the artisans and mechanics, to become of prime importance as the struggle with England grew more serious.

If society throughout the more settled portions of the colonies was English, it was, however, English with a difference,—a difference that may be noted in many ways. It was not merely that the "American language" was already beginning to diverge from English by the retention of many Elizabethan words which had become obsolete in the old country but also by the introduction of new ones. The American psychology itself was becoming subtly different. Owing to the influence of many conditions, the American had become more gentle in his instincts. In spite of cock-fights, eye-gouging, and more or less brutality, the more cruel sports of the days of colonization, such as bear baiting by dogs which delighted English audiences, had never been brought over here. On the whole, our legal punishments were much lighter than those in England, and, probably owing to better economic conditions, violent crimes, especially those involving property, were comparatively rare with us. Duelling never had as much vogue here as in Europe, and the American was already becoming something of a pacifist as regards war.

Humor is often a subtle key to the intricacies of national psychology, and it is notable that in Franklin's writings we already find American humor to have become the reverse of English, ours being founded in absurd exaggeration of statement whereas the English derives from under-statement. Class feeling had much shallower roots in our soil than in the old country; and the life and opportunities of the New World had tended to develop a greater sense of independence in the individual. There was, nevertheless, ample loyalty to King and empire, so long as claims to authority might not be pushed too far. All spoke of England as "home" and scarcely an American had any thought of fatal disputes with the mother country.

More than a century and a half had passed since Virginia had been first planted, and many of our institutions, such as churches and schools, were more than a century old, while many families traced their purely American ancestry for longer than that. A New Englander, New Yorker, Virginian or South Carolinian considered himself quite as good as any stay-at-home Englishman, was proud of his colony, and confident of the future. He thought only in terms of his own colony and England, and on the whole there was little love lost between the colonies themselves, the old jealousies still persisting. The last thing that almost any colonial politician would have thought of in 1763 would have been of the possibility of placing them all under one government.

There were, nevertheless, other forces at work in America. We have thus far spoken chiefly of the rich, but most colonists were not rich. America was far from being peopled only by those who lived in the big Georgian houses and dressed in brocades and satins and lace. We need not here speak of the several hundred thousand slaves, who were so submerged in the scale as to not require thinking about at that time except for the fear, constant in every plantation owner's heart, of a possible insurrection. But there were some hundreds of thousands of submerged Americans who were to be of immense importance in the next twenty-five years.

It is true that the general economic and social level of the entire white population was higher in the America of 1763 than anywhere else in the world, but the American of whatever nationality, whether he was recent immigrant or descendant of early settler, had become something different from the European he or his ancestor had been in the Old World. The first had come here fleeing from intolerable conditions at home, in England, Ireland, Germany or elsewhere, lured often by fantastic hopes. On the voyage over, the immigrant had usually suffered almost unspeakable hardships, sometimes two thirds of them in a vessel in the early eighteenth century dying on the way. Often cruelly fleeced by business sharks on arrival, the new-comer settled down or started for the frontier with anger and the grim determination to make his way. Descendants of the older English settlers could also hark back enviously to the earlier and simpler days when life was easier for the poor man.

Except for the scrabble for existence in the most primitive beginning of any settlement, there had always been distinction even in earliest America between the rich and poor, but that distinction had been steadily increasing. While the rich had progressed from the first rough shacks to the Georgian houses, there had been no such advance for the poor. In a new country where land was the prime source of capital even when not its final form, the rich and favored of the governor's set had been securing their huge holdings by means denied to the poor and socially lowly. There had been practically no improvement in agricultural implements, and the work of tilling an original grant of fifty acres or so had become no more remunerative and no less back-breaking in a century and a half. In New England the favorites of even the Puritan legislatures could manage to get grants of townships and farm lands by the ten thousand acres, and gradually become rich merchants in the seaboard towns or "Lords of the Valley" along the Connecticut. We have already noted the huge grants and landholdings of the favored in New York and the South.

With the increasing scale of business operations the small man found it more and more difficult to compete, whether in the size of boats for trading or the size of crops to be marketed. In the South the great increase in slavery in the century had brought its special problems. The planter who at the beginning could afford to buy slaves and breed them had a tremendous advantage in control of power to develop his land over those who could not; and as the numbers of black laborers rapidly increased after 1700 and racial pride came into play, the poor white farmer found himself not only poor but working on a level with the despised African.

In the early days, when land had been plenty, a man could find land for his sons not too far from his own home, but as population grew and land became scarce both from that reason and from the huge engrossing of tracts by the rich, the young generation found themselves more and more forced out to the frontier. In the beginning the frontier had been at every one's door and all had shared its hardships, but now with the settled life of the seaboard, the frontier was not only far off and open to dangers long past in the old settlements, but the frontiersman was beginning to be looked down upon as an ignorant, uncouth fellow. In New England when a man did go out to some new town which speculative grantees had opened for settlement, he often found that the favored owners had retained all political rights in their own hands, and that the settler had nothing to say about taxation, the building of roads or other matters in the town which he was building himself for their benefit.

Although the suffrage was much more widely extended than in England, it was limited by qualifications which disfranchised many growing classes, such as servants, artisans, small shopkeepers, and others even in the old settlements. The frontier counties in practically every colony, how-

TO BE SOLD on board the Ship *Bance-Island*, on tuesday the 6th of *May* next, at *Ashley-Ferry*; a choice cargo of about 250 fine healthy

NEGROES,

just arrived from the Windward & Rice Coast. —The utmost care has already been taken, and shall be continued, to keep them free from the least danger of being infected with the SMALL-POX, no boat having been on board, and all other communication with people from *Charles-Town* prevented.

Austin, Laurens, & Appleby.

N. B. Full one Half of the above Negroes have had the SMALL-POX in their own Country.

ADVERTISEMENT FOR SALE OF NEGROES ON BOARD THE "BANCE-ISLAND" AT CHARLESTON
From a broadside in the Library of Congress.

ever, had a special grievance in this respect. For example in Pennsylvania, when Lancaster was erected as an outlying county in 1729 it was allowed only four votes in the Assembly instead of the eight which each of the older counties had. Although the population further out grew rapidly, no new counties were created for twenty years, and when they were they were given only two votes each. When, with the further spread of population, it was necessary to create two more counties, these were yet more discriminated against by receiving only one vote each.

By one such method or another, in all the colonies, the frontier was thus almost disfranchised, and the control of the politics of the colony was retained by the old settlements. In all of the colonies a few families were usually in political control. John Adams said that six or a dozen at most ruled Connecticut in company with the clergy. In New York it was the Smiths, Duanes, Schuylers, de Peysters, and a few others. Family influence, the alliance of business with the legislatures, the growing power of the rising class of lawyers, favoritism of the governor,—all these and other forces seemed to be nullifying the power and opportunity of the common man. In 1763 there was special discontent as the dislocation of the economic life due to the recent war, with its high wages and prices and subsequent collapse, had created much debt and distress.

There were thus two marked cleavages beginning to show in the life of the period. There was a growing conflict between rich and poor, voters and non-voters in the older settlements; and also against those older settlements as a whole was ranged the entire frontier from Maine to Georgia, becoming angrily resentful over the denial of its rights. From time to time there were armed clashes here or there, and both aggrieved classes, in old and new counties everywhere, were beginning to find leaders from among themselves to voice their anger and their hopes. The dwellers in the Georgian houses, solidly conservative, were doing no little worrying, all along the coast, as to how these radical ideas among "the people" could be curbed.

CHAPTER V

THE INSOLUBLE PROBLEM OF THE NEW EMPIRE

THE British Government in England had colonial problems of a different sort to solve. Even if the statesmen across the water had not handled them very badly, as all English historians of today agree was the case, it is only fair to admit that the difficulties were practically insoluble at that stage of the world's political experience.

When the Peace Treaty of 1763 was being negotiated it was bitterly debated in England whether France should be made to cede Canada or the immensely rich sugar island of Guadaloupe. This conflict of views was of great significance for it indicated that a change was in progress in the theory of empire. According to the old Mercantile theory there was no question that Guadaloupe, supplying a valuable raw material,—sugar,—should have been taken rather than what were considered the vast and barren wastes of Canada and the savage infested Mississippi Valley. The old theory, as we have explained, envisaged only the building up of a self-sufficing *commercial empire* made up of the mother country and a group of colonies which would all contribute their particular share to the economic life of an empire which should thus be as independent as possible of all others. Such colonies were immediate and valuable assets to England, and involved no expense except that of naval protection, which England had always borne.

The change from that theory to the new one of *territorial empire,* in which huge tracts in foreign lands should be secured with an eye to the distant future and their potential value as affording, when populated, markets for British goods or homes for British subjects, was a momentous one. When the die was cast, and England chose the almost illimitable continental empire of the American North and West instead of the immediately valuable and easily governed island of Guadaloupe, it became evident that she would have to face a wholly new set of problems in imperial government and organization.

These fell chiefly into two sets: first, how should the new domain be organized and governed, and, second, as it was evident that the expense would be heavy, who should meet it and how?

Gradually during the eighteenth century a sort of standard type of colony organization had evolved. In most of the thirty or so colonies, island or continental, there were a royal governor and council, some royal customs and other officials, and an assembly elected by the colonists. Except for the regulation of trade by Parliament, the colonies had been left to a great extent to themselves, had raised their own taxes, and defended themselves on land with the occasional co-operation of the British fleet. This had been the case until the French and Indian War which ended in 1763.

Obviously such a scheme could not be put into operation in the Canada-Mississippi Valley territory, filled only with a few thousand recalcitrant French and several hundred thousand hostile Indians over whom French influence was still supreme. There was no use thinking of royal governors and popular assemblies there. What, for the most part, was called for were military posts and garrisons, and a unified control over the vast native population. The Indian policies of the thirteen colonies, with the partial exception of Pennsylvania, had always been both bad and conflicting. The Indians had continually been enraged by land-hungry settlers and by the English-American fur-traders who for the most part were a low and cheating crew. In 1754, when the magnitude of the impending struggle had become apparent in Europe, England had asked the colonies to devise some sound Indian policy in which they would unite, but, as we have seen, they had been unable to do so at Albany.

In addition to this first problem there was also that of expense. The colonists had not only been unable to agree on a common treatment of the important native question but the old theory that England should be responsible for naval defence had broken down. Although Massachusetts had been public-spirited, each colony had shown itself uninterested outside its own borders, and not always self-reliant even within them. More than half the total number of troops engaged on land, and a considerable part of the expense of even the colonial troops, had had to be provided by England. The debt of that country had risen to the then huge figure of about $650,000,000, and the annual cost of its army and navy from $350,-000 pre-war to $1,750,000 post-war.

Many in England felt that the Americans had not done their fair share in ridding their continent of the French, with whom, in the West Indies, they had even been carrying on a lucrative trade during the struggle. They felt, moreover, that the haphazard formation of western land companies, the pushing out of settlement, and the despoiling of the Indian hunting grounds, would keep the newly acquired territory, which had to be governed by England, in constant turmoil.

In the new British Government which came into office in 1763, Lord Shelburne at once set to work to decide how the Indian problem could be handled, whether an army would be necessary, and whether the colonies should be asked to defray part of its expense. Shelburne, who was young but had marked ability and was perhaps the best disciple of William Pitt, headed a group in Parliament which was thoroughly friendly, and sympathetic toward America, and the method by which he hoped to solve the difficult problem was not intended in any way to be hostile to the interests of the colonists. The plan evolved called for an administration of all the Trans-Alleghany Indian lands which would assure the savages that they would not be interfered with until honest purchases had been made. A line was to be run between the English and Indians, which would be slowly advanced westward as settlements proceeded based on treaties. Ten thousand troops were to be sent to maintain order, the cost to be borne at first by England and later shared by the colonists in some way which might be agreed upon as least objectionable and burdensome. Unfortunately these plans were interfered with by events on the American frontier and in the English Cabinet.

In spite of the Treaty of Peace, the French had been stirring the savages to revolt against the English, suggesting that France was sending an army to help them and pointing out how their hunting fields were never interfered with by French traders, whereas the English settlers cleared them of game as they moved steadily westward. The incitements of the French fell upon ready ears, for the colonists, as always, had been encroaching rapidly on Indian lands, and in doing so and in their fur trading subjected the Indians to abuses, thinking only of immediate and personal profit and without consideration of either justice or sound policy. In May, 1763, the savages rose under an able native leader named Pontiac and in a few weeks captured all the posts in the Northwest, from Pennsylvania to Lake Superior, except Detroit and Fort Pitt, the latter being saved by Colonel Bouquet with 500 Highlanders. That same summer, owing to political changes in England the Grenville-Bedford party came into power, and Shelbourne was replaced by the Earl of Hillsborough, of whom even George III was to say some years later that he had never known a man "of less judgment." On that, at least, the King was right, and that such a politician should have been placed in charge of American affairs at such a critical juncture was the first of the colossal blunders which the British Government was successively to make in the next decade.

Frightened into quick action, without ability and with inadequate knowledge of America, Hillsborough within six days prepared the Proclamation of 1763, as it is called, which established a dividing line between the colonists and the Indian territory. (See map on page 101.) The line so hastily adopted, running, roughly, along the Appalachian watershed, took no account of settlements already long made. Nor did it of territory granted to certain colonies in their charters, and within which grants had been made to land companies. Moreover, future sale by the Indians, except to the Crown, was prohibited by the Proclamation, settlers who had already entered the now forbidden territory being required to withdraw. Outside of the Indian preserve, the Proclamation also set up on the continent three new royal provinces,—Quebec and East and West Florida. The Americans were naturally deeply resentful toward what they considered an unjustified attempt to keep them from developing the western country, which they had, in part at least, helped to win for the empire.

The British Government had been right in its basic assumption that the vast hinterland could not be left to be exploited, governed and defended by thirteen wrangling colonies which had never been able to agree on anything. The ministers had been extraordinarily careless and clumsy, however, in taking the initial step to govern it themselves. That step taken, the second problem of cost at once came up. Meanwhile, George Grenville, who was hostile to America, had little knowledge concerning it, and possessed the mind of a bureaucrat, had become Prime Minister. Dangerously for a statesman, he began with statistics, and found that owing to colonial smuggling connived at by royal officials, it cost England $35,000 a year to maintain American custom houses that produced only $10,000 revenue.

As we have seen, molasses was the base on which New England commerce, at least, rested, and had the old Molasses Act of 1733 with its prohibitive duty been observed by the colonists they would have had no money to buy goods in England. All of the colonies, without exception, were always hard put to it to find enough exchange to pay their English debts. Grenville, with the intention of reducing the duties on molasses to a point at which they might be paid and collected, secured the passage, in 1764, of the so-called "Sugar Act," lowering the duties from 6d. to 3d., and also imposing duties upon other imports into America, such as wine from the Azores and Madeira, coffee and the products of the East and the foreign West Indies. Moreover he showed that he intended to see that the new laws should be obeyed. Warships were sent to the American coast, naval officers given power to collect duties, and prosecutions for smuggling were taken from the colonial courts and put under the jurisdiction of Admiralty courts.

An act was also passed declaring any future issue of colonial paper money not to be legal tender, thus extending to all America the prohibition which had been enacted against New England only in 1751. This greatly frightened the colonists, who, from the constant scarcity of coin, had had frequent recourse to issuing paper. What perhaps frightened them most of all was the provision that customs duties were to be paid into "His Majesty's Exchequer," which they mistakenly assumed meant that the gold or silver paid for all duties and fines would be shipped to England and leave them with nothing with which to pay their foreign trade balances. It was really intended, although not worded clearly by the government, that this money should remain in America and there be used to pay one third of the cost of maintaining the ten thousand troops, whom Parliament undertook to station there, England expecting to pay the other two thirds herself.

The fear of a gold drain affected all the colonies but the class most alarmed by the new customs duties in the "Sugar Act," and even more by the prospect of duties really being collected, were the merchants of New England. Uneasiness had already been caused in that Puritan section by a rumor that an Anglican bishop was to be appointed with all North America as his see, which made the still influential body of congregational clergy hostile to the thought of any encroachments by England on complete local liberty of action.

In addition, there was in Boston one of the most remarkable Americans of the period. Samuel Adams was the son of a well-to-do brewer and had been educated at Harvard. He had no capacity for business and managed to lose the comfortable estate which he inherited. In 1764 he was in debt and his family were partly dependent upon charity. In later life, after the Revolution, he was to show no more capacity for constructive statesmanship than he had for business. He was narrow and provincial, but in the single groove in which his mind ran it operated so powerfully and cut so deep that he may be counted as one of the men who have profoundly influenced the course of history in their day.

That one groove, into which flowed the whole of his intellectual and emotional nature, was bitter hostility to England, and insistence upon the complete freedom of the citizens of Massachusetts. For him, that colony was all that existed in the political world, and almost alone among Americans of this period he seems early to have conceived the thought of achieving independence of the empire. He was extremely provincial and, not unlike some other Bostonians, felt that his town was the hub of the universe, and that salt had no savor outside of New England.

In December, 1765, his fellow radical at the other end of the colonies, Christopher Gadsden, had written from South Carolina that "there ought to be no New England men, no New Yorker, etc., known on the Continent, but all of us Americans." Such broader vision was beyond Adams, who even in later years only hesitatingly yielded to the necessities of nationalism. He had, however, consummate ability as a revolutionary agitator in manipulating the opinions and emotions of the ordinary people, and for the next ten years he was to devote himself to inflaming the public mind on every possible occasion.

When Grenville's plans for the new duties became known, a

town meeting in Boston appointed a committee to draw up resolutions for their representatives in the General Court, which Adams drafted. Committees of merchants in the leading seaports of several colonies had sent over protests to England, pointing out the disastrous effect on trade of the new laws, but Adams went far beyond this. "If our trade may be taxed, why not our lands? Why not the produce of our lands, and in short everything we possess?" If taxes are laid upon the colonists without "legal representation where they are laid," he added, "are we not reduced from the character of subjects to the miserable state of tributary slaves?"

This was a wholly new doctrine, advocated also by James Otis in his pamphlet entitled the *Rights of the British Colonies Asserted and Proved,* in which he suggested that the colonies be given representatives in Parliament. Hitherto the colonists had always accepted the doctrine that Parliament could pass Acts regulating imperial trade and laying duties. They had merely nullified the Acts by smuggling or pointed out their inexpediency without ever claiming that they were unconstitutional or tyrannical. The British Government could scarcely have been expected to acquiesce supinely in the new constitutional theories put forward by Adams and Otis but the vigor of the radical group combined with the remonstrances of the conservative merchants should have warned them to walk warily. Instead they made a fatal blunder.

Even although England expected to pay a large share of the future imperial expenses in America, it was considered that the Americans' own share would not be covered by the new duties, and Grenville had been looking about for additional taxation. One of the simplest forms is that of a stamp tax on legal or business papers, and this, already in use in England, had been discussed for some years as possibly applicable to the colonies. Grenville, in fact, had asked the opinions of the Colonial Assemblies about it and requested alternative suggestions as to forms that might be preferable to them, without getting any helpful advice.

It is clear now looking back that such a tax, being internal instead of external, might raise a storm of protest, but, little of a statesman as Grenville was, he cannot perhaps be blamed too heavily for not foreseeing the full effect of what he was doing. Even Benjamin Franklin, who was then in England, although he opposed the passage of the Act, did not think the colonists would object, and advised two of his friends at home to take office as stamp distributors, and Richard Henry Lee, the future patriot, also applied for the position in Virginia. In view of such opinions Parliament passed the Act without the slightest thought that there would be any serious objection to it, in spite of some speeches against it, notably by Colonel Isaac Barré. The Act, which received royal assent March 22, 1765, levied taxes of varying amounts on newspapers and almost all legal documents, the stamps having to be paid for in coin.

The news was received quietly for the most part in America as Franklin had anticipated. Then suddenly the storm broke. Two years before, out in the western mountain region of Virginia, a young man named Patrick Henry had won a case for the people against the payment to the local Anglican clergyman of his salary according to the terms of what was called the "Two Penny Act." Henry's case was weak and the verdict unjust but his success won him rousing popularity in the frontier section, and before news of the Stamp Act came he had been sent to the legislature as a member of the House of Burgesses, where he was regarded with fear and dislike by conservative Virginians.

On May 29, 1765, when the House was considering what action to take on the Stamp Act, Henry leaped to his feet and proposed a series of resolutions in a speech which, although often quoted, has not come down to us in authentic form. It called forth a rebuke from the Speaker, who avowed that Henry had uttered treason. Passage of the resolutions was bitterly opposed by such men as Peyton Randolph, Edmund Pendleton, Richard Bland, and George Wythe, who were all to become prominent on the American side, and it is imposible to tell just how many of the proffered resolutions were actually passed by the House. However, six were published in the newspapers, and, as "the Virginia Resolves," they ran like a flaming torch up and down the entire coast. It was claimed in them that the local legislature was the only body which had any legal right to tax the Virginians.

Economic conditions were bad in America and had been made worse by the Acts of the preceding year. At first the merchants had suffered most from them but the Stamp Act brought the newspaper editors and lawyers into sharp opposition to Britain, and the whole population feared stagnation of business both from the new taxes (which in reality were light), and from the mode of their collection. Massachusetts called for a meeting of representatives from all the colonies to be held in New York in October. Before that, some action had to be taken. America was almost a unit against the imposition of the new Stamp tax. The only question was how to avoid it. In many colonies the merchants agreed not to import English goods until the law was repealed, and that summer American orders in England declined £600,000.

Organizations called "Sons of Liberty" were formed almost everywhere, mostly from the extreme radical groups. Stamp distributors were threatened, and personal violence used against them. Mobs broke windows, burned houses, and intimidated people from using the stamps had any one been so inclined. In Boston the costly home of the Chief Justice, Thomas Hutchinson, was sacked. All his furniture and the priceless documents which he had collected for writing his *History of Massachusetts,* were thrown into the street and burned. America was in turmoil from one end to the other, the mobs often getting out of hand. In some colonies business was suspended and in others carried on without use of the legal stamps.

One strange feature was the slight interest taken in the meeting of the Stamp Act Congress in October. Only nine colonies were represented, and its proceedings passed almost without notice in the newspapers of the day. In spite of the difficulty of reconciling the views of the twenty-seven delegates, resolutions were passed claiming, as Virginia already had done, that the colonies could not be taxed save by their own assemblies where alone they were represented. It was found difficult to claim rights common to all if based on varying charters, and the broader ground of "natural rights" was therefore entered upon from this time.

The people at large, however, were not interested in fine-spun political or constitutional theories. With them it was rather a surge of emotion at interference with their accustomed freedom and fear of what might come, instilled into them by such men as Christopher Gadsden in South Carolina, Henry in Virginia, and Adams in Massachusetts, with others of like sort elsewhere. "No taxation without representation," "the rights of man," and "tributary slaves" were words which burned deep into the minds of the crowds, and the search for a legal basis for constitutional relations was left to the intellectuals.

When in March, 1765, chiefly as a result of pressure brought to bear on Parliament by the English merchants, the Stamp Act was repealed, the news was received almost as emotionally as had been that of its passage. America went wild with rejoicing, and no attention was paid to the Declaratory Act passed simultaneously asserting the right of Parliament to bind the colonies in all cases whatsoever and denying their claim to taxation solely by their own legislatures. Even Pitt, who with other statesmen had demanded the repeal in Parliament and had declared that he rejoiced that America had resisted, stated that he believed in the full parliamentary control over the colonies except to take "money out of their pockets without their consent."

The fact is that unconsciously the two parts of the English race had drifted far asunder in fundamental political ideas. The change had come about so gradually that neither had realized it. The idea of representation is a case in point. In England, Parliament was considered to be representative not of individuals but of classes. If some members of the landed interest and of the commercial and professional classes could elect representatives, then those classes and interests were considered to be represented. Representation, until long afterward, was not thought to have anything to do with territory or numbers. There were great centres of population in England which had no direct representatives at all. Yet these considered themselves represented because all classes in them were represented by men elected from members of their particular class elsewhere.

The Englishman thus found it hard to understand why the American landowner or merchant claimed that he was unrepresented merely because he did not himself vote for a member of Parliament. On the other hand, from historical reasons a new system had grown up with us and seemed almost the order of nature. In spite of our limited franchise and many abuses, the general theory had early developed that as new towns or counties were formed they should be given representation, and thus the idea of representation came with us to be connected with numbers and locality. So much so that by this time the practice was almost universal of electing a representative from the district in which he lived. "No taxation without representation" thus meant something quite different on the two sides of the ocean, as did Pitt's taking of money without "consent."

Again, in England, Parliament, as the great body representative of the whole nation, had come to be supreme. There was nothing it could not do in legislation. With us there had developed an idea of a fundamental law, derived from our constant reference to the charters in squabbles with governors or the home government. From this we slipped easily into the eighteenth-century doctrine of "natural rights," rights inherent in every individual simply as a human being. This was as little likely to be taken seriously by the British statesmen when demanded only by Americans as it would have been by us in 1765 if demanded by our 400,000 black slaves.

Finally, we had come to look upon our local legislatures as practically co-ordinate with Parliament, glimpsing a sort of commonwealth of nations such as the British Empire is now becoming. Such a theory offers many difficulties in practice even today, and in 1765 it was quite outside the realm of political realities.

The ideas of English and Americans were largely the product of their environment in each case. It seemed natural to the Englishman at home to accept a system into which he had been born, just as it seemed natural to the American to adapt that system to the new conditions of colonial life. A small farmer in Yorkshire who never had voted for a member of Parliament did not trouble his head about it, but a small farmer in a Massachusetts town or Pennsylvania county who had been accustomed to personal representation in the legislature and moved out on the frontier to settle a new town or county, did not see why he should be disfranchised for doing so.

In a new country not only does the new environment operate on old ideas and ways of doing things, but the absence of any accumulated stock of traditions, institutions, and vested interests allows of the rapid growth of new ideas. In my boyhood, for example, I remember that the then small town of Cheyenne, Wyoming, had electric lights when New York had only gas in its streets, and was running electric trams when New York had horse cars. It was not due to any superior virtue in Wyoming but to the fact that it was perfectly free to install the new without considering the old, whereas in New York the new came into conflict with all sorts of established interests connected with the old.

How fast new America had moved as compared with old England is shown by the fact that it was the conservatives in America who were closest in thought to the most advanced liberals in England. Had each of these classes been in control in the respective countries, an adjustment of the quarrel would have been likely. In the mother country, however, the most die-hard of the politicians held the power at critical stages, and in America the extreme colonial radicals kept stirring trouble.

It has been said that America was like a boy who had grown up and could no longer be kept in subjection. There is truth in the simile and at the same time danger for clear thinking. A father who does not let his boy go his own way after a certain age and become independent is naturally considered stupid or tyrannical, but there is no similar code of conduct for nations or empires when a part wishes to secede from the whole. The British statesmen of this period assuredly could not have justified themselves if, without a struggle, they had simply allowed the Americans to disclaim every shred of authority over them by Parliament, any more than a century later we ourselves allowed the Southern States to secede peaceably because they desired to do so. Nor would we allow any part of our nation or empire to do so today solely of its own volition. The British statesmen were stupid, but they were also confronted with a problem which was practically insoluble.

Briefly, our political philosophy had become different from the British. Our interests seemed to us the most important in the empire, as England's did to her. They conflicted at several points. We quickly realized, once the quarrelling started, that even if we could send some representatives to Parliament we would merely confer supreme power on that body with only a trifling minority of members from America. "No taxation without representation" could only mean that we must forever deny to Parliament any power of the purse over us. The difference which had been tacitly accepted in the past between internal and external taxation came to seem no difference at all when analyzed. English logic had to insist on the power of Parliament to legislate for the empire or there was no empire. American logic led to an almost total denial of such power.

With the good feeling, and the innate loyalty to the empire existing in the minds of most Americans, affairs might have slipped along with little friction had English statesmen let sleeping dogs lie or had there been no extremists in the colonies like Adams and Henry and Gadsden. This was true in spite of bickerings with the governor in Massachusetts over demands for damages on account of the Stamp Act riots or with General Gage in New York over the operation of the Act (1765) quartering troops.

In 1766, in a new Cabinet in England, Charles Townshend became head of the exchequer. Undeterred by the views of Pitt, who as Earl of Chatham was nominal head of the Cabinet, but ill, Townshend at once set himself to get money out of America. Few statesmen can ever have handled delicate situations worse. In 1767 he secured the passage through Parliament of a number of acts, all calculated to arouse the resentment of the colonies. In one of these a duty was laid upon tea, red and white lead, glass and painters' colors, designed to produce a revenue of about £40,000 a year.

In part this was to be applied to the support of the army in America and in part to paying the salaries of the colonial governors and judges, thus removing them entirely from control by the assemblies. It also provided for a new administration of the customs service and made it clear that every Navigation Act of the old commercial system from 1660 on, most of which had been dead letters, were to be enforced. Writs of Assistance were also legalized, although it had been James Otis's fiery denunciation of these which had first made him a popular leader in 1761. Another bill suspended the New York Assembly on account of its refusal to furnish supplies for the troops, and another created a board of commissioners to supervise the collection of duties in America. Having sown this field of dragon's teeth, Townshend let himself out by dying, and was succeeded by Lord North as Secretary of the Exchequer, Hillsborough occupying the new office of Secretary of State for the Colonies.

Protests were sent to England and to a great extent the non-importation agreements were put into force again. In Philadelphia John Dickinson, a Pennsylvania lawyer who had received his legal training in the English Inns of Court, began publishing his famous *Letters of a Farmer* which, reprinted everywhere, were perhaps more widely read than any of the rest of the rapidly increasing literature of controversy. He declared that laying duties to raise a revenue instead of to regulate trade was an innovation, and that although there was a certain power in Parliament (which like all Americans he found more and more difficult of definition), "we

---

(6)

cause, for *three shillings* and *four-pence*, was tried, all the people of *England*, with anxious expectation, interested themselves in the important decision ; and when the slightest point, touching the freedom of *one* colony, is agitated, I earnestly wish, that *all* the *rest* may, with equal ardour, support their sister. Very much may be said on this subject ; but, I hope, more at present is unnecessary.

With concern I have observed, that *two* assemblies of this province have sat and adjourned, without taking any notice of this act. It may perhaps be asked, what would have been proper for them to do ? I am by no means fond of inflammatory measures ; I detest them. I should, be sorry that any thing should be done, which might justly displease our sovereign, or our mother country: but a firm, modest exertion of a free spirit, should never be wanting on public occasions. It appears to me, that it would have been sufficient for the assembly, to have ordered our agents to represent to the king's ministers, their sense of the suspending act, and to pray for its repeal. Thus we should have borne our testimony against it ; and might therefore reasonably expect that, on a like occasion, we might receive the same assistance from the other colonies.

* *Nov. 5.*   A FARMER.

Concordia res parvæ crescunt.
Small things grow great by concord

The day of King WILLIAM *the Third's landing.*

(7)

LETTER II.

Beloved Countrymen,

THERE is another late act of parliament, which appears to me to be unconstitutional, and as destructive to the liberty of these colonies, as that mentioned in my last letter ; that is, the act for granting the duties on paper, glass, &c.

The parliament unquestionably possesses a legal authority to *regulate* the trade of *Great-Britain*, and all her colonies. Such an authority is essential to the relation between a mother country and her colonies ; and necessary for the common good of all. He, who considers—these provinces as states distinct from the *British empire*, has very slender notions of *justice*, or of their *interests*. We are but parts of a *whole* ; and therefore there must exist a power somewhere, to preside, and preserve the connection in due order. This power is lodged in the parliament ; and we are as much dependant on *Great-Britain*, as a perfectly free people can be on another.

I have looked over every *statute* relating to these colonies, from their first settlement to this time ;
B 4   and

THE BEGINNING AND ENDING OF TWO LETTERS FROM *DICKINSON'S
LETTERS OF A FARMER,* PUBLISHED IN LONDON IN 1768
From the Ford Collection in the New York Public Library.

---

are only as much dependent on Great Britain as one perfectly free people can be on another." He suggested that three successive lines of action might be taken against England,—first, remonstrance and petition, second, refusal to buy British goods, third, as a last resort only, forcible resistance to the Acts of Parliament. For the first time he suggested, not independence, but the thought that the colonies were beginning to form a nation. They are separated, he

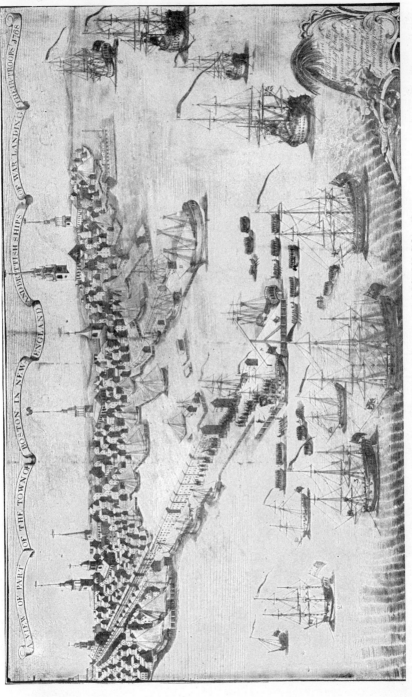

BRITISH TROOPS LANDING AT BOSTON IN 1768

The description reads that after landing at Long Wharf "they marched with insolent parade, drums beating, fifes playing and colors flying, up King Street, each soldier having received 16 rounds of powder and ball.

From the engraving by Paul Revere in the Stokes Collection, New York Public Library.

THE ABLE DOCTOR OR AMERICA SWALLOWING THE BITTER DRAUGHT

From an engraving by Paul Revere after a caricature in "London Magazine," April, 1774. In the Spencer Collection, New York Public Library.

wrote, "from the rest of the world, and firmly bound together by the same rights, interests, and dangers." It was indeed danger, forced upon them by the mistakes of English statesmen, which was beginning to make them feel, in Dickinson's words, that "they form one political body of which each colony is a member."

The new board of customs commissioners made their headquarters in Boston, and from the imperial standpoint the improvement in the service was notable, the American duties collected rising from £2000 a year to £30,000. Owing mainly to the unenforcement of the early Navigation Acts and of the impossible Molasses Act, smuggling had ceased to be looked upon in America as reprehensible. Every one, even leading merchants like John Hancock, smuggled regularly. Hancock was the richest man in New England, and because of his wealth was later to be chosen President of the Continental Congress. Owing to the lightness of his character, his excessive vanity, and love of popularity, unballasted by either moral depth or intellectual ability, his motives for joining the patriot party are difficult to appraise correctly or even, perhaps, fairly, but there was no question of patriotism in much of his smuggling. That was for profit.

The new customs commissioners had several times asked for a ship of war to patrol the coast and had been growing more and more angry over the smuggling they could not prevent when a particularly outrageous case occurred. There was a duty of £7 per tun on Madeira wine, and merchants did their best to make an additional profit by avoiding this. In the spring of 1768 the man-of-war *Romney* had finally been stationed in Boston Harbor, and, not long after, Hancock's sloop *Liberty* arrived from Madeira. The customs inspector who went on board was confined in the cabin and the cargo hurriedly unloaded at night. The commissioners on hearing of this ordered the sloop seized and had her towed out and anchored off the *Romney*. At once the mob, now ready to rise on every occasion, attacked the houses of the commissioners, who took refuge in Castle William. There had been similar outbreaks elsewhere, and in October the British Government stationed two regiments in Boston to maintain order. Events were marching.

Early in the year the Massachusetts House of Representatives had sent a circular letter to the other colonies suggesting that they all unite both in discussing the situation and in petitioning the British Government with regard to the Townshend Acts. The royal governor in Massachusetts, Francis Bernard, was peculiarly lacking in tact, knowledge, and judgment, and unhappily it was this incapable official, always at loggerheads with his somewhat troublesome Bostonians, who formed the official opinions of his equally incapable superior, Hillsborough. The earl instructed Bernard to demand that the House of Representatives rescind the Resolutions in connection with the circular letter, and to dissolve that legislative body if it declined. He also sent instructions to the governors of all the other colonies to dissolve their assemblies if they should act favorably on the request of Massachusetts. The House of Commons backed Hillsborough and were for even more extreme measures.

Massachusetts voted in the House, 92 to 17, not to rescind, and the legislature was promptly dissolved. An extra-legal convention of delegates from all the towns then met in Boston, and adopted resolutions similar to those which under the leadership of Samuel Adams had been drawn up on many occasions. Parliament, which with utter lack of statesmanship had brought on this new crisis, now lost its head yet more and sent an address to the King asking that the inciters of "rebellion" be brought to England for trial for treason under an old and inapplicable statute.

All the colonies were deeply stirred and in the Virginia House of Burgesses, George Washington introduced a set of Resolutions, known to history as the "Virginia Resolves of 1769," which had been drawn up by George Mason. They marked a distinct advance in clarity of thinking over the earlier ones and proclaimed that the Colonial Assembly, with the approval of King or royal governor, was the only body which could tax the colonists. They also stated that the colonists had the right to petition the King for redress of grievances, and that to transport any person overseas to stand trial for "any crime whatsoever" was "highly derogatory" of his rights as a British citizen.

It was not only in the legislatures that the growing confusion was evident. The attempt to renew the non-importation policy led to much bitter feeling and actual violence among the colonists themselves. The chief financial loss of such a policy fell on the merchants who instead of entering upon the policy willingly were to a large extent coerced. In South Carolina, for instance, they were forced to suspend imports only by threats of personal violence from the Sons of Liberty led by the radical Gadsden. In Boston, Adams had his mob ready, and intimidation, destruction of property, and tarring and feathering were freely used to bring the merchants into line with the radicals' political plans, as in New York and elsewhere.

Meanwhile, following the death of Townshend, there had been another change in Cabinet posts in England, and Lord North, who now became Prime Minister, decided that the government was stirring up resistance in America for little actual gain. He therefore secured the passage of a bill in Parliament voiding all the new duties of the Townshend Acts, except that on tea which was kept as a symbol of the right of Parliament to levy duties. The administrative machinery erected for the American customs was also retained as were the older established duties.

It is a mistake to think of the colonists as all burning with "patriotism" and hatred of England. We must recall that although events were fast bringing about unprecedented unity of sentiment and action among the several colonies, they were still very distinct from one another. A Virginia planter, for instance, would have felt much more at home with an English squire than with a Boston merchant. Speaking broadly, however, there were three groups which severally developed the same attitude toward England in all the colonies. Two of these were comparatively small, the ultra-Loyalists at the top, who defended all that England did, and the extreme Radicals at the bottom. In between was the vast mass of Americans who wanted above all else to be allowed to live their lives and earn their bread in peace, unmolested by new and annoying British laws or the violence of American radical mobs. They were willing to stand up for their rights, and were made both angry and anxious at the trouble that the injustice and stupidity of the politicians in Parliament were making, but hoped for a change. They also, however, feared the growing violence and breakdown of order in America.

As we have seen, there were many grievances felt here by different classes and sections,—artisans in the towns, men of the frontier, and others. America was full of combustible material, and with the growing unrest of the times it was easy to kindle this with a spark. Within a few years popular leaders had sprung up whose power and local importance came from stirring up all the discontented elements. They played with mobs, and not always with the single-ness of purpose and hatred of a Sam Adams against English policy. All sorts of local aims were also being served. As in all such cases, the influence of these popular leaders depended upon the stirring up of emotion and the creating of a seeming constant need of their leadership.

In Massachusetts, Adams had proved a master at keeping the public mind in ferment. Opinions will always differ widely about him but I think he was consistently honest in his purpose. His nar-row mind, however, was always as firmly convinced that he was indubitably right as was ever that of old John Endicott himself. On the other hand, we are all human, and he could hardly escape, un-consciously, the effect of finding himself, after a life of somewhat humiliating failure, in a position of tremendous influence over the populace, with his real talents for drawing up remonstrances and inciting to revolt in constant demand. His whole importance, unlike that of John Adams, Washington, and other greater men, was dependent upon keeping alive the passions of the mob. This he did constantly, in public meetings, in the legislature, in news-papers, and more mysterious ways, "cooking up articles, paragraphs, occurrences" as John Adams said of him.

Steadily throughout the two years the British soldiers had been in Boston, Adams had seen to it that their presence should create as much friction and be as thoroughly resented as possible, although the soldiers had maintained perfect discipline. Finally, on the very day that Lord North moved the bill doing away with the Town-shend duties, March 5, 1770, the long-expected clash occurred be-tween citizens and soldiers in Boston.

A sentry at the Custom House was pelted with snowballs by some young roughs and called out the guard. A crowd gathered, and one soldier was knocked down and another beaten with a club. Mis-taking a shout for an order to fire, the soldiers did so, killing four of the crowd. The officer in command at once surrendered to the civil authorities, and at the trial, in which the soldiers were de-fended by John Adams and Josiah Quincy, Jr., all were exonerated except two of the privates, who were convicted of manslaughter and burned in the hand as punishment. Immediately after the affray the two regiments had been removed to Castle William by Lieutenant-Governor Hutchinson. This "Boston Massacre," brought on by the constant incitement of Adams and others, was long used by them to stir up feeling against the British, and passionate orations were delivered for some years on each anniversary.

The news of the repeal of the Townshend duties was received by the merchant class everywhere with feeling of deep relief, and they and other conservative elements decided to stop further bickering with England. The quality of British political life was at perhaps the lowest point it ever reached, but there were constant changes and as long as a working compromise seemed to have been brought about and England had made a partial retreat it was

New-York May 10ᵗʰ 1770.

The FEMALE PATRIOT, Nᵒ. I.

ADDRESSED TO THE

TEA-DRINKING LADIES of NEW-YORK.

WHEN ADAM firſt fell into SATAN's Snare,
   And forfeited his Bliſs to pleaſe the Fair;
GOD from his Garden drove the ſinful Man,
And thus the Source of human Woes began.
'Jwas weak in ADAM, for to pleaſe his Wife,
To loſe his acceſs to the Tree of Life:
His d ar bought Knowledge all his Sons deplore,
DEATH thir Inheritance, and SIN their Store.
But why blame ADAM, ſince his Brainleſs Race
Will 'oſe their ALL to obtain a beautious FACE;
And will their Honour, Pride, and Wealth lay down,
Rather then ſee a lovely Woman frown.
The Ladies are not quite, ſo compliſant,
If they want TEA, they'll ſtorm and rave and rant,
And call their Lordly Huſbands Aſs and CLOWN,
The jeſt of Fools and Sport of all the Town.
A pleaſent Story lately I heard told
Of MADAM HORNBLOOM, a noted Scold,
Laſt Day her Huſband ſaid, " My deareſt Life,
My Kind, my Fair, my Angel of a Wife;
Juſt now, from LONDON, there's a Ship come in
Brings noble News will raiſe us Merchants Fame,
The Fruits of our non-importation Scheme.
The Parliament, dear Saint, may they be bleſt
Have great part of our Grievances redreſt:"
" Have they indeed," replies the frowning Dame,
" Say, is there not ſome Tea and China come."
" Why, no! We can't import that Indian Weed,
That Duty's ſtill a Rod above our Head."
" Curſe on your Heads, you naſty fumbling Crew,
Then round his Shoulders the hard Broom-Stick flew,
Go, dirty CLOD-POLE! get me ſome Shuſhong,
This Evening I've invited MADAM STRONG.
— Silence — you BLOCKHEAD — hear, the Lady
           knocks!
Get to your Cock-Loft or expect ſome Strokes "
    — " Your Servant Madam, Tea is on the Board
I really tho't you once had broke your Word."
" I aſk your Pardon, dear Miſs HORNBLOOM,
My ſpraling Brats kept me ſo long at Home;
My ſtupid Huſband too has gone aſtray
To wait upon the SONS of LIBERTY.

A BROADSIDE CONDEMNING TEA-DRINKING
LADIES
From the original in the New York Public Library.

thought that the more or less theoretical disputes could be shelved.

Moreover, the merchants had not liked at all the coercion practised on them by the radicals to force them not to import, and the conservatives had all become alarmed by the disorders brought on by the Sons of Liberty and the dangerous turmoil of mob-rule. If they did not wish their profits interfered with or their liberties infringed by England, neither did they want to find themselves controlled in America by the lower classes, as they considered them, of town or frontier, in whose ability to govern they had no confidence whatever. The complete breaking off by John Hancock of relations with Sam Adams was symptomatic of what was going on elsewhere. The merchants soon began importing freely again, and business began to boom at last after the hard years.

To be sure, the British government was still intent on collecting what duties remained, and smuggling continued. It was merely for profit's sake, however, and was on a huge scale. Occasionally there were physical clashes with customs officers, and in June, 1772, the revenue schooner *Gaspée* was seized and burned in Rhode Island waters. It was the third vessel so destroyed in that nest of smugglers and the royal commission could get no witnesses who would testify against their friends and neighbors.

In the autumn a rumor came over that England was contemplating paying judges' salaries out of the customs revenue, and Sam Adams, who had been doing his best throughout the past two years of prosperity and calm to keep the political pot of protest boiling, seized on this as a new and intolerable grievance. In a town meeting he secured, not without much opposition, the appointment of twenty-one men as a "committee of correspondence," which was to state the rights of the colonists "as Men, as Christians, and as Subjects," and to correspond on the subject with committees from other towns. Gradually radicals in other colonies formed similar committees, and thus a revolutionary organization was built up throughout America, and did its best to stir the people, as Sam Adams said, from "stupor and inaction."

It was not so much stupor as it was the Anglo-Saxon's mental habit of not bothering about fine-spun theories, and of letting matters drift and adjust themselves so long as there is no crisis to get excited about. The country generally was prosperous. The merchants, who could afford to lose one complete cargo of tea in three and yet make large profits, were contented. In spite of all the agitators from Adams in Massachusetts to Gadsden in Carolina, the substantial classes everywhere refused to consider their liberties in danger. The country had settled down to calm after the storm, and was glad to do so. Then suddenly the English Government made what was to prove an irretrievable blunder.

Until 1773 the East India Company, and not the British Government, was the ruler of India. It had been in frequent trouble with native princes, and several times in financial difficulties. The interests were vast and in 1773 an Act was passed which gave Parliament a voice in administration. The company was in trouble and had 17,000,000 pounds of tea stored in London. North decided, solely with thought of the extrication of the company and with none at all of American colonial policy, to allow the company to sell this tea in the colonies, paying the regular American three-penny duty but none of the charges and duties imposed in England. The idea was that this would clear off the company's surplus and at the same time allow the colonists to buy their tea cheaper than ever, even when smuggled.

The effect, however, was to give the company, temporarily at least, exclusive rights in America, where the radicals at once raised the cry of "monopoly." For three years they had been trying to find an issue without success, and they probably would have failed again on tea had all American merchants who had been tea importers been made the agents for the sale of the government-company tea. Instead of this, certain agents only were appointed, most of whom were unpopular from having taken sides against the great bulk of American merchants in previous troubles. What Sam Adams had been unable to accomplish was now achieved by Lord North, who threw the powerful American merchant class over to the side of the radicals again, just when they themselves were least inclined for such an unnatural union.

When the first tea ships arrived under the new plan, they were nowhere allowed to discharge their cargo except at Charleston. From some ports they were forced to return to England, but Boston staged its famous "tea party." Governor Hutchinson, who had become extremely unpopular, refused to sign clearance papers permitting the ships to leave until their cargoes had been discharged. A number of public meetings had been held, and feeling ran high. It is hard to say which was the more stubborn, the royal governor or the radicals. The latter might have allowed the tea to be landed as in Charleston and stored in warehouses without its being permitted to be sold; or Hutchinson might, like other governors, have allowed the ships to sail. As it was he played straight into the hands of Sam Adams.

According to a preconcerted plan, when the governor's final decision was made known to a great public gathering in the old South Meeting House, a band of men disguised as Indians boarded the vessels and threw all the tea into the harbor. Opinion in America was divided on the action. Even some New England town meetings condemned it, speaking of "liberty degenerating into anarchy," and although John Adams applauded it such patriots as John Dickinson and Benjamin Franklin heartily disapproved. One of America's best friends in England, William Pitt, then Earl of Chatham, denounced it as "criminal."

The work of the mobs in Boston, New York, and elsewhere was once more beginning to make the owners of property fearful and to cause them to withdraw their new support temporarily given to the radicals on account of the Tea Act when yet another blunder by the British Government, which seemed determined to force conservatives and radicals together in America on every opportunity, caused a vast wave of united sentiment, hostile to England, to flow over the whole of the colonies.

If American conservative opinion was opposed to the destruction of private property in Boston, English governmental opinion was furious about it. In March, 1774, at Lord North's request, Parliament passed a bill, since known as the Boston Port Act, removing the Custom House from that town and closing its harbor to all inward and outward commerce until restitution should have been made to the East India Company for the destroyed tea, which was estimated to have been worth £15,000 Sterling. The Act went into operation June 1, and on that day Governor Hutchinson sailed for England and turned the province over to the commander-in-chief of the British forces in America, General Gage. The news of the terrifically severe punishment which had been meted out to the

Quebec

to Quebec
QUEBEC ACT
LINE 1774

LOUISIANA
(to Spain 1763)

PROCLAMATION LINE 1763

FLOR. (Br.1763-83)

THE THIRTEEN COLONIES

Montreal

Quebec

L. Ontario

Fort
Niagara

Lake Erie

NORTHWEST
TERRITORY

NEW YORK

Crown Point
Ticonderoga

Saratoga
Mohawk R.
Albany

Bennington

Concord
Boston

Cape
Cod

NEW
HAMP-
SHIRE

Champlain L.

Connecticut R.

MASS.

Hudson R.

Delaware R.

CONN.
Hartford
R.I.

Newport

West Point

PENNSYLVANIA

Morristown
New York
Brooklyn
Princeton
Trenton
Philadelphia

LONG I.

Valley Forge

N.J.

Ohio
River

Boonesboro

Baltimore
(Washington)
Mt.Vernon
Potomac R.

Delaware Bay

MD.
DEL.

Chesapeake

VIRGINIA
Richmond
James R.
Williamsburg

Yorktown

ATLANTIC OCEAN

an R.
Roanoke R.
Guilford
Court House
Raleigh

NORTH CAROLINA

King's Mountain

Cowpens
Camden

Wilmington

Savannah R.

SOUTH
CAROLINA

Augusta

Charleston

GEORGIA

Savannah

FLORIDA
(to Spain)

St.Augustine

GENERAL BATTLEGROUND OF THE REVOLUTION AND (INSET) THE
LINE ESTABLISHED BY THE QUEBEC ACT, 1774

third largest port in America roused all the colonies. Resolutions of sympathy and cargoes of food poured from the whole continent into the closed town.

Three other Parliamentary Acts relating to Massachusetts were also soon passed. The first of these altered the charter of that colony and provided that the members of the council should thereafter be appointed by the Crown, that minor officers were also to be appointed instead of being elected, and that no more town meetings could be held without the consent of the governor. Another provided that officials charged with capital crimes might be sent to England for trial, together with all the witnesses, and a final Act renewed in somewhat harsher terms the earlier one as to quartering of troops. General Gage was made governor. There were voices raised in Parliament against the severity of all these Acts. Notably Chatham pointed out that the day was coming when the colonies would vie with the mother country in arms and arts, and that the colonists should be treated as children worthy of their sire. But the members generally were overwhelmingly on the side of coercion.

In the same session of Parliament another Act, the Quebec Act, was passed without thought of our thirteen colonies, but was considered by them as aimed at themselves. The problem of the government of Canada had never been satisfactorily solved, and this Act was directed to that end. The French were guaranteed freedom of religion, and certain administrative arrangements were made. In addition, the province was extended southward to the Ohio, which conflicted with the claims westward to lands which Massachusetts, Connecticut, and Virginia all believed were theirs under their charters. This was a mere blunder on the part of the English statesmen, but such careless blunders are costly, and this Act, which with the other four came to be known as the "Intolerable Acts," did much to unite the sentiment of the colonies against England.

Meetings now followed one another in quick succession in America, from those of towns and counties to State conventions. Then, at the suggestion of Virginia, heartily welcomed by the other colonies, the first Continental Congress met at Philadelphia, September 5, 1774, delegates being present from all the colonies except Georgia. Among others were John and Samuel Adams from Massachusetts; Roger Sherman from Connecticut; Stephen Hopkins from

Rhode Island; John Jay and Philip Livingston from New York; John Dickinson, Joseph Galloway, and Thomas Mifflin from Pennsylvania; Cæsar Rodney, Thomas McKcan, and George Read from Delaware; George Washington, Patrick Henry, Peyton Randolph

ADVERTISEMENT.

THE Committee of Correspondence in New-York, having on Monday Night laſt proceeded to the Nomination of five Perſons to go as Delegates for the ſaid City and County, on the propoſed General Congreſs at Philadelphia, on the 1ſt of September next; the five following Perſons were nominated for that Purpoſe,

Philip Livingſton,
James Duane,
John Alſop,
John Jay,
Iſaac Low.

The Inhabitants, therefore, of this City and County, are requeſted to meet at the City-Hall, on THURSDAY next, at 12 o'Clock, in order to approve of the ſaid five Perſons as Delegates, *or to chooſe ſuch other in their Stead, as to their Wiſdom ſhall ſeem meet.*

By Order of the Committee,

ISAAC LOW, CHAIRMAN.

TUESDAY, 5th
July, 1774.

THE SELECTION OF DELEGATES FROM NEW YORK TO THE FIRST
CONTINENTAL CONGRESS

From a broadside in the New York Historical Society.

(who was chosen President), and Richard Henry Lee from Virginia; Richard Caswell from North Carolina; and from South were Edward and John Rutledge and Christopher Gadsden.

Opinion ran from ultra-conservative to extreme radical, and the action of the Congress was a compromise. The Declaration of Rights drawn up to be sent to England was moderate and dignified. The rights of the colonists were based upon nature, the British constitution, and the charters. As the colonies could not properly be represented in Parliament, the Declaration asserted, their local assemblies should have exclusive power of legislating, but, it was added, for the best interests of the whole empire, the colonists would submit themselves to Parliamentary Acts designed solely for the regulation of trade. It was also stated that the colonists could not submit to an enumerated list of Acts which had been passed since 1764.

An association was entered into by which the colonies bound themselves not to import or export goods to or from English ports, nor consume English goods, until redress of grievances was obtained. Committees were to be appointed in every town and county who were to report the names of such as refused to sign the association agreement or who violated it. This was the most important part of the work of the Congress, and these local committees became of extreme importance as the struggle advanced into its later stages. Before adjournment provision was made for a new Congress to meet May 10, 1775, unless grievances had been redressed before that date.

Meanwhile, Gage was in Boston with 5000 troops, and warships lay in the otherwise empty harbor. He had been ordered to seize Sam Adams and John Hancock and ship them to England for trial, but had failed to catch them. Regardless of the royal governor, Massachusetts was governing herself by a Provincial Congress. The winter of 1774–75 passed peacefully for Gage in Boston but he knew the country everywhere outside was buzzing as with angry hornets. In September he had made a foray a few miles beyond the town limits and seized some powder, but almost before he was back, the country "minute men," estimated at 40,000, had swarmed after him.

As spring came on he decided to make an effort to capture stores which he understood had been gathered at Concord. On the famous 19th of April, 1775, a detachment of British regulars marched through the streets of Boston on what was to become one of the most celebrated military expeditions in history despite its apparent unimportance at the time. Few, if any, undertaken lightly for a minor objective have had such resounding consequences.

Although the troops started before daybreak, the alarm was at once given and Paul Revere and two others rode through the country to rouse it, so that by the time the thousand advancing British soldiers reached Lexington they found about fifty men blocking

By *the* LION *&* UNICORN, **Dieu & mon droit,** *their Lieutenant-Generals, Governours, Vice Admirals, &c. &c. &c. &c.*

A H U E *&* C R Y.

WHEREAS I have been informed, from undoubted authority, that a certain PATRICK HENRY, of the county of Hanover, and a number of *deluded followers,* have taken up arms, chosen their officers, and, styling themselves an *independent company,* have marched out of their county, encamped, and put themselves in a posture of war; and have written and despatched letters to divers parts of the country, exciting the people to join in these *outrageous* and *rebellious* practices, to the *great terrour* of all his Majesty's *faithful* subjects, and in *open defiance* of *law* and *government ;* and have *committed other acts of violence,* particularly in *extorting* from his Majesty's Receiver-General the sum of 330l. under *pretence of replacing the powder* I *thought proper* to order from the magazine; whence it undeniably appears, there is *no longer* the least security for the *life* or *property* of any man: Wherefore, I have *thought proper, with the advice of his Majesty's Council,* and in *his Majesty's name,* to issue this *my* proclamation, strictly charging *all persons,* upon their *allegiance,* not to *aid, abet,* or *give countenance* to the said PATRICK HENRY, or *any other persons* concerned in *such unwarrantable combinations ;* but, on the contrary, to oppose *them,* and *their designs,* by *every means,* which designs must otherwise inevitably involve the *whole country* in the *most direful calamity,* as they will call for the *vengeance* of *offended Majesty,* and the *insulted laws,* to be *exerted here,* to vindicate the *constitutional* authority of government.

Given, *&c. this 6th day of May,* 1775.

D * * * *

G * * d * * * the P * * * *

A BROADSIDE OF 1775 DENOUNCING PATRICK HENRY AND HIS FOLLOWERS
From the original in the Library of Congress.

the way. Eight of these were killed, and the column proceeded. Most of the stores at Concord had been removed, but the British destroyed what little remained, and then started on the return march to Boston. By that time the whole countryside was alive with minute men, who shot at the moving British column from behind trees, stone fences, rocks, and any shelter. The retreat became a rout,

THE MARCH OF DEMOCRACY

WILLIAMSBURG, Saturday, *April 29, 1775.*

LATE laft night an exprefs arrived from Philadelphia, with the following melancholy advices from the province of Connecticut, forwarded to the committee of correfpondence in this city.

The blow (fo much dreaded by our noble friend Lord Chatham*) is now ftruck, a great deal of blood fpilt, and much more, it is likely, than the prefent advices communicate. That great man, in his fpeech upon the neceffity of withdrawing the troops from Bofton (delivered in the Houfe of Lords the 20th of January laft) fays:* "*Perhaps, even whilft I am now*
"*fpeaking, the decifive blow is ftruck, which may involve millions in the*
"*confequences; and, believe me, the very firft drop of blood that is fpilled*
"*will not be a wound eafily fkinned over; it will be* irritabile vulnus, *a*
"*wound of that rancorous and feftering kind, that, in all probability, will*
"*mortify the whole body.*"

PHILADELPHIA, *April 24, 1775.*

An exprefs arrived at five o'clock this evening, by which we have the following advices, viz.

Watertown, *Wednefday morning, near* 10 *o'clock.*

To all FRIENDS of AMERICAN LIBERTY.

BE it known, that this morning, before break of day, a brigade, confifting of about 1000 or 1200 men, landed at Phipps farm, at Cambridge, and marched to Lexington, where they found a company of our colony militia in arms, upon whom they fired, without any provocation, and killed fix men, and wounded four others. By an exprefs from Bofton, we find another brigade is now on its march from Bofton, fuppofed to confift of 1000 men. The bearer, Trial Briffet, is charged to alarm the country, quite to Connecticut; and all perfons are defired to furnifh him with frefh horfes, as they may be needed. I have fpoken with feveral, who have feen the dead and wounded. Pray let the Delegates from this colony to Connecticut fee this; they know Col. Fofter, one of the Delegates.

J. PALMER, one of the committee.
A true copy from the original, by order of the committee of correfpondent of Worcefter, April 1775.

Attefted and forwarded by the committes of Brookline, Norwich, New London, Lyme, Saybrook, Killingfworth, E. Guilford, Guilford, Brandford, Newhaven.

Fairfield, Saturday, *April 22, 8 o'clock.*
Since the above written, we have received the following, by a fecond exprefs.

Thursday, 3 *o'clock after noon.*
SIR.

IAM this moment informed, by an exprefs from Woodftock, taken from the mouth of the exprefs at two of the clock after noon, that the conteft between the firft brigade that marched to Concord was ftill continuing this morning at the town of Lexington, to which faid brigade had retreated; that another brigade, faid to be the fecond mentioned in the letter of this morning, had landed with a quantity of artillery at the place where the firft did. The Provincials were determined to prevent the two brigades from joining their ftrength, if poffible, and remain in great need of fuccour.

HOW THE NEWS OF LEXINGTON AND CONCORD WAS RECEIVED
BY THE OTHER COLONIES
From a broadside in the Library of Congress.

and even when reinforced by 1500 troops under young Earl Percy who had hurriedly been sent to their aid, the exhausted British reached Boston and safety only with difficulty. More than 270 were killed, wounded, or missing, and the successful Americans settled down to besiege the town, closed this time by Massachusetts and not by Lord North. On that 19th of April, the shot had been fired "that was heard round the world." The great empire so hardly won in 1763 had begun to dissolve in blood.

CHAPTER VI

THE REVOLUTION

THE news that the long years of bickerings, arguments, appeals and legal reprisals had at last ended with open warfare between colonists and British troops was carried rapidly down the whole coast by messengers on horse-back. The fact that, although the galloping horsemen travelled with great speed for those days, they took five days to reach Philadelphia and six to give their tidings in Virginia, which were not heard at Edenton, North Carolina, for two weeks, helps us to understand some of the difficulties which both Congress and the army would have to face. Everywhere the startling news of fighting called forth resolutions of protest against England, and stirred the war spirit.

On May 10 the Second Continental Congress met in Philadelphia as agreed the previous year, and that same day Ethan Allen with a force of Vermonters surprised the British commander of Fort Ticonderoga. According to Allen's story in later years, he demanded the surrender "in the name of the Great Jehovah and the Continental Congress." However, one of the witnesses of Allen's triumph, giving a different version, reported that what Allen really said to the British officer was "You d——d old rat, come out!" which sounds more authentic. At any rate, a most welcome addition to the scant stores of colonial powder was secured and two days later Crown Point was also captured.

In Boston, the 6000 or more British regulars were besieged by a motley crowd of possibly 20,000 New England militiamen, whose only "training" (a rather bibulous and festive one) had been from two to four days a year. The town was at that time connected with the mainland by only a narrow neck, and was dominated by two eminences, Breed's Hill and Bunker Hill, the peninsula from which they rose being likewise connected with the mainland by another—Charlestown-neck.

THE FIGHT ON LEXINGTON COMMON

From a painting by Howard Pyle.

THE BATTLE OF BUNKER HILL

From a painting by Howard Pyle.

On the morning of June 17, the British were unpleasantly surprised to discover that Breed's Hill had been fortified in the night. Colonel William Prescott and his regiment, who had done the work, were entrenched there, with none too much ammunition. Had the British seized the Charlestown "neck" they would have trapped the Americans, but with a folly equal to Prescott's rashness, a council of war determined upon a frontal attack up the hillside by troops ferried across from Boston. General William Howe, in command, was a brave officer with a high reputation, and in the face of galling fire he led his lines up the steep incline again and again. The carnage was terrific, from one third to a half of the British being killed by the New Englanders who held their deadly fire against the enemy each time until they could aim "at the whites of their eyes."

Suddenly the firing stopped. The American ammunition was exhausted. Without disorder the Americans retreated to the mainland, and the British occupied the peninsula. In spite of the retreat, the "battle of Bunker Hill," as it came to be called, was an overwhelming victory for American morale. The British had obviously had to show the greater courage, but the fact remained that raw New England militia had faced British regulars and inflicted heavier casualties than any other enemy had done in the whole Seven Years' War. The English had met English.

Lexington, Concord, Ticonderoga, Crown Point, Bunker Hill settled the matter. With these attacks on British troops and with a Congress of all the colonies sitting in Philadelphia, there could be no turning back for America, nor could any English statesman of the eighteenth century have considered anything except the putting down of what was open rebellion. On June 15 Congress appointed George Washington Commander-in-chief of the American forces.

This action, the wisest and most pregnant with good of any that the Continental Congresses took, was due chiefly to the conflicting ambitions and jealousies of the various sections. New England disliked the thought of a commander from outside her borders, but the rest of America feared even more a New England army commanded by a New Englander. Much to the chagrin and mortified pride of Hancock, who had hoped for the post, John Adams, seconded by Sam, engineered the compromise, although after the matter was settled the formal nomination was left to a Marylander. Although

Washington had a high reputation throughout the colonies, one of the main reasons for picking him at this stage was that he was one of the richest and most prominent men in Virginia, which was a much more populous and important colony than Massachusetts. Moreover, he was one of the few colonials who was well known for his military experience, and for all these reasons, his choice to head the rebel army would carry unusual weight both in England and the colonies. The choice would help to show positively that New England did not stand alone in her resistance and that a Southerner of wealth and influence, with everything to lose, was willing to stand in the very forefront of the rebellion.

On July 3 Washington reached Cambridge and inspected his army. Numbering 20,242 officers and men, of whom 17,215 were present for duty, it was such only in name, and we may here glance at some of the difficulties which were to beset Washington throughout the entire war. He never in truth had more than the nucleus of an army. It is a mistake to think of our America of the Revolution as a nation of patriots all rising to their own defence. When Independence came, John Adams thought that one third of the people were in favor of it, one third opposed, and one third neutral. The New England historian Channing suggested forty per cent of the population as a fair percentage to be considered "militant revolutionists."

This estimate should give us, from a population of 2,200,000 whites, about 250,000 revolutionists of military age. In the Boer War in 1900, a population of 300,000 Boers put over 40,000 men into the field, and if we had done as well in our own self-defence from 1776 to 1783 we might have had 280,000 combatants. Yet Washington never had over 18,000 in any one engagement or over 22,000 at one time in his army, and during much of the war only a fraction of such a force. Of course, owing to short terms of enlistment and constant changes in personnel, many times those numbers served during the course of the struggle for a few days, weeks or months. On the other hand, however, Van Tyne, the leading authority on the subject, estimates that 50,000 of the Americans who remained loyal to England served with the British forces.

When Washington had had time to look over the situation at Boston he was nearly in despair. He found many of the officers, who were elected by their men and stooped to curry favor with them instead of enforcing orders, thoroughly incompetent. He made, as he wrote, "a pretty good slam" among these and discharged some for cowardice and others for fraud. Officers went off to their farms, taking privates with them to work, and drew pay for both. "Such a dirty, mercenary spirit pervades the whole, that I shall not be surprised at any disaster that may happen," was one of many such comments that the new commander wrote of those under him. Some of the higher officers, such as Major-General Schuyler, were so disgusted with the greed and selfish spirit manifested that they were restrained with difficulty by Washington from throwing up their commissions.

The militia, Washington wrote, could be depended on for only a few days at a time, when they would get tired, ungovernable, and slip off to their homes. By February, 1776, half the army had melted away. In time, he gathered a group of able officers, but throughout the war there was always the same difficulty with the troops. Wherever fighting occurred, the farmers could be counted on to swarm in from the countryside and take irregular part in the engagement, but it was extremely difficult to secure men to enlist, even with the offer of high bounties in cash. Not only have we always been a pacific and unmilitary people, but the scarcity of labor, the anxiety over the women and children left at home on the farms, the poor pay in rapidly depreciating paper money, the lack of supplies of all sorts in the army, all made the service extremely unpopular.

Given the general conditions of the time and the lack of public spirit on the part of most, of which Washington, John Adams, and other leaders constantly complained, all praise is due to the officers and the comparatively small band of Continental Regulars who stood by their commander throughout the duration of the war and under every discouragement. It was these men and not those who would occasionally run from their farms to take a pot-shot at the enemy or enlist for a month or two who saved the cause.

If the colonists generally did not support Washington, neither did the government give him efficient backing. Congress did not dare to tax the people, and all its decisions were made as the result of compromise among the representatives of thirteen jealous States, each thinking in terms of itself. Even the eight generals commissioned to serve under the commander-in-chief had to be chosen, like a modern President's Cabinet, to balance competing geographical sections and provincial jealousies rather than for their abilities.

There was no efficient War Department, and during most of the war the army was in straits for everything an army needs. There were scarcely any uniforms, and often only rags. The "Continental" uniform of portraits and popular pictures was mostly mythical. Shoes, food, ammunition, supplies for the sick, everything was always in arrears or never arrived at all. The Medical Department during the whole Revolution presents mostly a picture of quarrelling doctors and incompetency. Of the four Directors General, one was court-martialled and two were dismissed from the service. As Colonel Ashburn, the historian of our Army Medical Department, records, there is little or nothing in this aspect of the struggle in which we can take pride.

The point is not, however, our pride but the truth as to the sort of difficulties Washington had to overcome. What was true of the Medical Department was true also of almost every other. There were times when the troops nearly starved in the midst of rich farming districts. For lack of an adequate Commissariat, wherever the army marched or camped, it almost created famine in the neighborhood. Moreover, farmers and tradesmen, patriots as well as Tories, profiteered shamelessly at the expense of the soldiers. In the terrible winter at Valley Forge, Washington could scarcely get enough food to keep his men from starving, the farmers preferring to sell it for high prices in gold to the British in Philadelphia. Sometimes for weeks at a time his troops had no powder except what was in their cartridge boxes.

On the other hand, the British also had their difficulties. Although their troops far outnumbered ours, they had perforce to be broken up into several bodies. Almost all military supplies had to be transported three thousand miles across the ocean by uncertain sailing vessels. In America, transporting large bodies of troops by land was almost impossible, and uncertain by water. The great valley of the Mississippi is bound together by the river that traverses it with its branches, but one of the factors which had kept the thirteen seaboard colonies separate and provincial was the fact that no rivers

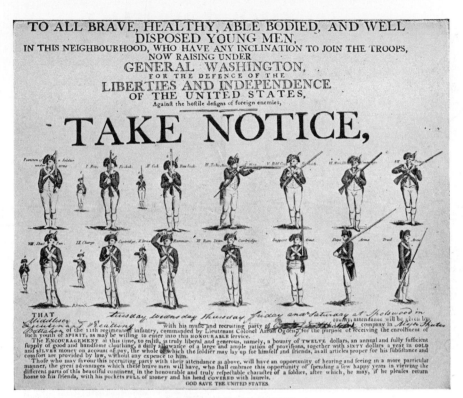

A RECRUITING POSTER

It reads in part: "The encouragement at this time to enlist, is truly liberal and generous, namely a bounty of twelve dollars, an annual and fully sufficient supply of good and handsome cloathing, a daily allowance of a large and ample ration of provisions, together with sixty dollars a year in Gold and Silver money on account of pay, the whole of which the soldier may lay up for himself and friends, as all articles proper for his subsistance and comfort are provided by law, without any expense to him. . . . Those . . . who shall embrace this opportunity of spending a few happy years in viewing the different parts of this beautiful continent, in the honorable and truly respectable character of a soldier, after which, he may, if he pleases return home to his friends, with his pockets full of money and his head covered with laurels.

From the original in the Pennsylvania Historical Society.

PROSPECT HILL.	BUNKER's HILL.
I. Seven Dollars a Month.	I. Three Pence a Day.
II. Fresh Provisions, and in Plenty.	II. Rotten Salt Pork.
III. Health.	III. The Scurvy.
IV. Freedom, Ease, Affluence and a good Farm.	IV. Slavery, Beggary and Want.

HANDBILL SENT AMONG THE BRITISH TROOPS ON BUNKER HILL
From the original owned by the Massachusetts Historical Society.

THE EVACUATION OF CHARLESTON BY THE BRITISH, DECEMBER, 1782

From the painting by Howard Pyle.

joined them. The short streams, which ran from mountain to sea, even such as the Hudson and Potomac, were inter-colonial barriers, not highways for those travelling up and down the coast.

Nor was there any one vital spot in America the possession of which would determine the conflict. As Chatham said, it was impossible to make war against a mere map. Nor, again, was the American army an objective. It was not Washington's forces, sometimes numbering only two or three thousand, but the swarms of country people ready to rise for a few days anywhere who were the real enemy. It was as though in the jungle one had been called upon to fight not a single specimen of big game but innumerable hosts of insects that were everywhere and nowhere, that would swarm and sting to death and then disappear.

The British had been badly misinformed about colonial sentiment by many of their governors and other officials. Everywhere in the eighteenth century the poorer people were thought of no importance, and a large proportion of the rich, with whom the governors came into contact, were in truth on the side of England in the controversy. This was particularly true in Boston, where such a wealthy patriot as John Hancock was an extreme exception. The jockeying for political advantage between the powerful families in New York led some of them to the patriot side, but the New York "aristocracy" was pretty solidly Tory. A larger proportion of rich and distinguished families went over to the American side in Virginia than in any other colony, but the British were right in believing that everywhere in America, even in recalcitrant Boston, they would be supported by a considerable part of the most important people, and others.

As we have seen, the number who joined the British fighting services was very large. The patriots greatly disliked to be called "rebels," believing, as the Southerners did in our later Civil War, that they were merely fighting for their legal rights, but on the other hand those Americans who espoused the British side of the argument and fight believed that they were on the side of law and order, of maintaining the established basis of society. They felt quite naturally toward those who were taking up arms against the English Government as today conservative people, rich or poor, even if they are "Sons" or "Daughters" of the American Revolution, feel toward Socialists and others who would alter the established social scheme. We must recall that although our Revolution was less bloody than most, nevertheless there was much mobbing and disorder, so that many even of those who believed that England was wrong dreaded a possible disastrous overturn of order in America by the lower classes more than temporary inconvenience or suffering from bad British laws.

But, although such people were numerous and in many cases individually powerful, they were not organized, and after the first bloodshed at Lexington the revolutionary committees all through the colonies took over control. Not only were freedom of speech and of the press entirely suppressed but those who were thought to be on the Tory side were threatened, persecuted, and disarmed. As the war went on and laws against them were passed in the heat of passion by the various States, in many cases Tories were imprisoned, tarred and feathered, gathered into concentration camps, ostracised socially or economically, and forced to cease carrying on their callings as lawyers, doctors, teachers or merchants, while their property was confiscated on a heavy scale. In a number of States any one who acted or spoke against Congress could be imprisoned or fined, the fines sometimes running up to $20,000, and as half of them went to the informer, the way was open for vast injustice. Imprisonment was a far heavier punishment than the word suggests. All prisons were vile in those days, though few were so terrible as the almost incredible one in Connecticut far below ground in the shafts of the copper mine at Simsbury, where physical and moral conditions were indescribable.

Occasionally a Loyalist may have been a source of danger to the patriot cause in his community but such cases were comparatively rare, and as the war went on and persecution became fiercer, and laws providing for confiscation of property more severe, they can be attributed mainly to the spirit of lawlessness, cruelty, and greed which revolution always breeds. A man would be accused of being a Loyalist by a prejudiced jury, and his property ordered confiscated. This would then be sold and would be bought, often for a small fraction of its value, by "patriots" who made large profits on it. Many of the finest estates in Massachusetts, including Governor Hutchinson's (which even under these conditions brought £98,000), as well as some of the largest in New York and other colonies, were thus seized.

The suffering was not confined to the rich, for a farmer who coveted his neighbor's acres or even a little straightening of boundaries, would find it convenient to obtain them in this way if any case, though of the flimsiest, could be made out against the owner. Such Loyalists alone as later turned in their claims to the British Government listed confiscated properties to the total amount of £10,000,000, of which the Claims Commission disallowed only £1,000,000. Many of the Tories were exiled penniless, a list of 300 in Boston including many of the families who had been most notable in the life of the colony from its very founding. In all, willingly or unwillingly, between sixty and a hundred thousand left America for Canada, the West Indies or England.

This aspect of the war, which brought bitterness and suffering to hundreds of thousands of those Americans who left and those who stayed, should not be forgotten. In almost every village, neighbor was divided against neighbor, and not seldom even the members of the same family against each other. In many communities it was the rich, educated, and conservative who remained loyal to the old order, so that the radicals were left more and more in control.

Opinion in England was also divided. Not only did America's defenders in Parliament stand by her, but the City of London showed its dislike of the war throughout. Many writers produced pamphlets upholding our actions, just as others, like Doctor Johnson, wrote in the pay of the Ministerial party against us. The English merchants were naturally opposed to war, as we owed them some £5,000,000 at its outbreak, of which the Virginians alone owed over £2,300,000. It was said in British newspapers of the day that one half of the English people had given their voices against their own country. The British landed interests were most strongly against us, and the merchants and common people for us. Of course as the war continued, the feeling developed among many that, right or wrong, England would have to see it through, a sentiment which grows in any nation in any war, whatever public opinion may have been at its outbreak.

We were, however, only at the beginning of all this when Washington was trying to organize an army actually in the face of the enemy at Boston. In September, 1775, he spoke of the situation as "inexpressibly distressing," the army without clothing or supplies, ready to melt homeward at the first touch of cold weather, and not a dollar in the pay-chest. However, an expedition against the British in Quebec met with the Commander's approval, and two small forces proceeded to try to make a joint attack, the one, under General Schuyler, advancing up the old route of Lakes George and Champlain, and the other through the Maine forests under command of Benedict Arnold, a capable and at that time wholly patriotic officer.

Owing to Schuyler's illness General Montgomery took his command, and although the difficulties of supplies, organization, and transport were almost insuperable, he captured Montreal with his forces November 12. Leaving detachments to garrison St. John's and Montreal, and losing a good part of the remainder of his troops who left him for home, he pressed on with only 300 men to join Arnold before Quebec. The joint assault was made in a heavy snowstorm on December 31, Montgomery, a gallant officer, being killed at the very beginning of the action, and Arnold wounded. The assault failed, and some months later the entire expedition had to be abandoned as a failure.

Apart from extremely bad organization, the lack of success was due to the rank and file of our troops. Montgomery complained that the New England soldiers were "the worst stuff imaginable," refusing to obey orders, and continually deserting because they were homesick. John Adams asserted that if they continued to run away as they had at Quebec and "the Cedars," the American cause would be lost. One of the objects of the expedition had been to unite the Canadians to ourselves but this also resulted in failure, in part on account of the conduct of our soldiers who were licentious and who pillaged houses and scoffed at the Catholic religion of the French. In spite of all, however, the expedition was to bear important fruit, as we shall see later, and happily success elsewhere was to encourage the Americans for the moment.

Washington managed to keep an army together through the winter, and in March he determined to drive the British from Boston. Seizing and fortifying Dorchester Heights, he commanded the British position by cannon dragged from Ticonderoga. At first the British thought of a counter attack, but a storm prevented this and then a complete evacuation was decided upon. It took ten days to make the preparations but finally on March 17 General Howe, who had succeeded Gage in command, sailed away in the British

Two favorite SONGS,

made on the Evacuation of the Town of BOSTON,

by the *British Troops*, on the 17th of March, 1776.

IN feventeen hundred and feventy fix,
  On March the eleventh, the time was prefix'd,
Our forces march'd on upon Dorchefter-neck,
Made fortifications againft an attack.
  The morning next following, as Howe did efpy,
The banks we caft up, were fo copious and high,
Said he in three months, all my men with their might,
Cou'd not make two fuch Forts as they've made in a night.
  Now we hear that their Admiral was very wroth,
And drawing his fword, he bids Howe to go forth,
And drive off the YANKEES from Dorchefter hill :
Or he'd leave the harbour and him to their will.
Howe rallies his forces upon the next day,

IT was'nt our will that Bunker Hill
  From us fhould e,er be taken :
We thought 'twould never be retook,
  But we find we are Miftaken.
The foldiers bid the hill farewell,
  Two images left fentreis,
This they had done all out of fun
  To the American Yankees.
A flag of truce was fent thereon,
  To fee if the hill was clear,
No living foul was found thereon,
  But thefe images ftood there.

ONE FORM OF POPULAR REACTION TO THE EVACUATION
From the original broadside in the Massachusetts Historical Society.

fleet, with about 11,000 British troops and 1000 Loyalist refugees. Washington took possession of the town, ordered the militia home, left five regiments to garrison the Massachusetts capital, and within three weeks was on his way to New York with the remainder of the army.

Meanwhile, the British, like the Americans in Canada, had tried a stroke at the extreme end of the colonies, hoping to capture an important town and rally to their side those who sympathized with them. In the beginning of 1776 a joint naval and land expedition was set on foot to capture Charleston, South Carolina, and to combine with the Tories to gain control of the far southern colonies. The land forces of British and Loyalists were defeated, however, at Moore's Creek, February 27, and the fleet, long delayed, failed in June in its attack on the little fort defending Charleston. This side expedition of the British had proved even less successful than the American one to Canada.

While all these acts of plain warfare had been occurring, the relations of the colonies to England were anomalous. It is true that Congress by declaring war, taking over the army, advising Massachusetts to resume its old form of government and to consider the "Intolerable Acts" as void, by making loans, issuing paper money, corresponding with foreign governments, fitting out war vessels, and by other acts had obviously become a revolutionary body. On the other hand, it denied, and honestly, any thought of independence. Indeed, in July, 1775, the more conservative men in it secured the passage of another Petition to the King, which the Monarch declined to receive. Nevertheless even as late as January, 1776, North Carolina, Maryland, Pennsylvania, New Jersey, and New York were instructing their delegates to have nothing to do with voting for independence, and men like Anthony Wayne and Washington had been violently protesting against it.

In that month came the news that Parliament had passed an Act prohibiting all nations from trading with the colonies, and making any ships engaged in such trade lawful prizes of war. Next came news of fighting in Virginia. Norfolk was strongly Tory and Governor Dunmore was using it as a base to spread British influence. Had he been a little wiser in action he might have come near succeeding in establishing a powerful British faction in the colony, but forced to take to sea by the more radical patriots he made the mistake of bombarding the town and setting fire to it before leaving, thus greatly strengthening the propaganda of the patriots.

About this same time there appeared a book which perhaps more than any other, with the possible exception of *Uncle Tom's Cabin,* nearly a century later, has inflamed American public opinion. The literature of the Revolution was extensive, although thus far we have mentioned only James Otis and John Dickinson as having contributed notably to it. Both in the years of discussion leading up to the struggle and in those of the actual fighting, the presses were kept busy issuing books, pamphlets, and newspaper articles dealing with the controversy, while ministers, such as J o n a t h a n Mayhew, Samuel Cooper, Charles Chauncey, George Duffield, and others, discoursed from their pulpits. To a great extent, the writings of the period dealt with the constitutional aspects of the problems which were splitting the empire. In Massachusetts, for example, John Adams wrote out his views at length, while Daniel Leonard took the Tory standpoint, as Joseph Galloway did in Pennsylvania. In p o e t r y, the revolutionary f e r v o r and new patriotism found l y r i c a l expression in the work of Francis Hopkinson and satirical in those of Philip Freneau and John Trumbull. Important as the writings of these and many others were in the intel-

COMMON SENSE;

ADDRESSED TO THE

INHABITANTS

OF

A M E R I C A,

On the following interesting

S U B J E C T S.

I. Of the Origin and Design of Government in general, with concise Remarks on the English Constitution.

II. Of Monarchy and Hereditary Succession.

III. Thoughts on the present State of American Affairs.

IV. Of the present Ability of America, with some miscellaneous Reflections.

A NEW EDITION, with several Additions in the Body of the Work. To which is added an APPENDIX ; together with an Address to the People called QUAKERS.

N. B. The New Addition here given increases the Work upwards of one Third.

Man knows no Master save creating HEAVEN,
Or those whom Choice and common Good ordain.
THOMSON.

PHILADELPHIA PRINTED.

And sold by W. and T. BRADFORD

FACSIMILE (REDUCED) OF THE TITLE-PAGE OF PAINE'S *COMMON SENSE*
In the New York Public Library.

lectual discussion or emotional stimulation, they all paled before those of Thomas Paine.

Paine was a born revolutionist and was later to take part in the French Revolution. He had been dismissed from his small government post in England in 1774, and had come to Philadelphia, where he knew Franklin and other leaders. In January, 1776, his small volume entitled *Common Sense* was issued from the press, soon to run up to the then colossal sale of 100,000 copies. It was neither learned nor profound but its terse, vigorous style embodying the emotions that thousands were beginning to feel made it run like a prairie fire through the whole colonial mind from Maine to Georgia. Its sentences were to be the common-places in America for a century and to be recited by every schoolboy. "Of more worth is one honest soul to society, and in the sight of God, than all the crowned ruffians that ever lived." "Every spot of the old world is overrun with oppression. Freedom hath been hunted round the globe. Asia and Africa have long expelled her. Europe regards her like a stranger; and England hath given her warning to depart. O! Receive the fugitive; and prepare in time an asylum for mankind."

To understand the full effect of such passages, we must recall the circumstances under which great numbers of the poorer colonists of recent years had then come to the colonies, as well as the general restlessness of the discontented classes we described earlier. America, he said, must always be secondary to the interest of England if tied to her. It was absurd to think of 3,000,000 people running to meet every ship in order "to know what portion of liberty they should enjoy." It was "madness and folly" to have further trust in Britain. England and America belonged to different systems, "England to Europe, America to herself!" American affairs were too complex, too important to be handled by ignorant men three thousand miles away. "The period of debate is closed. Arms, as the last resource, must decide the contest." "The last cord now is broken." As compared with the best literature of the controversial period, Paine's book was superficial and crude, but it was incomparably written to reach the hearts of plain men and to stir them to action. It created a vast wave of feeling in favor of complete independence. It appealed to passion, but the overwhelming passion of the day, whether of Puritan patriot in Boston, of Virginia planter who wished to govern the "old Dominion" himself, or of the frontiersman smarting under the rule of the seaboard, was for liberty. To this the book was a flaming beacon.

Throughout the colonies, moreover, the control of events was fast slipping from the hands of the conservatives. In Pennsylvania, for example, the Assembly which had formerly defied the frontier had yielded step by step until it was taking its orders from the revolutionary Committee of Safety. In Virginia, although the Assembly sat, the real power had passed to the revolutionary Convention, which drew up a new constitution for the State, including a Declaration of Independence from England. In May, 1776, the Convention instructed the State's delegates to Congress to move a Resolution declaring the colonies "free and independent States."

The temper of Congress itself was becoming more radical, and in the same month, May, that body recommended to all the colonies that they form new governments for themselves. By June 7, Richard Henry Lee of Virginia introduced resolutions to declare the colonies independent, to n e g o t i a t e foreign alliances, and to form a Confederation of the new States. There was still some struggling between the conservative and radical elements, the former from the Middle Colonies and South Carolina, but the latter won, and a committee was appointed to draft a Declaration of Independence, although some good patriots, such as John Dickinson and Robert Morris, still thought the action premature.

Written by Thomas Jefferson, with some minor changes made by John Adams and Franklin, it was brought up for debate on July 2. The day before, on a test vote, New York and Pennsylvania had been against making the Declaration, Delaware was divided, and South Carolina asked for time. On the 2nd, however, all voted

A R T I C L E S

O F

Confederation

A N D

Perpetual Union

BETWEEN THE

S T A T E S

O F

New Hampshire, Massachusetts Bay, Rhode Island, and Providence Plantations, Connecticut, New York, New Jersey, Pennsylvania, Delaware, Maryland, Virginia, North Carolina, South Carolina, and Georgia.

W I L L I A M S B U R G:
Printed by A L E X A N D E R   P U R D I E.

From the original in the Library of Congress.

in favor, except New York, and on the 4th the draft made by the committee was accepted with certain alterations, and copies ordered to be sent to all the Assemblies and revolutionary Conventions and Committees. New York agreed on the 9th and the signatures of the members of Congress were appended, at various dates, to the engrossed copy which was not prepared until August 2.

The news of the passing of the Declaration was received with wild rejoicing throughout America. Bells were rung in the churches, bonfires blazed, and untold quantities of liquor were drunk to innumerable toasts. It is true that the Loyalists and many of the conservatives, who took the American side with heavy misgivings, believed the action rash and unjustified, and were deeply saddened at the severance of ties with the country from which they had sprung. But the die was now cast and such men, even if they remained in America, were to have no further influence.

Much of their criticism of the document itself was justified. It is not as easy as it was a century and a half ago to agree unqualifiedly with some of its most resounding statements, largely drawn from the philosopher Locke. In spite of all that can be said against it, it remains nevertheless one of the great milestones in the history of man. The greater part of the Declaration was taken up with a recital of the crimes of George the Third. Stupid and stubborn as the King was to prove, most of these were in reality merely the workings of the old Colonial System which the Americans had now outgrown, but the indictment had been made, and the trial was to take place, —trial by battle. We may have found that it is not so simple to resolve political questions by "the laws of nature and of Nature's God," but such phrases as "all men are created equal," "are endowed by their Creator with certain unalienable rights," that governments "derive their just powers from the consent of the governed," were dynamic forces which sent the world on a new course the end of which is not yet in sight.

As we have seen, Washington, appreciating the strategic position of New York, had gone there direct from Boston. He at once strengthened the lower defences of the city, and later built Forts Lee and Washington on either side of the Hudson about what is now 183d Street. Howe was also aware of the value of the city, and on June 25 arrived in the harbor with a fleet from Halifax. He was later joined by the troops returning from South Carolina and, August 12, by Lord Howe with fresh troops from England, including the first detachment of the hired Hessians from Germany. In all, the British landed about 32,000 troops on Staten Island. "On paper" Washington had about the same number, but in reality only slightly over 20,000 present for duty. Of his five divisions, one had been sent over to Brooklyn to intercept an approach of the British from Staten Island by that route which was to prove the one chosen.

On August 22, Howe ferried 15,000 troops over to Long Island, reinforced three days later by 5000 more, and camped about eight miles from the American lines, where Washington had 7000 of his men. General Greene, who was to have been in command, was ill, and the battle of August 27 was fought without a head, ending in disaster for the Americans, who lost about 1000 men, though Washington managed to rescue the remainder by a masterly retreat across the East River at night. The situation forced him to evacuate New York by September 12 and in the process, three days later, there was a disgraceful panic among the Americans as they were pursued by the British, Washington himself, while trying to rally his men, nearly being captured. In the battle of Harlem Heights, however, on the 16th, his troops gave an excellent account of themselves, and their morale was restored.

Little by little, however, the Americans were forced to give way. In the battle of White Plains, October 22, they met well a direct frontal attack, but again had to retreat, and Forts Lee and Washington, with over 2800 prisoners, soon fell into the hands of the British. Washington took up a temporary position at Newark, with only 6000 troops, but was forced southward by the British, who now believed the war almost over. Many of the New Jersey and Maryland militia marched off to their homes, and the American Army dwindled to less than 3000 soldiers whose enlistment would be up in a month.

Washington then retreated across the Delaware, urging General Charles Lee to join him as rapidly as possible. Lee, however, who from jealousy was a traitor to Washington, moved with extreme slowness, and at Basking Ridge was taken prisoner by the British, whereupon he turned traitor also to the whole American cause. That cause, by this time, seemed almost hopelessly lost, but to Washington's surprise, Howe, instead of pursuing him, went into winter quarters in New York, leaving garrisons in Princeton and some other Jersey towns.

Determined to deliver a brilliant counter-stroke, the American Commander, on Christmas night, 1776, ferried his army across the ice-filled Delaware, and after a quick march to Trenton attacked the Hessians there, who had been celebrating Santa Claus with too deep potations and were mostly sound asleep. On the morning of December 26 they were driven from the town with heavy loss, and although they returned with reinforcements some days later, Washington eluded them by the trick of leaving his camp fires burning, and on January 3 made a surprise attack on Princeton. The terms of enlistment of all his men had expired on January 1 but he had induced them to remain for another six weeks by promising a bounty of ten dollars each above their regular pay, and after Princeton, joined by the remnants of Lee's army, he pushed on to Morristown, where, unmolested by the British, who evacuated all of New Jersey, he settled down for the winter. This unexpected turning of the tables, at the very moment when all seemed lost, was declared by Frederick the Great to be the most brilliant operation in all military history. The shattered morale of the Americans was restored, and Washington's own prestige enormously and fortunately strengthened.

The following year was to prove the most fateful of the war. If throughout its duration Washington was to be hampered by the interference of Congress, the British also had their difficulties from the fact that military operations were planned by men largely ignorant even of American geography and terrain, 3000 miles from where such plans were to be carried out. In war after war the Hudson River-Lake Champlain route to Canada had always figured, and the British now planned that General Burgoyne should lead an army along it southward from Montreal to be met by Howe advancing northward from New York. Ever since the American attack in Quebec, troops had been kept in Canada, whom it was now proposed to use with heavy reinforcements from abroad. The orders sent to Howe were conflicting, and, as we shall see, he did not attempt to carry out his part of the joint plan. It was, in any case, much too complicated a one for local conditions in America.

As spring came on, Washington, with a much augmented army, was watching to see what Howe would do in New York. There had been skirmishes which signified nothing when, on July 5, the British General unexpectedly embarked a large part of his troops on transports, and after being held by calms until the 23d, disappeared from view over the horizon. There was complete uncertainty as to where he would appear next, and meanwhile news came that Burgoyne, moving south with 7000 troops, nearly half of whom were hired Brunswickers, had captured Ticonderoga.

When Howe's fleet appeared in Delaware Bay, Washington at once moved to the defence of Philadelphia, but Howe again disappeared, and it was thought he had headed south for Charleston. The suspense was not for long, for the British fleet was next discovered in Chesapeake Bay, having been able to sail two hundred miles up that body of water without having been seen. After landing troops for the capture of Philadelphia, the ships once more cleared out to sea. On September 11, the Americans and British met at the Brandywine, where the former sustained a bad defeat, and after some additional fighting, notably at Germantown on October 4, Washington was obliged to abandon the capital city to Howe and to take up winter quarters at Valley Forge while the British enjoyed themselves in Philadelphia. Had Howe followed up his advantage at the Brandywine with a few energetic blows, he might, instead of settling down comfortably for the cold weather, have ended the war completely and at once. He missed his opportunity, however, as he had at the battle of Long Island, with momentous effects on the history of the world.

Burgoyne had been meeting disaster in the North where his transport service in the wilderness had broken down. He was short of supplies, and the New Englanders, roused like angry hornets, were hanging on his flanks. While at Fort Edward he decided to send an expedition eastward to Bennington to capture stores which he understood had been collected there, but the Vermonters at once got wind of his intent. General John Stark hastily raised a force of about 2000 farmers and August 16 attacked Lieutenant-Colonel Baum and his Germans, capturing or killing the whole of them, the few British and Indians with them escaping. A second detachment, which had been sent to Baum's aid by Burgoyne, was met and defeated by Colonel Seth Warner with more militia, and in all Burgoyne lost about 800 men out of the 6000 he had after leaving a necessary garrison at Ticonderoga.

The British commander had been ordered to count on help from Colonel St. Leger who was to advance along the Mohawk Valley to meet him, but this expedition had been defeated by the Americans under Benedict Arnold at Oriskany, and all hope was lost from that direction. He had also been told that Howe would meet him by way of the Hudson, but that officer had gone to Philadelphia. The army of the unfortunate Burgoyne was encumbered with about 300 women and an absurd amount of household stuff. The Americans felled trees and in other ways impeded both his advance and his lines of supply to the rear. By September there were about 20,000 Americans, chiefly short-term local militia, surrounding him, and his position was becoming desperate. His army was like a great clumsy antediluvian animal caught in a quagmire.

The American regulars were commanded by Gates and occupied high land, known as Bemis Heights, overlooking the Hudson, below which Burgoyne would have to pass. Believing that General Clinton in New York would be sent to his support by Howe, Burgoyne tried to push on, but suffered heavy losses in several engagements. His army was on half rations, but, although in spite of the difficulties, retreat was clearly the only course left to him, he now made no move.

It has been said that he temporarily lost his mind and it is impossible to explain his acts at this period. Finally the retreat was begun but his army was completely surrounded by the Americans and on October 17, after some days of negotiation, the British were surrendered at Saratoga with the loss of all their arms, although the troops were to be permitted to march to Boston and be transported to England on condition of not serving again in the war. Gates had made a great blunder in not insisting, as he well could, on absolute surrender, but even as it was the disaster to the British had resounding consequences in Europe and for America.

France had been watching England's civil war with the colonies with intent interest. Smarting from the defeat of 1763 she had been longing for revenge. The situation was well understood in America, and Franklin had been sent to Paris to try to negotiate a treaty of alliance, but France, which had no interest in building up an American republic, was wary. Although a good many French officers had come to America, some merely to make money and a few like Lafayette, young and ardent, inspired by the dream of liberty, the French government had only the thought of injuring England and of protecting her own West Indian islands, and no intention of committing itself until it should become evident that the old lion was going

FACSIMILE OF WASHINGTON'S OATH OF ALLEGIANCE
In the War Department, Washington.

to be so heavily attacked by her cubs as to make it safe to join the fray. This was what the surrender of Burgoyne achieved.

When the Americans showed that they would be able to divert a large part of England's strength, France at once made two treaties with us, February 6, 1778, one of alliance and one of commerce. She recognized the independence of the United States of America, and agreed that if she and England should go to war she would serve as our ally until our independence had been acknowledged by England also. Neither America nor France was to make a separate peace.

For long we had been receiving surreptitious aid from Europe. Not only had such officers as the French De Kalb, the Pole Pulaski, and the Prussian Baron von Steuben proved highly useful, but we had been allowed to receive supplies from both France and Spain. The treaty of alliance, however, greatly changed the situation. England and France were at war, of course, within a few weeks of France's action, and although Spain did not join until 1779, and then as the ally of France only and not of us, the war was widening fast for England. It was no longer a matter of rebellious colonies but of a struggle for life against the second greatest naval power in the world.

It was well for us that France's selfish policy coincided with our needs, for these were almost hopelessly great when the treaties were signed. In spite of the victory at Saratoga, our most important cities were still in the hands of powerful British forces, while Washington at Valley Forge had an almost destitute army, half-naked, unshod, suffering severely and steadily dwindling. In all, at Newport, New York, and Philadelphia, the British had nearly 34,000 troops whereas the Americans had only 15,000, also scattered, which Washington hoped to be able to increase to 20,000.

When we recall that the number of Americans of military age was at least 300,000, we can understand the despair of those who were leading the revolt when only 15,000 of these could be induced to serve. Not only were men, supplies, and money lacking, but the old jealousies between colonies and individuals had broken out again. Most serious of all, efforts were being made, largely by New Englanders, to get rid of Washington and to put the incompetent Gates, who owed the victory at Saratoga mainly to Arnold, in his place. This intrigue, known as the Conway Cabal from one of its active instigators, General Conway, an Irishman who had come from France, was happily crushed, but the winter of 1778-9 was dark indeed for the American cause. In spite of all, however, when England sent commissioners to negotiate peace on any terms except the acknowledgment of American independence, all offers were spurned. Had it not been that the French alliance had been concluded, it would have been folly not to have accepted the olive branch.

From the entry of the French, although the war continued in America, England realized that that theatre was not the principal one for the events to come. Had General Howe had the energy of Washington he might easily have crushed him with greatly superior forces almost any time during the winter, but fortunately the British general found the life of Philadelphia too agreeable to bother, and in

May, 1778, he was recalled to England, and succeeded by Clinton from New York.

Clinton had orders to send 8000 of his men to the new seat of war in the West Indies, and to move the remainder to New York. Marching from Philadelphia overland across New Jersey, with a baggage train twelve miles long, his slow progress offered a chance to Washington who attacked him at Monmouth. Charles Lee, whose treachery had not been known and who had been exchanged by the British, was given the post of senior Major-General in the fight, and whether traitorously or not, acted so incomprehensibly as to rouse Washington to anger and to permit Clinton to escape. The "damned poltroon," as the Commander-in-Chief called Lee to his face, was later dismissed from the army.

Philadelphia, however, was once more in our possession, and there was to be no more fighting of consequence in the North. A minor affair, an attempted co-operative movement of the American troops and the French fleet under d'Estaing, against the British in Newport, failed of success and created some ill-feeling against the French on account of what was considered their unnecessary leaving of the Americans in the lurch. However, Newport was evacuated by the British in 1779, the troops being taken south for the operations in Carolina, and more of the New York troops were moved to the real seat of war, the West Indies.

Washington, however, did not feel strong enough to attack the British in our chief port. Each winter his army fell to only about 3000 men, and the fact is that we Americans were heartily sick of the struggle. The New England colonies as well as others were nearly bankrupt. Our Continental paper money was nearly worthless. The economic suffering had been great. For the most part our war, which had now developed into a tremendous struggle of England against France, Spain, and Holland, had been transferred to other parts of the world, mainly the high seas. We were, as even Washington admitted, at the end of our own rope. We had not achieved independence, and were waiting for the result of the conflict of greater forces than our own far from our shores.

All fighting within our own limits, nevertheless, was not yet over. In the North there is little to record except the indecisive capture of Stony Point by the Americans, and the unhappy treason of Arnold.

That officer had been one of the finest in our army. Wounded at Quebec, the conqueror of St. Leger, the real hero of the capture of Burgoyne, active and able in the American cause, he had been most ungenerously treated by both Gates and Congress. He also had a beautiful but extravagant wife to whom he was devoted. Finally after four years, he decided to change sides and betray his country. For £10,000 he offered to try to deliver West Point to the British, asking another £10,000 if he were successful and a commission as Major-General in the British army. No definite terms appear to have been agreed to by the enemy, but negotiations were entered into.

The discovery and foiling of the plot was one of the dramatic incidents of the war and will always be recalled for the tragic fate of the young English officer who was used as go-between by Arnold and Howe. Major André was one of the most attractive of the younger men in the British service, a man of the highest honor and popular with all who knew him. After the negotiations had been proceeding for some time, he was sent up the Hudson in a small vessel to meet Arnold and arrange certain details in person.

Howe had ordered him not to wear a disguise nor to penetrate the American lines, but a change in Arnold's arrangements led to André's going ashore. While there, the vessel to which he expected to return was shot at and made to drop down stream, André being thus forced to attempt to make his return by land. With a pass signed by Arnold, he managed to fool an American sentry, but the following morning he was held up by four volunteers who had posted themselves near Tarrytown to prevent farmers from driving cattle toward New York for sale to the British. Their suspicions having been aroused, they forced André to undress in the bushes and discovered incriminating documents in his stockings. Turned over to the American military authorities, the fate of the young Englishman was sealed, and on October 2, 1780, he was hung as a spy at Tappan. Although his doom provoked much sympathy even among his enemies, there was no question of his guilt, and he himself met his end with great fortitude, regretting only that he could not be shot instead of being hung like a criminal. Arnold escaped to the British and lived long and unhappily, despised by them and Americans alike. Apparently he was paid between £6000 and £7000 for his unsuccessful treachery.

There had been more or less fighting along the western frontier from the beginning of the war, the British from Detroit and other interior posts stirring up the Indians against us. We ourselves had used Indians against the French but their employment by the English aroused much resentment, and in 1778 Lieutenant-Colonel George Rogers Clark moved westward from Virginia and in a brilliant campaign, with less than 200 men under him, captured Cahokia and Vincennes. The territory north of the Ohio thus passed into American hands with the exception of Detroit, and the western, like the northern, phase of the war was over. The final scenes were to be enacted in the South.

The British had always believed the Loyalist element to be particularly strong there, and at the end of 1778 captured Savannah and overran Georgia, re-establishing the royal government. They next attacked South Carolina, the plan being to advance northward, conquering one colony after another. When this became evident, Washington despatched General Benjamin Lincoln to the new centre of operations. That officer was able to seize Charleston but failed in a joint attack with d'Estaing's fleet on Savannah, d'Estaing hurrying away from fear of the hurricane season.

The French fleet out of the way, Clinton sailed south with 7000 troops and recaptured Charleston, Lincoln having unwisely allowed himself to be shut up in that town instead of retreating. The surrender of that not very astute general with his entire force of 5000 was a serious blow, and left the South defenseless. Guerrilla leaders, such as Thomas Sumter, Francis Marion, and others, dealt swift and unexpected strokes against British forces but could make no great impression, and Clinton, believing South Carolina captured, returned to New York, leaving Lord Cornwallis and 5000 men to hold it.

Washington wisely wished to send a new army to the scene under General Greene, but was overruled by Congress, which sent its pet Gates instead. By August 14 Gates had reached a point about thirteen miles from Camden where Cornwallis lay with about 4000 men, of whom 800 were ill. Gates, almost incredibly, believed he himself had 7000, although he had in reality only a little over 3000 present and fit. On the night of the 15th both he and Cornwallis had each determined to make a surprise attack on the other, and at two o'clock on the morning of the 16th the armies came into contact, both getting a surprise.

The result was a complete disaster for the Americans. Gates's force, half of which was made up of raw militia, had been weakened by bad food the day before, and fled in a panic when attacked, throwing away their arms and fleeing in complete rout. Kalb was killed and Gates himself did not stop his personal retreat until he had got 180 miles away, after having lost 2000 troops as against a loss of only 300 British. Washington now had his way, and Gates, who had become a laughing stock, was replaced by Greene, one of the ablest generals produced by the war. Before he reached the South, the British had received a severe check at King's Mountain from bands of North Carolina frontiersmen, who organized themselves under their own leaders.

Greene had at first only 2300 men when he reached that State and waited for reinforcements before entering upon a campaign against Cornwallis. In a minor action, however, a small part of his force under Daniel Morgan won a brilliant victory over the British Lieutenant-Colonel Tarleton at Cowpens, January 17, 1781. After Morgan rejoined Greene the combined forces amounted to about 5000 men, of whom less than 500 had ever been in action. Cornwallis had only 2250 but all were veterans. The American militia, although excellent for certain sorts of fighting, had nearly always proved weak in regular battle, and Cornwallis did not hesitate to attack the larger force at Guilford Court House on March 15.

Although he claimed the victory, his losses, nearly a third of his entire force, were so great that he immediately retreated to Wilmington where he might get in touch with a British fleet. Greene, in a masterly campaign, now operated against minor British bodies and cleared the Carolinas to near the coast. Meanwhile Cornwallis had marched northward to join Arnold with his 5000 troops in Virginia, where they had been harrying the country. Although the British pursued the American forces operating in that State under Lafayette, and even made their way as far as Charlottesville, nothing was gained, and in August Cornwallis made his base at Yorktown, which he fortified.

The end of the fighting in America was now approaching. Cornwallis had 7000 men of whom over 5000 had been sent from New

York, cooped up behind his fortifications on the bank of the York River, an arm of Chesapeake Bay. Lafayette was watching him with 3500. Washington was waiting to strike at New York with an army of 7000 of whom 5000 were French and only 2000 Americans. Suddenly word came that the French Admiral de Grasse would be at the mouth of the Chesapeake about September 1 with a fleet and 3000 more French troops. Washington at once decided to make Cornwallis's army his objective, and marched rapidly southward across New Jersey.

It had been clear for some time that the great struggle between England and her foes would turn on sea power. The Americans had had a small navy and about 2000 privateers at sea, but although these inflicted much damage to commerce and in such fights as those between the *Bon Homme Richard* under Captain John Paul Jones and the English frigate *Serapis* brought glory to American sailors, they were in no way decisive of the final result. Jones was one of the most picturesque figures which emerged from the Revolution and although he was a properly commissioned officer of the American navy, having been made Captain on May 9, 1777, the English persisted in regarding him as a mere privateersman and even a pirate.

On the two cruises in British waters which he made first in the *Ranger* and later in the *Bon Homme Richard* he affronted the pride of our enemy by daring to appear and fight in waters which they considered peculiarly their own. The romantic story of his having landed a party at the mouth of the Dee to seize the Earl of Selkirk as a hostage and having failed in this, due to the Earl's absence, of his returning $500 worth of silver plate which he found his men had carried off, appealed to Americans, as did his capture of such ships superior to his own as the *Drake* and the *Serapis*. The British, however, did not relish having him appear off Dublin, cruise in their home waters, threaten to burn Leith in reprisal for British burnings in America, and the other exploits in which he indulged. Perhaps no other American was so hated by them, and his name was a bogy with which to frighten children. After the war, he took service with Catherine of Russia, and added to the romance of his life somewhat at the expense of his reputation.

If the doings of Jones were more romantic than influential, the French navy was an important factor in the later struggle, and Cornwallis was lost unless the sea could be kept clear between him and Clinton at New York. A fleet under Admiral Graves had been sent to the Chesapeake for that purpose by Rodney, but de Grasse proved more energetic than d'Estaing, and having reached the Chesapeake first at once sailed out to give battle when Graves appeared. The English were badly defeated and had to run for New York, leaving Cornwallis helpless on his peninsula. Steadily the siege went on, the French and Americans almost equally divided in numbers, pressing their works closer day by day.

Finally, on October 19, 1781, Cornwallis surrendered his entire force, although a week before he had had word that Clinton was preparing to relieve him with Graves's fleet and 7000 more men. His case, though extremely serious, did not appear to be absolutely desperate, and it has remained a question whether he was justified or not in his sudden decision. In England, when Lord North was given the news, he threw up his arms and exclaimed, "It is all over."

Throughout the war, Washington had been most anxious to recapture New York, and when, as a result of his masterly combination with the French fleet, he had disposed of Cornwallis and his 7000 men, he urged de Grasse to combine with him for an attack on New York. The admiral, however, wished to return the French troops he had borrowed from Hayti as quickly as possible, and declined. Clinton thus remained unmolested for two more years while Washington was forced to remain inactive, but on guard.

Although the fighting in America was over, it continued elsewhere and by the end of 1781 England had lost all her West Indian possessions except Antigua, Barbadoes, and Jamaica. The next year the Spaniards captured Minorca and were besieging Gibraltar. Ireland was in rebellion, and in India Sir Eyre Coote was struggling, successfully, against the Sultan of Mysore. The British fleet was much outnumbered by its combined opponents but in April, 1782, Rodney inflicted a severe defeat upon de Grasse. A powerful body of opinion in England, however, had long been opposed to the continuance of the war. It was realized that America was in any case lost to the Empire, and nothing was to be gained by keeping up an aimless struggle against France, Spain, and Holland.

The North Ministry resigned in March, 1782, and under the new one, which included the Marquis of Rockingham, Fox, and Lord

Shelburne, negotiations for peace were opened with the representatives we had had in Paris for that purpose, Franklin, John Adams, and John Jay. Franklin had been representing American interests in France since 1776. He had already spent sixteen years in England before the war, and without losing a whit of his racy Americanism, he knew Europe as did no other American of his day. Shrewd, humorous, a genuine child of the eighteenth-century philosophy, serene, imperturbable, realistic, infinitely curious, accepting life as it came in experience, one of the notable scientific investigators of his day, tolerant and mellow, unaffected, full of common sense, knowing how to make the best of every situation and of his peculiar qualities and characteristics, always Benjamin Franklin, whether carrying a loaf of bread under his arm in the streets of Philadelphia, talking with kings or being adored by French society, he had become the rage in Paris and done much to make the French idealize the life and character of his own new nation.

Both Adams and Jay we shall meet again, and it is unnecessary to follow in detail the negotiations of the three Commissioners. The Treaty of Alliance with France had provided that neither nation should make a separate peace, but wisely the Americans did not trust the French Minister Vergennes who, happily for us, having used the American war for his own purposes, had no wish to see the United States made any more powerful as an independent republic than he could help. In addition he was sympathetic toward the desires of Spain to strengthen herself in the New World, and had some thought of a possible future French empire in the Mississippi Valley.

In fact, although later the wily minister pretended to be offended because the Americans negotiated with the English more or less independently of him, he had wished that they might do so in order to have a free hand for himself to play off conflicting claims after the Treaty of Alliance had lapsed by the attainment of its American object, with the acknowledgment of our independence by England. Without the French we could not have won our independence, as Washington and other leaders admitted on various occasions. The men, money, and supplies that they sent direct to America and the weight of their power and Spain's were all necessary to us. A few distinguished individuals, like Lafayette, were genuinely on our side, as was a part of the French people. Without minimizing in the least the importance of the French aid or the generosity of individual Frenchmen, it is nevertheless unwise to wax sentimental over the Treaty of Alliance. The French are, and always have been, an extremely realistic race, and there was nothing sentimental on their side about the Treaty. Our revolt gave them the long desired opportunity to wipe off scores with England and they seized it. It was solely with self-interest in view and without the slightest desire to aid us in establishing a republic that the Bourbon government of France before its Revolution made its treaty with us.

Our negotiators, therefore, made their own peace with England, keeping strictly, however, to the terms of the Treaty with France by providing that the Peace Treaty with England should not become effective until peace had also been made by that country with our ally. In the preliminary treaty with England our complete independence was acknowledged and it was provided that our boundary line should run approximately up the St. Croix River, thence along the forty-fifth parallel to the St. Lawrence, passing from there along the middle of streams and lakes to the Lake of Woods, down the Mississippi to the thirty-first parallel, along that to the Chattahoochee River, down that to its confluence with the Flint, and so east to the Atlantic Ocean again.

Although Florida, the whole Gulf coast, and all west of the Mississippi remained in the possession of Spain, the Americans were given right of free navigation along the river. Thanks to John Adams's determination we also, against much British opposition, secured our accustomed right of fisheries on the Newfoundland and Canadian coasts. It was further agreed on our side that no impediment would be placed in the way of the just collection of debts owed by Americans to English, and that Congress should recommend to the several States repeal of the laws against Loyalists. These agreements were reached by the end of November, 1782, but it was not until nearly a year later, September 3, 1783, when a general peace was signed by all parties to the war, that the Anglo-American treaty also became operative.

Meanwhile the American Army had been disbanded some months earlier but not without threat of a serious *coup d'etat*. As we shall see in the next chapter, the finances of the Confederation were in utter confusion. The army had long been unpaid, and both men and officers feared that if they went separately to their homes they would never receive their pay. There had also been much talk about a new government for the independent States and the advantages of a monarchy. In March, 1783, a paper was circulated among the officers at Newburg suggesting that they meet to consult as to the future and suggesting that they, unpaid, should not be the chief sufferers by

the war. Hearing of this dangerous move, Washington issued an order against secret meetings and called a public one for the 15th. Gates, who had been one of the plotters, was asked to preside at this as senior officer and had taken the chair when to that officer's surprise Washington himself appeared.

The Commander-in-Chief advanced to the platform and began reading from a prepared address. After a few words, he paused, drew his spectacles from his pocket, and said that after growing gray in his country's service he now found himself growing blind. Continuing, he explained the difficulties of Congress, urged that on their honor the officers would express their detestation of any one who would destroy their country's liberty, promised that he would do his best to see justice done to them, and left the room. Immediately the officers passed resolutions of loyalty and denounced the secret circular. Congress voted full pay for five years, and with great difficulty gathered together enough for actual pay for three months, and soon after the proclamation of April 19, 1783, declaring the war at an end, the army was peaceably disbanded.

It would have been easy, with a devoted army at his back, for Washington to make himself dictator or even, possibly, as many wished, a king. Instead he kept a mere remnant of his troops until New York was at last evacuated by the British in November, on the 25th of which month he took his last leave of his officers in Fraunces' Tavern, and travelled to Annapolis to surrender his commission to Congress. Throughout the war he had declined all pay for his services, and returned to his beloved Mount Vernon with only the blessing of his country and the hope expressed by the President of Congress that God might give him that "reward which this world cannot give."

A century later one of the greatest historians of that English nation which Washington had fought was to write of him that "it was only as the weary fight went on that the colonists learned little by little the greatness of their leader, his clear judgment, his heroic endurance, his silence under difficulties, his calmness in the hour of danger or defeat, the patience with which he waited, the quickness and hardness with which he struck, the lofty and serene sense of duty that never swerved from its task through resentment or jealousy, that never through war or peace felt the touch of a meaner ambition, that knew no aim save that of guarding the freedom of his fellow countrymen, and no personal longing save that of returning to his own fireside when their freedom was secured. It was almost unconsciously that men learned to cling to Washington with a trust and faith such as few other men have won, and to regard him with a reverence which still hushes us in presence of his memory." To-day, his statue stands in the heart of London, the very centre of the British Empire, a gift graciously accepted by the British people from their oldest colony, Virginia.

CHAPTER VII

THE FEDERAL UNION FORMED

THE end of the war brought relief and rejoicing to the colonies. The eight years precisely, from the 19th of April, 1775, when the first really warlike engagement between Americans and the British had occurred at Lexington, to the 19th of April, 1783, when the formal announcement was made that the war was ended and independence won, had been years of suffering, anxiety, and turmoil. There had been so much passion spent over "slavery" and "liberty," that, liberty gained, the world seemed to open in endless vistas of prosperity and happiness. Nevertheless, although there was much truth in the belief that the American colonies when united as an independent nation had a future which would have been denied to them as outlying provinces of an European empire, the prospects of an immediate leap into the millennium were to be rudely shattered by actual conditions.

It has been claimed by some historians that America was prosperous in the last year or two of the war. It is true that after 1778 there was increasing importation of foreign goods and even luxuries. It is also true that, as compared with most wars of equal importance, the actual destruction of American property had been slight. Over ninety per cent of the population was engaged in agriculture, and even within the zones of actual military operations there had been little damage done to farm property. It has even been said that the great bulk of the population went on with their farming undisturbed by the fact of war. Such statements, however, do not appraise fairly the vast dislocation that occurred in the economic life of the people, and the false basis for even such prosperity as existed.

There was bred, of course, as in all wars, a class of new rich, of men who had been shrewd enough to take advantage of conditions for their private benefit, who had profited by army contracts, or had been lucky in speculation or privateering. The respectable firm of Otis & Andrews in Boston, for example, were charging the government 100 per cent profit, and at one time the United States owed them nearly £200,000 lawful money. Such families as the Derbys in Salem and the Cabots in Beverley grew rich from privateering. Sudden profits called for unwonted luxuries. On the other hand, many firms were ruined. To a large extent the God of Chance had ruled. The loss of a ship or two to the enemy might cripple a merchant of standing whereas a capture of one or two enemy vessels might make some upstart rich. One of the most marked changes in Boston at the end of the war was the great alteration in the personnel of its "leading" citizens. If in that town after 1778 there was much dissipation and extravagance there was also much pinching poverty and economizing. What was true of Massachusetts was largely so also of the other colonies.

Apart from the influence of war on various occupations, such as the disastrous effect on the fisheries or the substitution of speculative privateering for the old substantial merchandise shipping, the factor that counted most in disturbing economic life was the colossal depreciation in the paper money, and the corresponding advance in prices.

Because of their fear of taxation, the colonies refused to grant to Congress any power to raise money by that means, and as they failed miserably in making voluntary grants to the central government, that body had to carry on the war by the simple but disastrous method of turning out paper money on the printing press. Over $240,000,000 was thus issued by Congress and an equally large sum by the several colonies. The steady increase of the amounts outstanding, and the decreasing prospect of its ever being reduced as promised, naturally led to its decline in value as measured in coin or goods.

Over and over, the United States pledged its "sacred honor" that the bills would be redeemed at their face value. They were forced on the people at times regardless of depreciation. General Putnam issued an army order that any civilians declining to take the paper money at its face value in exchange for goods should be imprisoned and suffer forfeiture of their merchandise. The Council of Safety of

Pennsylvania added banishment as the punishment. Yet the paper fell steadily until, like the German mark after the World War, it became practically worthless, and the Congress which had so often pledged our honor to its redemption finally redeemed it in new paper at one in forty after it had fallen to one in a hundred and twenty for coin.

The reverse of this movement was a fantastic rise in the prices of merchandise, farm produce, and all other goods, and in wages, though as usual wages did not rise in proportion to the cost of living. As we know well from our recent experiences, any such great readjustment in prices has very unequal effects on different classes and even individuals in a community. The rapid rise in prices gives the effect of a feverish prosperity, while many persons suffer and the whole community is on an unsound basis.

After a time, it became almost impossible to trade in terms of money, and barter was widely resorted to. The relations between debtors and creditors became impossible. If a man borrowed money or held up payment for purchases, all he had to do was to wait with the assurance that he could pay his debts for a half, a quarter or less than when he had contracted them. Creditors of all sorts, shop keepers with open accounts, lenders of money, mortgagees, persons whose property was held in trust, were often ruined. Even Washington refused to have his agent accept payments in the paper, declaring that although he would gladly sacrifice his entire estate in a common cause he would not consent to be ruined in such a dishonorable way while others were prospering. Bitterly did he complain that "idleness, dissipation, and extravagance," "speculation, peculation, and an insatiable thirst for riches seem to have got the better of every other consideration, and almost of every order of men."

Farmers who were getting high prices seemed on the one hand to themselves to be getting rich, yet on the other, their labor supply was greatly interfered with, and when the men were at the front it sometimes was almost impossible, even with the help of the women, to raise the crops. Moreover, the farmers paid equally high prices for such articles as they had to buy, and it must be recalled that the great mass of farmers did not raise their crops for sale but for their own consumption, so that they gained little or nothing on the high farm prices and lost on high merchandise ones, being at the same time under the psychological influence of the general extravagance engendered by the overturn of all the old standards of living.

Many States, wholly unsuccessfully of course, tried to fix prices by law, as had been done, so Pelatiah Webster said, from the beginning of the world, though such efforts never had had more effect than "sprinkling water on a blacksmith's forge." When the Continental money was at last funded in 1790 at the rate of one cent in the dollar, the wake of ruin that it left covered the whole country, a ruin of spiritual quite as much as of material values. The $200,-000,000 of paper money issued by the several colonies had also heavily depreciated and in addition most of them had accumulated debts to an extent that could not be liquidated by ordinary taxation. It is, I think, as unhistorical to speak of America as prosperous at the end of the war as of a man with nervous excitability and a high fever as being well. John Adams described the situation better when he said that the war was "immoderately gainful to some, and ruinous to others." The letters of his wife describing the hardships on their farm due to high prices and lack of labor give a very different picture from the account books of the privateering Derbys and Cabots, or the inventories of shops catering to the new rich or the foolishly extravagant.

There was, however, prosperity for certain classes, and with the return of peace all hoped to share in it. Rather naïvely, we expected the trade of the world to be open to us. We had hoped to negotiate with England a treaty of commerce as well as of peace, but England had declined. We had forced her to acknowledge our complete independence, and in her view we were, as in truth was the case, a foreign country. By our rebellion we had not only deprived her of the most important part of her empire but had become the ally of her immemorial enemy, France. She saw no reason for giving us special privileges in her imperial trade, though Lord Shelburne and others had a wider vision and would have tried to unite the two nations closely in sentiment and commerce. Unhappily, narrower views, such as those advocated by Lord Sheffield in his *Observations of the Commerce of the American States,* were to prevail. In the war, England had found herself almost alone in a hostile world, with her fleet heavily outclassed, and she now determined to make no concessions which might build up American shipping at the expense of her own.

In 1783, by Orders in Council, she excluded our vessels absolutely from Canada and the West Indies, thus putting us on the same footing as any other nation, and she did the same when she allowed our vessels in her own ports precisely the same privileges as those of any European power. On the other hand she did admit free of duty all our raw materials, to be carried direct from America to England in either our vessels or her own, on the old basis of colonial days. This concession was an important one, but our exclusion from the West Indies played havoc with our old triangular trade routes. We were not, it should be noted, excluded from trading with the islands but from doing so in our own vessels. The owners of these were forced to hunt for new sources of trading and were rather unjustly irritated against the British, who may have been narrow-minded but were certainly within their rights. Their policy, from the point of view of statesmanship, was unwise for the long run, but on the other hand we were rather illogical in demanding at once independence and those old special privileges in her trade which we had enjoyed as part of the empire.

France also reduced the privileges she had accorded us as allies in the war. In 1783 she excluded our vessels from her West Indies and although the following year she opened some of her ports there to us for certain articles, they had to be carried only in small vessels which were required to ply directly between the islands and our own ports. In so far as our triangular trade was concerned, therefore, she interfered with our shipping as much as England did. To a great extent, however, these foreign Orders in Council became dead letters and by 1785 we had begun to trade with the British West Indies much as we had been accustomed to do.

The Dutch and Danish islands had always been open to us, and Spain opened the ports of Santiago and Havana in Cuba. Our commerce returned to normal, and the economic life of the new States was also on a sounder basis from the rapid increase which had perforce taken place in manufacture during the non-importation periods and the war. Manufactories of firearms, iron works, textile mills, and other industries had been started and prospered, and these reduced to some extent the necessity of such imports, helped our trade balance, and gave greater variety to our occupations. There was a severe depression, as we shall note, in 1785, as usually happens two or three years after the close of a great war. Then there was increasing prosperity until our first national panic came in 1791.

If our commerce gradually fell into the old grooves again, there had been one immense change wrought by the war, more momentous than any other save the fact of independence itself. That was the opening of what was then "the West." The old Proclamation Line of 1763 which the British had hoped would keep us from too rapid expansion and Indian complications had vanished. Even before the war its uselessness had become partially manifest. It could cause irritation but it could not prevent all emigration any more than the imaginary line of the equator affects the waves that flow across it. In 1769 pioneers had founded a small settlement on the Watauga in Tennessee, and the picturesque Daniel Boone had been several times across the mountains when, with a group of settlers, he built a fort and established Boonesboro in 1775. The following year Kentucky was made a county of Virginia, and gradually both Kentucky and Tennessee saw the pouring in of what may be considered our first great western movement, hordes of settlers tramping over the mountains through Cumberland Gap and other passes from Pennsylvania, Virginia, and the Carolinas.

The boundaries and claims of the old colonies were vague, and the words "over the mountains" had deep significance. Restless, discontented, poor, and ambitious spirits had always been moving from older to new settlements further out, from the earliest days of colonization. There had been, as we have seen, jealousies and grievances on the part of new settlements against old. But this new frontier, "over the mountains," was isolated from the eastern States as none of the old "frontiers" had been. The old frontiers had been merely rougher and rougher fringes of settlement on the advancing edges of a society that was based on the seaboard.

The new frontier over the mountains, by the enormous difficulties of transport, no longer looked to the eastward ocean ports but westward to the Mississippi. As the pioneers came through the passes or gaps in the mountains, the magnificent valley of the Father of Waters, 2000 miles wide, lay before them. Here was a vast new empire to be conquered, the outlet of which was not by way of Boston, New York, Philadelphia, or Charleston, but by way of the great river, Spanish New Orleans, and the Gulf. The interminable forests, infested with savages, covered "the dark and bloody ground" of Kentucky and stretched away to where Spanish America lay across the river, or down to the swamps and bayous of Louisiana.

The pioneers who had crossed the mountains before the war had been but the vanguard of the masses to follow. By 1790 there were probably about 150,000 people living in the land that looked westward. There had been land companies formed and men like Richard Henderson, one of the greatest of our land speculators, had tried to build new States. But for the most part the movement was one of individuals and families, who governed and defended themselves. In one year, 1788, over 18,000 men, women, and children went down the Ohio on rafts, and perhaps an equal number tramped over the southern passes. Various State organizations were proposed, —Transylvania, Westsylvania, Franklin,—but these came to nought in the uncertainty as to ownership under the conflicting claims of the older eastern States derived from their colonial charters.

These claims on the part of some States also made for jealousy among the others, and Maryland, fearing Virginia's enormous western domain, refused to sign the articles of Confederation in 1777, aimed at a closer and more effective union, unless the States with western claims should cede them to the Confederation for the common good. In 1780 and 1781, New York, Connecticut, Massachusetts, and, in part, Virginia consented to do so, so that when the Treaty of Peace was signed, it was the *United* States and not the *several* ones that became the sovereign of the West north of the Ohio. The new States later to be created there thus had a national origin and never looked to colonial charters as the basis of their liberties. The southern section of the West also passed to the Federal Government a few years later.

The West was to be national in another sense. The immigrants who so rapidly poured into it came from all the colonies, and commingled as did none of the populations "back East." A Connecticut Yankee and a South Carolinian clearing the forest in adjoining patches felt themselves closely united as Americans and Westerners, and the old provincial jealousies of the East were largely sloughed off. On the other hand, the mountain barrier and the geographical unity of the great valley and river tended toward a new sectionalism, and the Westerners came to feel a corresponding unity in their

LAND CLAIMS OF THE THIRTEEN STATES

interests as contrasted or even conflicting with those of both Northern and Southern sections in the East.

In part, the conflict of interests was to arise from the failure of both Americans and British to carry out the terms of the Treaty of Peace. America had fought through most of the war with scarcely anything that could be called a central government. Although a

Confederation had been urged in 1776 it was not until May 1779 that the States could agree upon its terms, and owing to the western land problem, Maryland did not join until 1781, so that it was not until March 1 of that year, scarcely more than six months before Yorktown, that Congress had authority as the representative body of the Confederated States.

The form of government then inaugurated was both clumsy and weak. There was no executive, the President of Congress being merely the presiding officer elected by that body, which itself sat as a single chamber. The Congress itself had no power of taxation, of regulating commerce, or of enforcing its measures on the several States. The acts it was allowed to perform, such as declaring peace and war, making treaties, sending and receiving ambassadors, determining boundary disputes, regulating Indian affairs and coinage, had to be agreed to by the representatives of nine States, each of the thirteen having a single vote each. No amendments could be made to the Articles except by the unanimous consent of all.

When it came to carrying into effect terms of a Treaty which might be unpalatable to any State or its citizens, such a government was quite evidently helpless. In the Treaty with England there were two unpopular clauses, those relating to the Loyalists and to the payment of private debts to English merchants. Congress, as the Treaty demanded, did recommend to the States that they should restore confiscated Loyalist property and refrain from any further confiscations, but there being no means of coercion, the States to a considerable extent failed to take action. The Loyalists were heartily hated, and although much of their property had been unjustly seized, practically none was restored. This gave the British Government the chance to claim that the Treaty was being violated, though it is doubtful if the clause in it relating to Tories had been considered by the English Peace Commissioners as more than a gesture.

A much more legitimate grievance on the part of England was the disregard of the clear promise in the Treaty that no impediment would be placed in the way of the collection of just private debts by English creditors. This clause was unquestionably violated by some of our States, with Virginia in the lead. Nearly twenty years later, after endless litigation and negotiation, we admitted that we had been in the wrong, and the United States Government paid £600,-

ooo to England as a compromise sum to settle the adjudicated debts.

However, in the years immediately following the peace in 1783, it was only too clear to foreign governments, and to our own ambassadors abroad, such as John Adams in London, that the so-called government of the United States under the Confederation was merely a rope of sand ostensibly binding together thirteen semi-independent small nations which did as they pleased and which, internationally, were wholly irresponsible.

Moreover, although the Confederation was to be brilliantly successful in inaugurating a national land policy, it failed, as the old colonies had, in an Indian policy, and proved itself powerless to prevent conflict between the lawless settlement by hordes of immigrants and the legitimate rights of the savages to their hunting grounds. By the Treaty we had come into possession of that immense territory north of the Ohio River which came to be known as the "Old Northwest," and in which, at the end of the war, there were practically no white inhabitants except Canadian fur traders, and a few French farmers about Detroit and the other military posts where, since 1763, there had been English garrisons for maintaining peace with the Indians.

All these posts were on the American side of the new boundary line. The very valuable fur trade was the only apparent asset in North America which England had saved from the war, and the Canadians, much chagrined to find where the boundary had been placed by the British negotiators in Paris, urged the government not to give up the posts, at least until they could get their merchandise out and reorganize the trade. Not to hold them, they pointed out, would be the ruin of Canada. The British Government, therefore, made no haste to recall their troops from American soil, and soon the obvious weakness of the Confederation, and the failure on our part to live up to the clauses in the Treaty about Loyalists and debts, gave the British an excuse for declining to carry out the clause about the evacuation of the posts until we had observed our part of the agreement.

Moreover, it began to look as though the United States might break up, and if it did, it was evidently to British interest to have grappling hooks on the great Northwest. We shall later notice events in the East which made even Washington fear that anarchy was coming, and consider here only the West. We need merely note that Vermont, which did not join the Union until 1791, was still intriguing with the British as an independent power. In the West, the British chance of detaching the new settlements from the Confederation was even brighter.

The interests of the new communities were, as we have pointed out, largely distinct from those of the East. The settlers rightly considered their future possibilities of development as boundless, but the barrier which separated them from the seaboard is shown clearly enough by the fact that it was easier to ship produce from the Ohio River to Philadelphia by way of New Orleans than it was direct by the few hundred miles of rough and rocky road which straggled over the mountains. Moreover, the East cared little or nothing about the new West. In fact, many conservatives on the seaboard intensely feared its growth, with the threat of radicalism and eventual shift in the balance of political power. In 1786 John Jay even proposed to Spain that we consent to the closing of the Mississippi for twenty-five years in exchange for new privileges in her ports in Europe. The West properly felt that its vital concerns were not safe in a government controlled by Easterners.

Both Spain and England realized the loose nature of the bonds which united the two sections of the new nation, and played for time until the West might become independent or fall into their several hands. Thus, while England retained military posts which should have been evacuated in the North, Spain likewise encroached on our territory from the south, maintaining garrisons at Natchez and elsewhere, and opening the river to the western traffic as a grace and not as a Treaty right. Many leading Westerners were in Spanish pay and were intriguing to secede from the United States with the thought, however, of founding an empire of their own which might come to include a good part of Spain's American possessions. The whole section was covered by a tangled net-work of intrigue in which no one trusted any one else, not even those in their own pay.

If conservative Easterners feared the West, they also had an ample supply of anxieties in the East itself. We have seen how as the Revolution advanced, control had fallen more and more to the radicals. The catch-words of the movement,—the talk about tyranny and slavery, the slogans about "no taxation without representation," the declaration that "all men are created equal," that "governments derive their just powers from the consent of the governed"—had all, combined with the constant mobbing, the tarring and featherings, the Tory confiscations, and other war-time commotions, given a tremendous impetus to what were considered radical ideas, and the demands of the common man.

The conflict between conservative and radical was well displayed in the drafting of the new State constitutions, some of which proved over-conservative, as in South Carolina, and others over-democratic and radical as in Pennsylvania. In the former, the large planters of the seaboard strongly entrenched themselves in control. The new constitution perpetuated the old under-representation of the western counties, and established a fifty-acre freehold as qualification for the suffrage, an estate of £2000 for election to the Senate, and £10,000 for election to the Council or Governorship. Pennsylvania went to the other extreme. All qualifications for the suffrage were abolished except payment of a State tax, thus giving the western counties control of the State, and there was no governor and no Upper House, in this new super-simplified democracy.

Although the new State constitutions thus varied greatly, in general there was a broadening of the suffrage and a democratizing of the fundamental laws in all of them. In Virginia, within a few years, primogeniture, entails, and the slave trade were abolished, and in Jefferson's Statute of Religious Liberty a complete separation was established between Church and State. What few relics remained of feudalism, such as quit-rents, were everywhere swept away. The strong feeling against anything resembling an aristocracy or class distinctions was evidenced in the violent opposition to giving the officers of the army half pay for life, and in the absurd alarm raised by their forming an association, the Cincinnati, to perpetuate the friendships and memories of their service. On the other hand, few or none in the upper classes had any confidence in the ability or honesty of the lower in political matters, and in a few years their worst anticipations seemed on the verge of fulfillment.

In Massachusetts, in spite of the wild talk of the radicals, such as Sam Adams, in the twenty years of controversy and war, the governing class had always insisted, as far as possible, upon a narrow suffrage and the right of the "wise, the rich, and the good," or in

John Adams's phrase the "well born" to rule. In the new constitution adopted in 1780, the property qualification for the franchise had been doubled just when Vermont was abolishing every restriction and New Hampshire was giving the vote to every male over twenty-one who paid a poll tax. Now that the war was won, "no taxation without representation" was considered radical doctrine, and the propertied classes were looking about for safety from the possible attacks of the non-propertied ones. By 1786, forty per cent of the entire taxation of the State was being raised, with scandalous inequity, from the poll tax alone.

Meanwhile, the feverish and unhealthy prosperity of the end of the war had come to an end everywhere in the colonies. The fictitious war-time prices for farm produce collapsed. The new manufacturing enterprises suffered from British competition. The currency was in confusion. Enormous purchases had been made of British goods, which it was impossible to find exchange to pay for. The shoe was suddenly put on the other foot, and the debtor class now found itself in unexpected difficulties. As ever under such conditions there was a strong demand for "cheap," or paper money. The general crisis was most clearly marked in Massachusetts, where the incoherent policy of the legislature did much to precipitate it.

The whole of the State appears to have been in trouble. In Groton every third or fourth man between 1784 and 1786 suffered from one to a dozen suits for debt, and in Worcester County there were 4000 suits in one year in a total population of 50,000. Farms could not be sold for enough to satisfy the owner's creditors. In 1785 the legislature laid no taxes; then the next year levied them so heavily that they could not be borne. In June the town meeting of Groton chose a "Committee of Correspondence" as in revolutionary days, and conventions were held in many counties to consider the grievances of the people.

A "reform" legislature, when elected, did nothing. Then open rebellion broke out under the lead of Captain Daniel Shays, who had had a good record in the war, and others of standing in their several communities, although the mass of revolters were farmers, mechanics, and laborers, numbering, it was reported, in the western part of the State one fifth of the population. Among other grievances, the various conventions reported that the rebels objected to the mode of taxation and of paying the State debt; the method of representation; the existence of the State Senate; lawyers and their high fees; and the lack of a circulating medium.

Nothing was done to remedy the real abuses and even Sam Adams joined the reactionaries in Boston in denouncing the right of the people to voice their grievances! The court calendars were overflowing with suits for debt which meant ejectment of the owners from their farms or shops, and failing to obtain justice, the next step of the "rebels" was to close the courts. This was done by armed crowds in the autumn of 1786, at Northampton, Great Barrington, Worcester, Concord, and elsewhere. Sam Adams, of all men, began to denounce the mobs, and at a mass meeting in Faneuil Hall refused to consider the demands of the people, claiming, with his old fixed idea, that the trouble was caused by British emissaries. Without touching the real troubles, the legislature temporarily suspended the sitting of the courts.

At Mount Vernon, Washington was deeply troubled at the growing anarchy, but his advice to investigate the grievances, and if they proved real to remedy them, and if unreal, to put down the movement by force, was not acted upon. The beginning of the next year the situation was worse. Convinced that neither the legislature nor the "wise and good" would make any move to remedy the distress, the insurgents grew more violent, and at last the legislature put a force under General Lincoln in the field against them. Within a few weeks, "Shays's rebellion," as it is called, was crushed, the leaders captured or fled, and, having had a thorough scare, the legislature at last took some action on the people's complaints.

Watching events in Massachusetts, multitudes besides Washington had been profoundly alarmed for the foundations of society. Economic conditions were bad everywhere, and the grievances of the poor not limited to the Bay State. The rebels had shown how easily the old revolutionary machinery of committees and conventions could be initiated again, not against England, but against the newly established and unstable State governments. It was realized as never before that the central government of the Confederation was helpless and powerless. Our weakness in dealing with trade, commerce, and foreign nations had long been evident, but now that we had glimpsed alarming social revolution at home, the tide turned toward the possibility of a better union and a stronger government, there even being talk of a monarchy. Daniel Shays was in truth one of the chief fathers and begetters of our Federal Constitution.

There had already been many suggestions of the possibilities of strengthening the Confederation, but nothing had been attempted. Any action toward that end, in view of the attitude of the people and the jealousies of the States, had hitherto been outside the range of practical politics. These jealousies had been particularly manifested in the tariffs which the various States placed on the importation of foreign goods and even on goods imported from one State into another; and in questions arising between colonies as to navigation in waters, like New York Harbor and Chesapeake Bay, on which two or more States might border.

A dispute of the latter sort between Maryland and Virginia had been of long standing when, in 1786, Virginia, extending the range of the negotiations, suggested to all the States that they send delegates to a convention to be held at Annapolis to consider their relations to the trade of the United States. The meeting, held in September, was attended by delegates from only five States, but although there was little interest in it, the opportunity was seized by the more far-sighted among those, such as Washington, Alexander Hamilton, and James Madison, who were anxious for a stronger government. At Annapolis, Hamilton took the lead, and secured the passage of a resolution suggesting the holding of a convention, to be authorized by Congress and approved by the States, for the purpose of improving the form of government. Virginia at once endorsed the plan and chose delegates to the proposed convention. Other States followed her lead, and Congress forwarded an invitation to all of them to send delegates to the convention to be held in Philadelphia on May 14, 1787.

When the convention assembled in Independence Hall in that city as appointed, all the States were represented except Rhode Island, which had opposed the suggestion, and Vermont, which had not yet joined the Union. The fifty-five delegates formed as notable a gathering as had the first Continental Congress, but there were many changes to be observed. The more extreme radicals of the early days of the Revolution were now absent. Neither Sam Adams nor Christopher Gadsden had been chosen by their States to attend. Patrick Henry had been included in Virginia's delegation, but had declined to serve. John Adams was in England as our first minister to that country, and Jefferson was in France.

The work of the first Congress had been essentially destructive, that of the convention was to be constructive; and the temper of the members was essentially conservative. Their duty was not to sever political old ties but to find some instrument of government to preserve new ones. Much the ablest delegation was that from Virginia, consisting of Washington, James Madison, John Blair, George Wythe, George Mason, and Governor Edmund Randolph. Rufus King, then only twenty-two years old, although the youngest of the Massachusetts delegation, was the most important member on it. Connecticut sent excellent men in Roger Sherman, William S. Johnson (recently elected president of Columbia College in New York), and Oliver Ellsworth, while New York's leading delegate was Alexander Hamilton, just thirty but already possessing a national reputation. Among the seven from Pennsylvania were James Wilson, Robert Morris, Gouverneur Morris, and the aged Benjamin Franklin. The other more important Northerners were John Dickinson from Delaware, William Paterson of New Jersey, and Luther Martin from Maryland, while South Carolina's delegation included two able representatives in John Rutledge and Charles Cotesworth Pinckney.

In running over the list of the total membership, one is struck happily with the evident calming down of the old passions of the war. Among the delegates, for example, there were Jared Ingersoll, who, as Stamp Distributor, had been subjected to personal violence by the Sons of Liberty; Dickinson, who had declined to sign the Declaration of Independence when in Congress; and Johnson who had been so lukewarm in the war as to have become unpopular. It is also interesting to note that of the fifty-five men who were to frame our Constitution, nine, or exactly one sixth of the total, were foreign born.

When the convention organized, Washington was made chairman, and although he took no part in the debates his influence throughout was great, quite aside from the occasional votes he cast.

His influence was, indeed, notable from the very outset. The convention met in the same room in which, in 1776, the Continental Congress had voted the Declaration of Independence, and which had already become clothed with historic memories. The first meeting was informal, noticeable among the members being Madison, shy, small, and slender; Hamilton, also short but handsome, young, and distinguished in appearance; old Benjamin Franklin, with the benign face of the philosopher which had bewitched the ladies of the French Court; Washington, tall and dignified, receiving the natural deference of all the other members; the Scotch-born Wilson, and Rutledge, and the two Pinckneys from South Carolina.

There was some preliminary discussion of what sort of constitution would be acceptable to the people, and many voiced the fear that only half measures would win popular approval in view of the jealousies of the States, and the many opposing opinions on almost all points of the public at large. With unusual seriousness, Washington broke incisively into the discussion. In words which the politicians of today would do well to remember and act upon, he expressed his own independent view. Few speeches so brief have carried so much weight. "It is too probable," he said, "that no plan we propose will be adopted. Perhaps another dreadful conflict is to be sustained. If, to please the people, we offer what we ourselves disapprove, how can we afterward defend our work? Let us raise a standard to which the wise and the honest can repair; the event is in the hand of God." Although subsequent compromises had to be made, the temper of the meeting at once rose from the plane of politics to that of statesmanship.

The greatest difficulty which had to be overcome was the old jealousy of the States for one another and their pretensions to complete sovereignty individually. How to reconcile the sovereignty of the several States with the creation of a general government which should have genuine power would have been an almost insuperable problem to solve even had the States been all of the same size and power, but to this was added the fact that they differed greatly, and that the small ones feared placing themselves under control of the larger ones. The combined populations of Rhode Island, Delaware, New Jersey, and New Hampshire, for example, were only 453,000, which was but slightly larger than that of Pennsylvania alone, less than Massachusetts, and only somewhat more than half that of Virginia with its 747,000.

The latter State on May 29 submitted what came to be known as the Virginia Plan, and in introducing it Governor Randolph frankly said that it was intended to create not a "federal government" but a "strong *consolidated* union." It separated the executive, legislative, and judicial branches, and provided for a Congress of two Houses, the lower elected by the people of the several States, and the upper of persons nominated by the State legislatures, both in proportion to population or State tax quotas.

The Virginia Plan thus gave control to the larger States and around this point debate raged for a fortnight until Paterson of New Jersey introduced the "New Jersey Plan," which provided for equal representation in a one-chamber Congress by every State instead of resting it on the basis of population. Paterson's suggested Federal Government was in some ways an improvement over the old Confederation, especially in that it made the Acts of Congress and treaties negotiated by it the supreme law of the land and gave that body at least the theoretical right to coerce a State which did not pay its requisitions for taxes.

The chief difficulty, however, and the one which threatened to ruin the work of the convention, was that mentioned of how to provide for a fair balance of power in Congress between the big and little States. For weeks the wrangling went on, and as the weather became hot in July so did the tempers of the delegates. Franklin suggested praying to God for help and Hamilton is reported to have answered curtly that they needed no "foreign aid." It was not until the 16th that what is known as the "great compromise" of our Constitution was finally adopted, providing that representation in the lower branch of Congress should be according to free population plus three fifths of the slaves, and each State should have equal representation in the Upper House or Senate. There were several stages in reaching this fundamental compromise, and in connection with the slave apportionment neither South nor North was wholly satisfied.

Although the debates over representation had evolved from State jealousies, larger sectional cleavages also appeared. The East as a whole feared the West, and the possible development of large population and political power there. North and South split not only over the slavery question but also, as the former was becoming commercial and industrial and the latter was agricultural, over giving to the Federal Government the power to regulate commerce. This particular point was agreed to only after the South believed it had protected itself by the clause which prohibited Congress from passing any law placing an export duty on our produce. As a result of compromise after compromise, the Constitution gradually took form, and on September 17 it was signed by those present. According to the terms on which it had been drawn, however, before it could go in operation, the approval of at least nine of the States would have to be obtained.

The new compact was an immense improvement over the old Confederation. An executive was provided for in the person of a President, who was to be elected for four years by electors specially chosen by each State as its legislature might direct, the number of electors of any State being equal to the total number of senators and representatives it sent to Congress. These electors were to meet in their own State and the person who received the greatest number of their votes in all the States was to be President, and the one receiving the next highest number to be Vice-President, provided that in each case the person voted for received a majority.

If two tied for the highest number of majority votes, the election for President went to the House of Representatives, where, for this purpose, each State should have only one vote, and in case of a tie for Vice-President, the election went to the Senate. If no one received a majority of all the votes in the Electoral College, the House of Representatives should choose a President from among those having the highest five votes. These provisions were altered later by the Twelfth Amendment, adopted in 1804, which was to provide that the President and Vice-President should be voted for separately by the electors, and if no one received a majority for President, then the choice should be made by the House of Representatives from among the highest three receiving the greatest number of electoral votes.

The President was made Commander-in-Chief of the Army and Navy; given the right to demand the advice of the heads of all departments of the government; the power to veto Acts of Congress, unless repassed by a two-thirds vote; the power "by and with the advice and consent of the Senate" to make treaties, provided two thirds of the senators concurred; to appoint ambassadors, judges of the Supreme Court and all other officers of the government, also with the advice and consent of the Senate; was required to give Congress information as to the state of the Union; to see that all the laws were executed; and the right to convene Congress in extraordinary session, and to adjourn it when he thought proper if there were a disagreement between the two Houses. He could be impeached and removed from office for treason, bribery or "other high crimes and misdemeanors."

The legislature was to consist of two Houses, the Senate and House of Representatives, the former to be composed of two senators elected by the legislature of each State for a term of six years, each senator having one vote. The Vice-President of the United States was to be President of the Senate until, on account of death, resignation or inability to perform his duties on the part of the President, he might succeed the latter in office.

The House of Representatives, in which all money bills had to be initiated, was to be composed of members chosen every second year directly by the people, the electors in each State having the same qualifications for voting as were required for electing the members of the lower House in the legislature of such State. The number of representatives was not to exceed one for every 30,000 inhabitants (excluding Indians and counting three fifths of the slaves), and although the Constitution did not require that a representative should be a resident of his particular district the growing habit of localism in American representation, which we noted earlier, received sanction in the requirement that he must be a resident of the State from which he was returned.

Numerous and varied powers were conferred upon the new legislature. It could lay and collect both direct and indirect taxes, provided these were uniform throughout the nation; it could borrow money on the nation's credit; regulate both foreign and interstate commerce; establish uniform laws as to naturalization and bankruptcy; coin money, regulate currency, and regulate weights and measures; establish post offices and post roads; provide for patents and copyrights; constitute courts inferior to the Supreme Court;

declare war, raise and support an army and navy; call out the militia to execute the Federal laws, suppress insurrections and repel invasions; exercise complete jurisdiction over a tract ten miles square to be chosen as the location for the national Capital; dispose of or govern all territory belonging to the United States; admit new States to the Union; and make all laws necessary for carrying its powers into effect.

Certain things it was forbidden to do. It could not suspend the privilege of the writ of Habeas Corpus except in cases of rebellion or invasion when the public safety might demand it. It could not pass any bill of attainder or *ex post facto* law; could lay no direct tax except on the basis of population according to the census; could give no commercial preference to the ports of one State over those of another, nor oblige any vessel to enter, clear or pay duties in passing from one to another; nor could it grant any title of nobility. It was to guarantee a republican form of government to every State.

The judicial department of the central government was to be vested in a Supreme Court, and such inferior courts as Congress might create. It was provided that the power of the Federal judiciary should "extend to all cases in law and equity arising under this Constitution, the laws of the United States, and treaties made, or which shall be made, under their authority;—to all cases affecting ambassadors, other public ministers or consuls;—to all cases of admiralty and maritime jurisdiction;—to controversies to which the United States shall be a party;—to controversies between two or more States;—between a State and citizens of another State;—between citizens of different States;—between citizens of the same State claiming lands under grants of different States, or the citizens thereof, and foreign States, citizens or subjects." This creation of a Federal judiciary with such wide jurisdiction and powers was, perhaps, the most daring of the moves made toward a strong nationalism in the Constitution, and from it was to arise the process of judicial review by the Supreme Court over the Acts of Congress itself.

Passing from the organization of the central government to the States, we may note that, on the one hand, each State was required to give full faith and credit to the public acts, records and judicial decisions of every other; that the citizens of each were to be entitled to all the privileges and immunities of those in all the others; and that a criminal fleeing from one to another was to be given up to the jurisdiction of the first, and that a person "held to service or labor" (such as slaves) under the laws of one State and escaping to another should be returned to his owner. On the other hand, no State was to be permitted to make any foreign treaty or alliance; to coin money or emit bills of credit; to make anything but gold and silver legal tender; to pass any *ex post facto* laws, bills of attainder, laws impairing the obligation of contracts, or to confer titles of nobility; nor in general to lay any duties on imports or exports.

At the end of the Constitution were added the provisions for amending it which are still in force.

Such was the extraordinary document to which the delegates appended their signatures in September, 1787. Many had contributed their ideas to it and worked for final harmony, but unquestionably the master spirit had been James Madison, who combined great constitutional knowledge with a firm grasp upon the actualities of the situation. It was in the latter point particularly that Hamilton, whose great work was to be done later, was lacking, and during the later sittings he was not even present. Next to Madison, it was either Wilson or possibly Washington who had the greatest influence in bringing about the final result, which was at once forwarded to the Congress of the old Confederation in New York. By that body it was transmitted to the several States so that it could be everywhere submitted to conventions for ratification or rejection, the latter appearing all too likely.

Meanwhile, the old Congress had itself been engaged in momentous legislation, ending what was to prove its final session with one of the most statesmanlike measures which has ever been enacted. The members had been struggling with the problem of the western lands for many years, and in 1785 had passed an ordinance providing for a survey and the division of the territory into townships six miles square, made up of sections of 640 acres each, one section in each being reserved for a school fund and four for the Federal Government.

Believing that the land should be made a source of revenue, it was arranged that it should be sold at not less than one dollar an acre. This had proved too costly for most pioneers, but speculators, such as those forming the Ohio Company, had purchased tracts as large as 1,500,000 acres, the price for such wholesale transactions being reduced by the government, and the companies had undertaken to plant settlers. Rapid development, however, called for administration, and in July, 1787, while the Federal Convention was sweltering in Philadelphia over a new organic law for the nation, the old Congress was also drafting one for the Northwest territory.

This "Ordinance of 1787," passed in New York on the 13th, organized the Northwest into a district to be administered by a governor and judges appointed by Congress, but provided that when it should have 5000 free male inhabitants over twenty years of age, they could elect a legislature of their own, and send a delegate, without vote, to Congress. The territorial government thus provided for followed somewhat closely the old colonial governments as devised by England. It was to have a popularly elected assembly as the lower House of the legislature, but the governor was to be appointed by Congress, which body also made selection of the councillors, or members of the upper House, from names submitted by the lower.

The whole territory was eventually to be cut into not less than three or more than five States, which were severally to be admitted to the Union, when any one had a population of 60,000, "on an equal footing with the original States in all respects whatever," except that slavery was forever forbidden. The way was thus wisely opened for an expansion of our people westward with no permanent loss of political rights. There was to be no colonial status or subordination, and the easy transition from wilderness through territorial government to full Statehood was made possible by the old Confederation, which had otherwise been growing weaker and less competent each year.

The plan was not one which would work well for an empire scattered in all parts of the world and made up of diverse races. Close geographical contiguity indeed, seems essential for its success, since it has not proved satisfactory even in Alaska, but it solved our continental problem extremely well as we moved westward until the original States became forty-eight and their citizens had come to share the benefits and responsibilities of the Federal Government from the Atlantic to the Pacific.

The wisdom of the measure has deserved all the praise bestowed upon it, but it is only fair to point out as we have suggested, that it was not a general solution of the "colonial problem." So long as any portion of our national domain has remained in a territorial or dependent status, as Alaska, Hawaii, the Philippines, Porto Rico, and other portions yet do, we have found ourselves forced to govern much as England did in the eighteenth century. We have declined, as England did, to accord complete self-government, have appointed officials, legislated for and even taxed the inhabitants without their consent, and done many if not most of the things for which we so heavily blamed England. The fact is that the colonial problem, like that of racial or other minorities, has not yet found a theoretically perfect solution at the hands of any government, our own no more than others. As in many situations in life when seemingly legitimate interests of different groups conflict, the best that can be hoped for is a moderately satisfactory working compromise.

II

When the suggested framework for a new Federal Government was offered to the people of the old thirteen States in 1787, by the Constitutional Convention, it was far from certain that they would accept it. Throughout the country, newspapers and pamphlets voiced the opposing views of those who were soon called "Federalists" and "Anti-Federalists," according as they approved or disliked the suggested plan of union. There was much appeal to prejudice but on the whole the debate was carried on upon a high and serious plane. From 1763 the people had been arguing constitutional problems, and perhaps no other nation was ever so well prepared to consider so important a question. The preparation had been so long and thorough that it is certainly questionable whether we would be as competent today to consider such a matter as our ancestors were in 1787. Then as now, however, many did not care to bend their minds to serious discussion, and for such there were innumerable squibs published in which the question was brought down to the level of their mental laziness or incapacity.

The lack of a Bill of Rights was one of the most influential arguments against the Constitution on all sides, and one of the more humorous pamphlets complained, its author thought only in jest, that we were not guaranteed the right to drink. Washington and the other delegates, sipping their port and Madeira, could hardly have foreseen the need for that. The best controversial articles in the whole discussion were those written by the New Yorkers Hamilton and Jay and the Virginian Madison, which were published together in the volume called *The Federalist,* which has become an American classic. That none of these were New Englanders is but another evidence of the loss of that section's former intellectual predominance.

When we study the proposed form of government and contrast it with the niggardly grant of power to the old Confederation, recalling the jealousies of the States and their long training in opposition to authority from outside as hitherto represented by King and Parliament, it appears remarkable that there was any chance of ratification. Some of the small States ratified promptly, Delaware December 7, New Jersey December 17, 1787, Georgia January 2, and Connecticut on the 9th, 1788. Meanwhile there was a great struggle going on in some of the most important ones.

In Pennsylvania the majority of the people were probably opposed to the suggested Constitution, but those in favor of it rushed a call for a convention through the assembly before their opponents had time to organize, and ratification was announced December 12, 1787. In the convention in Massachusetts the Anti-Federalists were in a majority, and ratification, after much anxiety, was attained only by a sharp political deal with John Hancock, the presiding officer, who was inveigled into thinking he might be the first Vice-President if the new government were formed, and by gaining over other delegates by appropriate means. Sam Adams, provincially minded as ever, was also opposed, but in February the Massachusetts convention by a very narrow margin voted for ratification provided that certain amendments might be offered to the other States for adoption.

Just as the revolutionary Adams opposed the Constitution in Massachusetts, so did Patrick Henry in Virginia, and the contest in that most important State of all was prolonged and bitter. He who in Stamp Act days had proclaimed that there should be no Virginians or New Yorkers but only Americans, now declaimed as violently against the preamble of the Constitution because it began, "We, the people of the United States" instead of " We, the States." Like many, he feared a "consolidated" government, and the loss of State's rights. Not only Henry but much abler men, such as Mason, Benjamin Harrison, Monroe, and R. H. Lee, were also opposed and debated with Madison, John Marshall, Wythe, and others in what was the most acute discussion of the question carried on anywhere.

As in all the colonies, the richer tidewater section was on the whole overwhelmingly in favor of a strong government. Shays's Rebellion was still fresh in mind, and the proposed Constitution protected property. In Virginia, however, the far western section, looking to problems of interstate trade and the enforcement of the Treaty with England, was also, for different reasons, in favor of ratification. Won in Massachusetts by only 19 votes out of 355, approval was won in Virginia, even with the west in favor, by only 10 votes in 168, June 25, 1788. In New York the opposition between the small, rich group on the coast and the interior farmers had no make-weight as in Virginia, and New York City had to threaten to secede and enter the Union without the rest of the State before a favorable vote could be secured, and then by only 3 votes in 57.

By that time all the other States, except North Carolina and Rhode Island, had ratified, and there remained no question as to the establishment of the new government. The last of the Southern States came in on November 21, 1789, and of the Northern May 29, 1790. Owing to the way in which the conventions were held, the great opposition manifested everywhere, and the management required to secure the barest of majorities for ratification, it seems impossible to avoid the conclusion that the greater part of the people were opposed to the Constitution. It was not submitted to the people directly, and in those days of generally limited suffrage, even those who voted for delegates to the State conventions were mostly of the propertied class, although the amount of property called for may have been slight. No one can question that, had the Constitution not been ratified, the old Confederation would have broken down, and the States become a quarrelling lot of small independent sovereignties. Had the America of 1787 been a pure democracy based on manhood suffrage, such a breakdown would seem to have been inevitable.

Nevertheless, the sharp corner had been turned. It was announced by the old Congress that the new form of government had been ratified, and the States proceeded to the choice of electors. The unanimous vote of these in all States was for Washington as President, and, by a lesser number of votes, John Adams was chosen Vice-President. New York was picked for the temporary capital, and the government was to be started on March 4, 1789. Whether "we, the people of the United States" had really wished it or not, all acquiesced, and the most momentous step since the Declaration of Independence had been taken in peace.

CHAPTER VIII

THE NEW NATION GETS UNDER WAY

IT was with genuine regret that Washington felt obliged once more to obey the call to his country's service. The eight years of war had placed a terrific strain upon him, and although only fifty-seven he spoke of himself as already "in the evening of life." He loved, as a large planter, to manage his beautiful estate overlooking one of the most peaceful and lovely stretches of the Potomac, and might well feel that he had done his duty and that the task of statesmanship might now be taken up by others. Throughout the war his thoughts had ever turned to his beloved "Mount Vernon," and his one ambition, second only to that of serving his country, had been to return thither and take up again the life of country gentleman, interested in all which had to do with his farms and the affairs of the neighborhood. He had, indeed, become a world figure, and so many guests were to claim his hospitality that he at times, somewhat regretfully, spoke of his home as "an inn," but it was around that home that his affections centred. Unallured by the glamour of high office or the glare of publicity, he would have infinitely preferred to remain the Virginia planter than to accept the election to the Presidency.

He was, however, indispensable as the head of the new and untried government, the establishment of which had been opposed by probably a majority of the citizens. No one else commanded the universal trust and reverence which he did in 1789, and as always in a crisis the people turned instinctively to a strong leader. Others, however able, were sectional. Washington alone held the confidence of the entire nation, and him only would the people follow in the dangerous work of establishing a government that would be honeycombed with local jealousies, and which might be saved only by belief in the even-minded justice of the man at its head. Wearily, and prompted only by a compelling sense of duty, Washington started on his journey to New York.

The whole trip was one long ovation. Cannon roared salutes, children sang by the roadsides, bridges were festooned with flowers, there were banquets at every halting place. The roads were still bad, and the members of the new government assembled but slowly in New York. Instead of March 4, the inauguration could not take place until April 30, on which day Washington, standing on the bal-

View of the TRIUMPHAL ARCH, and the manner of receiving General Washington at Trenton, on his Route to New York. April 21ˢᵗ 1789

THE TRIUMPHAL ARCH WHICH GREETED WASHINGTON ON HIS ENTRY
INTO TRENTON ON APRIL 21, 1789

From "The Columbian Magazine" of May, 1789, in the Historical Society of Pennsylvania.

cony in front of Federal Hall at the corner of Broad and Wall Streets, took the oath of office in full sight of the crowds. The procession which had accompanied him from his house in Cherry Street, along what is now Pearl Street, to Broad, and thus up to the yet unfinished Hall where the Sub-Treasury now stands, had passed along the narrow winding streets, lined with sight-seers, offering a strong contrast to the inaugural parades of today. The crowd which watched the Chancellor of New York administer the oath to him on the balcony was full of the color of the gay clothes of men as well as women. Artisans were there in their yellow buckskin breeches, checked shirts, and red flannel jackets; while the richer gentlemen were notable in their three-cornered cocked hats, heavy with lace, their bright-colored long coats, with lace at the cuffs, their striped stockings, short breeches, and silver-buckled shoes. Unlike the artisans, their long hair was tied in a cue and heavily powdered. Their ladies were gorgeous in brocades and taffetas, high hats with tall feathers rising from them, and their skirts puffed out nearly a couple of feet on either side. As Washington took the oath, shouts rose from the crowd of "Long live George Washington, President of the United States," while the guns of the Battery roared their salute. The brief ceremony over, the new President retired to the Senate Chamber to deliver his first inaugural address.

There were at that time no political parties. At the beginning of the war, people had divided into Whigs and Tories, or Patriots and Loyalists, but the result of the struggle had left only the Whigs. During the discussion and ratification of the new Constitution there had been Federalists and Anti-Federalists, but the adoption of that instrument seemed to end the reason for the existence of the latter. Nevertheless, there was an ample supply of groups and of cleavages from which parties might in time arise. There were the frontier and old sections; the rich and the poor; the agricultural and the commercial classes; the men whose property was in land and those who owned securities; those who believed in a strong central government and those who stood for the fullest possible sovereignty of the component States; those who believed the Constitution should be interpreted as strictly as might be and those who wished to give its clauses the widest possible interpretation. But on the 30th of April, 1789, there were no party organizations nor, as yet, clearly defined parties. Washington thus had a clear field from which to make his appointments, and he also believed that the Presidency should not be a partisan office.

If there were no parties, there was also at first scarcely any government. Everything had to be organized. During its first session Congress passed the Judiciary Act, which gave form to the Supreme Court; approved sixteen amendments to the Constitution, ten of which, after being accepted by the States, were declared operative in 1791; and, in addition to much other legislation, created the four departments of State, Treasury, War, and Justice. War seemed remote, our international relations were slight, but our fiscal problems were pressing, so that the most important post was easily that of Secretary of the Treasury. Washington appointed to it Alexander Hamilton of New York, making Jefferson Secretary of State, General Knox, of Massachusetts, Secretary of War, and Edmund Randolph, of Virginia, Attorney-General. Two of these, Hamilton and Jefferson, were not only so important in their own day but their ideas and policies have continued so to dominate American thought that we must consider them in some detail.

Hamilton, at that time thirty-two years of age, was the illegitimate son of a Scotch planter and a French woman of the Island of Nevis, his mother being unable under the laws of that day to secure a divorce in order to legalize her union with Hamilton's father. He had come to New York for his education, and as a youngster had eagerly espoused the cause of the Revolution. Handsome and brilliant, he had secured a place on Washington's staff and although his career as a soldier was not distinguished in the field, he had won the affection and respect of the Commander who employed him as Aide and had led one of the storming parties at Yorktown. Less than a year before that episode he had married the daughter of General Philip Schuyler, and so had become allied to one of the most powerful families, socially and politically, in New York, where, at the end of the war, he became one of the leading lawyers.

New York political life was notoriously sordid, and the cleavage between the rich families who endeavored to rule and the general mass of the people, of whom a larger proportion were city dwellers than in any other State, made politics more "aristocratic" than anywhere else except perhaps South Carolina. Hamilton, who had reached America as a poor boy, with a blot on his birth, and who by his own abilities had risen to high position and become a member of the ruling caste, became, as often happens in such cases, more of an "aristocrat" than the "aristocrats" themselves, if that were possible, in his views as to government.

Those views of Hamilton are of great importance, for he is one of the half dozen or so of men who have most conspicuously moulded not only the nation of his own day but that of our own. His fundamental thesis was that most men are not good and wise but vicious and not to be trusted. Government cannot rely upon their good qualities but must depend upon careful manipulation of their passions. Each class, he believed, had its faults, but those of the rich were less likely to prove inimical to prosperity and sound government than those of the poor. The latter might sometimes mean well but they could not reason rightly as to how to secure good ends. He denied totally that the voice of the people was the voice of God. This, he said, was opposed to the real facts, which were that "the people are turbulent and changing; they seldom judge right or determine right." The people constantly needed to be checked.

For these reasons, he believed in the necessity of a strong central government, which should have power to control both the people and the States, which should be kept as far from democracy as possible, and which should derive its strength from the rich. Basing government on men's passions, he found the two most influential ones to be ambition and self-interest. Give men a large financial stake in the maintenance of a form of government, he thought, and they can be counted upon to support it. Ownership of government securities would be one such incentive. The larger the moneyed class would become, the more stable the government. The farmer, with no interests outside his own acres, or the town artisan, might easily be led to revolt. Not so the owner of government bonds, the manufacturer, the banker, and all those who in one way or another received special favors from government. A tariff, for example, would not only build up the moneyed class by developing manufactures but would also create a body of citizens dependent upon government for special privilege. A privilege of any sort binds a man closely to the conferrer of it.

Hamilton was not an orator and his style was diffuse, but his mind was brilliantly clear and his thought more impeccably logical than that of any other statesman we have had. Based upon propositions that seemed to him self-evident,—that democracy had always failed, that the people were incapable of self-government, that they must be governed, that for this a strong government was essential, that strength must be derived from those with heavy stakes of self-interest,—his system led straight, as it has ever since, to the final use of special privileges as the strongest ties between the individual and government or party.

Jefferson's views were the antitheses of these. Born in 1743, in the Blue Ridge section of Virginia, he had been brought up among the best and soundest of the frontier yeomanry of that State. Married at twenty-seven to a beautiful and rich young widow, he built Monticello on its hill top near Charlottesville, and no one can visit that delightful estate without realizing that, whatever his political views might be, its owner was, in the best sense, an aristocrat to his finger tips.

Jefferson, however, unlike his New York opponent, had a deep and abiding faith in the ability to govern himself inherent in the common man, or, rather, the comman man as Jefferson then found him in the America of his day. Jefferson knew London and Paris and some of the other cities of Europe. He had no faith in the common man when living under such crowded and unsatisfactory conditions, "steeped in the vices" which such situations bred. If we also should come to have manufacturing, great, crowded cities, and to approximate to European social and economic conditions, our electorate, Jefferson believed, would also become corrupt and incapable of self-government. But American conditions, he considered entirely different, and so long as we could keep the simplicity of our life, the door of opportunity wide for every man to own his own home, and the chance to make a comfortable living in a wholesome way, he believed the American common men could safely be trusted to govern themselves and others. Looking westward, he thought he saw sufficient free land for the maintenance of such conditions for a thousand years ahead.

This then was Jefferson's major premise,—belief in the common man. From it he deduced his views on government. He wished as little of it as possible. Later, in his first inaugural as President he was to define what he considered "the sum of good government," as "a wise and frugal government that shall restrain men from injuring one another, shall leave them otherwise free to regulate their own pursuits of industry and improvement, and shall not take from the mouth of labor the bread it has earned." He feared the power of wealth, the change from agriculture to manufactures, the creation of a strong central government. He would keep all matters of government, even the selection of those who should administer justice, as close to the people as possible.

Hamilton thought from the Federal Government downward; Jefferson from the parish or county upward. Jefferson was for free trade and no special privileges for any one, and although we may call him an idealist as contrasted with the realist Hamilton, there is no question but what he incarnated the dream that we Americans have always dreamed as Hamilton did not. Hamilton's mind, more powerful and coherently logical than Jefferson's, might have worked out its syllogisms and system of government as readily in any historic period and any Old World country as in the America of 1789. Jefferson voiced the peculiar hope and aspiration of the people of that time and place as he had done in the Declaration of Independence. For Hamilton that document was war-time propaganda; for Jefferson it was still a living faith. Today we pay lip homage to Jefferson but time and men's daily passions and desires have been on the side of the realist Hamilton who believed in the innate corruptibility of all of us.

The America of today, with its prohibitive tariffs, its special privileges, with its constant demand for more and more gifts and interference from "government," has developed from the Hamiltonian formulæ. We must not get too far ahead of our story, and have taken a glance forward merely to indicate the lasting nature of the conflict which was to arise in Washington's Cabinet, and the magnitude of the two men who were to lead the parties soon to be formed. Beside the two giants, Hamilton and Jefferson, the other two officials, Knox and Randolph, assume mere antiquarian interest.

Congress had had many things to attend to before organizing the Departments. The new government had got going more or less piecemeal, for although Washington was not inaugurated until April 30 enough members of the House had arrived by April 1 to permit of organizing that body, and the Senate was able to do so on the 6th. As the old Continental Congress had expired on March 4, the nation was without a Federal government of any sort for more than a month, but as soon as the new one had been started it set itself to the most immediately pressing task of all, that of providing money. James Madison at once proposed a tariff, which he wished to have for revenue only, and the discordant interests of sections and occupations were quickly disclosed.

New England wanted a low rate on molasses and a high rate on the rum they made from it. Pennsylvania wanted its rum free and a duty on steel, which it had begun to manufacture. New England

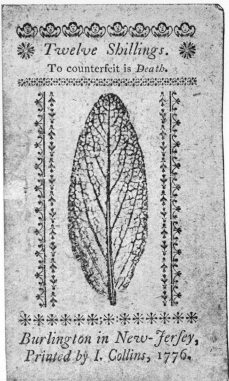

OBVERSE (TURNED) AND REVERSE OF TWELVE–SHILLING NOTE OF THE
COLONY OF NEW JERSEY, MARCH 25, 1776
From the collection of George R. D. Schieffelin.

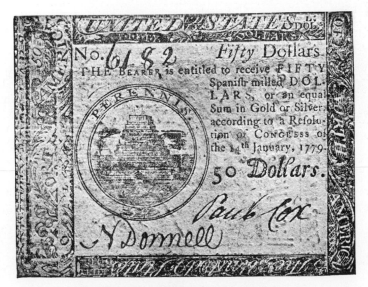

PAPER MONEY ISSUED BY CONGRESS IN 1779
From the American Numismatic Society Collection.

A PENNSYLVANIA LOAN OFFICE CERTIFICATE REDEEMED BY THE ACT
OF AUGUST 4, 1790

According to the records of the Pennsylvania Loan Office now filed in the Treasury Department, the original of the certificate, issued in favor of Benjamin Say, remains outstanding.

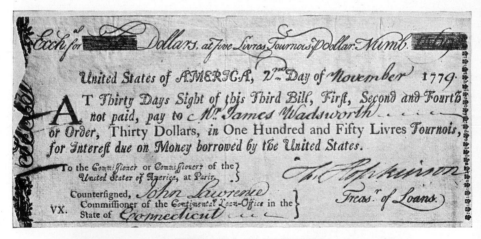

A THIRD BILL OF EXCHANGE

Issued by the Connecticut Loan Office under authority of an Act of Continental Congress of September 9, 1777, in payment of interest due on Loan Office Certificates representing money borrowed by the United States at Paris from funds advanced by the French Government. The bills were issued in sets of four, and the first one of any set to be paid automatically voided the rest.

From the Chase Bank Collection of Moneys of the World.

and South Carolina wanted no duty on steel, which would increase the cost to them of ship-building and of agricultural implements. South Carolina asked a duty on hemp which was opposed by Pennsylvania and New England because it would increase the cost of rigging ships.

So it went. The process, with which we have since become so familiar, of "log-rolling," that is of each congressman voting for a duty not wanted in his district if a vote could thereby be obtained for a duty that was wanted, began within the very first week of the national government. It was made evident at once that a tariff, even for revenue only, would be involved in sectional and class interests, and was bound to be regarded in the light of protection and special privilege, and to bring about bargaining and lobbying.

It was only later in the year that Congress could organize the Departments, and Washington could appoint the Secretaries and create his Cabinet. Hamilton, who took office on the 2nd of September, 1789, was at once asked by Congress to report a plan for the support of the public credit, and set to work. Jefferson did not take his desk at the State Department until the following March, so slowly as a whole did the government get under way.

By January, 1790, Hamilton was able to report to Congress and it was at once evident that this young Secretary of the new Treasury could rival any Finance Minister of the Old World in the daring and scope of his proposals. Our foreign debt was about $11,710,000 including the unpaid interest; the domestic debt about $42,400,000; and the debts of the individual States about $25,000,000. Hamilton proposed to pay the first in full, to fund the second in new bonds, dollar for dollar without any consideration of their depreciated value or the price they were selling at, and to have the Federal Government assume the full payment of the State debts.

No objections were made to the meeting of our foreign obligations but the other two suggestions aroused a storm of protest. We had repudiated the old Continental currency almost entirely, and the Loan Certificates for the debt had fallen to below twenty per cent in 1786 and were quoted at only forty per cent in 1789. They had been sold and resold and it was uncertain how many were in the hands of the original lenders to the government. When Hamilton's unexpected plan was made public, shrewd men sent agents on fast ships to the South or on horseback through the country to buy up Certificates for as low as twenty which Hamilton was proposing to refund at one hundred. His suggestion was a wise and far-sighted one for the restablishment of the fallen credit of the United States but to most it looked like a deal to allow speculators to feed at the public trough.

The assumption of the State debts was also bitterly opposed by some of the States. Massachusetts and South Carolina had the largest debts, and were well satisfied, but Virginia had paid off nearly all of hers and did not see why she should be now taxed again to help pay off those of less thrifty commonwealths. As usual, it came down to a question of self-interest on the part of each. The intrigue by which Virginia's opposition was overcome and enough votes secured to pass the measure has never been fully explained. Jefferson, apparently innocently, was mixed up in it. In any case, Virginia finally voted in favor of the assumption of the debts, and Congress voted to locate the new national capital, which had been a bone of contention, on the banks of the Potomac River. Although not quite in the way he had proposed them, all of the Secretary's measures eventually passed, and by the following summer U. S. Government six per cent bonds were selling at a premium in Europe, a notable triumph for the new nation.

Hamilton had to a great extent followed English precedent in his funding measures, and he wished to facilitate yet further the building up of the moneyed interests by the establishment of a bank similar to the Bank of England. In December, 1790, he offered a report on the subject, and, against much opposition, the bill creating the Bank of the United States was passed by both Houses, and sent to Washington for approval. So much criticism had been aroused, however, that the President hesitated, and asked for opinions as to the constitutionality of the measure.

The conflict between Jefferson and Hamilton now clearly emerged. The former claimed that according to the Tenth Amendment to the Constitution, "all powers not delegated to the United States by the Constitution, nor prohibited by it to the States, are reserved to the States respectively or to the people," and that the power to charter a bank had not been expressly given to the Federal Government in any of its clauses.

On the other hand, Hamilton defended his position, claimed that the Federal Government was "sovereign," that the power to create corporations is an attribute of sovereignty, and that the clause authorizing Congress "to make all laws necessary and proper for carrying into execution the enumerated powers" would cover the case. In other words, he invoked the doctrine that there existed "implied" as well as "enumerated" powers.

Opinion will always differ as to the merits of the two sides of this controversy, which has run throughout our national history. There would seem to be no doubt, however, that Jefferson expressed the will of the people, and that, dubious as the ratification of the Constitution had been in any case, it could never have been brought about had the Hamiltonian doctrine of implied powers been put forward as the way in which the Constitution would be interpreted if adopted. Washington was convinced, nevertheless, and signed the bill.

In December, 1791, Hamilton went a step further and presented to Congress his celebrated Report on Manufactures. It contained practically every argument which has since been used in favor of a high protective tariff, and its author's purpose was clearly expressed. This was in part to protect "infant industries," but such infants have a way of never growing up in the opinion of their parents who inevitably continue to demand more and not less favors at the public expense the bigger and stronger their infants become. The copper, steel and certain other industries are assuredly far from being infants today, yet the demand for pap has also far from diminished. It is impossible to say what Hamilton would think of the development of his theory in practice, although an opinion may be ventured that he would not be greatly shocked, for he had, in fact, a political quite as much as an economic end in view in his tariff policy. That was chiefly to gain another large body of citizens who would be linked to the new government by the strongest ties of economic self-interest, but Hamilton was, as yet, a little ahead of his time.

The Secretary's vigorous handling of the national finances, and the rapid rise in the price of government stocks, had induced a period of wild speculation. There was as yet no organized stock market but people everywhere sold government scrip from hand to hand, and its enormous advance, with the attendant easy profits, soon led the speculation into other channels, notably land. Business in general had been getting better since about 1786 and this, with the speculation in national securities, probably helped greatly to float the new government safely, and recovery from the temporary crisis of 1791–2, our first panic under the Constitution, was rapid.

The differences between Hamilton and Jefferson, and the schools of thought they represented, were, however, becoming more marked as the Secretary of the Treasury rapidly pushed his policies. Hamilton, young, brilliant and successful, self-confident and conceited, took little pains to explain his views or to conciliate Jefferson and the opposition whose convictions were derived from quite different political bases. Jefferson, Madison, and many others felt that Hamilton was twisting the new government into a shape that had never been contemplated, and not only did they disagree with him on fundamental constitutional interpretation, but the sectionalism and class favoritism of his policies also repelled and alarmed them.

Both manufacturing and the ownership of liquid capital in government or other securities were for the most part concentrated in the northern seaboard communities. The South and the frontier West were agricultural, and began to dread the rapid rise of a powerful Northern moneyed interest which might control banks, manufacturing, tariffs, and the form of taxation. Moreover, although Hamilton was personally honest, he was surrounded by men who were not, and there was no lack of scandal in the advantages taken by congressmen to profit personally by advance knowledge. Hamilton himself took no pains to hide his belief in the necessity of corruption, and in the advantage of a monarchical form of government, though he admitted the impracticability of the latter in America. His cynical view of the art of governing may have been the correct one, and Jefferson's an impossible dream, but Jefferson did represent the hope and belief of the common man and many who were far above his level, and these began to see little difference between government as advocated by Hamilton and that of George the Third with his bought Parliamentary seats. Before the end of Washington's first administration the rift in his Cabinet had become dangerously wide.

During that period the work of the State Department was complicated but less spectacular and important than that of the Treasury.

Our impotence at the end of the old Confederation was well known in Europe and we were treated with the contempt meted out to a tenth-rate nation. France, indeed, went so far as to give her consuls in the United States extra-territorial powers similar to those that foreign consuls have had in such countries as China and Siam, and the French Vice-Consul in Norfolk did not scruple to seize a ship captain, put him into irons, and was only at the last moment prevented from shipping him to France for trial.

Spain owned at this time not only Florida and the Gulf coast but practically all the country between the Mississippi and the Pacific, and when war was threatened between her and England over the right to trade in furs at Nootka Sound in Vancouver Island, we became alarmed at the possibility of this vast territory passing into British hands and finding ourselves hemmed in, not by the waning power of Spain but the rising one of the British Empire. The latter still held the northern posts in her military control, and Spain took advantage of the situation to occupy two more on our side of the Mississippi. The war cloud blew over but in the tangled negotiations and in our continuous efforts to secure from Spain the rights of navigation of the great river and of deposit at New Orleans, Jefferson had come to realize the full importance of the West.

New parties had not yet taken definite shape, but it was evident that Hamilton would lead the commercial and financial interests of the North, whereas Jefferson stood for the inchoate mass of men everywhere, though more particularly in the South and West, who objected to a too powerful central government, and to the rise of Hamilton's money power. The strongest group of anti-Hamiltonian men in the North, not only artisans and other city workers but the families who had always contended with those allied to the Schuylers and their crowd, was in New York. Jefferson's party, when it might be formed, would thus find itself in alliance with these. In 1792, however, the situation had not crystallized, and both Jefferson and Hamilton urged Washington, much against his will, to run for another term. He was unanimously elected, and John Adams again became Vice-President, although the "Republicans," as those opposed to the Hamiltonian theory of the State were beginning to be called, tried to defeat Adams and elect George Clinton of New York in his place. Affairs in Europe were soon, as always, to have sharp repercussions on our side of the water, and in this case to bring about the sharp alignment of the developing political parties.

The French Revolution had broken out in 1789, and at first we all followed its course with enthusiasm. It was easy to get drunk on abstract liberty in the eighteenth century, and the French people seemed to be only following in our footsteps. Washington had been in office but a few weeks in his second term when news arrived that caused a revulsion of sentiment among a large part of the Ameri-

THE CONTRAST
A cartoon comparing American and French liberty in 1789.
From C. C. Coffin's "Building the Nation," New York, 1882.

cans. The increasing bloodshed and brutal violence of the French movement had culminated in cutting off the head of the King after the Declaration of a Republic, and France had declared war on England and Spain. Not content with putting her own house in order, she had, like modern Soviet Russia, called on the people everywhere to rise against their monarchs,—practically a declaration of war against every European State. These events killed the sympathy of many Americans, as did the news that the revolutionists had forced Lafayette to fly from Paris. There was, nevertheless, a large body of American opinion still in favor of the Revolution, an opinion shared by Jefferson.

The position of our government was extremely delicate. Under the Treaty of Alliance we had guaranteed France possession of her West Indian Islands, which would undoubtedly soon be attacked, and had also, somewhat vaguely, agreed that in case France was involved in war we would not give shelter to privateers of other nations. England, believing we would attack her on the side of France, as perhaps most Americans in an outburst of emotion wished to do, began to impress seamen from our vessels and enlarged the list of contrabrand by declaring that all food stuffs destined for French ports could be seized. In the course of the war hundreds of our vessels, particularly those trading to the French West Indies, were destined to be captured, although the profits of the trade must have been great or the risks would not have been taken.

The immediate problem which faced Washington on receipt of the news in April, and the further notification that the Revolutionary government was despatching a French Minister to us, was whether to enter the struggle or to remain neutral. Hamilton urged strongly that the Treaty of 1778 had been made with the government of the Bourbon monarchy, and that that monarchy having been overthrown, we were in no way bound to carry out the treaty provisions in favor of an entirely different government. This would seem to have been a reasonable interpretation, for assuredly no one today would feel obliged to carry out with the Russian Soviet government treaty obligations incurred with the old Czarist régime. Washington, however, adopted Jefferson's view that the treaty was not dead but merely suspended, and on April 22, 1793, issued a Proclamation of neutrality. Three weeks later the French Minister, Edmond Charles Genêt, arrived in Philadelphia by way of Charleston, South Carolina.

Genêt was the Frenchman at his worst. Vain, impractical, puffed to bursting with the presumed importance of France, ignorant of other nations, he at once entered upon the most absurd and fantastic career which any foreign diplomat has displayed for our amusement or annoyance. At Charleston he formed a Jacobin Club, fitted out a privateer, and from that city satiated his vanity to the full by receiving the plaudits of the partisans of France all the way up the coast.

The President and members of the government in Philadelphia, even Jefferson, realizing his character, treated him with cool civility. Genêt, however, attempted to use American ports as bases for attacks on British commerce, to organize an expedition in the West to attack Spain, and in general to act as though America were French soil and we had never declared our neutrality. Finding himself rebuffed by the government, he lost his head completely, if he ever had any, and tried to appeal directly to the people through letters to Congress as though the President and the Cabinet did not exist. In August, by a unanimous Cabinet vote, France was requested to recall him immediately, which was done. The comic opera Minister, however, who had no desire to return to Paris to lose his head literally and not metaphorically, married a daughter of Governor Clinton of New York, and settled down on the banks of the Hudson.

Meanwhile, we were also having trouble with England. Not only was that country seizing our ships, impressing our seamen, and in general disregarding the somewhat vague rights of neutrals which she had never recognized, but the question of the Northwest was also becoming acute. The first British Minister to be accredited to us, George Hammond, was a painstaking but not very tactful youth of twenty-seven, who arrived at his American post in 1791. As we have noted, neither the British nor ourselves had fully carried out the terms of the Treaty of 1783, and the new Minister started to thresh out the old straw, with new grievances. Jefferson turned on him with demands for the evacuation of the western posts and compensation for the slaves the British had carried away at the end of the Revolution.

The fact was that the British were anxious to use our own derelictions in carrying out the Treaty as an excuse for altering the boundary line on the North. There was talk of creating a great neutral Indian Territory embracing the lands north of the Ohio River, and Lieutenant-Governor Simcoe of Canada was intriguing with the Indians against us. The seat of the Canadian Government had actually been transferred to our own side of the boundary and additional posts had been established on American soil. Our West was restless, loosely attached to the United States, pinched between British and Spanish encroachments, and there were vaguely known but certain conspiracies being hatched up among its people.

The situation was becoming intolerable. John Adams's prediction in 1785 had come true. If we did not carry out the Treaty in every particular, England, he had said, would not either and would probably use the excuse to infringe it further. We had not carried it out but England was becoming the worse offender. It began to look as though she had no intention of ever giving up the posts and the Northwest to us, and her depredations on our commerce were serious. Jefferson, Madison, and the gradually forming Republican Party were for measures of retaliation of a commercial sort. On the other hand, in New England the important mercantile class which formed the backbone of the Federalist Party was against any such measure. Hamilton pointed out that our imports from Great Britain in 1792 had been over $15,250,000 and from France only a little over $2,000,-000, and that three fourths of all our trade was with the former country.

During all the time that these war clouds had been gathering, there had been war within the Cabinet itself. Under a party system two such diverse statesmen as Hamilton and Jefferson could never have been expected to act together, for their differences, as we have said, were not merely of judgment on particular courses of action but of fundamental political philosophy. Hamilton, who regarded himself somewhat in the light of an English Prime Minister and not merely the ranking member of the President's Cabinet, interfered in all the other departments instead of confining himself to his own sphere of the Treasury. It must be admitted that with all his dazzling qualities, he had a taste for low intrigue, and he had for long been attacking Jefferson in the public press in articles which he signed with assumed names or initials. Washington did his best to bridge the widening breach between his highest two officials, but finally, December 31, 1793, Jefferson, who had long wished to do so, resigned his office and retired to Monticello.

Washington had frequently taken his advice as against Hamilton's but the latter Secretary was more and more attempting to force himself into all departments of the government, and to dictate the foreign as well as the fiscal policy. His services had been very great but he was beginning to make the mistake of thinking that his was the master-mind which must control the nation, a mistake that in a few years was to ruin his party and bring him to his own death.

The difficulties with England demanded settlement if war were to be avoided, and in April, 1794, the President appointed John Jay as Special Envoy to proceed to London and arrange all matters in dispute. The envoy was a man of high patriotism, unblemished character, and wide experience, but as the English Foreign Minister was advised in a confidential report on his psychology, "Mr. Jay's weak spot is Mr. Jay." Lord Grenville undoubtedly made the most of this weak spot. It is only fair, however, in considering the treaty made by Jay, execrated at the time and much criticized since, to admit that even if he allowed himself to be somewhat outplayed by his English opponent it was imperative that he make some treaty and not return empty-handed.

Jefferson's successor in the State Department, Edmund Randolph, did not count, and Hamilton was running that Department, as well as his own. He was at the height of his power, and he had explained to Washington that the very life of the United States depended on avoiding war with England. Moreover, he carelessly destroyed one of Jay's strongest weapons,—the possibility of the United States joining Sweden and Denmark in an Armed Neutrality,—by telling Hammond that such a move would be against our policy. It is true that England, for good and sufficient reasons, did not want war with us either, but whereas it might have been impolitic for her, it would, in the opinion of the Federalists who had sent Jay, have been fatal for us. The envoy was not a strong negotiator but he was thus sent to the enemy with his hands partly tied, and in the midst of the negotiations, word of what Hamilton had said to Hammond snatched his best weapon from him.

By the terms of the Treaty England agreed to turn over the Northwest posts to the United States by June 1, 1796, although Grenville refused to agree that both nations should not influence the Indians of the other, or to promise that in event of war the savages should not be used as allies. The old colonial debts, certain boundary disputes, and compensation for such captures made at sea as might have been unlawful, were to be settled by commissions. Nothing was said either of compensation for slaves taken in the Revolution or of impressment of seamen. There was to be complete freedom of trade between British ports in Europe and the United States, as well as in the East Indies.

The West Indies were to be opened to our vessels, if not over seventy tons, but in exchange for this Jay, who evidently overlooked, even if he knew of, our growing production of cotton, agreed that while the West Indies were open to us we would not export in American vessels any cotton, sugar, coffee, and cocoa. As a matter of fact,

England did not know either that we were beginning to raise cotton, and the enumerated articles were all supposed to be foreign products as far as the United States was concerned. This last article in the Treaty was struck out by the American Senate, and West Indian ports were kept open just the same until the War of 1812, for, if the commerce were essential to us, so also fortunately was it to the Islands.

Although Jay had secured the return of the Western posts, which were duly surrendered to us, it was considered that he had ransomed what rightly was ours by surrendering our interests in other quarters. The West gained much by the Treaty but the mercantile East felt that far greater concessions should have been won for trade. In weighing Jay's work it must be recalled that since 1783 England had treated us with disdain as an insignificant power, which in truth we were, and it was only in 1791 that she had even consented to send a minister to us. That she had now made a Treaty with the United States was, as Admiral Mahan has pointed out, a matter of epochal significance.

The Americans, however, did not so regard it. A howl of rage went up when the terms became known. Jay was burned in effigy and was execrated in the press and public speeches. The Treaty, with the West India clause excluded, barely passed the Senate by the requisite two-thirds vote, but the President, who felt that it sacrificed American interests and would bring down a storm of obloquy on himself, signed it after mature consideration as preferable to war. "If this country is preserved in tranquillity twenty years longer," he wrote, "it may bid defiance in a just cause to any power whatever," but he knew far better than the public that that time had not yet come.

The Treaty also helped to clear our relations with Spain, and the following year, 1795, that nation recognized the 31st parallel as our southern boundary and accorded us the right of deposit at New Orleans as well as that of navigating her section of the Mississippi. It took her three years more to make a leisurely evacuation of her posts on our soil, but by 1798 both Spanish and English had left us in possession of our own territory.

Western affairs were clearing, and the West was developing. Kentucky had been admitted as a State in 1792 and Tennessee was to follow in 1796. While the English had been in possession of the posts, trouble had broken out with the Indians, and Governor St. Clair of the Northwest Territory had suffered a terrible defeat November 4, 1791. This had been retrieved by General Wayne who crushed the

BURNING OF JOHN JAY IN EFFIGY
From a drawing by Darley.

natives at the battle of Fallen Timbers in August, 1794, just before Jay's Treaty was signed. The subsequent Treaty with the Indians, negotiated at Greenville August 3 the following year, gave the United States all of the territory below a new boundary line, including about two thirds of Ohio, and certain localities, such as those where Chicago and Detroit are located. The opening up of these new lands to settlement gave another great impetus to the westward movement, and after Cincinnati, which had been settled in 1788, came Dayton and Chillicothe in 1795 and Cleveland in 1796.

At the very moment when we were fighting the savages, the militia of four States, under Federal orders, was also putting down a rebellion of our own people. In 1791, as part of his general fiscal policy, Hamilton had secured the imposition of an excise tax on whiskey. An excise was considered by Americans as the most odious form of all taxation, and the Continental Congress had declared it to be "the horror of all free States." In 1793 the gross return from the whiskey excise was only $422,000, and allowing for drawbacks and the cost of collection this was reduced to only about $100,000 net, and in subsequent years it dwindled to much less. From various bits of evidence it had apparently been Hamilton's idea in part that its unpopularity might result in a minor insurrection somewhere, which could be put down by the Federal Government, thus helping to make clear its strength and paramount authority.

This is precisely what occurred, and in 1794 the people of the western counties of Pennsylvania held meetings, appointed a committee of safety, and attacked both sheriff and excisemen. But as an English pamphleteer had written, an excise "hath an army in its belly," and Hamilton was ready for his opportunity. He induced Washington to call out State militia and quell the revolt by force.

Although the rebellion itself was unimportant, the effect of the prompt suppression of resistance to the execution of Federal laws was lasting and wholesome. From the utter weakness and prostration of the old Confederation in 1789 to a treaty with England, an energetic war against the Indians in the Northwest, and a putting down of a popular uprising by the President of the United States with troops under Federal orders, all in 1794, the advance had been almost miraculous considering the hopelessness of the prospect in the earlier year. Most of the credit for the extraordinary success and vigor of the new government must be given to Washington and Hamilton.

When the government had been inaugurated, its cost had been much dreaded by the people, who complained loudly about senators and congressmen receiving such a huge sum as six dollars a day while attending to their duties. The Secretary of the Treasury had been given a salary of only $3500, and Hamilton, who was not rich though he lived with the rich, resigned his office January 31, 1795, as innumerable public men have been forced to ever since because they could not continue to serve the public for what the public was willing to pay. So great, however, had been his influence that he continued, from his law office in New York, to be the real leader of the Federal Party until the split with John Adams, which we shall soon reach. Jefferson, at Monticello, had been quietly but most efficiently gathering together the elements, North, South, and West, which were to form the "Republican" Party, a name which must not be confused with that of the present Republican Party formed in 1854.

Party spirit was beginning to run high, and the various acts of the government in its first eight years,—its fiscal policies, the excise, the Jay Treaty, the refusal to befriend France, and the apparent desire to placate England,—had all roused furious antagonism among a large part of the people. Republics are notoriously ungrateful, and peoples tire of their greatest men. A violent partisan press had also come into being, and no President, not even Roosevelt or Wilson, has been more bitterly assailed than was Washington in his second term.

The man who had served throughout the Revolution without pay was denounced as avaricious. His character was declared to be false and he was compared to the British tyrants. Immediately after his retirement from office, Franklin's grandson, B. F. Bache, in *The Aurora* wrote that every heart should beat with happiness to think that "the man who is the source of all the misfortunes of our country, is this day reduced to a level with his fellow citizens" and that "the name of *Washington* from this day ceases to give a currency to political iniquity, and to legalize corruption." Tom Paine called him either "an apostate or an imposter," "treacherous in private friendship, and a hypocrite in public life." Such was the reward meted out by a considerable part of the electorate to the man who had done more than any other to win independence for them and to establish their new nation.

Sixty-five years old, thoroughly weary of public life, Washington wisely declined to allow his name to be used again as a candidate, and so laid the first stone in the valuable tradition limiting the Presidency to two terms, a limitation not mentioned in the Constitution.

On September 17, 1796, shortly before the election of that year, he issued what has come to be known as his "Farewell Address" in which he summed up the political wisdom garnered from his experience. He stressed the immense value of the national Union to every citizen, and the danger of setting local politics above it or of forming parties based on sectional interests, "Northern and Southern—Atlantic and Western." He urged the importance of the division of governmental powers and warned against the encroachment of any one division upon the spheres of the others. Religion and morality, he noted, were indispensable supports to government, and added that national morality could not prevail if religious principles were destroyed. Looking abroad to the Europe of his day, he pointed out that that continent had a set of primary interests with which America had nothing to do, and that it would be unwise for us to entangle ourselves politically by alliance or otherwise in the Old World system. "Permanent, inveterate antipathies against particular nations and passionate attachments for others," he continued, "should be excluded" and "there can be no greater error than to expect or calculate upon real favors from nation to nation."

He was clearly thinking of England and France, and the advice to make use of our geographical isolation to develop peacefully into maturity and strength was urgently needed by those numerous citizens whose emotional sympathies for or against one or the other of those two countries would have led us into European entanglements. We must consider the Address, as later the Monroe Doctrine, against the background of the circumstances of the time, but for generations both were to prove the soundest of policies for the development of the New World, even if no policy can be literally adhered to through centuries of infinite changes. Nor was Washington's advice, wisest of all for his own day, followed by the people,—as events were soon to prove.

For one thing, the sectionalism that the President warned against was made evident in the election a few weeks later. It was the first which was fought on a party basis, and the Republicans decided to have their electors vote for Jefferson and Aaron Burr. The latter was a grandson of Jonathan Edwards and son of the president of Princeton; and at the time was a prominent lawyer in New York and a bitter political foe of Hamilton, with nothing as yet having occurred to smirch his public career. The Federalists decided upon

John Adams and Thomas Pinckney, to balance, like the Republicans, the North and South.

There were no "tickets" in the modern sense, and although the party leaders might agree among themselves whom they wished for President and Vice-President, the system, which we have noted, provided that the man receiving the largest number of votes in the Electoral College should receive the first office and the next highest the second. Attempts were made to have votes cast in such a way as to ensure the election of Adams and Pinckney but when they were counted it was found that Adams had received seventy-one and Jefferson sixty-eight. The Presidency was thus filled by Adams, a Federalist, and the Vice-Presidency by Jefferson, a Republican. If the Administration was curiously mixed, the geographical alignment was clear. Every State from Virginia southward had gone Republican and every one from Maryland northward Federalist.

Adams had been a distinguished patriot in the Revolution and was to found the most notable family in American annals. Sprung from simple farming ancestors, he had graduated from Harvard and after becoming a lawyer in Boston had taken prominent part in the controversies leading to the rupture with England. He had been a member of the Continental Congress, a member of the committee to draft the Declaration of Independence, Minister to Holland, where he had rendered valuable service, a member of the commission to negotiate peace with England, and the first minister to that country from America, These were but the more important offices he had filled, and his voluminous writings on controversial and constitutional questions had been of considerable influence. He was rather vain and somewhat fussy about etiquette but of strong mind and character and, like his descendants, of extreme independence in thought and action. His views on government naturally affiliated him with the Federalists but no Adams could be a party man in the strict sense of the word for he would always have to insist upon the integrity of his own mind when in conflict with party policies.

Such was the man who at sixty-two years of age succeeded Washington as our first party President, March 4, 1797. Hoping to continue Washington's policies, Adams made the disastrous error of continuing his Cabinet in office. There was not a man of outstanding ability in it, and several of them, including Timothy Pickering of Massachusetts, and Oliver Wolcott of Connecticut, were to prove traitors to the President, taking their orders from Hamilton and acting as his spies, Hamilton insisting upon being the actual, and regarding Adams as merely the titular, head of the government.

When Adams took charge, relations with France were difficult. The guillotine had been fast at work in Paris, and the Directory of five who were governing the country had dropped all the earlier idealism of the Revolution and had adopted the policy of military supremacy in Europe which is always at the back of the French mind. Washington had recalled our minister in 1796 and the Directory had refused to accept C. C. Pinckney as his successor. We were thus unrepresented at the French capital, where our Treaty with England was regarded as an offence which called for retaliation. By the summer of 1797 France had captured over 300 of our vessels and was far out-distancing any injuries the English had done us, besides employing a tone toward us which was indecently offensive.

Adams thought of sending Jefferson as envoy but Jefferson declined, wisely, as the office was not compatible with his duties as Vice-President. France was over-running her neighboring states, and the war with England continued. Adams, like most of the Federalists at this time, was bent on remaining neutral in spite of great provocation, and the Republicans still maintained their traditional French friendship. Although the Directory refused to accept an American Minister until their so-called grievances were redressed, Adams despatched a mission of three to see what could be gained by diplomacy, while to some extent preparing for war.

The envoys, C. C. Pinckney, Elbridge Gerry, and John Marshall could make no headway in Paris, the Directory insultingly declining to receive them at all. Hamilton and a large part of the Federalists began to believe that the only solution was to join England and to declare war against the French, who had conquered their other victims. Meanwhile, in Paris the American envoys were approached by mysterious go-betweens who, with threats as to what would happen to the United States if their demands were not complied with, asked for a loan of $10,000,000 and a personal gift to Talleyrand of $250,-000 as a preliminary to negotiations. On receiving word of this, Adams announced to Congress that he "would never send another minister to France without assurances that he will be received,

respected, and honored as the representative of a great, free, powerful, and independent nation."

The Republicans demanded proof of the need for such language,
and early in 1798 the President sent the damning despatches from
the envoys to Congress complete, except that the letters X, Y, and Z

CONGRESSIONAL PUGILISTS
During a session of Congress in Philadelphia in February, 1798.
From the Library of Congress.

had been substituted for the names of the go-betweens. Talleyrand
became the laughing stock of Europe, and the French party in
America was completely broken. The excitement throughout America was intense; "Millions for defence but not one cent for tribute"
became a rallying cry; and war seemed inevitable.

The French Treaties of 1778 were declared at an end; a Navy
Department was created; fourteen American men-of-war put to sea,
as did a couple of hundred privateers; the U.S.S. *Constellation* cap-

tured the French frigate *L'Insurgente;* 10,000 volunteers were called for a term of three years; and war with France apparently had come. The New England Federalists were delighted, and Hamilton was dreaming marvellous dreams of heading an army which should co-operate with the British fleet and capture all the Spanish possessions in North America, including Mexico. Indeed we were so near to war that the usual squabbling had begun as to chief command of the forces, involving Hamilton and Adams in an irritable controversy. The Hamiltonian Federalists completely ignored Washington's advice to keep out of European broils if possible with honor, but Adams believed in it, and was working hard toward that end, knowing, however, that he could no longer trust either his party or his highest officials. The French bluff had been called. France had no wish to add us to her enemies at sea, and it was intimated to Adams that if we sent a minister he would be honorably received.

By this time the President had learned that he could not trust his Cabinet which was disloyal to himself while supplying his enemy Hamilton with information of the most confidential sort. The situation was one of the most disgraceful in our history. No one with the instinct of a gentleman could have remained in the Cabinet, pretending to serve the head of the government with fidelity in a confidential post while in reality acting as a spy for an outsider. It must also be considered a blot on the nature of Hamilton that he was willing to be served in such fashion and to endeavor to secure his ends by a system of moral debauchery which if more than an isolated incident in our history would prevent any President from being able to trust his most intimate advisers as provided for him in the Constitution.

With characteristic courage, Adams acted without consulting any one. The Federalists, happy in the thought of war, were debating their plans in Congress when, like a thunderbolt, they received a message from the President enclosing the offer of peace from Talleyrand, and the nomination of William Vans Murray as American Minister. The Federalists could not take the responsibility of plunging the country into war when a clear road to peace had been opened, but Hamilton and all the leaders were furious. Adams alone had saved the nation and carried out Washington's wise policy. The treachery toward him justified him in acting without consultation, but he knew he was thwarting the wishes of the party leaders. It was an act of high courage on which he justly prided himself the remainder of his life.

Every difficulty was thrown in his way. The suggested single minister was replaced by a commission of three, and Pickering, by mean subterfuges, managed to hold up even the sailing of these for some weeks in the hope that something would turn up to defeat his chief. Arriving in France early in 1800, the envoys were received by Napoleon, and after seven months made a treaty of commerce with him. The following day, however, unknown to us, he forced Spain to cede to France the whole of the Louisiana Territory, so that our West once more faced a first-class European power across the Mississippi, and New Orleans became an outpost of the most dangerous nation of the Old World.

The war excitement had as usual brought a crop of hysterical legislation. In 1798 a new Naturalization Act was passed prolonging the required term of residence from five to fourteen years before citizenship could be obtained, and placing all foreign residents under surveillance. An Alien Act gave the President the power to expel from the country any alien whom he might judge dangerous to our peace and safety. A Sedition Act, in almost the precise wording of the law we passed in the World War, made any person punishable by fine or imprisonment who should speak or write against the President or Congress with "the intent to defame" or "bring them into contempt or disrepute."

No action was taken under the Alien Act but a few Republican editors were got out of the way under the Sedition Act. Among them was Thomas Cooper, later to become president of the University of South Carolina, who was fined $400 and jailed for six months. Although the persecutions and the infringement of the right to freedom of speech guaranteed by the Constitution were comically mild as compared with what went on during the Civil War and even more during the World War, our ancestors cared more about liberty than we do, and there was much opposition to these legislative Acts of the Federalists. The State of Kentucky passed a set of Resolves, written by Jefferson, which declared that, if Congress transcended its powers, each State had the right to determine for itself both the wrong and the mode of redress. Virginia also passed a set, drawn up by Madison, which similarly suggested the compact theory of the Federal Government and the doctrine of States' Rights.

No other State took action, but the Kentucky and Virginia Resolves marked another step forward in the crystallization of a section of public opinion as to the nature of the Federal Government which was diametrically opposed to the Federalist theory. It is worth noting that Madison, in his later life, explained why he and Jefferson had split with Hamilton by saying it was because the latter was deliberately trying to turn the government into "a thing totally different from that which he and I both knew perfectly well had been understood and intended by the Convention who framed it, and by the People adopting it."

No one had a deeper understanding or wider knowledge of what went on in the convention which adopted the Constitution than Madison, to whose painstaking notes, made day by day, we owe the most of what we know ourselves. It is only reasonable, therefore, to lay great stress upon his opinion, and when we are inclined to think of the Constitution as something immutable, it is well to recall that it has been gradually twisted and altered far from its original intention

New-York, December 21.

Columbia Mourns!

IT is with the deepest grief that we announce to the public the death of our *most distinguished* fellow-citizen *Lieut. General George Washington.* He died at Mount Vernon on Saturday evening, the 13th inst. of an inflammatory affection of the throat, which put a period to his existence in 23 hours.

The grief which we suffer on this truly mournful occasion, would be in some degree aleviated, if we possessed abilities to do justice to the merits of this *illustrious benefactor of mankind*; but, conscious of our in-

ANNOUNCEMENT OF WASHINGTON'S DEATH

From *The New York Gazette and General Advertiser*, December 21, 1799.

In the New York Historical Society.

through a century and a half, notably by Hamilton in its first decade.

The election of 1800 was to bring on the first serious contest between the Federalist and the Republican points of view. The old harmony was gone, and America was entering upon a new era. As if to mark the passing of the old, Washington, the one symbol of unity, sickened and died after a few days' illness, on the 14th of December, 1799. Everywhere there was mourning. Shops and offices closed, bells tolled all day, and memorial services were held in village after village as the news reached them. In Congress, Henry Lee uttered the now hackneyed words, "first in war, first in peace, first in the hearts of his countrymen." But it was noted that although the Federalist newspapers had heavy black borders and columns, the Republican journals used only a narrow band and that merely around the notice of his death.

CHAPTER IX

JEFFERSONIAN DEMOCRACY

BEFORE continuing the narrative of political events we may pause to consider what the young nation was like on the eve of events momentous for democracy.

In the quarter of a century from 1775, one of the most significant points to be noted is that the population of perhaps 3,000,-000 (including negroes) at the earlier date had increased to 5,300,000, or almost doubled. The whole of Great Britain and Ireland had only 15,000,000, and as the rate of increase in the Old World was small compared with the phenomenal one in America, the date seemed not far distant when our own nation would outnumber the mother country.

There were, moreover, striking changes in the sectional distribution of our people. Virginia, indeed, with 880,000 remained the most populous State, but in addition the Southern States as a group in the decade preceding 1800 gained 416,000, whereas the New England States had gained only 229,000. Rhode Island had stood practically stationary, and had fallen far behind such a new Western State as Tennessee. Kentucky with 221,000 was not much below Connecticut with 251,000, and there were 50,000 new settlers in the territories of Ohio and Indiana. There had also been heavy increases in New York and Pennsylvania, so that New England was falling rapidly behind the rest of the nation, largely due to the westward migration of its people. On account of the Napoleonic wars, there had been little immigration from Europe, and our national increase and local changes had been chiefly owing to native births and to economic factors.

A Federal Government had made little change in sectional characteristics, and New England, the Middle States, the old South, and the new West were as sharply differentiated as they had been, and as they were long to remain. In New England the religious impulse

195

had largely lost its effective power, and the old social-religious structure of the community had tended to harden into a steam-roller-like political machine. The clergy, it is true, no longer retained their minute inquisitorial control over the lives of their parishioners, but in conjunction with the groups of conservative ruling families they maintained a great influence over the political lives of their communities. The anti-religious excesses of the Revolution in France gave them an opportunity of preaching against all that savored of democracy, and a man denounced by them for religious infidelity or democratic beliefs, which they considered much the same, did not fare well if brought up for any reason before the civil magistrates.

In and about Boston the political group known as the Essex Junto represented the most extreme die-hard element in the Federalist Party, and there was little in the higher circles in Boston, twenty-five years after the Revolution, of what we call Americanism. Even the "man of the people," Sam Adams, had long since become a hard-shelled Conservative. Channing and Buckminster, who were to lead the Unitarian movement and do much to liberalize stagnant New England thought, were as yet only boys just graduated from Harvard in 1798 and 1800 respectively.

The old intellectual stream of the section had mostly dried up, and there was nothing to indicate the full harvest to be garnered a few decades later. As Henry Adams has noted, scarce a half-dozen names survive from the period of 1783 to 1800 which can even be recalled for any intellectual work in Massachusetts,—"not a poet, a novelist or a scholar," only a geographer like Jedadiah Morse, a minor historical chronicler like Jeremy Belknap, or a utilitarian mathematician like Nathaniel Bowditch, whose handbook, *The Practical Navigator,* adapted from an English work, began its long and useful career in 1799.

The valuable product of Boston points the way toward which Massachusetts' major interests were tending at this time. As a French traveller observed of the New Englanders, formerly so obsessed with theology, "commerce occupies all their thoughts." In 1790 Captain Robert Gray returned to Boston Harbor in the ship *Columbia* after having traversed nearly 42,000 miles of ocean in three years and laid the foundation for what was to prove a most lucrative trade, that of buying furs on the northwest coast of America

BALTIMORE IN 1752

The earliest known view of the city, when it had less than two hundred inhabitants.
An engraving from a contemporary sketch made by John Moale, courtesy of Mr. Russell W. Thorpe.

PITTSBURGH IN 1796

A second known view signed by Joseph Warin, but possibly by Collot.
From the Stokes Collection in the New York Public Library.

MOUNT VERNON

From the aquatint engraving by Francis Jukes, after Alexander Robertson, 1800.
Courtesy of The Mabel Brady Garvan Institute of American Arts and Crafts, Yale University.

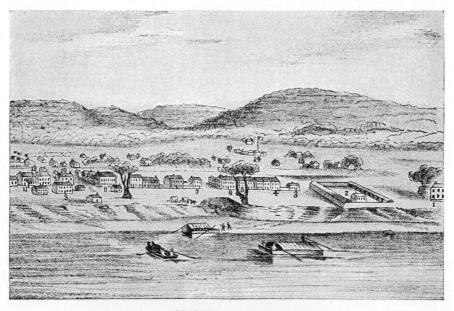

CINCINNATI IN 1802

1. Maj. Wm. Ruffin. 2. Artificer's Yard. 3. Charles Wattier. 4. James Smith. 5. David Ziegler. 6. Griffin Yeatman. 7. Martin Baum. 8. Col. Gibson. 9. Joel Williams. 10. Israel Ludlow. 11. Green Tree Hotel.

and selling them in China. Within two years this new trade,—Boston, Alaska, Canton, Boston,—was well established, and fortunes began to be made. It was a romantic route that these traders followed, rounding boisterous Cape Horn, stopping for supplies and rest in the unspoiled islands of the Pacific, buying furs from the northern savages, and disposing of them to the Chinese merchants at Canton in exchange for the products of the Orient, with which Boston wharves and warehouses were soon piled high.

Bostonians like William Sturgis and Thomas H. Perkins, starting with nothing, quickly accumulated wealth, while in Salem families like the Crowninshields, Derbys, and Princes were also doing so from a wholly different Oriental trade. Salem, only a few miles from Boston, preferred for some reason to traffic with the East by way of the African instead of the South American cape.

A Bargain !—For Sale

A MORTGAGE over 240 acres of Land, situate in the Townſhip of Greenwich, State of Connecticut, contiguous to Boſton Poſt-Road, and joining the Sound, formerly the property of Captain John Gregg, deceaſed, 36 miles from hence. There is ſtill unpaid and due from ſaid Eſtate, upwards of 1600l. including intereſt.—will be ſold cheap for Caſh, as the proprietors demands are urgent, and cannot conveniently wait the iſſue of foreclosing.

ADVERTISED SALE OF AN ESTATE IN CONNECTICUT TO ANTICIPATE FORECLOSURE

From "The New York Gazette and General Advertiser," December, 1799.

In Connecticut there was less wealth and shipping, but a somewhat livelier intellectual life, although the poetical and other outpourings of the so-called "Hartford Wits,"—Timothy Dwight, John Trumbull, Joel Barlow, and others,—make but dull reading to-day. At the beginning of the nineteenth century the section was as poor economically as it was intellectually, in spite of the growth of shipping fortunes. Agriculture was a scrabble for a mere subsistence; manufactures were yet in their infancy; and a banking capital of about $5,000,000 sufficed for the needs of all five States, Maine being then a part of Massachusetts.

New York had no more intellectual life than New England, if as much, except for the theatre. In drama it was to take the lead for the next quarter of a century, its large population, unhindered by religious scruples, affording excellent audiences. The first American comedy to be produced by a professional company, Royall Tyler's *The Contrast,* had been given in 1787, but William Dunlap was a far more important figure, and, especially as an adapter of French and German plays, exercised a considerable influence. For a number of years he was manager of "the Old American Company" which had its headquarters in New York, although playing also in other cities, going completely broke on one occasion when it tried Newport instead of its regular stands in the South.

New York, however, although much more cosmopolitan than Boston, was even more commercial. The politics of the State were still dominated by the alliances and feuds among the great families, most of them of Dutch descent. These families were still those with landed estates, the rise of the new types, such as the Astors or the Vanderbilts, lying just ahead in the next few decades. Religion had never been taken very seriously in this colony and State, and instead of a working compact between the rich families and the clergy the rich quarrelled

OPERA-HOUSE, Southwark,

THIS EVENING, the 27th of June, will be presented,

A CONCERT;

Between the parts of which will be delivered *(gratis)* A MORAL LECTURE, in Five Parts, Called,

Filial Piety;

Exemplified in the History of the

Prince of Denmark.

" —I have heard,
" That guilty Creatures, fitting at a Play,
" Have, by the very Cunning of the Scene
" Been ftruck fo to the Soul, that prefently
" They have proclaim'd their Malefactions:
" For Murther, though it have no Tongue, will fpeak
" With moft miraculous Organ.'
Shakefpear's HAMLET.

The whole will conclude with

Bucks Have-at-ye-All.

AN ADVERTISEMENT OF A THEATRICAL PERFORMANCE OF 1788, DISGUISED AS A MORAL LECTURE

From "*The Pennsylvania Packet and Daily Advertiser*" of 1788, *in the New York Public Library.*

among themselves, and each group had its following among the "mob," the country farmers and town workmen.

Hamilton, with the Jays, Schuylers, and others formed the Federalist faction, while the Livingstons, Aaron Burr, George Clinton, and their group formed the Republican faction, allied to the Virginians under Jefferson. These landed families, with their henchmen among the city working classes, made New York politics different from those elsewhere. The western part of the State was an empty wilderness. Rochester and Buffalo were unmarked sites in an uninhabited forest. Albany had a population of about 5000, and

GEORGE FREDERICK COOKE AS RICHARD III
Painted by Thomas Sully in 1811.

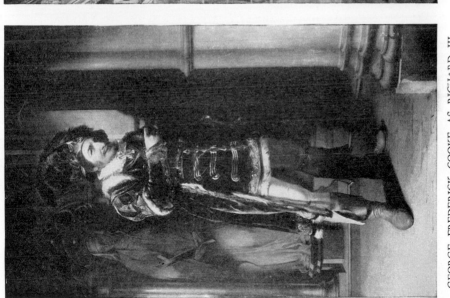

CHARLES WILSON PEALE IN HIS NATURAL HISTORY
MUSEUM
Painted by the artist in 1822 when the museum was located in the
State House, Philadelpha.a.

From the originals in the Pennsylvania Academy of Fine Arts.

OLD CITY HALL, NEW YORK, SHOWING THE EXTERIOR AS
REMODELLED BY L'ENFANT

Taken from Wall Street. One of the very few known impressions of an engraving by Tiebout.

From the Stokes Collection in the New York Public Library.

SECOND STREET, NORTH FROM MARKET STREET, WITH CHRIST
CHURCH, PHILADELPHIA

From an aquatint engraving by M. Marigot, 1807.

*Courtesy of The Mabel Brady Garvan Institute of American Arts and Crafts,
Yale University.*

Utica, just a year old, had perhaps fifty households. New York City, however, dominating the State, as always, with its 60,000 inhabitants, was more than twice the size of Boston or Baltimore, which latter in its sudden growth had just shot ahead of the New England metropolis.

That New York City, with comparatively small back-country, should have become the leading commercial port of 1800 requires explanation. Its advance had been due neither to its unexcelled harbor nor to the Hudson-Mohawk route to the West, both of which were to count heavily in its favor later. New York, like Massachusetts and Pennsylvania, had always been interested in shipping, but in the eighteenth century the great exporting States had been Virginia and Maryland, the leading staple for export being tobacco, until outdistanced by cotton in 1803. The following table, however, shows the astounding change that came over American commerce between 1790 and 1800.

Year	Exports of Domestic Products	Exports of Foreign Products
1790	$19,666,000	$ 539,000
1791	18,500,000	512,000
1792	19,000,000	1,753,000
1793	24,000,000	2,110,000
1794	26,500,000	6,526,000
1795	39,500,000	8,490,000
1796	40,764,000	26,300,000
1797	29,850,000	27,000,000
1798	28,527,000	33,000,000
1799	33,142,000	45,523,000

Had our export trade continued to consist chiefly of our domestic produce of all sorts, the sixty per cent increase noted above in that item would not have shifted the balance from the Southern to the Middle and Northern States. It was the nearly 900 per cent increase in our re-exports of foreign goods which brought about the new sectional alignment. The South had led in exports under the old commercial régime, dependent upon agriculture and local produce, but had possessed almost no shipping of its own. With the Napoleonic wars raging in Europe we took over, as a neutral, much of the trade which had hitherto been carried on by English or French vessels between their respective countries, their colonies, and the rest of the world. We now transported to Europe the products of the tropics, those of the West and East Indies, and the Far Orient, all of which were for the most part brought to our ports first and then reshipped.

It was thus not the States which had exported our own big staple crops but those which had capital invested in shipping which naturally derived the vast profits from this colossal increase in foreign exports as contrasted with the domestic export business. The North was clearly travelling faster than ever on the road toward becoming a commercial, banking, manufacturing, shipping section, whereas the South, especially after cotton was so soon to become king and make slavery appear to be an indispensable basis for economic prosperity, was settling down more and more inevitably to an agricultural slave-holding culture.

Forty Shillings Reward.

RAN away this morning from the subscriber, an Apprentice BOY named James Hoy, near 18 years old, about 5 feet 8 inches high, fair complexion, and hair tied behind. He took with him a brown jean coat, grey surtout, new shoes, round felt hat, and many other articles of cloathing.———Whoever brings him back or confines him in gaol, so that he be had again, shall receive the above reward.

JOHN FARRAN.

Philadelphia, June 26. 3fp

AN ADVERTISEMENT IN *THE PENNSYLVANIA PACKET AND DAILY ADVERTISER,* 1788

From the New York Public Library.

If New York was just on the verge of rapidly outrunning Philadelphia as a commercial entrepôt, the latter city was in every other respect the most important in the United States, the one to which all foreign travellers flocked and which they always praised highly. If it had not become quite the "garden city" of Penn's dreams it was the best planned on the continent, and its wide shaded streets and public buildings made it notable even for tourists. It had the best water supply, the best paving, and was the best lighted, as well as the largest, of our cities. Its citizens were both public-spirited and broad-minded, and led the world of that time in efforts to improve the treatment of criminals and the insane. Their city was also the centre of American manufacturing and of the best system of roads into the interior. Its banking capital of $15,000,000, including the Bank of the United States which was located there, made it our financial centre as well.

Until the summer of 1800, when the national government moved to the ludicrous jumble of unfinished buildings on the hills and in the swamp hollows of what was called the city of Washington, on the Potomac, Philadelphia had also been the national political capital. It is not without interest to speculate on what might have happened had it remained so, and if the Federal Government, instead of having had to establish itself as a sort of hermit kingdom in a No Man's Land outside the boundaries of any of the jealous States, had continued to function in our leading metropolis. We should then have had a real centre of our national life, a centre to which, as in Rome, Paris, London, and other great capitals, the wealth, art, literature, business, and politics of the nation would have flowed together, to the social and intellectual broadening, perhaps, of all of them.

Such a capital Philadelphia was until 1800, combining all the leading streams of national interest. Its society, however, was more to be noted for its charm and culture than for any outstanding intellects. Men like William Bartram, the naturalist, Alexander Wilson, the poet and ornithologist, H. H. Brackenridge, the satirist, many cultured doctors, lawyers, and others, gave a tone to social life. On the other hand, we may note that New York and Philadelphia had oddly exchanged the two men who had perhaps the widest reputations,—Charles Brockden Brown, the novelist, who had been born in Philadelphia and gone to New York to escape the plague and edit a magazine; and Philip Freneau, the poet, who, born in New York, had gone to Philadelphia, likewise to edit a magazine. Brown's novels, such as *Arthur Mervyn* and *Wieland,* attained great popularity in Europe as in America, debauching the public taste with their romanticism and melodrama, while Freneau's poetry was sufficiently recognized abroad to be plagiarized by no lesser men than Campbell and Walter Scott, both of whom borrowed lines from him without acknowledgment. It may be noted, as indicating an increasing restlessness and mobility even in the settled East, that Brown later went back to live in Philadelphia, and Freneau spent the latter part of his life in New Jersey.

Pennsylvania was perhaps the most broadly democratic of the older States. Property was not only rather evenly distributed but the presence of twenty religions prevented any such alliance between the rich and the church for political purposes as existed in New England, and there were no dominating families or great landed estates as in New York and the South. The Quaker influence was strong, both politically and spiritually, but that of the Germans was negligible in introducing any intellectual impress from the land of their origin. Goethe and Klopstock were probably as completely unknown in Germantown as they were in New York or Boston. Although Philadelphia continued to grow rapidly, after 1800 it settled down to a quiet town with a marked flavor of its own, losing the commercial primacy to New York, and the Presidents and statesmen to Washington.

Except for Baltimore, a hustling new town, struggling like the other seaboard cities for the business of the new West, there was no other city worth the name, south of Philadelphia until we reach Charleston, South Carolina. Magnificent plans had been made for the new City of Washington by the Frenchman, Major L'Enfant, but scarcely a start had been made in 1800. One wing of the Capitol was ready for occupancy and the other was nearly finished, but between them was merely an empty gap where the great central portion now stands surmounted by its dome. All around it was unkempt waste land. There was one good tavern not far off, and a few dwelling houses were being put up. Pennsylvania Avenue was a quagmirish dirt road leading down through an alder swamp and up to the White House.

The latter was still only partially plastered, without the main staircase, which was not as yet begun, with a leaky roof and sagging floors, due to poor material and workmanship. Here and there were boarding houses rising out of the wilderness, where lived unfortunate senators and congressmen. So crowded were these hostelries that at one of the best, where Jefferson stayed, he was the only boarder who could have a room to himself. The so-called streets were merely ruts in the sticky Virginia red-clay, almost untraversable in wet weather. The comfortable little hamlet of Georgetown on its hill afforded a retreat but was too far, considering the roads, for most officials to live in. In the summer, the swamps bred fever and ague, and even Jefferson declined to stay in the dangerous neighborhood.

Across the Potomac to the south the traveller entered the section of farms and great plantations, of slave labor, of little or no commerce and of slight financial interests. Here life for the most part was going on almost precisely as we found it in 1763. There had been a good deal of talk of gradually abolishing slavery, and such men as Washington and Jefferson had been in favor of doing so, it being a question whether a system of free labor might not be more profitable. The far South, however, with its unhealthy climate, its rice fields, and now its cotton, had decided the question in the negative, for there seemed to be no other system of labor which could be substituted.

Slavery had been legalized in the Constitution, but as a compromise the slave trade had been prohibited after 1808, and as the enormous increase in the cotton production demanded a corresponding increase in labor, and the supply could no longer be added to from Africa, the price of slaves rose rapidly, and consequently the Southerner's economic interest in that form of property also increased. A dozen slaves which had cost no more than a few mules or cows, were one thing, but a dozen which represented an invested capital of $15,000 to $25,000 were another.

The one great change from our picture in 1763 was due to this increase in cotton. As has so often happened in the last century or more, one invention was reinforced almost simultaneously by another, quickly changing the conditions of a whole industry. Whitney's cotton gin, which solved the problem of cotton from the standpoint of production in America, coincided with the inventions of Hargreaves, Arkwright, and others in England which revolutionized the commercial use of the plant by introducing textile machinery. The demands suddenly became enormous, and our exports rose from 200,000 pounds in 1791, to 18,000,000 in 1800, and 64,000,-000 in 1807.

Most of this mounting export trade passed through the port of Charleston, whose population was fast approaching that of Boston. There the great rice and cotton planters had their town houses, and mingled with the merchants and bankers, all growing rich together with the rise in the price of lands and slaves, and with the great new staple crop to be exported. It was a question whether the theatre of Charleston or Philadelphia was the finest in America, and for a while no other city could boast of a more brilliant social life. It possessed a good library; book stores throve; dressmakers and milliners imported the latest French modes for the ladies; the racecourse was notable even in the South; and there was also a golf club, as there had been for some years in the much smaller communities of Savannah and Augusta.

Charleston, however, was a unique phenomenon in the South, and even there the type of life and mind being evolved was quite different from that of any Northern city. The seaboard of Carolina had 30,000 whites ruling a population of 100,000 negroes. Throughout the whole South, with the exception of a few families in Charleston, in the absence of commerce, banking, and business, there was no career open to a young man other than that of planter, lawyer or politician. The ambitious man who did not wish to emigrate to the West looked to a career in public affairs, and the mind of the South became preoccupied with problems of statesmanship or politics and not of economics.

As we pointed out earlier, the Southerner came rather to look down upon commerce, and without opportunities in finance and business he grew more and more out of sympathy with the Federalism of such men as Washington and Marshall, and turned to the tenets of Jefferson. Although steeped in classical literature, used in graceful allusion in oratory in courts or legislature, the Southerner had also ceased to be a creative factor in our literature. At this period the leading author of the South was the Virginian lawyer, William Wirt, whose *British Spy* attained a popularity incomprehensible today and which indicates the depths to which the literary taste and production of the section had sunk by 1803.

A quarter of a century of independence, our growing commercial importance, the accumulation of wealth, our illimitable resources in the West, and our astounding fecundity as shown in population figures, were beginning to make America very conscious of itself. Our self-satisfaction was all too obvious to foreign travellers who complained that we seemed to think that no one had any brains except in the United States. Even the House of Representatives suggested that we announce to the world, in 1796, that we were "the freest and most enlightened [nation] in the world!" To quote part of Henry Adams's list, however, the European looked in vain amongst us for a worthy contemporary to Goethe, Schiller, Mozart, Haydn, Kant, Fichte, Scott, Wordsworth, Shelley, Beethoven, Hegel, Cuvier, and other poets, philosophers, scientists, musicians, and like contribu-

CHARLESTON, SOUTH CAROLINA

*From the original painting by S. Barnard, 1831. Courtesy of The Mabel Brady Garvan Institute of
American Arts and Crafts, Yale University.*

THE CITY OF WASHINGTON IN 1800

From an engraving by Parkyns in the Library of Congress.

GIRARD'S BANK, PHILADELPHIA, IN 1831

From an engraving by Sears after a drawing by Barton.

tors to the common fund of world culture found at the time in Europe.

In only one art did we strike out with some originality. Our colonial period was over, and with it passed our colonial architecture, the Georgian and earlier styles. The new, which came in about the turn of the century, was based on the formalism of the classic design. Our political literature had been fused through and through with classic thought and precedents. Having founded a Republic on what was erroneously considered to have been more or less classic lines, we turned instinctively to classic examples for the new houses and public buildings which our individual wealth and new governmental needs demanded.

In this we were ahead of Europe, instead of following her. The temple design for the new capitol in Virginia preceded the first in Europe, the Madeleine in Paris, by twenty-two years, as did other of such buildings in America. The first "crescent," now so often seen in English cities of the Regency period, originated not in England but in the work of Charles Bulfinch in Boston. Jefferson was the earliest advocate of the new style, but was followed by the rise of our first professional architects, men like Bulfinch, Samuel McIntyre of Salem, or John McComb in New York. The new style, in all its variations, was not limited to any one section, but for the next thirty years or more may be found in plentiful examples throughout the whole country. The new buildings were not only larger and more pretentious than the old Georgian ones but in the private dwellings indicated an increasing desire for the amenities of life, such as diversification of the rooms for their particular purposes, and such hitherto unknown niceties as the addition of dressing rooms to the bedchambers. The new houses, too, were beginning to be filled with beautiful examples of furniture made by such American craftsmen as Duncan Phyfe and Samuel McIntyre, following the English styles of Adam, Hepplewhite and Chippendale.

If luxury were thus developing in the homes of the rich in the seaboard States, there was otherwise but little change in physical conditions since before the Revolution. The owner of one of the big new houses, whether in Massachusetts or South Carolina, might insist upon a dressing room off his bedroom, but when he was travelling away from his own home, he was lucky if he did not have to sleep eight or ten in a room in the inn, or even two or more strangers in one bed, in which the linen was only occasionally changed. There were some inns which were clean, and in which this "vulgar, hoggish custom," as it was called by Europeans, did not obtain, but it was fairly universal. The Duke de la Rochefoucauld-Liancourt was but one of many who noted that a traveller fell into the first bed he could find in a roomful, preferably choosing one that did not already have an occupant.

The roads on the whole showed no improvement. Perhaps one of the worst on the main line north and south was the stretch between Elkton, Maryland, and the Susquehanna Ferry, in which the ruts were normally so deep that the passengers in the stage coach, at the cry of the driver, had to go from one side to the other, as if ballasting a sailboat, to keep the coach upright. The rivers were by no means always spanned by bridges or crossed by ferries, and out of the eight which Jefferson had to cross in riding from his home at Monticello to Washington, five had neither bridges nor boats.

The stage coaches were hardly more than big boxes, with no steps, nor glass in the windows or doors. In bad weather the openings were closed with leather curtains. Their progress was slow, four miles an hour between Bangor, Maine, and Baltimore; and not seldom they were upset or their axles were broken by the bad roads. In winter the crossing of such rivers as the Hudson or the Susquehanna in small boats amid the waves and tossing ice was sometimes fatal, the danger not being lessened by the frequent drunkenness of those in charge. The trip between New York and Philadelphia, partly by stage and partly by boat, took a day and a half, but the several stages that ran daily from Philadelphia to Baltimore took three days for the journey. South of the Potomac, the roads were even worse, and except for one stage that ran between Charleston and Savannah, all travelling south of Petersburg, Virginia, had to be done on horse-back.

There was a mail route which extended from Maine to Georgia, a letter passing the entire way taking 20 days in transit. There was daily service between New York and Virginia, but only thrice weekly between New York and Boston, and mail from Philadelphia to Nashville took 22 days. Writing was an expensive matter in those days, the rates of postage having been established on a sliding scale

COPY OF AN OLD STAGE–COACH SIGN AT THE TURNPIKE ENTERING WINSTED
FROM NEW HARTFORD

CHURCH AND MARKET STREETS, ALBANY, 1805, SHOWING THE OLD DUTCH
CHURCH BUILT IN 1715 AND DEMOLISHED IN 1806

*From a lithograph after original contemporary sketches. Courtesy of The Mabel Brady Garvan Institute
of American Arts and Crafts, Yale University.*

GOWNS OF THE PRESIDENTS' WIVES

1. Martha Washington, 1789–1797. 2. Abigail Adams, 1797–1801. 3. Dolly Madison, 1809–1817. 4. Mrs. Van Buren, 1839–1841. 5. Mrs. Lincoln, 1861–1865. 6. Mrs. Garfield, 1881. 7. Mrs. Roosevelt, 1901–1909. 8. Mrs. Harding, 1921–1923. 9. Mrs. Coolidge, 1923–1929.

From the collection in the Smithsonian Institute.

according to distance in 1792. Thus a letter could be carried up to 30 miles for 6 cents, between 30 and 60 miles for 8 cents, with increases up to 450 miles or more, for which the charge was 25 cents. Yet even in 1800 the government operated 20,000 miles of postal routes with 900 offices, handling, at a rough estimate, nearly 3,000,-000 letters, which illustrates clearly the huge physical problem which beset us then and was to explain much in our future development. Compared with the compact, small European nations, our tasks were to be colossal.

The educational system throughout the nation had, if anything, retrograded instead of advancing after Independence, in spite of the rise of the "academies" and the enactment of many excellent laws, most of which were imperfectly observed. Our oldest college, Harvard, was actually graduating fewer students between 1790 and 1800 than it had during the years of the Revolutionary War itself. The medical school, founded in 1783, was turning out two doctors a year for the whole of America. There was not much to choose between the sections, and before 1800 thirty of the new "academies" had been established in North Carolina as against only seventeen in Massachusetts.

The dress was still that of the eighteenth century, and men of the upper classes wore gaily colored satin or damask coats and waistcoats, with knee-breeches, shirts with ruffles down the front and hanging over the hands, cocked hats and wigs. Among the beaux, French fashions were replacing the more sober square-toed shoes, silver buckles, and black silk stockings of the conservatives. Skin-tight trousers, almost impossible to sit down in, started almost at the arm-pits and ran down into high yellow or white topped boots. The blue or green coats ended in long tails cut to a sharp point. The women's dress, even more absurd, followed every whim of fashion imported from abroad, although often of exquisitely beautiful materials.

We have thus far spoken only of the seaboard States, but beyond the mountains a new empire was rising, remote both in fact and feeling from the East. We have already noted its beginnings but the emigration had been constant, until by 1800 about 400,000 persons were living beyond the Alleghanies. There were several main roads along which the incessant streams of emigrants travelled. One ran along the Mohawk Valley into western New York; a second from Philadelphia to Pittsburgh; and a third from the Potomac to the Monongahela; a fourth through southwestern Virginia and the Cumberland Gap to the Ohio River. Charleston, which lay nearer Nashville and that section than did any other Eastern seaport, was also planning a road which would divert Western business to itself. By whatever route the emigrants who tramped or drove their Conestoga wagons to the Western slopes made the journey, once across the mountains the rivers became their highways, and flatboats carried them and their goods down to the sites of new clearings or settlements.

The long land journey made the transport of produce to market in the East impossible, but with the opening of the Mississippi by Spain in 1795, the great river traffic began and a million dollars of produce was shipped out by that route in 1800, a sum to be more than doubled in the next two years. This gave the West its first purchasing power, which was immediately reflected in the shops of Eastern merchants, those of New York, Philadelphia, Baltimore, and Charleston all competing for the trade.

In 1796 Congress had passed a more liberal land Act, but even under that a settler could not buy less than 640 acres at $2.00 an acre, half the amount to be paid at once, and half at the end of a year. Few of those passing westward, however, could have afforded $1280 for land alone, without counting stock, household goods, and transportation. In 1799 the Northwest Territory had developed sufficiently to permit it to have an agent in Congress and William Henry Harrison was chosen for the office. Kentucky and Tennessee had both become States but Harrison, who knew his West well, was the first representative from the public domain north of the Ohio, and at once urged the passage of a new land Act, which was approved in 1800. Under this, land could be sold locally in half-sections, or 320 acres, the payments being spread in 4 instalments over 4 years, so that a settler could get legal title by an initial payment of only 50 cents an acre, the total amount involved being only half that of the minimum under the preceding Act. Although the law hastened settlement, it also did much, owing to innumerable unpaid instalments, to break down the business integrity of the settlers.

Once over the mountains, the pioneer found himself in a world as unlike the East as it was remote from it. There were no Georgian houses or new classical mansions there or clothing of satin and brocade. The settler was considered well-housed when he was able to replace a rough open lean-to with a log-cabin raised in a few days with the help of neighbors. A hunting shirt, deer-skin or linsey-woollen trousers, and moccasins were the summer clothes of the men, with a white blanket coat added in winter. Boots were rarities, and, indeed, throughout the States among the poorer people shoes of any sort were not much worn by any in the summer, men and women working barefoot in the fields. Even back in New England boys went barefoot to church on Sundays, and the little girls carried their shoes and stockings in their hands, to be modestly put on behind a bush before they entered the meeting-house.

But it was not merely the poverty of the West which set it off from the East. Not only was there neither inherited nor accumulated wealth there, but no classes, institutions, and as yet only rarely schools or churches. To be sure there was soon to grow up that peculiar trait of ours which mixes culture, education, and religion with Chamber of Commerce boosting. A few years later, Timothy Flint, a missionary to the western wilds, wrote that when he went to a town religion was considered to be contemptible, and he was opposed by the whole settlement. Why, then, he continues, did they invite me here? "On speculation. A minister—a church—a school—are words to flourish in an advertisement to sell lots."

There was a strong leaven of Scotch Presbyterians at first, but as swarms came from Congregational New England, from the Anglican South, from almost every one of the old settlements East, every religion practised in America came to be represented, as well as every type, good and bad,—splendid pioneering material and the lowest riff-raff. It was an existence which stimulated the emotions rather than the mind, and civilized standards of thought and custom tended to be dropped with other too heavy baggage on the way over the mountains or in the hard work of clearing the wilderness. Baptist and Methodist missionaries and preachers began to minister to these people without churches, and occasional camp-meetings, which too often developed into emotional orgies lasting for days, replaced the regular and decorous Sunday church-going of the old days in the East. On the other hand, the pioneers in the sections far from the old settlements owed no small debt to many of the better sort of preachers who ministered, somewhat crudely perhaps, but still effectively, to spiritual needs. Riding on horseback from one settlement to another, these "circuit riders," as they were called, were often imbued with the genuine spirit of the missionary, and the amount of work which they did in a year was extraordinary. The most noted man in the Methodist Church, Bishop Asbury, had to supervise all the Conferences between Maine and southern Georgia, riding annually between 5000 and 6000 miles. It was said that he had seen more people in America than any other man, and certainly none could have been better known himself than the Methodist leader.

The life of the settlements, however, tended to be rough and brutalizing, infinitely hard on the women in especial, and was of a sort in which only later novelists have found romance. The grinding toil, the unutterable dulness and loneliness, the poverty, and often the discouraged shiftlessness, broke down the morale of many who started with high hopes of a new life in the new country. Lowest of all were the boatmen, "half-horse, half-alligator, with the cross of the wild-cat" as they were described, who gathered for their wild dissipations in the river towns which for long enjoyed evil reputations. Behind the first pioneers, however, who were forever moving on with the disease of eternal restlessness in their blood, came settlers who were thrifty and substantial, and who, not always to sell lots, built schools and churches and established law. As usual on the frontier, all stages of civilization and all sorts of standards and morals were mixed incongruously.

One thing which the frontier bred above all else was democracy. In the self-confident, equalitarian life of these dwellers in log cabins, there was at once an insistence upon the worth of the individual, and a distrust of those who were different. Wealth, social position, even education came to be both disliked and feared. These people wanted not only to govern themselves with no outside interference, but wanted in office, as their representatives, men only like themselves whom they could understand and whom alone they felt they could trust. Always enmeshed in debt for their first settlement, and with little opportunity for making money, they hated and feared the moneyed interests of the East, and any political power which was not close to themselves and in their control.

Government seemed to them a simple matter, and one which they could easily manage. In the constitution for Ohio, which after some delay was admitted to the Union as a State in 1803, the democratic tendencies were more clearly marked than in any which had yet been drawn. The governor had neither appointing power nor the right to veto legislation. The supreme court judges, instead of being appointed for life by the executive, were to be elected by the legislature for seven years if not removed for bad behavior before that time. All men were declared equally free and independent, and the franchise was given to all white men over twenty-one provided they had paid "or were charged with" a State or county tax.

In spite of the fact that the scope of the franchise had been very much widened generally throughout the country as compared with pre-Revolutionary days, we were yet far from the manhood suffrage of the 1830's, and it has been estimated that only about one-fifteenth of the white population had votes. Moreover, usually the voter had to announce publicly the way he was voting, which obviously would often call for much courage or for suppression of his real wishes. Apportionment of votes by districts was also such as tended to nullify popular choice. In Virginia, for example, a hundred voters in the tidewater section secured as much representation in the State Assembly as a thousand in the western region. There was similar heavy discrimination against the upland part of South Carolina in favor of the coast, and in such States as New York, Massachusetts, and others, districts were so arranged as to interfere with popular representation in the legislatures. As the legislatures chose Presidential Electors it is evident that even the fifteen per cent of the "people" who could vote at all might have their wishes thwarted as to the party or President elected. For somewhat different reasons, the same holds true even today, and it has repeatedly happened that a President is elected who has received only a minority of the popular vote. In the important election of 1800, which we shall now have to discuss, we shall have to go behind the actual votes cast in the Electoral College to understand the result.

The issue between the Federalists and the Republicans, or Democrats as the Jeffersonian Party had also begun to be called, was clear.

It stemmed back to the difference in political philosophy between Jefferson and Hamilton which we have already discussed. Caucuses of the two parties in Congress selected respectively President John Adams and C. C. Pinckney as Federalist candidates, and Jefferson and Aaron Burr as Republican, a Northern President with Southern Vice-President, and vice-versa. The campaign was one of extreme bitterness, the Republicans being denounced as Anti-Christ in New England, and every possible slander being everywhere heaped upon the several candidates.

Hamilton was the "boss" of the Federalist Party, but, as we have seen, had come to hate Adams, who, nevertheless, after a tour of New England, Hamilton realized had to be the party candidate. Blinded with passion, Hamilton wrote for private circulation a pamphlet in which, with a complete breakdown of political sense and ordinary decency, he declared at length that Adams was utterly unfit for office but that Federalists should vote for him so as to bring in the party. Some of the saner leaders, such as George Cabot, urged its suppression but one of the printed copies fell into the hands of Aaron Burr who immediately saw to its publication. When the Electoral votes were counted it was found that Jefferson and Burr each had seventy-three, Adams sixty-five, and Pinckney sixty-four.

It was a Republican victory, revealing markedly distinct sectional and class cleavages. The West and the entire South up to Maryland voted for Jefferson, as did Pennsylvania and New York. Maryland was divided evenly, but Adams, who also got some votes in North Carolina and Pennsylvania, carried the whole of New England. The adroit political manipulation of Burr in New York decided the final result but two facts stood out. One was that the agrarian South and the frontier West were strongly Democratic and anti-Federalist, and the other was, on a closer analysis of the local returns everywhere, that the poorer people, the farmers and town artisans and others, were Democratic whereas the main Federalist strength came from the mercantile and other monied interests.

Although Adams had run on the Federalist ticket, he was by no means of the full Federalist faith, and this as well as Hamilton's hostility and the bitterness of those who had so sorely resented Adams's preserving the nation from war with France, contributed to his defeat. He had agreed on the whole with the Federalist doctrine of government by the "wise and good," who he thought were more likely to be found among those who had enjoyed opportunities by the possession of a reasonable degree of wealth. On the other hand, wealth to him meant landed property, and he had no sympathy with a government in the interest of a mere stock-jobbing, monied class feeding at the public trough on special favors.

Moreover, Adams distinctly recognized that if in a pure democracy there was great danger that the propertyless class would vote away property from others, yet there was also danger that a rich class in complete control might, with its superior knowledge and financial ability, win for itself the greater part of the wealth of the country. He believed, however, in a strong central government, and one of his last acts in office before leaving the half-finished White House to his successor was to appoint to the Chief-Justiceship of the Supreme Court, John Marshall, who in the next decade was to do even more perhaps than Hamilton in moulding the yet malleable Constitution into an instrument for a powerful and highly centralized government, emphasizing the rights of property over those of man.

Jefferson and Burr being tied for the first place, the election had to be carried to the House of Representatives, where, after taking thirty-five ballots, no decision had yet been reached by February 17, 1801, although a President had to be inaugurated on March 4. The Federalists had been trying to defeat the known wishes of the Republicans to make Jefferson President by electing Burr instead, but having reached a complete deadlock, and Hamilton being opposed to the election of his bitter New York rival, three Federalists cast blank ballots and Jefferson was elected by a majority of two votes. The Republicans had also won good majorities in both houses of Congress, and in 1804 the Twelfth Amendment to the Constitution, submitted in 1802, provided against such a dangerous situation as had arisen from the tie vote between Jefferson and Burr by requiring that the Electors vote separately for candidates for the highest two offices.

The new President, when inaugurated in a simple but dignified ceremony, fully realized the sectional and class foundations of his power, but perhaps no other Presidents except Washington, Lincoln, and the two Adamses have entered upon office with a greater desire to conserve the interests of the entire nation. In his Inaugural

Address he called upon all citizens to remember (what it would be well for us to recall today), the "sacred principle," as he called it, "that though the will of the majority is in all cases to prevail, that will, to be rightful, must be reasonable; that the minority possess their equal rights, which equal laws must protect, and to violate which would be oppression." "Having banished religious intolerance," he went on, "we have yet gained little if we countenance a political intolerance, as despotic as wicked, and capable of as bitter and bloody persecutions."

No one, Jefferson added, would wish to dissolve the Union, and

yet all of y[m] inculcat[?] Honesty, truth, temper[ce] gratitude, & the love of man, acknolg[?] & adoring an overruling providence, which by all it's dispensations proves that it delights in the happiness of man here, & his greater happiness hereafter: with all these blessings, what more is necessary to make us a happy and a prosperous people? still one thing more, fellow citizens, a wise & frugal govmt, w[ch] shall restrain men from injuring one another, shall leave them otherwise free to regulate their own pursuits of industry & improvement, and shall not take, from the mouth of labor, the bread it has earned. this is the sum of good govmt, & this is necessary to close the circle of our felicities.

A FACSIMILE (REDUCED) OF THE CONCLUDING LINES FROM THE THIRD
PAGE OF JEFFERSON'S INAUGURAL ADDRESS, MARCH 4, 1801
From the original in the Library of Congress.

in that sense we all were both Federalists and Republicans. As for a "strong" government, he believed ours the strongest in the world, but to be strong and to enjoy the loyalty of its citizens they must be allowed to govern themselves. "Sometimes it is said, that man cannot be trusted with the government of himself. Can he then be trusted to govern others? Or, have we found angels in the form of kings to govern him?" We may recall that he did not believe in the power of self-government of all men under all circumstances and that it was safe only under our American condition of free land and free men. In his address, however, he spoke of our country as having "room enough for our descendants to the thousandth and thousandth generation," so hidden in the future were all those mechanical inventions which were to enable us to sweep across the continent and subdue it within a century. He proposed a "wise and frugal government," bestowing exact justice on all of every station, creed or belief; "friendship with all nations, entangling alliances with none"; the maintenance of State governments as the surest bulwarks of liberty; the honest payment of all public debts; the diffusion of education; freedom of the press, religion, and the person.

In his later years, looking back over his long and varied life, Jefferson spoke of the election of 1800 as a "revolution" as great as that of 1776. It was not that, and circumstances were to force Jefferson into acts which were in some cases opposed to his principles as he had laid them down for the people. But the defeat of the Federalists by the Republicans was the first of those great movements among the democratic elements in our population which in each generation have had for their object the bringing back of government from too great subservience to what in a literal sense have been "privileged" classes to a government that should carry out the spirit of the Declaration of Independence.

It was the man who had written that Declaration who was the standard bearer in the first revolt when the Federalists, who had done much sound work in the organization of the new nation, became too markedly the purveyors of privilege to certain economic and social groups in a single section of the country. John Adams had risen above his party to save the country, but that party had no roots in the soil of the common people,—their hopes, fears, and emotions, —and Adams fell with it.

The inauguration of his opponent was welcomed throughout the land, except in Federalist strongholds, with greater rapture than had been shown since the signing of peace in 1783. The new President entered upon office with the noblest of aspirations and the highest of hopes, hopes doomed to deep disappointment from the same currents of European policies which had whirled us round and round, and brought bitter dissension among us ever since we had thought we had attained to an independent national life.

CHAPTER X

THE PRESIDENCY OF JEFFERSON

JEFFERSON, whose wife had died many years earlier, did not immediately move to the White House, or "President's House" as it was then called, but remained at Conrad's boarding house for some weeks until he could set off to his beloved Monticello. In those days a President was not overwhelmed with the mass of detail work which unquestionably interferes with the efficiency, as it tends to break the physical strength, of a chief magistrate of today, and Jefferson spent about a quarter of his time, or an aggregate of over two years during his two terms, in the healthy and happy atmosphere of his own estate.

By the end of April, 1801, however, he was in Washington and ready to undertake his duties there. He hoped to be able to unite the country and in spite of the vile slanders of the campaign, which he never publicly noticed, to win over to the Republican way of thinking many who had been alienated from what he believed a true Americanism only by fear of the excesses of the French Revolution.

He well knew that the leaders of the Federalist Party were his inveterate foes, and did not make the mistake which Adams had made of placing in his Cabinet any but men whom he could trust to be in sympathy with himself and his policies. For Secretary of State he chose James Madison of Virginia, and for Secretary of the Treasury Albert Gallatin of Pennsylvania, the latter the best financier of his time. Both of these were far abler men to serve in their offices than any who had occupied them since Hamilton and Jefferson himself. His Secretary of War, Henry Dearborn, and Attorney-General, Levi Lincoln, were both from Massachusetts. If Massachusetts could offer no stronger men for Cabinet rank, it was not Jefferson's fault that, as the Federalist fire-eater, Josiah Quincy, complained a dozen years later, the government had "been composed to all efficient purposes of two Virginians and a foreigner." Gallatin had, indeed, been born in Switzerland, but Hamilton, the Federalist boss, had been born in the island of Nevis, and Gallatin was in the United States before the Constitution was adopted.

The problem of office-holding was presented to Jefferson as the first President who had to deal with it. Washington had properly put into government positions those who were favorable to the new form of government, as yet weak and untried. On his second election there was no need of change, nor, although parties had developed, did Adams, who was of the same party as his predecessor, have to make any considerable change in 1797. For Jefferson, the situation was wholly different. When he entered office there was not a single office-holder of his own political beliefs, and the hostility of his enemies was unbelievably bitter. The leading Federalist newspaper in Connecticut, for example, claimed that the followers of the new

MAD TOM in A RAGE

A CARTOON SHOWING JEFFERSON, ASSISTED BY SATAN, PULLING DOWN A COLUMN REPRESENTING THE FEDERAL PARTY

From the Emmet Collection, New York Public Library.

President denied "the propriety of the marriage covenant, of the tender connections of life, of the obligation of a promise, and the quiet possession of *individual property*." A couple of years before, the dyed-in-the-wool Federalist clergyman, Timothy Dwight, one of the leaders of the State, had claimed in a Fourth of July oration that if the Democrats attained power the churches would be turned into "temples of reason"; "that we may behold a strumpet personating a Goddess on the altars of Jehovah"; and "our wives and daughters the victims of a legal prostitution . . . the loathing of God and man."

With the defeated party indulging in such maniacal frenzy it could hardly be expected that a President would consent to have all the offices below Cabinet rank held by the enemy. As he explained, vacancies occurring "by death are few; by resignation none." Great pressure was also brought to bear upon the President by his own followers who demanded, as party leaders and adherents always do, some of the spoils of victory. Jefferson himself had always believed in rotation in office aside from party, and if in the course of his first term he replaced Federalists by Republicans in about half the places at his disposal there was no reason for Hamilton's accusation against him of "ineradical duplicity."

With all his idealism, Jefferson was an able organizer and administrator, and with a good working majority of Republicans in Congress he set to work initiating a number of reforms. A minor change was made in the mode of communicating his first message to Congress in December, 1801. Washington and Adams had always appeared in person to read their messages with a certain degree of ceremony, but in accord with his belief that government should be as simple and unostentatious as possible, the new President merely sent his to the legislature in writing by messenger, a practice always maintained since down to President Wilson more than a century later.

One of the first measures passed by the new administration was the abolishing of the hated excise tax on whiskey. Provision was also made for a much stricter accountability of public officers for their expenditure of public moneys. No fraudulent practices were found in the accounts of the Federalists but the old system of voting money in single large sums without specific appropriations for particular purposes left altogether too much discretion to the heads of departments; and money appropriated with the intention of having it spent in one way could be spent for quite other ends.

Although the new system of specific appropriations has led to abuses in "log rolling" it would be hard to believe that the older system would not have led to yet graver ones. Jefferson also carried out his pledge of economy and reduced public expenditure in his first year from $7,500,000 to $5,000,000, and although, not including sinking funds, the Federalists had increased the national debt over $8,000,000 between 1792 and 1800, the Republicans reduced it, between 1801 and 1810, $27,500,000 or, counting in the $15,000,000 paid for Louisiana out of the Treasury, $42,500,000.

The navy was reduced in accordance with an Act which had been passed by the last Federalist Congress, and Jefferson also cut down the army from 4000 to 2500 men but at the same time took a great step toward its increased efficiency by establishing the Military Academy at West Point. His interest in letters and education was shown by the enactment of a copyright law and the founding of the Library of Congress.

Although always a determined opponent of war if it could possibly be avoided by more peaceful and reasonable methods for settling disputes, Jefferson was never a pacificist, as had been shown clearly enough in the Revolution, and one of the early events of his first term showed him a more resolute defender of American rights by force than either Washington or Adams had proved themselves. The rulers of the Barbary States,—Algiers, Tunis, Tripoli, and Morocco—had long been in the habit of preying on the commerce which passed along their shores, and England and the other European powers had regularly bought immunity by paying tribute to the pirates. We had followed suit and in the ten years down to 1800 had sent over $2,000,000 to buy the corsairs off.

Jefferson determined to try force even before the Bashaw of Tripoli, dissatisfied with the amount he was receiving, declared war on us. An American squadron was sent to the Mediterranean, followed by others under command of Commodore Preble, during the next three years, and on February 16, 1804, Lieutenant Stephen Decatur with a handful of men rowed into the harbor of Tripoli, where the pirates had anchored our captured ship *Philadelphia*. Driving her Tripolitan crew overboard, Decatur set her on fire, and escaped safely to his own vessel, having accomplished what Admiral Nelson called the most daring act of the age. Tripoli was bombarded and in 1805 its ruler was forced to sign a treaty guaranteeing that Americans should be unmolested, although the other Barbary powers were not brought to book for another decade. In view of what we shall have to say later about impressment of our seamen by the British it is interesting to note that Captain Bainbridge, of the *Phila-*

delphia, who was a prisoner in Tripoli, called Commodore Preble's attention to the fact that more than one half the crew of our war ship were English sailors not naturalized in America.

The neat little war which we had waged against the Tripolitan pirates was a trifling matter as compared with the diplomatic contest which Jefferson entered upon with perhaps the greatest bandit of all time, the Emperor Napoleon.

"Louisiana," as the territory, roughly, between the Mississippi River and the Rocky Mountains, New Orleans and the Canadian boundary, was called, had been ceded by France to Spain in 1763. The southeastern part included both banks of the River and a strip of the Gulf coast. By our treaty with Spain in 1795 we had been granted, for three years, the right of navigation and of deposit at New Orleans, and we have already noted how rapidly commerce increased in the West after the river had thus definitely been opened to us. The westerners took it for granted that the rights would not be revoked, and in fact after the treaty expired Spain did nothing to alter the situation until 1802.

In July of that year the Intendant, or Spanish governor, at New Orleans received orders to withdraw the right of deposit, that is of landing goods at that port without payment of any charges while being transshipped. The West felt that a hand had suddenly grasped its throat and was about to throttle it. There was a wave of indignation in the whole section, none too tightly bound to the East politically in any case. Jefferson fully realized the need for action and for making the West believe its rights and interests would be defended by the Federal government, but declined to be hurried. The Federalists, who had never had any love for the West but who were anxious to put Jefferson in a hole, immediately clamored for war with France, for although the Mississippi had been closed by Spain that nation had secretly retroceded Louisiana to France by the Treaty of San Ildefonso on October 1, 1800.

Napoleon, whose schemes of empire and conquest had become grandiose, was dreaming of re-establishing France both in the Far East and in America, and had secured the retrocession of Louisiana by offering the King and Queen of Spain an Italian kingdom with at least a million inhabitants for their son-in-law to be carved out of Tuscany. Some months after the deal was consummated, Jefferson heard of it and the sailing of Napoleon's brother-in-law with troops for the conquest of Santo Domingo in November, 1801, threw a lurid light on the possibilities if Napoleon were to try to extend his power to North America, come into possession of both banks of the Mississippi at its mouth, and secure a territory, blocking us on our entire western boundary, somewhat larger than the United States itself. Spain was a comparatively peaceful neighbor and a declining power. To substitute for her the man who was setting civilization ablaze was a danger of appalling magnitude.

While the Federalists were doing their best to force a war, Jefferson went quietly to work. He envisaged the possibility of war as a last resort, and more than hinted at it to the French Minister. He also wrote his famous despatch to our minister, Livingston, in Paris, in which he announced that the day on which France should take possession of New Orleans we would have "to marry ourselves to the British fleet and nation," and in concert with them hold all of the two American continents for the common purposes of Britain and the United States, a measure far from desirable but one which Napoleon would have forced upon us. Jefferson's message to Congress in December, 1802, however, was peaceful in tenor, though the news of the withdrawal by Spain of the right of deposit had reached us only a few weeks earlier. The President contented himself with mildly suggesting that if the rumored transfer to France should take place it would cause a change in our foreign relations.

The next month, January, 1803, he secured the appropriation by Congress of $2,000,000 to be used "in relation to the intercourse between the United States and foreign nations," and the same day nominated James Monroe to be Minister Extraordinary to France, explaining in a letter to him that the Federalists were trying to force the nation into war and, failing that, to win the votes of the West for the election of the next year. In April Monroe reached Paris.

Meanwhile much had been happening in Europe. War between England and France had come to a temporary end with the Treaty of Amiens in March, 1802, but Napoleon's attempt to conquer Santo Domingo had ended in ignominious disaster. War and, more especially, yellow fever had reduced the number of French troops from 28,000 to 4000, and General Le Clerc himself had died. The negro patriot, Toussaint L'Ouverture, was successfully defying Napoleon, who was also chafing from loss of prestige from the state of peace in Europe. In March, 1803, he threatened war with England and that country took up the challenge again on May 18. The Emperor had got sick of his plan of colonial expansion, made one of his sudden changes in policy and decided on seeking new laurels on the battlefields nearer home. He now had no wish to send more troops to Santo Domingo; to spare others to garrison the vast territory of Louisiana; or to have the United States throw its weight on the side of the enemy and seize Louisiana as a spoil of war.

Jefferson had instructed Monroe and Livingston to negotiate for the purchase, for not more than 50,000,000 francs, of New Orleans and the two Floridas, which would give us the Gulf coast along our South, and the control of the outlet of the great river. If they could not make this deal they were to offer about 37,000,000 francs for New Orleans alone. If they could make no purchase they were to insist upon a perpetual guarantee of right of navigation and deposit. If even that could not be obtained, they were at once to negotiate with England with a view to joining her in war on France.

Livingston had begun negotiations before Monroe arrived but Napoleon had not matured his policy. Suddenly he did so. He needed money for war. He no longer wanted Louisiana. He decided to sell the whole thing if he could, cancel his liability for administering it, remove the American menace, and raise cash by doing both. When Livingston on April 11 suggested again that we buy New Orleans he was startled to have Talleyrand ask him suddenly what the United States would pay for the whole of Louisiana. Monroe arrived in a day or two and although they had no instructions to make any such stupendous bargain, they did not hesitate, and after a week or two of haggling over terms, they signed the papers on May 2 (antedating them to April 30), which gave us the whole of the territory described for approximately $15,000,000.

We thus came into possession of the Mississippi from source to mouth, and the area of the United States at a stroke of the pen increased from less than 900,000 square miles to over 1,800,000. So well had Gallatin handled the national finances that when called upon to make payment he could do so without asking Congress for a cent. What we had bought, however, was more than a little uncertain at the time. Napoleon did not have a shadow of right to sell Louisiana and broke both faith and law to do so. He had, first, never fulfilled the conditions of the cession from Spain. Secondly, he had agreed that he would never cede the territory to any other power but that if France did not occupy it it should be delivered back to Spain. Finally, under the French constitution, he was forbidden to alienate French territory. However, Spain, having no other course to pursue against him, acknowledged the transfer, and at New Orleans in November handed over the province to the French, who, in turn, transferred it to us in December. Its boundaries were vague, and various interpretations of old records and treaties could make it include either or both of West Florida and Texas, and its northern limit was equally indefinite. But there was no question of the magnitude of the step America had taken.

Jefferson, however, was staggered and put in an extremely awkward situation. The purchase of New Orleans or of a bit of the Gulf coast might be considered as a mere rectification of our boundaries under the Constitution, but to double the size of the nation, to create a domain from which enough new States could be carved to upset completely the balance of the old, could not by any stretch of logic be made to fit the strict-construction theory of the Constitution which Jefferson and the Republicans had insisted upon. On the other hand, apart from the immense addition to our territory, the advantages of securing the whole of the Mississippi, of being forever relieved from the danger of a foreign nation to the west of us, and of clearing ourselves from innumerable possibilities of being entangled with Europe in all its conflicts, were so great as to admit of no denial.

All this, Jefferson realized, and when the Senate confirmed the treaty with France the President signed it, believing the nation would sustain him and later pass an amendment to the Constitution legalizing what had been done. It cannot be claimed that he was inconsistent, and he frankly declared that if, as was suggested to him, he could consummate the deal under the "general welfare" clause there was then no Constitution at all. The nation, however, was less bothered with scruples, and the amendments Jefferson wished were never passed. With negligible exceptions the people hurrahed and acquiesced, although the New England Federalists grumbled furiously at such a complete shift in the balance of sectional power as they foresaw in the future.

The Federalists had other grievances against Jefferson. Just before they had been forced from office they had passed a new Judiciary Act which President Adams had signed on February 13, 1801, three weeks before he left the White House. This had added sixteen judges to the Federal circuits. An Act had also been passed and signed on the 27th which provided, among other things, for as many Justices of the Peace in the District of Columbia as the President should deem necessary. Adams had made all the appointments of the Federal judges, as well as that of Marshall to the Supreme Court and forty-two Justices of the Peace, in the closing days of his administration, and the Republicans not unnaturally felt that they should have been left for them.

The nominations of the Washington Justices of the Peace had been made by Adams March 2, confirmed by the Senate on the 3d, and Jefferson took office on the 4th. He decided to withhold commissions from seventeen of these; and Congress repealed the Judiciary Act which had created the sixteen Federal judges, this action infuriating the Federalists, who absurdly claimed that the very foundations of liberty and property were undermined.

Twenty-five Justices for the District were ample to care for the business but Jefferson's withholding of the others' commissions raised a more important question and resulted in a decision of the Supreme Court which was perhaps the most far-reaching and fundamental that that body has ever handed down. In December, 1801, William Marbury and three others, whose commissions were being held up, applied to the Supreme Court for an order requiring the Secretary of State, Madison, to show why a writ ordering the handing over of the commissions should not be issued. The decision was not handed down until February, 1803, and then by Chief Justice Marshall.

Ever since the adoption of the Virginia and Kentucky resolves, Marshall had been pondering the question as to where the final authority lay in our government as to what was and what was not law throughout the nation. He had reached his conclusion and had been waiting for an opportunity to affirm it in such a way as to make it, if possible, the accepted one for all time. He chose the case of Marbury vs. Madison for the purpose. By the time the decision was handed down the case, in so far as concerned the plaintiffs, had become unimportant, but Marshall's opinion has been of vast influence ever since.

The powers of the legislature, he declared, were limited. To indicate and preserve those limits was the purpose of the Constitution. That instrument, therefore, controls any legislative act that may be repugnant to it. "A legislative act contrary to the constitution is not law." All laws repugnant to it must be void, and "it is emphatically the province and duty of the judicial department to say what the law is." There had been nothing in the Constitution giving the courts the right to pass on the constitutionality of laws, but Marshall was right in that the final right to decide on what *is* law must reside somewhere, and his assertion that it resided in the Supreme Court has ever since been acquiesced in.

The repeal of the Federalists' Judiciary Act, and the subsequent proceedings of Jefferson were followed up after Marshall's decision, by what the Federalists claimed to consider a wholesale attack on the Courts by the Republicans. A certain Federal Judge, John Pickering of New Hampshire, had become both a heavy drinker and insane. He was impeached and tried in the United States Senate and, in spite of the plea of insanity made on his behalf by his son, was found guilty and dismissed from the bench, on which he was obviously incompetent to sit. The same day on which the Senate voted on Pickering's case, the House of Representatives decided also to proceed against Samuel Chase, one of the Associate Justices of the U. S. Supreme Court. More than once Chase in addressing juries had spoken with great violence against the Republican Party and its policies, but such harangues were not uncommon in that day, and although that party in the Senate had a two-thirds majority with which to convict him on merely party grounds, had it wished to do so, nothing warranting conviction was found against him and he was acquitted.

These events, and more particularly the acquisition of Louisiana, led the die-hard Federalists of New England, who believed the salvation of the country rested solely on themselves and that democracy spelled anarchy, seriously to consider the question of secession. Timothy Pickering and the rest of the Essex Junto in Massachusetts, with Connecticut leaders of the same stamp, planned a new Northern Confederacy, to be made up of New England and New York, which should set up for itself and cut loose from the growing control of the South and its allied West.

Hamilton was taken into the secret but disapproved of the plan. The plotters then approached Burr, whom although a Republican they knew to be dissatisfied with the treatment he had received from his party since the election of 1800, the success of which had depended so greatly on his own control of the pivotal State of New York. They offered to support him with Federalist votes if he would run for governor of New York as a Republican in consideration of his swinging the State into secession and the new Confederacy, of which they agreed to elect him the first President. Hamilton, however, by his influence among the New York Federalist voters, prevented Burr from becoming governor, and the whole scheme failed. In the course of the episode, Hamilton had also made charges seriously reflecting on Burr's honor, and the latter, now ruined politically, challenged Hamilton to a duel about six weeks after the election. Hamilton, although opposed to secession, himself believed the nation was drifting to anarchy under Republican rule, and that the day was coming when he might be called upon to save it. He felt that if a stigma were even unjustly placed upon his courage he would be prevented from playing the part he wished in the future he foresaw. Therefore he accepted the challenge, and on July 11 at six in the morning he crossed the Hudson to meet his antagonist.

When the men faced one another, Burr took careful aim and mortally wounded Hamilton, who died the following day. Settling affairs of honor by a duel was then a common practice. Hamilton's own eldest son had been killed in one only three years earlier, but there was a revulsion of feeling after the great leader to whom the nation owed so much had been shot down in cold blood, and although Burr went back to his chair as presiding officer of the Senate he was now completely discredited.

So also, however, was the Federalist Party, which had lost its ablest leader in Hamilton. The people had seen that Jefferson had protected trade, as in his attack on the Barbary pirates; that he had stood by the West; that he had carried out his pledges of economy and good government; and as contrasted with the secession policy of the Federalists the President had doubled the size of the country by the purchase of Louisiana, an act which had proved enormously popular.

Federalist leaders might grumble that the nation was being ruined by the Republicans but the people believed, on the contrary, that its power, prestige, and prosperity were being greatly augmented. In the election of 1804 Jefferson was overwhelmingly re-elected by 162 votes to only 14 for his opponent, C. C. Pinckney, the Federalists carrying only Connecticut in New England itself, and outside of that stronghold no State but Delaware. Even Massachusetts, the very heart of Federalism and the seat of the Junto, went solidly for Jefferson in the Electoral College.

Had the President retired at the end of his first term he would have gone down into history as perhaps the most completely successful Chief Executive who ever sat in the White House. Unfortunately the nation was now on the eve of being again involved in what seemed the endless Napoleonic struggle; and Jefferson's second term was to be as troubled as his first had been brilliant. Practically all of his difficulties came from his efforts to deal with the European situation but we may glance first, a little out of chronological order, at the end of his former Vice-President Burr.

The details of what is called the "Burr conspiracy" are still shrouded in the mystery which hangs over all the many plots which were hatched in the West. He had been dropped by his party, and the new Vice-President was George Clinton of New York. Before leaving Washington, the ruined Burr made a somewhat fantastic offer to the British Minister to bring about a secession of the West from the Union for $500,000, but England was not interested in either the project or its author. Burr then went to the Ohio River, and by his charm of manner won many to his side, including even Andrew Jackson, appearing to some as a patriot and apparently confiding to others his schemes for secession or for the building up of a new empire in Mexico. General Wilkinson, still in the secret pay of Spain although our Governor of Louisiana and the ranking general in the American Army, discussed plans with Burr, the precise nature of which is still unknown.

Back again in Washington after having been as far as New Orleans, Burr managed to get $10,000 from the Spanish Minister, although he apparently intended to attack Spain in Mexico. In the summer, 1806, he was again in the West floating down the river with about sixty followers. Nobody knew what was in his mind, but Wilkinson, who was always a traitor to every side, now sent word to Jefferson that Burr was involved in a great plot to break up the Union. After the President had received similar messages from others whom he believed he could trust, he issued a proclamation for the capture of Burr, who was caught, taken to Richmond, and tried for treason before Chief-Justice Marshall. No proof sufficient to warrant conviction was forthcoming, and the indictment against the former Vice-President broke down ignominiously, doing a good deal to undermine in many quarters the popularity of Jefferson, who had pressed the case.

Meanwhile much more important complications were developing abroad. France and England had become locked in a life-and-death struggle, Napoleon having become practically supreme on land and England at sea. Neither cared in the slightest for the rights of neutrals, of whom the United States was by far the most important. As had happened in the earlier war a vast increase in the carrying trade fell to our share, and the ship owners were making large profits, even allowing for the many captures. England invoked what is call the Rule of 1756, which forbade a neutral to carry on a trade in war time which was denied to him in peace, and claimed that we were transporting French West India produce to French ports in violation of the rule. They also claimed that even if the cargoes were brought to America first and then re-shipped the voyage was a "continuous" one, a theory which we ourselves invoked during our Civil War but which was against our interests in the earlier period. An attempt to settle matters by negotiating a treaty with England in the summer of 1806 failed, and soon after the Orders in Council issued by England and the decrees put forth by Napoleon seemed to leave no scope whatever for American commerce.

In December, 1806, Napoleon issued the "Berlin Decree" which proclaimed the British Isles to be blockaded, prohibited all intercourse with them and declared that all merchandise coming from them was lawful prize, and that no ship which left an English port would be admitted to a French one or those of any allied nation.

England replied in January with an Order in Council prohibiting all trade between any two ports in the possession of France or her allies. The following November she added another prohibiting all neutral trade with any port from which British ships were excluded unless the ship called first at a British port and paid duties. Napoleon then retorted with his "Milan Decree" authorizing the confiscation of any vessel which paid duty to the English or sailed to or from any port anywhere in the British Empire.

Both nations not only preyed on our commerce in accordance with these Orders and Decrees but infringed our rights even within three miles of our own coast, and used our harbors for war purposes. Between the reopening of the war in Europe in 1803 and our entry in 1812, the British captured 917 of our vessels and the French 558, the French inferiority in sea power evidently being made up for in greater activity in captures and confiscation. Our own navy was small in comparison with those of the belligerents, and the cost of defending our coasts appeared prohibitive. Jefferson, on the advice of his naval officials, had about seventy small gunboats built by 1807, but these were absurdly inadequate for any purpose.

If there were nothing to choose between the two European powers in their utter disregard of our rights, or what we claimed as such, there was one point of dispute which in practice, though not in theory, embroiled us with England rather than with France. All nations at that time, including the United States, denied the right of a native-born citizen to shed his responsibilities by becoming naturalized in a foreign country. If a French or an English vessel came within our three-mile limit and had on board deserters from the American Navy, even if they had become naturalized French or British subjects, we would have had the right to seize them and put them back in our ships. On the other hand, England and France had similar rights as to their citizens even though they had become American subjects.

The problem never arose with the French, as owing to the difference in language and for other reasons there were practically none of the naturalized citizens of either nation serving in the ships of the other. Nor did we have to exercise our right as against the English, as no American deserters wished to serve in their navy. The right of search and impressment thus had value only for England against us, as the bad conditions in her navy and better economic possibilities in America led great numbers of her men to desert and enter our service, both in our navy and merchant marine. We have already noted that after the European war had begun in 1803, over one half the men on our ship, the *Philadelphia,* at Tripoli were English sailors who were not even naturalized American citizens.

Had England confined herself to taking bona-fide British-born citizens off our ships when within three miles of her coasts, we could have had no complaint. But in the first place, she claimed that she had the right to do so wherever she met one of our vessels on the high seas, and also, owing to the practical impossibility of telling whether an Englishman, a Scotchman or an Irishman had been born in the British Isles or in the United States, she impressed great numbers of men who were genuine native-born American citizens. There was much fraud in our issuance of citizenship papers, and the British claimed, rightfully enough, that these could not be relied upon as proof. British officers were never supposed to impress native Americans, but in fact several thousands were so taken, and complaints were constant. The practice was bound to lead to gross injustice and abuse, and was extremely irritating. Finally an incident occurred which nearly precipitated war.

Some French frigates were lying in Chesapeake Bay and some from the British Navy were hanging off the Capes in wait for them. A good many of the English seamen had deserted ashore and, it was thought that they, with their ringleader, a man named Ratford, had enlisted in the American service. Our Navy Department claimed that it had searched for him on our few ships and had not been able to find him.

On June 22, 1807, our frigate *Chesapeake,* under Commodore Barron, left Norfolk and set out to sea, her decks still littered with supplies and with most of her guns not even mounted. She was followed by the British frigate *Leopard* from the British squadron, and when about ten miles off-shore the British ship, which had overhauled the American, signalled to her to stop. Barron, without fear of danger, did so, thinking the British wished to send despatches. When the small boat which put off from the *Leopard* reached the *Chesapeake* the officers who boarded her demanded that they be allowed to search the ship for British deserters. Barron answered that the only deserters on his vessel were three men who were native Americans and who had already been wrongfully impressed once.

In reality, although without the commander's knowledge, Ratford was also among his crew, but Barron declined to allow the search, and immediately after the British officers had again reached the *Leopard* that ship fired a full broadside into the *Chesapeake,* followed by two more. Twenty of our men were killed or wounded, and Barron, having taken his vessel to sea in a completely helpless condition, struck his flag and surrendered. The British then came aboard once more, mustered the crew, caught Ratford, and carried him and three Americans off to the *Leopard,* the *Chesapake* returning crippled to Norfolk.

As soon as the news of the insult spread over the country the excitement was intense and there was a wave of indignation which would have carried the nation united into war had Jefferson so willed. From England, the foreign minister, Canning, at once expressed regret and said he would take all proper steps called for as soon as an investigation was made. Jefferson, however, in his instructions to our minister in London, Monroe, ordered him not to accept any offer of reparation or apology that did not include a complete renouncing by England of her claim to impress her men from our vessels. This Canning declined to agree to, and in fact orders were issued in October directing British officers to impress British seamen on foreign vessels to the fullest extent possible. Meanwhile, Jefferson had issued a proclamation ordering all British war vessels out of American waters, forbidding others to enter, and prohibiting all intercourse with them.

America was wholly unprepared for war, and Jefferson, who had always been interested in the possibility of substituting economic pressure for armed force, decided upon making the experiment. He did not, in fact, expect to avoid war in the end but hoped that by bringing heavy pressure to bear there was a chance that England might do us justice. He also realized that we had as many grievances against France as against England but decided to settle with England first and then, as he said, "trust to the chapter of accidents" to see what could be done with Napoleon.

Congress met in October but it was not until Canning's despatches had arrived that Jefferson sent his message on the situation. In April, 1806, a Non-Importation Act had been passed prohibiting the importing of certain enumerated British goods, a measure which had been designed to strengthen the hands of our negotiators at that time, and quite clearly drawn from the precedents of the American Revolution. This, however, had not been put into effect.

Jefferson now tried the same sort of pressure on a far wider scale, and on December 22, 1807, secured the passage, with little debate, of the Embargo Act, prohibiting the export of any produce whatever from the United States or the clearing of any American vessel for a foreign port. Believing that American trade was essential to both belligerents he hoped by cutting them off to secure the revocation of the British Orders in Council or the French Decrees, or both. In fact, owing in part to non-observance of the measure and in part to the economic situation, the Embargo proved to have not only little coercive power over our enemies, but a disastrous effect on ourselves.

Although the original Act was passed in December, two additional ones were required in January and March, 1808, to close loopholes, and the big ship owners had ample time to clear many of their vessels before they could be stopped. Once abroad, they could go on cruising and trading for their owners, and although the risks were great the profits were correspondingly so. The French West Indies suffered some inconvenience but Napoleon confiscated every ship he could find in a French port, and did not fare badly. English-manufactured goods were smuggled in over the Canadian boundary, and also found new markets in South America.

On the other hand, although some merchants, whose ships were out of American jurisdiction, made good profits, others, whose vessels were tied up in our ports, were ruined, and the price of American agricultural products fell to disastrously low figures for the farmers and planters. It is usually said that New England and New York suffered the most, and this is possibly true, but the sufferings of the South have largely been ignored.

The value in normal times of the exports of domestic produce from the Middle States was twice as great as those from New England, and in the South three times, but whereas the loss in such ex-

THOMAS JEFFERSON
From the portrait by Sully in the American Philosophical Society, Philadelphia.

CITY ELECTION AT THE STATE HOUSE, PHILADELPHIA.

From the original water-color signed John Lewis Krimmel, 1815. Courtesy of the Historical Society of Pennsylvania.

ports due to the Embargo was only about 75 per cent in the two northern sections it was 85 per cent in the South. Of the total exports, of both domestic and foreign products, New England's fell from $24,278,000 to $6,000,000 or 75 per cent in 1808 as compared with 1807, those of the Middle States from $43,500,000 to $9,800,000, or 78 per cent, and those of the South from $35,900,000 to $5,300,000, or 85 per cent. Although New England and New York lost heavily

THE EMBARGO,

A SONG COMPOSED AND SUNG AT DOVER. *JULY* 4th, 1808.

[TUNE—Come let us prepare—

DEAR Sirs, it is wrong
　To demand a *New Song*;
　I have let all the breath I can spare, go;
With the Muse I've confer'd,
And she won't say a word,
　But keeps laughing about the EMBARGO.

I wish that I could
Sing in *Al°gro* mood,
　But the times are as stupid as *Largo*;
Could I have my choice,
I would strain up my voice,
　'Till it *snapt* all the *strings* of EMBARGO.

Lest Britain should take
A few men by mistake,
　Who under false colors may dare go;
We're manning their fleet
With our Tars, that retreat
　From poverty, sloth, and EMBARGO.

What a *fuss* we have made,
About rights and *free trade*,
　And swore we'd not let our own share go;
Now we can't for our souls
Bring a Hake from the *shoals*,
　'Tis a breach of the *twentieth* EMBARGO.

PART OF A BRITISH POLITICAL SONG ON THE EMBARGO
From the original in the New York Historical Society.

in shipping, on the whole the South suffered more severely than any other section.

Agitation against the measure was most vociferous, however, in New England, although more votes against the Embargo measures were cast in the South than North. The fact that New England made the most noise in strenuous opposition was partly due to the fact that such ships as did not sail were tied up to their docks, a dead loss, and their crews were without employment. The Southern planter who could not dispose of his tobacco or rice still had his plantation to live on, and his slave labor was as well taken care of as ever. The second reason was that New England was the stronghold of what remained of the Federalist Party, bitterly hostile to Jefferson, and anxious to make the most of every count against him. Such men as Timothy Pickering spread the absurd lie that Jefferson favored the Embargo only to aid Napoleon and to ruin New England.

By March, 1809, Timothy Dwight of Connecticut was preaching sermons on the text "Come out therefore from among them, and be ye separate, saith the Lord," and a new movement toward secession got under way. A Convention of representatives from the New England States had also been proposed to meet and nullify the Embargo measures. Manufacturing in that section was being stimulated and the manufacturing interest was rapidly growing but the Federalist leaders were connected with the shipping interest and paid no attention to any counterbalancing advantages in other directions.

Town meetings and State legislatures passed more and more denunciatory resolutions; smuggling and violence became more rampant; and at last, after fourteen months of the experiment, Jefferson yielded to the storm. On March 1, 1809, he signed a bill which had been passed by Congress repealing the Embargo completely, and passing in its stead an Act which merely prohibited trade with Great Britain and France until one or the other should suspend their obnoxious Orders and Decrees. Intercourse could be resumed by Executive order as soon as either nation complied with the demand. Three days later Jefferson's term expired and James Madison became President.

Jefferson had "kept us out of war" but at a price which the people were unwilling to pay, and his hope of showing Europe that instead of armed action there are "peaceable means of repressing injustice by making it the interest of the aggressor to do what is just and abstain from future wrong" had proved vain. It is impossible to say whether he might have been successful had the people stood by him, not engaged in smuggling and had kept their ships at home. The Federalists who blamed him most were the worst offenders in undermining his policy, and in any case he underestimated that preference for profit to patriotism which is always in evidence in every crisis and which a statesman has to allow for.

A few weeks before Jefferson's retirement, the Assembly of Virginia passed a vote of thanks to him for the services he had rendered, naming among them, justly, the decline in the number of public officials, the reduction of the national debt by $33,000,000, the peaceable acquisition from the Indians of 100,000,000 acres for settlement, the doubling of the size of the national domain by the purchase of Louisiana, the lesson taught the Barbary pirates, and the inviolate preservation of freedom of speech and of the press.

In thought, no man who has ever been President has so permanently influenced every generation of Americans, and without belittling the great work done by Hamilton and the Federalists before the latter lost their senses and became mere carping provincialists, it may be said that of all men of his period, the mind of Jefferson was the greatest moulding force in what we consider the typical American spirit. He himself laid little stress on the Presidency and many years later, when contemplating his end, he asked that the only words to be placed on his tomb should be: "Here was buried Thomas Jefferson, Author of the Declaration of Independence, of the Statute of Virginia for Religious Freedom, and Father of the University of Virginia; because by these as testimonials that I have lived I wish most to be remembered."

CHAPTER XI

THE WAR OF 1812

AFTER his second election Jefferson had stated that on no condition would he be a candidate for a third term, thus being the first to strengthen the precedent made by Washington. The President, however, had never concealed the fact that his own choice for a successor was Madison, who was by no means generally accepted by the party which had begun to feel the effects of severe strain. Madison, although an able thinker on the theory of government, was not at all a capable executive or manager of men, and many leading Virginians wished Monroe to be Jefferson's successor. In the North there was much talk about Southern dictation and a "Southern dynasty," and George Clinton felt that the office should fall to him. Some strength was added to his pretension in that he had been Vice-President under Jefferson as Jefferson had been under Adams, and Adams under Washington.

The campaign was one of local politics and jockeying for position by political machines, particularly in Virginia and New York, in which latter State the Republican Party was being split between George Clinton and his nephew De Witt Clinton, the Federalists flirting with each faction. In spite of the revulsion of feeling due to the Embargo, and of the effects of local politics, which swung New Hampshire, Massachusetts, Rhode Island, Connecticut, and Delaware once more into the Federalist fold, the Republicans won easily even with a divided vote from New York, Maryland, and North Carolina, and Madison was elected with George Clinton again as Vice-President.

The new President's inaugural address was colorless, and the make-up of the Cabinet disappointing. Gallatin, the only strong man in it, was retained at the Treasury but at a time of peculiar international difficulty the office of Secretary of State was given to

Robert Smith of Maryland, a man rich in family connections but poor in ability. He and Gallatin clashed for two years before Madison finally asked for Smith's resignation and appointed James Monroe in his stead.

At the very beginning of the new administration, however, it seemed for a few months as if Jefferson's policy might really have borne fruit. Early in 1809 Canning instructed the British Minister in Washington, David Erskine, to agree on the part of England to have the objectionable Orders in Council withdrawn, and to make atonement for the *Chesapeake* outrage, provided, however, that the United States would maintain Non-Intercourse with France while restoring trade with England. He further insisted that we should recognize the Rule of 1756, and agree to the seizure of American ships by the British Navy when found trading with countries observing Napoleon's Decrees.

These conditions were, of course, out of the question, but the minister, realizing this and being anxious to bring about accord between the two nations, exceeded his instructions, which he did not divulge to our State Department, and made an agreement with us that England would rescind the Orders in Council in exchange for our reopening trade with her, and continuing Non-Intercourse with France. Madison, keen as Erskine for peace, accepted this arrangement, raised no question as to impressment, and, the agreement signed, proclaimed trade open again with Great Britain. America hailed the move as a diplomatic victory, and from all our ports ships quickly cleared for British ports.

Then came the disillusionment. Canning repudiated both the agreement and the minister who had made it contrary to his instructions. Erskine was recalled and a certain Francis James Jackson who had a Prussian instead of an American wife, as had Erskine, was sent to Washington in his place. Jackson was not tactful and Smith, not yet deposed from office, was diplomatically clumsy. Madison notified the British Minister that any further discussions would be futile, and the diplomat asked for his passports. There was nothing further for Madison to do but to issue again a Proclamation of Non-Intercourse with England, and the situation, like an infected wound, became worse than ever.

Meanwhile, shippers had again tasted the sweets of action and

By the Virtue, Firmness and Patriotism of

JEFFERSON & MADISON,

Our Difficulties with England are settled—our Ships have been preserved, and our Seamen will, hereafter, be respected
while sailing under our National Flag.

NEW-YORK, SATURDAY MORNING, APRIL 22, 1809.

IMPORTANT.

By the President of the United States.—A Proclamation.

WHEREAS it is provided by the 11th section of the act of Congress, entitled " An
" act to interdict the commercial intercourse between the United States and Great Bri-
" tain and France, and their dependencies ; and for other purposes,"—and that " in
" case either France or Great Britain shall so revoke or modify her edicts as that they
" shall cease to violate the neutral commerce of the United States," the President is au-
thorised to declare the same by proclamation, after which the trade suspended by the said
act and by an act laying an Embargo, on all ships and vessels in the ports and harbours of
the United States and the several acts supplementary thereto may be renewed with the
nation so doing. And whereas the Honourable David Montague Erskine, his Britannic
Majesty's Envoy Extraordinary and Minister Plenipotentiary, has by the order and in the
name of his sovereign declared to this Government, that the British Orders in Council
of January and November, 1807, will have been withdrawn, as respects the United
States on the 10th day of June next. Now therefore I James Madison, President of
the United States, do hereby proclaim that the orders in council aforesaid will have
been withdrawn on the tenth day of June next; after which day the trade of the United
States with Great Britain, as suspended by the act of Congress above mentioned, and
an act laying an embargo on all ships and vessels in the ports and harbors of the United
States, and the several acts supplementary thereto, may be renewed.

Given under my hand and the seal of the United States, at Washington, the nineteenth day of April, in the year of our Lord, one
(L. s) thousand eight hundred and nine, and of the Independence
of the United States, the thirty-third.

JAMES MADISON.

By the President,
RT. SMITH, *Secretary of State.*

PROCLAMATION OF APRIL 19, 1809, ANNOUNCING THE WITHDRAWAL OF THE
ORDERS IN COUNCIL TO TAKE EFFECT IN JUNE, 1809

From a broadside in the New York Historical Society.

238

profits, and the Non-Intercourse Act of 1809 was to expire with the session of the Congress then sitting. In another effort to solve the problem, the Legislature passed what was known as Macon's Bill No. 2, being the second bill introduced for the purpose by Nathaniel Macon of North Carolina whom John Randolph described in his will as "the best, purest and wisest man" he had ever known, and whom Jefferson called "the last of the Romans."

The first bill, which was in some respects better, had been killed as a result of the feud between Smith and Gallatin, but the second was allowed to pass and received the approval of the President. By it trade was to be reopened with all the world but if before March 3, 1811, either France or England should do us justice and rescind the restrictions on our trade and the other should not, then the President should proclaim Non-Intercourse against the nation which so declined.

Napoleon now took a hand in the game. He had been seizing and selling all American vessels he could catch in French ports, the seizures thus far having brought him between $8,000,000 and $10,-000,000, but on August 5, 1810, he issued a Decree that the Berlin and Milan Decrees were revoked and that after November 1 they "will cease to have effect," it being understood, he stated, that the English should revoke their Orders in Council or that the United States should cause its rights to be respected.

The ambiguous language was as sticky as flypaper, and intended to be. Were the French Decrees revoked on August 5 or November 1? Were they in truth revoked at all? John Quincy Adams warned Madison that Napoleon had merely laid a trap to embroil us with England, which was precisely what he had done. American vessels in French ports were not released, and in at least one case, a new one was seized. Moreover, Napoleon carried on the operation of the Decrees as respected other nations. Madison, most unwisely, decided to trust the French, and on November 2, 1810, he issued a Proclamation stating that as France had revoked her Decrees, all restrictions on our commerce with her should cease; and that, on the other hand, if England did not similarly revoke her Orders within three months we should be obliged to revive the Non-Intercourse measure against her.

The British Government, having had more experience with Napoleon and less childlike trust in him than had Madison, declined to believe that the Emperor had really revoked the Decrees. Certainly his actions gave no reason to believe that he had. At the moment there was, unfortunately, no British Minister in Washington. Jackson, who had represented the British Government there, had been withdrawn at the request of the United States and no successor had been appointed as yet, the somewhat absurd reason being that Jackson had been promised his post and salary for a year, and the British did not want to pay any other minister a salary until that year was up. In England, George III had finally lost his reason completely, and it was not until February, 1811, that a Regency was arranged. Until that had been done, it was difficult for the British ministry to take any important action. Pinkney, however, insisted upon their coming to an immediate decision as to American matters. The American Minister should have made allowance for the unfortunate crisis, which he might even have used for his purposes, but instead, with an irritation which was wholly unwarranted, he insisted upon leaving England and returning home. Thus it happened that at a most critical time neither nation had a minister at the capital of the other.

Madison had already made one great mistake when he had got caught in the Erskine fiasco. Now he would not acknowledge that he might have made another by having been duped by Napoleon. He had announced to the world that the Decrees had been revoked, and he stubbornly continued to declare that they had been in spite of all evidence. England rightly insisted that they had not been. We had fallen into the French trap as Adams had predicted. March 2, 1811, Madison proclaimed that Non-Intercourse was resumed as to England. If, however, France had not in truth revoked the Decrees, we were evidently not carrying out the terms of the Macon Bill, and were merely joining Napoleon against England.

While Madison was thus getting us completely involved in the toils of the astute Emperor, our peace was even more imperilled by the course of events in the West and in the new Congress. It is impossible to understand why we went to war with England unless we consider these carefully. Economic conditions in Europe in both belligerent countries were becoming such that at last Jefferson's policy of economic pressure was beginning to have a chance of success, and, even with our inept diplomacy, war might have been avoided had it not been for internal factors in our own national life.

The Northwest Territory had been developing rapidly. Ohio had been made a State in 1802, Michigan Territory was carved out of the old Northwest in 1805, and Illinois Territory (including the present Wisconsin), four years later. The American pioneer had long been a woodsman and he could not, or thought he could not, utilize the open prairies and plains of the farther West. Not only was the tough sod too much for his rude ploughs but the absence of timber for dozens of daily uses, including the two essentials of housebuilding and fire for cooking and warmth, made the "great open spaces" seem impossible of utilization. As the steady stream of settlers poured westward from the East, and the pioneers preceded it in a restless advance, the movement of population was thus turned northward instead of westward, from the Ohio-Illinois country.

But the Indians were in treaty possession of much of the Old Northwest, and across the international boundary were scattered English to serve as a reminder that there was an intangible but very real barrier to advance beyond the Lakes. Treaty after treaty had been made with the savages, only to be broken, reserving lands to them with an ever-retreating line against the inflow of the whites. In the dozen years preceding 1809, the savages had "sold" 48,000,000 acres, not seldom when made drunk for the purpose, and without any apparent satisfaction of the whites' insatiable demand for land.

Finally two leaders arose among the red men, Tecumseh and his brother who was called the Prophet, sons of a Shawnee. These two men, the finest perhaps that the savages developed in their history, conceived the statesmanlike plan of reforming the Indians, keeping them from drink, stopping the alienation of their lands, and uniting all the tribes into one great confederation which should hold itself aloof from contact with the whites and defend the natives' own mode of life. For a short while they were successful and even induced their followers to give up rum. A large settlement of Indians under the leadership of the two brothers was established at the junction of Tippecanoe Creek and the Wabash River, and it seemed at last as if they might be able to make a final stand against obliteration or submergence by the whites.

The latter were thoroughly alarmed. Hitherto a "good Indian" had been a dead Indian, but if the savages reformed, declined to drink and to make any bargains the whites offered them when drunk, and settled down to a civilized life, what would become of the easy method of dispossessing them of the lands the whites coveted? William Henry Harrison, Governor of Indiana Territory, which comprised all that was left of the Old Northwest after the creation of the State of Ohio and the Territories of Illinois and Michigan, decided finally to settle the question in frontier fashion. He got together a few Indians and made a "treaty" with them which transferred Tecumseh's hunting grounds to the whites, a treaty which Tecumseh rightly regarded as void.

The Indian leader's power grew, however, and more tribes joined him, until, while he was absent in the South trying to gain the Creeks over to his plans, Harrison moved swiftly with over 1000 troops to Tecumseh's settlement at Tippecanoe with the intention of forcing hostilities. At first the Indians attempted a peaceful discussion, but Tecumseh had already warned Harrison that a conflict might be difficult to avoid if the whites persisted in their policy. The presence of the troops, nicely timed by Harrison to coincide with the absence of Tecumseh, was a provocation, and the Indians fell upon them in the night. It has been claimed that Harrison had made a truce and that the attack upon him was treacherous. Under the circumstances, however, and considering the whole trend of Indian relations in the district it is not easy to see why all the morality should be expected on the Indian side. In any case, Harrison routed the attackers, forced them to flee, and then destroyed their entire village.

"Tippecanoe and Tyler, too" were made for a Presidential campaign many years later, but our interest in the episode in this chapter is in its bearing on our relations with England. The affair was a bit raw, and advantage was taken of the belief through the West that the British in Canada were egging on the Indians against us to divert any criticism from Harrison and our pioneer settlers to the hated English. The truth of this is still open to question, though the savages had secured arms from the British, but the country was made to believe that we had not only been right in fighting Tecumseh but that our Northwestern settlements were unsafe from Indian attack so long as the British remained in Canada.

Three days before the massacre by Harrison at Tippecanoe, Congress met in Washington. A little over a fortnight later, Monroe became Secretary of State with the hope of averting war, but there was a group of young new members in the Congress who were yet more insistent upon bringing war to pass. There had been a surprisingly large turnover in the membership of the House as the result of the election, and the "War Hawks," as the aggressive new comers were to be called, formed an important element, though all so young that they were either unborn or in their cradles when the Declaration of Independence had been signed. Henry Clay of Kentucky was their leader, thirty-four years old, and most prominent in the group were John C. Calhoun of South Carolina (twenty-nine), Langdon Cheves (thirty-five) from the same State, Felix Grundy (thirty-six) from Tennessee, and Peter B. Porter (forty) of western New York.

These young men and others who joined with them were of a wholly different generation of Republicans from Jefferson, Madison, and Monroe; were impatient with the older statesmen and their methods; and most of them were closely connected with the Western frontier. Grundy, for example, had had three brothers killed by Indians, and Porter had bought a large tract of land just this side of the Canadian border along the Niagara River. Quickly combining with sufficient other members to organize the House, they elected Clay as Speaker, thus controlling the appointment of committees.

None of these new members, soon to have their way with our foreign relations, had, it will be noted, any relation with New England and the shipping interests of the country. In spite of European difficulties the ship owners had been doing very well indeed since the passage of the Macon Bill, our exports in 1811 having risen to $67,000,000, half of our commerce being with England, until Non-Intercourse was revived. With the return of prosperity, no more complaints had been made about impressment of seamen,—a subject in which the War Hawks had no direct interest whatever. What these really wanted was the annexation of Canada, which they absurdly claimed could be conquered in six weeks if we went to war with England. As propaganda in the West, they talked of the perfidy of the British "scalp-buyers" who incited the Indians to attack our settlers, but as this was not a topic which greatly interested the East they also made fervid orations about "sailors' rights" and the freedom of the seas.

In May, 1811, Commodore Rodgers in the U. S. frigate *President* was patrolling the coast off New York to carry out the orders of the Secretary of the Navy issued two years before (during which time nothing had happened), to resist any infringements of our national dignity. Having heard that the British frigate *Guerrière* had impressed an American seaman, Rodgers gave chase to what he thought was the *Guerrière* and after a fight of several hours forced the British vessel, which proved to be only the sloop of war *Little Belt,* to strike her colors. This added to the popular desire for war and wiped out the disgrace of the *Chesapeake* affair in the popular mind.

New England, and the shipping interests generally, were bitterly opposed to bringing on a conflict with England but more and more pressure was being brought to bear on President Madison. He would come up for re-election in 1812 and so far his record had been rather a dismal failure. Much the most aggressive section of his own party, that of the War Hawks with Clay and Calhoun in the lead, demanded war for the sake of annexing Canada, and it has been said that they made war a condition of Madison's renomination.

This may not have influenced him, for Madison was an honest if not a strong man, but on May 19, 1812, despatches arrived from England in one of which the British Foreign Office declined to rescind any of the Orders in Council until Napoleon unequivocally rescinded his Decrees, and stated that Madison's acceptance of the Emperor's shuffling and treacherous statements was "utterly subversive of the most important and indisputable maritime rights of the British Empire." Madison, pressed hard by the War Hawks and unwilling to admit that Napoleon had duped him, asked Congress, on June 1, 1812, for a declaration of war on England, mainly on the grounds of violation of our three-mile limit, of paper blockades, Orders in Council, and impressment of our seamen. Napoleon and the Westerners had won, and New England was plunged in gloom. On June 18 war was declared.

We had no minister in France. Pinkney unhappily had left us

unrepresented in England in order to satisfy his personal sense of irritation. We had, however, a very able minister in Russia, John Quincy Adams, who pointed out that Napoleon's system of Decrees was nearing its downfall. Our *chargé d'affaires* at our deserted Legation in Paris warned Madison that Napoleon's sole aim was to inveigle us into a war with England to further his own aims. Within the past three years our genuine difficulties with England had greatly diminished and were mostly due to our having let ourselves into the trap set by the French Emperor, who according to figures submitted by Madison himself had seized in the ports of France, Denmark, Holland, Spain, and Naples, 558 of our vessels in the preceding five years as against 389 taken by the British. The President admitted that it was hard for him to understand what Napoleon meant but with extraordinary naïveté set that down to the Emperor's "ignorance of commerce"! In declaring war on England we thus joined the side of the tyrant who was overrunning and enslaving the whole of Europe.

England did not want war with us. Had we had a minister in London we should have known this fact. A good part of the blame for the war must be laid on Pinkney's peculiarly thin skin covering an inflated ego. England, fighting Napoleon for the good of the world, was almost at her last stand in 1811. Her debt was $4,000,-000,000, an almost unbelievably large sum more than a century ago. Her exports had declined a good third in 1811. She was being bled white. There were riots among the poor, and the madness of the King and the assassination of the Prime Minister had at critical moments interfered with her consideration of American questions. In May, 1812, the House of Commons was debating the suspension of the Orders in Council to conciliate us, even without action by Napoleon.

Unluckily, Percival's assassination delayed action by requiring a new Ministry to be formed, but on June 16 it was announced in the Commons that the Orders in Council would be immediately suspended, and the formal Order carrying out this promise was signed June 23. Had Pinkney not left in a huff, we should have known of the British attitude and intentions. When we did know, it was too late. We had declared war two days after the announcement suspending the Orders had been made in Parliament. Had there been a trans-Atlantic cable in those days there would have been no war.

Public opinion as to the conflict was much divided in the United States. Many agreed with John Marshall that he felt mortified that America should have submitted to Napoleon, who, the week after war was declared, started his campaign of complete European conquest against Russia. The war for "free trade and sailors' rights" found no sympathy in the chief maritime sections of our country, New England and New York. In the election of 1812, New Hampshire, Massachusetts, Rhode Island, Connecticut, New York, New Jersey, and Delaware were to vote solidly against Madison, and this may be taken as a rough indication of the sectional attitude toward the war, although a single Eastern State, Pennsylvania, may be said to have turned the scale in favor of hostilities against England. Pennsylvania, however, although it had twenty-five electoral votes, was not a section, and the sections solid for the war, the South and the West, had practically never had a sailor impressed and scarce owned an ocean-going ship. The South, almost solidly Republican, or Democratic, both names being then used for the same party, was traditionally in favor of France, though republican France had no similarity to the despotism of Napoleon; and the West wanted Canada. Both France and England had trampled on our rights. We had heavy grievances against both of them, but France had not impressed our sailors and, which was more important, had no territory we coveted in North America.

The United States has never prepared for any war in advance, even when hostilities may have been imminent for a long time before their actual outbreak. The War of 1812 was no exception, though for years the possibility of war had been before us. We had, perhaps, about 8000 troops, mostly located in the West at Indian posts. Our few frigates and the useless small gun-boats were insignificant in comparison with the navy of England, then the most powerful she had ever possessed.

Worst of all was the division of sentiment in the nation. In New England church bells were tolled and flags hung at half mast when the declaration of war was announced. Massachusetts, Rhode Island, and Connecticut refused to allow their militia to be ordered out as Congress required, and during the entire war the New England section, which had accumulated half the specie of the country, did all in its power to obstruct the financial operations of the government, and subscribed to less than $3,000,000 of the $41,000,000 which was raised by the Treasury. The War Hawks, however, were as optimistic as they were jubilant. Calhoun declared that within a month the most important sections of Canada would be ours, and Clay boasted about the men of Kentucky alone being able to effect the conquest.

Fortunately for us, England in the Spanish peninsula and elsewhere, as well as on the seas, was so desperately locked in the conflict with Napoleon that she could spare little strength or thought for ourselves as enemies. In spite of that, the first campaigns of the war were disastrous failures for us. We were to pour our troops into Canada in four expeditions, one by way of Detroit, one by way of Fort Niagara, one across the St. Lawrence at Kingston, and one by the old route up Lake Champlain. The plan, badly conceived, was even worse executed.

The 2000 men under an old Revolutionary soldier, General William Hull, forming the first expedition, had marched some 200 miles from southern Ohio to Detroit, and were at that post when news of the war reached them, with the orders to invade Canada. Hull crossed the border and started to besiege the British post at Malden. While there he heard that the British had captured our garrison at Michilimackinac, and the Canadian commander, the able General Isaac Brock, having brought up reinforcements to Malden, Hull fell back again on Detroit. There he had over 1000 men and ample arms and ammunition but when Brock pursued him with 700 troops and several hundred Indians, Hull, in a funk, surrendered both the fort and the entire American force, August 16, 1812, thus losing with Detroit the control of the whole of our own Northwest.

Instead of our conquering Canada, the Canadian border had been pushed down to the Wabash and Ohio Rivers, for Chicago, then Fort Dearborn, had also fallen. Brock carried off Hull and the Americans as prisoners of war to Niagara, to deal there with the second expedition. Later, Hull was tried by American court-martial and condemned to be shot as guilty of cowardice, but the President reprieved him on account of his old service in the Revolution.

Early in October the Americans and Canadians were watching

each other across the Niagara River, and on the 13th a small detachment of American regulars was ferried across to attack the British on Queenston Heights, Brock being killed in the subsequent engagement. Nothing was gained by the Americans, for the New York militia under General Van Rensselaer, who should have gone to support the regulars, refused to budge over the boundary line of their State, and almost incredibly, calmly sat and watched their fellow Americans being shot down by the British. Van Rensselaer and General Alexander Smythe of the regular army had quarrelled over every detail, and now Smythe took charge. There were 4000 men in the force but not over 1000 would agree to cross into Canada. Smythe, like Hull, lost his courage and blustered and funked alternately. Congressman Porter challenged him to a duel after accusing him of cowardice. The only result of the campaign thus far had been the exploding of the reputations of three generals.

Nothing came of the Kingston expedition, but General Dearborn was still at Plattsburg with a force of between 1000 and 2000 men. On November 19 he marched these to the Canadian border where they, like their brothers in the West, sat down and refused to cross the line. Dearborn calmly marched them back the twenty miles again, and the "conquest of Canada," which the War Hawks had promised should be completed in a month, was getting to be a roaring farce, at which even we Americans had to laugh between our fits of irritation.

For a while, however, we had better luck at sea, and a few famous fights cheered us greatly. On August 19, 1812, Captain Isaac Hull, a nephew of General Hull, redeemed both the family and national names from disgrace, three days after his uncle's cowardly surrender of Detroit, by battering the British frigate *Guerrière* to pieces and forcing her surrender. His own vessel, the *Constitution,* carried forty-four guns to the thirty-eight of the British, but the chief point was that the Britisher who had been most active in impressment had had to strike his colors to the American navy. In October news came that the American sloop-of-war *Wasp,* eighteen guns, had captured the British sloop *Frolic,* evenly matched and in fair fight. Then Commodore Decatur, in the frigate *United States,* turned up at New London with the British frigate *Macedonian* as a prize. That one of the best frigates in the British Navy should be taken into an Ameri-

THE DEATH OF TECUMSEH IN THE BATTLE OF THE THAMES

From the engraving by Wellstood after the painting by Chappel. From the Library of Congress.

THE CAPTURE OF THE *JAVA* BY THE CONSTITUTION

From the lithograph by Sarony and Major, 1846. From the Library of Congress.

can port as a prize was getting a bit too much for the English, who had regarded themselves as invincible at sea.

A few weeks later, however, Captain Bainbridge in the *Constitution* destroyed the equally powerful British frigate *Java* off the Brazilian coast, and in February, 1813, the U.S.S. *Hornet* sank the *Peacock*. We had forced three British frigates and three sloops-of-war to surrender in six months, and ourselves had lost only the gallant little eighteen-gun *Wasp*, which had been captured with small glory by the British seventy-four-gun frigate *Poictiers*. Moreover, our privateers, partly from New England but more largely from the Middle States, had been playing havoc with British commerce, capturing over 300 vessels. America was jubilant, and it was largely these early and striking naval victories in single battle, with Perry's later exploit, which left the impression that somehow it had been a glorious war for us.

In June, 1813, Captain Lawrence in the *Chesapeake* met the British frigate *Shannon* off the Massachusetts coast and in fifteen minutes was forced to surrender, and from then on the control of the sea

THEATRE.

The public is respectfully informed that the Theatre will be ILLUMINATED THIS EVENING in commemoration of the late GLORIOUS AND BRILLIANT VICTORY OBTAINED BY THE U. STATES FRIGATE CONSTITUTION.

On WEDNESDAY EVENING, February 24th, Will be performed (for the first time in America) the Historical Drama of, THE RENEGADE, By J. Reynolds, Esq author of Exiles, Free Nights, &c. as now performing in London with great applause,

Between the Play and Farce a Patriotic Sketch in one act, called America, Commerce and Freedom. View of the sea, the Genius of America, descends in a Car, the Temple of Naval Glory rises out of the ocean. A Letter Dance by the Infant Vestris, Miss Jones and Mast. Whale; in which the names of Hull, Jones, Decatur, and Bainbridge will be displayed. A naval column will rise from the Stage in honor of Hull, Jones, Decatur and Bainbridge, surmounted by a full-length portrait of COMMODORE BAINBRIDGE.

The whole exhibition to conclude with a painting in transparency, descriptive of the BLOWING UP OF THE BRITISH FRIGATE JAVA, On the 31st December, 1812.

In course of the sketch the following songs will be sung, America, Commerce & Freedom, by Mr. Darley—Yankee Chronology, by Mr. Yates; Yankee Frolicks by Mr. M'Farland.

To which will be added, HOW TO DIE FOR LOVE. The Box office will be opened on Friday morning.

GENERAL COMMITTEE.
☞ The members of the General Committee of Federal Republicans, are requested to attend a meeting of the Committee on Tuesday evening Feb. 23, at 7 o'clock, at Washington Hall. Feb. 22

UNION BANK.

CELEBRATION OF THE VICTORY OF THE *CONSTITUTION* HELD AT THE PARK THEATRE, NEW YORK

From an advertisement in "The New York Evening Post" of February 23, 1813, in the New York Historical Society.

became completely British. Our coast was blockaded from New London to the extreme South, and by the autumn we did not have a single ship of our own off the shores. How complete the blockade became is shown by the drop in exports from New York from $12,000,000 in 1811 to $200,000 in 1814 and a fall in those from Virginia from $4,800,000 to $17,500. England had bottled us up and put in the cork.

On the other hand, affairs began to look up inside our boundaries. Harrison took command of a new and much larger force in the West for the purpose of recapturing Detroit, and to support him Captain Oliver H. Perry built five additional ships on Lake Erie, and with his little fleet of nine vessels completely defeated a somewhat less powerful squadron of the British. The English vessels carried sixty-three guns to the American fifty-seven but ours were heavier, and in the end weight told, although Perry's tactics had been brilliant. His brief despatch telling of the victory to Harrison read simply, "We have met the enemy and they are ours; two ships, two brigs, one schooner, and one sloop."

Harrison had already suffered the defeat of two of the three columns he had directed toward Detroit but Perry's victory clearing the lakes caused the British general, Proctor, to abandon Detroit and Malden, which immediately thereafter were occupied by Harrison. He pursued the retreating British, defeating them in the Battle of the Thames, in which Tecumseh, who had naturally gone over to the English side, was killed. The Northwest was again in our hands, though that was slight comfort. Some additional fighting on land and another small naval engagement, on Lake Ontario, were indecisive, but the war on both sides was becoming more barbarous. On December 19, 1813, we burned the town of Queenston, leaving the inhabitants to shift for themselves on a bitter winter night. In revenge the British captured Fort Niagara, and destroyed Buffalo, then a small village, letting the Indians loose on the surrounding country.

By the spring of 1814 most of the incompetent higher officers had been cleared out of our army, and among the surviving major or brigadier generals were George Izard, Jacob Brown, Andrew Jackson, Peter B. Porter, and Winfield Scott. On July 3, Scott defeated the British at Chippewa in a well-fought action, and on the 25th

ENGLAND PREPARING TO REPLACE THE FLEET DESTROYED BY McDONOUGH

From a cartoon by William Charles in the New York Public Library.

Brown inflicted heavy losses on the Canadians at Lundy's Lane, although the victory lay with the latter, and at best the encounter must be considered as a drawn battle. Napoleon had abdicated in April, and the British were at last free to wage war against us in earnest.

Large reinforcements were sent to Canada, and by August over 10,000 veterans of the Duke of Wellington's Spanish campaigns, commanded by General Prevost, were in Montreal waiting to invade us by way of Lake Champlain, as of old. Prevost marched southward, reaching Plattsburg early in September, where he had prepared a flotilla of lake boats. We also had a fleet of small vessels under command of Commodore MacDonough, although it was much weaker than Prevost's, being capable of throwing a broadside of only 759 pounds against the British 1128. The Americans won in a brilliant little action, and Prevost having lost control of the waterway, there was nothing for him to do but to retreat with his 10,000 men, who had been opposed on land by only 1500 American regulars with some militia.

Good news was sorely needed, for affairs were otherwise going very badly. Our commerce had been almost annihilated, owing to the complete blockade, which in the spring of 1814 had been extended to Massachusetts. The government was nearly bankrupt, the blockade having cut off almost all revenue from customs duties, and New England having refused to contribute from its hoard of specie to the purchase of loans. The last loan offered had failed, and all banks south of Connecticut had suspended specie payment.

The British appeared to be in full control of all our coast, and with entire impunity had been landing marauding parties, burning farms and villages. In August they put ashore forces on the bank of the Patuxent River and marched unopposed for some days toward Washington, reaching Bladensburg on the 24th. The capital was wholly undefended, and every one there got in a panic. About 7000 militia, without training, were hurriedly raised to oppose the further advance of the enemy, but these raw recruits broke and fled in a rout at the first encounter. That night the British reached Washington and deliberately burned the public buildings and many of our national records. The President had to flee and hide in the woods, leaving his uneaten dinner on the White House table to be enjoyed by the British.

In the far South Andrew Jackson had been trying to carry out the cherished wish of the Southerners to possess themselves of Spanish Florida. The first year, after having started a little campaign of his own, Jackson was recalled because Madison did not wish to involve us in war with Spain. The next year, however, a rising of the Creek Indians in Mississippi Territory gave an excuse for a punitive expedition, and after having forced the Indians to sign a treaty giving us two thirds of the present State of Alabama, Jackson continued his march eastward, and captured the Spanish settlement of Pensacola. However, rumors of an important British attack on New Orleans led the War Department to order him westward, and with great reluctance our too casual Westerner had to abandon his attack on the possessions of a friendly power.

Meanwhile both England and ourselves were heartily sick of the war. The rescinding of the Orders in Council had really removed the cause of the struggle before it had begun, though we did not know it. The English people had never wanted the war with us, and now negotiations began almost immediately to terminate it. Had it not been for the Orders in Council of the British and the trap laid for us by Napoleon we would never have gone in. The Orders had been rescinded and Napoleon's perfidy had been fully proved. There seemed no reason why peace should not have been made in 1812 almost as soon as the affair started. The War Hawks, however, were determined to get Canada. This could not be avowed, and so some cause of delay in ending the fight until they got what they wanted had to be found. The war was thus fought from the beginning on the sole ostensible issue of forcing England to abandon the practice of impressment.

Yet New England, whose sailors it was, for the most part, who had been impressed, would have nothing of this issue. When Madison published a list of 6057 men who had been taken, a committee of the Massachusetts legislature reported that this number was "three or four times too large." The war was enormously adding to the manufacturing capacity of New England, just as the earlier measures of Embargo and Non-Intercourse had, but the Federalist

Party, now in power there again, was as yet a party of the shipping interest. Disaffection to the national government had been steadily increasing. Many acts of both governors and legislatures can hardly be regarded as less than traitorous, and finally, at the darkest moment of the war, in October, 1814, came a call from the Massachusetts legislature for a convention to meet at Hartford for the purpose, among others, of arranging for another convention from all the States to revise the Constitution.

The call created great alarm in the nation. It was absurd to talk of revising the Constitution in the midst of a war, and there is little doubt that the more violent Federalists, such as Timothy Pickering and some of the Essex Junto, had secession in view, the alternative, a new Constitution taking power from the South and West to bestow it on New England, being obviously out of the realm of practical politics. The convention met behind closed doors on December 15, and at last issued suggestions which were clearly the result of compromise. They did not suggest the desire for secession but did say that if the Union were to be dissolved it should be done in peace time, and that "States which have no common umpire must be their own judges, and execute their own decisions." The situation disclosed was serious, more for what was not publicly avowed than for what was.

While New England was thus toying with the thought of breaking up the Union, suddenly came the news that Andrew Jackson had completely defeated the British in a great battle at New Orleans. Sir Edward Pakenham with 50 vessels and 10,000 troops had arrived at the mouth of the Mississippi and moved against the city, which Jackson had been recalled from Florida to defend. The American forces were much inferior to the British but were composed of splendid marksmen from Kentucky and Tennessee, devoted to their commander. Pakenham delayed, and Jackson took up a strong position against which, with foolish hardihood, Pakenham determined to launch a frontal attack. There had been some skirmishes when the final assault was made on January 8, 1815. The frontiersmen simply mowed down the British regulars as they gallantly advanced according to the orders of Pakenham, who was himself killed. The foolhardiness of the attack was demonstrated

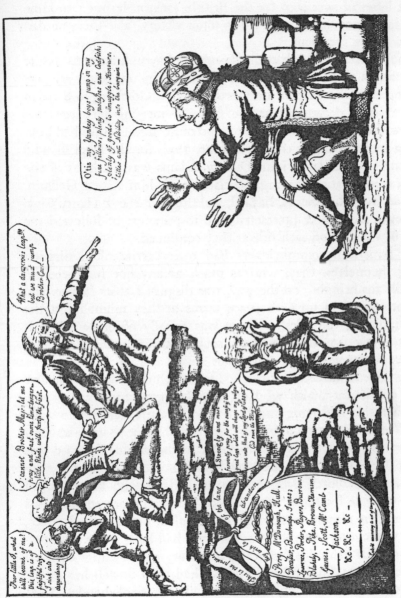

THE HARTFORD CONVENTION OR LEAP OR NO LEAP

George III urging the New England States to secede.

From a cartoon by William Charles in the New York Public Library.

by the Americans losing only eight killed and thirteen wounded against losses of over 2000 for the British. Jackson leaped into fame throughout a country longing for some victory, and the war had made a future President.

In point of fact, the battle was useless for, unknown as yet to Americans, a treaty of peace had been signed by our commissioners with the English at Ghent on Christmas Eve. Göteborg in Sweden had first been designated as the place of meeting but for some unknown reason had been changed, and our commissioners had been waiting in the Belgian city since June, 1814, for the English who came some weeks later. John Quincy Adams was the head of the American delegation, having associated with him Albert Gallatin, Jonathan Russell, James A. Bayard, and the War Hawk Henry Clay. The negotiations were protracted, and to some extent followed the course of victories on each side as they continued.

The American commissioners had many acrimonious disputes among themselves. Clay, who as much as any one had been responsible for bringing on the war, was disgusted at its failure, and was entirely taken up with peace terms as they might affect the Mississippi and the West. Adams was equally obstinate when it came to New England questions, such as the fisheries. The English negotiators were men of inferior ability and wholly lacking in tact. In the end a treaty was patched up which did not mention any of the objects for which we had ostensibly gone to war.

Neither side had won, and both were heartily sick of the stalemate. We could not do any more than we had done with scarce a ship against the strongest naval power in the world. England was licking her wounds after the long Napoleonic campaign and, staggering under colossal debts and taxes, had no wish to prolong a useless struggle for no apparent object. The two peace commissions disagreed on almost everything except that both wanted peace, which was signed December 24. The war had been worse than useless, for it left behind it for nearly a century hard feelings between the two nations. England believed we had tried to stab her in the back while she was engaged in an almost single-handed fight against the man who wished to make himself universal tyrant in Europe; and we, having chosen England instead of France as the enemy, began to develop the legend of her being our constant and inveterate foe. The only one who had gained from the War of 1812 between England and America was Napoleon, and when peace was made he was already in exile.

CHAPTER XII

THE ERA OF GOOD FEELING

ROM the very beginning of American settlement until
that Christmas Eve, 1814, when peace was made at Ghent,
Europe and our relations to it had been among the most
prominent of the mental preoccupations of the American
people. Throughout the whole colonial period our fairly constant
squabbling with Parliament or Royal Governors kept our depend-
ence upon Europe constantly before us. As part of an European
Empire we had been involved in all the wars started in the Old
World between the greater powers. Then came the Revolution, and
after Independence we were, as we have seen, caught in every eddy
of the Napoleonic conflicts. With peace both in Europe and America, however, there began an entirely new era. The Christmas present which the American people received in December, 1814, was
nothing less that an almost precise century of time in which to con-
centrate solely upon their own problems of organizing their government and society and of the physical conquest of the continent,
with scarce a thought of the Old World, its standards, ideals, or em-
broilments.

I do not mean that we were completely isolated, for we have never
been that, but our relations with Europe became matters for statesmen and secretaries of state to deal with rather than forces which
compelled the people at large to keep their eyes turned eastward
over-seas, diverting their energies, complicating their national policies and dividing us on questions with which we had no immediate
concern instead of on those naturally arising from our domestic
economic and sectional problems. In May, 1815, we sent Captain
Decatur with a small fleet to force Algiers, Tunis, and Tripoli to
respect our rights and to renounce all levying of tribute on us
for the future. It was a significant little gesture, and our final
shot in Europe until 1917. With immense zest we made a complete

right-about-face and turned our thoughts and energies from overseas eastward to the development of the natural resources in the West.

The attitude of the Federalists toward the war, and more especially the nation's extreme dislike of the proceedings of the Hartford Convention, had left the Federalist Party without a shred of power or influence save in Massachusetts, Connecticut, and Delaware, which States cast their vote for Rufus King in the Presidential election of 1816. There were then nineteen States in the Union, five west of the mountains, and every one of the nineteen, except the three named, went solidly for James Monroe, who was elected by 183 votes to King's 34. So certain was the result held to be in advance that there was no real contest anywhere. Four years later, in the election of 1820, the "last of the Virginia dynasty" was re-elected by an even more overwhelming vote of 231 to 1, a single dissenting vote only, from New Hampshire, preventing Monroe from sharing with Washington the honor of an unanimous election.

Largely from the absence of an opposition party, his eight years of office have been called the "era of good feelings." Rather it may be called the era of slack water, of pause before new and violent controversies were to be aroused by the problems and personalities now coming to the front. The old Federalist Party had disintegrated, but the Republican Party, by force of circumstances, had become more than half Federalist in its policies. From the acquisition of Louisiana by Jefferson onward, one measure after another, seemingly necessitated by the exigencies or opportunities of the moment, had come to make it difficult to distinguish a Republican in practice from a Federalist in theory. The break-up of the Federalists was so obviously complete that the Republican Party was alone left in the field, but that fact tended to obscure another which was that by a continual shifting of their ground and abandonment of clear-cut principles the Republicans also were preparing a break-up of their own party, impregnable as it seemed with its vote of 231 to 1 in 1820.

Inaugurated in March, 1817, Monroe made John Quincy Adams, son of old President John Adams and one of the most distinguished diplomats of the time, his Secretary of State. The appointment could not have been bettered, although it was in part made for geographical reasons. Of the five Presidents thus far elected, four had been Virginians, and if Monroe were re-elected, as seemed inevitable, the nation would have had a Virginian for chief Executive for thirty-two years out of the first thirty-six of its existence.

Antagonism was developing to this continued control by the South, and Monroe for that reason wished to put a New England man in the highest post in the Cabinet, although by doing so he disgruntled Henry Clay, who promptly declined the offer of the War Department, and was elected Speaker of the House. Calhoun accepted the War portfolio, and William H. Crawford of Georgia continued at the Treasury. With William Wirt of Virginia as Attorney General, the Cabinet was entirely drawn from the South with the exception of Adams.

Other than in trade, the losses of the war had not been great. Only about 1500 men had been killed in battle, although the total casualties were several times that number. With the exception of the destruction of our new buildings and of our records in Washington, there had been little serious damage to property on shore, raidings, along the coast, of farms or villages having been more exasperating than costly. The blockade had destroyed most of our trade temporarily, as we have noted, and in the fall of 1813 there could have been seen 249 ocean-going vessels, 90 of them among the largest owned, tied up at their wharves at Boston while the British patrolled the sea. With the return of peace, however, trade began to move again like a freshet thawed out in the spring, and in one month 144 vessels cleared from Boston for all parts of the world. Conditions were rapidly changing, however, and, partly due to the war and partly to other causes, the alignment between the three sections of the country was to become much sharper than ever in the next few decades.

Embargo, Non-Intercourse, and the blockade of the war had all acted as forced draughts under the development of American manufactures. In New England in 1807 there had been only 8000 spindles in the cotton mills. In 1815 there were 500,000. What was true of the textile industry in that section was also true of iron manufacturing in the Middle Colonies, and to a lesser degree of manufacturing generally in the North. New England did not yet realize that her future was in the factory and not on the sea, and the old

MILLS AT NORWICH FALLS, CONNECTICUT

From the engraving by H. Knecht, circa 1862, by courtesy of The Mabel Brady Garvan Institute of American Arts and Crafts, Yale University.

A COTTON PLANTATION IN THE SOUTH

From Lewis's "Das Illustrirte Mississippithal," Düsseldorf, 1854, in the Rare Book Room of the New York Public Library.

LE MARQUIS DE LAFAYETTE IN 1824

From the painting by Thomas Sully, owned by the City of Philadelphia. In the collection at Independence Hall, Philadelphia.

shipping merchants fought bitterly against the change, the interests of the two forms of employment of capital being diametrically opposed to one another, the shippers wanting free-trade and heavy importations, the growing manufacturers wishing protective tariffs and home markets limited to domestic goods.

By the end of the war it is said that 100,000 men, women, and children, mostly the latter two, were employed in New England in textile mills alone, and both this growing industrialism, and the increasing trade with the interior of the country, were rapidly developing urban centres of population. This was true of the North and to a lesser extent of the West but not of the South. Thus between 1810 and 1820 Boston rose from 32,250 to 43,300, New York from 96,400 to 123,700, Philadelphia from 91,900 to 112,800, and Baltimore from 35,600 to 62,700, whereas the metropolis of the South, Charleston, remained stationary at 24,700, showing an increase of only 69 persons in ten years. New Orleans, however, as the great entrêpot for all the direct export trade of the West, was advancing as rapidly as the Northern cities. The great trend toward urbanization of the population was not to set in fully until about 1820, continuing from that time to the present day, but the difference in that respect between North and South had already become evident.

For a time after the signing of peace, the Northern factories were hard pressed by what we would call today "dumping" by British manufacturers. Fearing the increasing American competition, the British deliberately shipped over all the goods they could at prices below cost of production, not for immediate profit but with the deliberate intent to throttle young and dangerous rivals. It was a policy which could not be indefinitely sustained and, in spite of our severe crisis of 1819, manufacturing had taken too deep root to be thus killed off.

Unlike agriculture, manufacturing called for considerable amounts of fluid capital, and this was being produced in the North and West but not nearly so rapidly in the South. The capital needed was coming from manufacturing itself, from shipping, and from various forms of quick trading, such as speculating in the rapid rise in values of real estate in growing cities. At the time of the Revolution, planters like Washington and Charles Carroll had been among the richest of Americans, but fifty years later no Southerner could vie in wealth with new men in the North. For example, Stephen Girard in Philadelphia, starting with shipping, was worth perhaps $5,000,000 in 1820, and John Jacob Astor possibly twice that in New York. The latter, a German immigrant who, unknown and almost illiterate, had arrived in that city in 1783, could, by 1808, invest $500,000 capital in one of his enterprises alone, the American Fur Company. Rough and unscrupulous in his methods, uncultured but coarsely vigorous, he thought imperially in business. His plan to establish the seat of his fur trading at Astoria in the Oregon country had been interfered with by the war, but otherwise the conflict had brought him large winnings in lucky shipping ventures, profits from a single voyage sometimes running to $70,000 cash.

In the South little or no such free capital was being created. In that section, capital was chiefly in the form of land and slaves. The export of tobacco fell off sharply after the war, and the increased production of Virginia had to compete with the richer soils of Kentucky and North Carolina. There was little or no surplus of any sort at the year's end in the old tobacco States, where the poorer whites scrabbled for an existence, and the richer saw profits eaten up by the need of keeping on the slaves and their natural increase. The lower South, the "cotton belt," was indeed enlarging its acreage and crops by surprising leaps, but somehow in plantation economy book profits have a way of getting turned back into the property for one need or another.

The new big cotton plantation of that day, run much like a Northern factory in that owner and hands were growing farther apart from all friendly contact, had the disadvantage that the labor supply could not be quickly adjusted to the demands of production or price. Where a Northerner was paying fifty cents or a dollar a day to a man or child whom he could turn off at a moment's notice, the Southerner had to buy his slaves at about $800 each in 1818, and incurred in addition the costly responsibilities of feeding, clothing, and looking after the slave in sickness, knowing that death meant a heavy capital loss. Sometimes an epidemic would carry off a third of the blacks on a plantation in a few weeks. Slack working, petty thieving, the difficulty of getting a good overseer, runaways, sick or dead negroes, all reduced profits.

Capital invested in land and slaves could be made profitable only by raising as large crops as possible, regardless of price. There was incessant demand for new and unworn lands, and the cotton belt spread ever westward. Many of the big old plantation homes were beautiful, and living in them was on a bounteous scale, but capital was not accumulating in liquid form, and the economic life, as well as the social structure, was becoming more and more "set" in the mould of one basic industry instead of being increasingly diversified as in the North. Only a very small proportion of all Southerners were rich enough to own slaves, and the slaveless whites, despised even by the slaves themselves, were driven on to poorer and poorer lands, or emigrated to the West, where they glimpsed a possibility of getting away from the hopeless poverty and the sinking in the social scale which seemed to be their fate in the slave States.

Southern wealth was passing from the old tobacco aristocracy of Virginia, and to some extent from the rice planters of Carolina, to the new cotton magnates, who too frequently had little of the cultural background of the older families. Life in the southern tier of States, with the somewhat enervating climate, the monotonous single industry, the big-scale management of slave labor, and the loneliness of the big plantations must have been dull, and little conducive to intellectual vigor and effort. No Washingtons, Jeffersons, Monroes, or Marshalls were to come from it. On the other hand, much of its most vigorous stock was passing steadily westward.

In 1790, when Washington was inaugurated, there were about 222,000 people living beyond the mountains, or a little over five per cent of our total population. By 1820 the number had risen to over 2,600,000, more than twenty-seven per cent of the whole. During the hard times in the East after the war the stream of westward migration rose to a flood. Emigrants poured along the old roads headed for the Land of Promise. Some were lured by good soils and pleasant situations as they journeyed, and along the Mohawk Valley route, for example, flourishing villages sprang up all the way to Buffalo.

Following the road from Philadelphia the pioneers struck the junction of the Alleghany and Monongahela Rivers, forming the Ohio, at Pittsburgh, and that town quickly became one of the great gateways to the West, where travellers and goods were trans-shipped from wagons to the boats plying down the river. By 1816 it was incorporated as a city, and had its shipyards, rolling mill, steel furnace, and other industries. The National Road, on the construction of which Congress spent $7,000,000, was completed in 1818, carry-

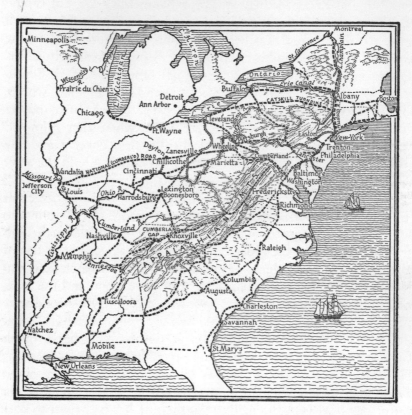

PIONEER ROADS

ing traffic at the rate of ten miles an hour by way of Cumberland to Wheeling, and for a time this road, connected with one from Baltimore, remained the chief route to the Ohio. It was an amazing improvement over any other we had had and greatly facilitated the ceaseless westward flow.

However, until the coming of the railroads, considerably later, land transportation remained costly as compared with water, and another great impetus to the building up of the West came with the development of the steamboat. In 1785, John Fitch had begun his efforts to make steam navigation practical on our rivers, and had tried a steamboat on the Delaware. In spite of his persistence and the regular running of a boat for a while in 1790, he was not to achieve success, and for the most part his experiments met with only jeers from the public. In any case, river boats could not facilitate travel up and down the coast to any extent, due to the direction in which the rivers flowed. In 1802, an uninterrupted line of stage coaches was inaugurated between Boston and Savannah, but these took four days from Boston to New York, one and a half from New York to Philadelphia, fifteen from Philadelphia to Charleston, and two more from that town to Savannah, or twenty-two and a half in all. The 1200 miles was traversed at an average speed of fifty-three miles a day, the hard journey costing $70 for transportation and about $25 more for board and lodging on the way.

River transport was much more important in the West, and also as a means of reaching that section. In 1807, Robert Fulton, to whom the success was to come which had been denied to Fitch, and also perhaps too much of the fame of establishing steam navigation in America, built the famous *Clermont,* which made her trial trip up the Hudson in August. Although her rudder did not work well, and the weight of her engine set in solid masonry was rather too much for the light craft, she reached Albany from New York in thirty-two hours, and a new epoch in our transportation had been opened. The following summer, the vessel ran regularly, and the way having been pointed out, others began to ply on many of our rivers, although their use did not become general until after the War of 1812. Some idea of the remoteness of even the nearer West may be obtained from noting the best time which could be made between New York and Pittsburgh after the *Clermont* had reduced the time up the Hudson to only thirty-two hours. The best route from New York was by way of Albany as that utilized possible water routes to the full, yet by a combination of boat and turnpike it took twenty-three and a half days to cover the 916 miles.

In 1811, an all-water route by steam was opened from Pittsburgh to New Orleans, a vessel named for the latter city making the long trip successfully, although for the next two years she ran only between the Gulf port and Natchez.

In 1819, the first steamship to cross the Atlantic, the *Savannah,* made the trip between New York and Liverpool, and the modern age was dawning. About the same time there were some three-score stern-wheel river steamers operating regularly between Louisville and New Orleans, transporting freight to the upper Ohio River towns for less than half the charge for carrying the same freight overland from Baltimore or Philadelphia. The magnitude of the western trade of the present and future was realized by the Eastern merchants and capitalists, and each city hoped to become the chief clearing point for it, and to hold it against the menace of the Mississippi route. The National Road gave a great advantage to Baltimore, but in 1817 New York State authorized the building of a canal 363 miles long to connect the Hudson at Albany with Lake Erie, and although not finished until 1825 this was to prove one of the determining factors in the forging ahead of New York City.

Canal Celebration.

On Wednesday last, the waters of Lake Erie were admitted into the Great Canal, and that stupendous undertaking completed. The navigation between the Atlantic and the Lakes is now open, and a direct intercourse established between this city and the fertile regions upon the borders of the Canal Friday next, the fourth of November, is fixed for the celebration of this great event. Preparations on a grand scale are making to commemorate the day. The details of the different institutions, societies, &c. have been published in the daily papers. These will form a grand aquatic procession, which will proceed to the Ocean, and having assisted in performing the ceremony of uniting the waters with the Ocean, will return to the Battery at three o'clock. National salutes will be fired from the different Batteries as the procession passes by, both in going and returning. In the evening there will be a Grand Ball in the La Fayette Circus, which is to be considerably enlarged and fitted up for the occasion, in a style of taste and elegance never surpassed in this city. We hope that no accidents will occur which may in any way disturb the rejoicings which are to take place.

NEWSPAPER ANNOUNCEMENT OF THE CELEBRATION ATTENDING THE OPENING OF THE ERIE CANAL

From "The Truth Teller" of October 29, 1825.

The completion of the "big ditch,"—it was only four feet deep,— was celebrated throughout the entire State. A gaily decorated flotilla of canal boats started from Buffalo on October 26, and as the mules drawing it tramped along the towpath, they were startled in every village by shouting crowds who cheered the slow-moving procession of boats on their way. At Buffalo, two kegs of water had been placed on the leading one, and when the flotilla reached New York, this was towed out to Sandy Hook, where Governor Clinton poured the water from the lake into that of the sea, with the inevitable flow of accompanying oratory. The cannon on the Battery roared a salute, and that night there were balls, dinners, and illuminations in the city which was rejoicing in the vistas of new prosperity opened to it.

By 1820 the West had filled with incredible rapidity. Ohio, which had had only 50,000 inhabitants when admitted to Statehood eighteen years earlier, had grown to 600,000, and had more people than Massachusetts. Wealth was accumulating in its rising cities, whose streets and houses seemed to duplicate those of the most conservative of New England towns. It was a far cry from the log cabin to the homes of the wealthy Ohio merchants. Nevertheless, the old Federalist fears of a shift in the balance of power seemed to be becoming realities. Louisiana had been admitted to the Union in 1812, Indiana 1816, Mississippi 1817, Illinois 1818, Alabama 1819, and, as we shall

JAMES BEDDO.

Proprietor of the Mail Stage, from Montgomery Ala. to Fort Mitchell.

INFORMS the Public, that his Stages are now in operation, and that he has made arrangements with Mr. Henry Crowell, and H. Knox, Proprietors of the Stage from Fort Mitchell, to Milledgeville, to keep up a regular LINE OF STAGES, twice a week, from Montgomery Ala. to Milledgeville Geo. leaving the Globe Tavern, Montgomery, every Tuesday and Friday, at 2 o'clock A. M.

ADVERTISEMENT OF THE MAIL STAGE RUNNING TWICE A WEEK FROM MONTGOMERY TO FORT MITCHELL, WHERE CONNECTIONS WERE MADE FOR MILLEDGEVILLE

From "The Mobile Commercial Register," May 19, 1823. By courtesy of the Mobile City Library.

presently note, Missouri was to come in in 1821 as part of the bargain by which Maine was added the year before. The two States of Louisiana and Missouri, the latter with over 70,000 inhabitants, both lay almost entirely on the west bank of the Mississippi River, and both pioneering and settlement had passed far across that stream. Following in part of the route of the Lewis and Clark exploring expedition of 1803–06, Astor's fur traders who bought in the Far West had penetrated overland to the Oregon coast.

In this new western empire there were already flourishing centres such as St. Louis, Louisville, Cincinnati, and other cities and towns, before long to far exceed in population any of the centres of the old South. Speaking of Cincinnati, for example, in the 1819 edition of *The American Universal Geography,* its author, Jedidiah Morse, notes that in 1810 its population was 2540, in 1815 about 6500, and in 1819 about 10,000. It possessed nine churches for different denominations and a stone flour-mill nine stories high, but after giving other statistics the author adds plaintively, "so rapid are the improvements in this and other towns, and indeed of this whole western country, that it cannot be expected that a geographer should be able to keep pace with them." We were, as Calhoun said, "rapidly—I was about to say fearfully—growing."

We were not, however, growing in the finer arts. The general level of culture, under the pressure of all this new economic exploitation, was lower than it had been a half century earlier. There were no painters to rank with the Copleys, Peales, and Wests of the late colonial period, and poor Morse, when speaking of the nation as a whole, had to stumble badly when he came to discuss "literature." "Few men, in America," he wrote, "have originally sufficient property to justify them in devoting their lives to the pursuits of literature . . . and Mæcenases are indeed but rarely found in a country where wealth or office is the general object of pursuit." If "men of learning of the English stamp" were seldom found in America, he noted, nevertheless, that nowhere else except in Scotland was general education so diffused among the entire people.

However, Washington Irving had published his *Knickerbocker's History of New York* in 1809. *The North American Review* had started on its long career in 1815, and *The American Journal of Science and the Arts* was established three years later. In 1817 *The North American Review* had printed Bryant's "Thanatopsis," though it must be admitted that when that and his "To a Waterfowl!" were submitted to the editors one of them claimed that there must be some imposition, as no one in America was capable of writing such verse.

The predominant interest of the period was material development, and the colossal work confronting us was that of providing for the material needs of a people multiplying and spreading with incredible speed,—needs of transportation, of housing, of financing, of almost everything. This task, combined with the hitherto undreamed-of size of the prizes which might fall to the fortunate,

FAIRVIEW INN, BALTIMORE, MARYLAND

A stopping-place on Frederick Road, on the route to the West at the beginning of the nineteenth century.

From a water-color in the collection of the Maryland Historical Society.

VIEW ON THE ERIE CANAL, 1830–1831

From a water-color drawing by J. W. Hill in the Stokes Collection, New York Public Library.

like Girard or Astor, inevitably deflected us away from the humane culture of our eighteenth century. On the other hand, Morse was also right in pointing to the diffusion of education as something to be noted.

We became, as we were long to remain, furiously materialistic in conquering, one might say, raping, the continent, but along with it at all times there has been the strain of idealism, expressed chiefly through the concept of democracy, and in this the West led, as might be expected. Mississippi demanded that the voter be either a tax-payer or a militiaman, but with this slight exception every Western State which was admitted to the Union came in with white manhood suffrage. More than that, they did not claim, as the older Southern States had done, any apportionment of representation based on slaves held, thus basing their constitutions solely on the right of the majority of free whites to rule regardless of any representation based on ownership of property. The reaction was felt in the East and between 1818 and 1821 manhood suffrage was practically adopted in Connecticut, Maine, Massachusetts, and New York.

Democracy could not flourish on the gigantic scale contemplated in the settlement of the American continent unless the sections could be linked together by convenient and rapid means of communication, and in this period we are continually being brought back to the fundamental question of how the West could be bound to the East, and where. In 1808 Gallatin, at the request of the Senate, had made his noted *Report on the Subject of Public Roads and Canals* in which he proposed, by the expenditure of about $20,-000,000 by the government, to build a series of combined roads and canals connecting East and West at various points. Jefferson believed in the importance of the object but had doubts as to the constitutionality of the government's embarking on such construction work and suggested amendments.

Nevertheless, when the Bill for the National Road from Cumberland to Wheeling was passed it received his signature. Doubts continued, however, and in 1817 Madison vetoed an important internal improvement bill sponsored by Calhoun, on the ground that he could not reconcile it with the constitution, his successor Monroe taking the same ground a few months later. Although the government had built the National Road it not only declined to undertake any further construction of roads and canals but even to appropriate money for the upkeep of that built.

Meanwhile Clay and Calhoun, always ardent nationalists, had been pleading for internal improvements. The one from the South and the other from the West, they realized the growing sectionalism of the nation. Two things were clearly necessary to bind the sections together—transportation and community of economic interest. Clay believed he had found the solution of the problem in what he called "the American System," outlined by him with perfect logical clarity, and made more popular and practical by such lesser minds as the Pennsylvanian Andrew Stewart.

Clay's theory, stemming from Hamiltonianism, was that by means of a protective tariff, and not one simply for revenue, manufactures would be deliberately built up. This would make us to a much greater degree self-supporting as to the articles manufactured, and provide employment for a large industrial population divorced from the soil. The feeding of this non-agricultural population would provide a domestic market for a large part of the agricultural produce of the growing West, which would, in exchange, buy Eastern manufactures. The South would do the same, in exchange for cotton sold to Northern textile mills. A considerable part of the revenue derived from the duties under the tariff which was to bring these happy results to pass was to be used for internal improvements, so much desired especially by the West, linking all parts of the nation together. The theory is alluring but does not allow for the antagonism of sectional, class, and occupational interests.

Owing partly to British "dumping" and the general unsettlement of post-war conditions, a tariff had been passed in 1816 which was only to a slight extent protective, but even so it had been opposed by New England, where the old shipping interest was as yet stronger than the manufacturing. On the other hand, the South was in favor of it, less from a hope, as has often been claimed, of building up manufacturing in that section than of providing a market for cotton in New England. The manufacturing Middle States were strongly in favor of protection, as they were always to remain.

The real struggle for the American system outlined by Clay lay ahead in the next decade, but the vote on the tariff bill of 1820, which failed of passage by only one vote, indicated that sectional changes were occurring and that however "national" a tariff system might be called, even as so brilliantly conceived by Clay, it was in reality a local question. In the House, New England's vote was divided eighteen in favor to seventeen opposed, showing the gain of the manufacturers on the merchants; the Middle States voted solidly in favor, with only one dissenting vote out of fifty-seven; the South now voted fifty against with only five in favor; and the northern Western States were in favor, while the lower tier, from Kentucky southward, were opposed.

In other words, the manufacturing Middle States and the Ohio Valley wished for as much protection as possible, whereas the great tobacco and cotton growers joined with the gradually declining shipping interest of New England to defeat it. The planters had begun to realize that a somewhat enlarged domestic market plus higher prices for manufactured goods was not so worth while as reliance upon the foreign market for export of crops and cheaper manufactured goods at home. We shall note the continuance of the struggle in the next chapter, and wish here only to mark its beginning and the great part played by Clay and Calhoun, who, following Hamilton, provided practically all the arguments that any protectionist has since used. There has always subsisted a difference of opinion, but the arguments have never altered, proof in itself of a fundamental and abiding clash of interests.

In 1819 the country was in the throes of the worst financial panic which it had yet suffered. It was largely due, as post-war panics are, to the economic derangement consequent upon war itself and to the psychology of all post-war periods. Such panics never ensue immediately upon the close of war but usually come only a considerable number of years later, when the factors have worked themselves out. The panic of 1791 occurred eight years after signing peace, and that of 1819 five years after. The war had cost the government about $200,000,000 , and partly due to the blockade and partly to the recalcitrancy of New England, the government finances had become disordered. In 1815 Alexander J. Dallas, then Secretary of the Treasury, had advocated the chartering of the second Bank of the United States to resume the functions of the first one which had been wound up when its charter had expired. Although there was a good deal of opposition, the bank was authorized by Congress in 1816 and began operations.

During the war, specie payment had had to be suspended by all banks outside the New England area, and bank notes had dropped to a discount of as much as thirty per cent. The currency was in confusion, and it was hoped that the new bank might provide a sound one. New England even yet declined to assist the government, and although most of the nation's specie was in that section it subscribed only $4,000,000 to the bank against $1,200,000 from Georgia! Philadelphia took $9,000,000 in stock and the bank opened January 1, 1817, with nineteen branches in the principal cities of the country. By the 20th of February specie payment had been resumed by the State banks, and the currency was once more on a firm foundation.

The banking system of the country, however, was not. Peace had led as always to a great outburst of extravagance on the part of every one. All wanted credit. The Northern manufacturers had been hard hit by British dumping, and were struggling against this unexpected competition. Speculation in land was rampant both in the South and West. Not only had planters and speculators on a large scale bought up tracts at high prices, but the innumerable emigrants to the West had borrowed heavily to pay for the lands taken up on government partial-payment grants and the cost of the move from their old homes. The State banks, many of them small, unsound, and in inexperienced hands, discounted paper for any one and every one who needed credit. In Kentucky at one session of the legislature forty banks were chartered, all soon to be closed.

The situation of the whole country was thoroughly unsound when in 1818 the United States Bank, which had been very badly managed and had done nothing to check the orgy of credit, suddenly instructed all its branches to accept no notes but its own, to demand immediate payment of all State bank notes, and to renew no personal loans. State banks crashed everywhere, the hollow credit structure collapsed, and ruin was widespread. Land values dropped in some cases by seventy per cent and staple products by fifty per cent. By the collapse of the local State banks and the foreclosures by the national bank, a large part of the city of Cincinnati, its hotels, iron foundries, unimproved real estate, warehouses, and so on

WALL STREET IN 1820

Aquatint engraving by R. Varus after an original contemporary painting.

Courtesy of The Mabel Brady Garvan Institute of American Arts and Crafts, Yale University.

SANDERSON'S FRANKLIN HOUSE, CHESTNUT STREET, PHILADELPHIA, 1835

"A new and beautiful hotel . . . having both a Restaurant and Ordinary . . . the accommodations are very superior . . . being so constructed as to form a parlour by day and a chamber at night."

Courtesy of The Mabel Brady Garvan Institute of American Arts and Crafts, Yale University.

passed in title to the Bank of the United States, and this story was repeated in other towns. The West was prostrate at the feet of what it had come to call "the Monster."

"The Monster," that is the Bank of the United States, had been unpopular in most of the newer States, as well as the older ones, and many of them had taken steps, notably by heavy taxation, to keep it from operating within their borders. Maryland had been one of these, and the Baltimore branch of the national bank had refused to pay the tax levied on its notes. The case had taken its course through the courts and in 1819 the verdict of the Supreme Court was handed down by Marshall, in what has been called one of the "greatest judicial utterances of all time." From the fact that McCulloch was the cashier sued by the State, the case is known as that of McCulloch *vs.* Maryland. It rested on the old question of the express or implied powers inherent in the Constitution, and as always Marshall was strongly in favor of the loosest construction, and the maximum of power for the central government.

In his opinion as handed down, he had to discuss, he said, "the conflicting powers of the government of the Union and of its members," a problem which must be decided peacefully "or remain a source of hostile legislation, perhaps of *hostility of a still more serious nature.*" From the method of adopting the constitution, he went on, "the government proceeds directly from the people . . . their act was final. It required not the affirmation, and could not be negatived, by the State governments." The national government is "emphatically, and truly, a government of the people. In form and substance it emanates from them. Its powers are granted by them, and are to be exercised directly on them, and for their benefit."

Having argued the power of Congress to create the bank he continued to argue against the power of a State to tax it. Finding no "express provision" covering the point he boldly claimed that there was "a principle which so entirely pervades the Constitution . . . as to be incapable of being separated from it without rendering it into shreds." "This great principle is that the constitution and the laws made in pursuance thereof are supreme; that they control the constitution and laws of the respective States, and cannot be controlled by them."

This he called an "axiom," from which he drew the corollaries that "a power to create implies a power to preserve," that "a power to destroy, if wielded by a different hand, is hostile to, and incompatible with these powers to create and to preserve," and that "where this repugnancy exists, that authority which is supreme must control, not yield to that over which it is supreme."

"In truth," as the great Chief-Justice said, the whole question was "of supremacy," and, if the States could tax the instrumentalities of the national government the declaration in the Constitution that it and its laws "shall be the supreme law of the land, is empty and unmeaning declamation." Marshall had not denied that the Federal Government was one of delegated powers, but insisted that in the exercise of those powers it had the right to choose the means by which they would effectively be put into action. In a word, the decision of the Court enabled the government to accomplish to the full the ends of its existence and to develop a vigor which would have forever been denied to it under strict construction not only of its powers but of the methods of exercising them. In the decision handed down by him in the case of Cohens *vs*. Virginia three years before, he had declared that the Supreme Court could set aside the decision of State courts or the laws of the State legislatures if found in conflict in its opinion with the Federal Constitution. In fact, the great work of the Chief Justice was not only to develop the theory of the Constitution but to give to the Supreme Court the power, which must reside somewhere, of determining what is in accord with the fundamental law and what is not. The ablest constitutional exponent whom America has produced, it is notable that in his long term on the Supreme Court bench he never but once, and then in an unimportant case, was found in a minority on a constitutional decision. As Lord Bryce once said, the Constitution as originally drafted was "rather a ground-plan than a city," and it was this mere ground-plan which was filled up by the Chief Justice. The work accomplished by him affords an interesting example of personality working in history, for John Jay, who had resigned the Chief Justiceship in 1795, and declined a reappointment when Marshall took the place, had done so on the ground that by its very nature the Supreme Court could never acquire a position of proper weight and dignity.

That it has become today probably the most important and influential national tribunal in the entire world is due chiefly to the strength of Marshall's mind and character. In spite of a somewhat discouraging number of cases decided on a basis of five to four, the Court performs an indispensable function in interpreting the Constitution, and in giving to what might have become a rigid document that living flexibility and accommodation to the changing needs of social and economic conditions which prevents that political fossilizing of the ideas of the past which is among the most potent breeders of revolution. Moreover, on the whole, its decisions have shown a remarkable independence of party spirit and a genuine desire to hold the scales of justice even. Many have felt, at times, that the Court might be too careful of the rights of property in comparison with those of man, but the honesty and ability of its members have scarcely ever been called into question. No other body in the nation has had so continuously a distinguished membership or has so retained the confidence of the people at large.

While Marshall was thus defining and extending the powers of the government the physical boundaries of the country were also being rounded out. Our only portion of the Gulf coast had been the somewhat uncertain and comparatively small stretch which had come to us with the cession of Louisiana, although in 1810 we had taken possession and kept against the protest of Spain the coast as far east as the Perdido River. We wanted not only all of the coast eastward but also the peninsula of Florida. This seemed clearly to belong to us geographically, but was unquestionably the property of Spain, which had three fortified posts there, including St. Augustine. That power, however, although required by treaty to keep the Indians from annoying us, made no pretense of doing so. With our discontented Creeks within our own borders and the Seminoles on both sides of the international boundary, episodes were bound to happen which could be conveniently turned to account.

Florida was an unpatrolled wilderness, and two Englishmen, an adventurer, Ambrister, and a trader, Arbuthnot, turned up there and began to stir the Indians to trouble. Our Seminoles did some scalping of settlers who were living on lands the Creeks had "ceded" to us, and President Monroe sent Andrew Jackson down to settle the trouble. Jackson chased the Seminoles over into Florida, caught and, after a summary trial, shot Ambrister and hung Arbuthnot, and then in true Jacksonian style started in to take possession of the Spanish posts.

England rang with denunciations of the killing of its citizens, but Lord Castlereagh, always friendly to us, and a wise statesman, declined to allow the demand for war to stir him. Adams in the Secretary of State's office took a high tone with Spain, and in an acidly sharp note informed her that she was not complying with her treaty obligations but leaving Florida to lie like "a derelict, open to the occupancy of every enemy," and that it served no earthly purpose except as a source of annoyance to us. Either Spain must maintain her authority or cede the peninsula to us. After a good deal of tortuous and rather amusing diplomacy we paid that nation about $5,000,000 for the whole of the peninsula and the Gulf coast up to what we already had. In the treaty which was signed in 1819, the Spanish Prime Minister showed himself a better bargainer than Napoleon had been.

In the same year there sounded through the nation a sudden dispute which Adams called a "fire bell in the night." The population of Missouri had steadily been growing, and in February a bill was introduced in Congress to admit her to statehood. Slavery had been fast dying out in the Northern States and increasing in the South but it had not as yet been at any time a national issue. It was, indeed, in the back of people's minds as a political problem.

The compromise adopted when the Constitution was framed providing that representation in Congress from slave States should be based on the white population plus two thirds of the slaves had never been wholly satisfactory to the North. If the blacks were mere property why, asked some of the Northerners, should five white men in the South be given as much representation as seven white men in the North? If there were a property basis for representation why should slaves count and not ships or factories? Nevertheless there had been no open agitation of the dangerous question. When the bill for the admission of Missouri was introduced, however, a representative from New York, General James Tallmadge, moved an amendment providing that all slaves born after the admission of the State should become free at twenty-five years of age, and that no more should be imported.

Owing to the much more rapid increase of population in the

North and Northwest than in the South, the number of Representatives in the House already stood at 105 to 81 in favor of the free States, although, as the number of slave and free States was the same, the Senate was equally divided. On Tallmadge's attempt to force Missouri to become free, what had been in the backs of people's minds suddenly leaped to the front. The amendment was lost and the matter went over to the next Congress, but the public discussion became bitter.

A vision had been opened of what the future might hold. From colonial days what is now the State of Maine had been part of Massachusetts, and the northern province had recently again expressed its wish to separate and become an independent State. This somewhat happy coincidence permitted of a way out of the Missouri discussion, and, by what is known as the "Missouri Compromise," it was agreed that Missouri should come in as a slave State and Maine as free, and that thereafter slavery should be prohibited in the remainder of the Louisiana Purchase north of the parallel of thirty-six degrees thirty minutes, approximately the southern boundary of Missouri. Although temporarily settled, Adams was right in appraising the unexpected controversy as merely the "preamble to a great and tragic volume."

Adams, who was the greatest Secretary of State we have ever had, had other problems on his hands than Jackson's two Englishmen and the Spaniards. For one thing, there were the questions left unsettled at Ghent. By Conventions entered into with England in 1818 the problem of our rights as to the Newfoundland fisheries was temporarily settled although it recurred at intervals to disturb relations for nearly a century. In the same year the undetermined question of ownership of the Oregon country was also compromised for a time on the basis of a joint occupation for ten years.

A far more important, and let us hope a perpetual, agreement was arrived at for American and British disarmament on the Canadian border. We both had boats on the Lakes, and the stage was set for a miniature race in armaments. We took the initiative in suggesting the complete "civilizing," in a very real sense, instead of the "militarizing," of the whole boundary, and Castlereagh happily fell in with the idea. For over a century, on a 3000-mile boundary between two of the greatest powers in the world, the British Empire and the

United States, there has been not a soldier, a fort or a naval vessel of importance, the greatest object lesson which the world has ever seen of how nations might learn to live together in peace and trust.

Meanwhile there were wars and confusion to the south of us. During the years that Napoleon had made himself master of Spain, her colonies had enjoyed a semi-independence, and although the Bourbon monarchy was restored, a movement toward complete independence had been started which found its leaders, and which Spain was to prove unable to control. The new governments set up by the successful revolutionists were republican in form, and much sympathy was aroused among our own people for those of the new states, as yet unrecognized by Spain, which were coming into being in South America.

Henry Clay in particular was eloquent in his appeals to Congress to recognize them, but Adams as Secretary of State took a more cautious and statesmanlike view. Although he wished the new republics well, and preferred that they should be independent of Spain he had none of Clay's emotional enthusiasm, and questioned how genuine their new liberty and republicanism might prove. Moreover he clung tenaciously to the policy, which on the whole had served us well, of complete neutrality in wars which did not immediately concern us. To Clay's disappointment, Congress passed a Neutrality Act in 1818.

England had considerable financial and commercial relations with the South American Spanish colonies, and Castlereagh at the Foreign Office had been watching the progress of the revolutions. An exchange of views between him and Adams came to nothing. By 1822 all of the former colonies had completely routed the remnants of Spanish authority, and in March we formally recognized the independence of Mexico, Colombia, Peru, Chili, and La Plata. A few months later Castlereagh was succeeded by George Canning as British Foreign Secretary. England's chief interest in South America, in so far as her policy was concerned, was to retain her trade and to ensure the safety of her investments there. She had hesitated to recognize the independence of the new nations, partly on account of the fact that it would be an unfriendly act toward Spain, on whose side she had just been fighting against Napoleon, and partly for fear of our continued expansion southward.

We have always honestly believed that we were not an imperialistic people and did not wish to expand, but other nations, quite rightly, have taken a different view of the probable course of our policies. They have also realized that expansion, when easily possible, becomes almost inevitable for any nation. Already by 1823 in our brief history we had doubled our territory by the purchase of Louisiana, tried to push its boundaries as far as possible, and then forced Spain to cede Florida to us. If South America, instead of being part of the Spanish empire, became filled with weak, and perhaps warring, States was it not likely that we would intervene and swallow them one after another? In that case, what might become of British South American trade was uncertain.

In the beginning of 1823, however, a new complication occurred. The Congress of Verona had decided that France should assist the Spanish King, Ferdinand VII, to rid himself of the constitution and restore him as a despot. This began to look as though France might join with Spain in reconquering South America and get a share of it for her pains, which would not have suited English policy at all. If the prospect of the United States taking a huge bite of the lost Spanish empire was disagreeable, that of finding France set up again as a great imperial power in the New World was startling.

Canning mulled the problem over and in the summer suggested to our Minister, Richard Rush, that England and the United States should join in a declaration warning France to keep her hands off, explaining that although he believed Spain could not reconquer her colonies England was not yet ready to acknowledge their independence. She had, however, no desire to acquire territory herself and would unite with us in pledging both nations against doing so in South America. It was a tempting bait, and both Jefferson and Madison swallowed it. The most powerful nation in the world, and our erstwhile enemy, was asking us to unite with her in redressing the balance of power in Europe and in determining the fate of half the New World. To act in concert might heal old sores, and with England pledged never to acquire additional territory in South America, a good part of the difficulties of European intervention on our side of the globe might seem to have been solved.

On the other hand, we had acknowledged the independence of

the new republics, and Canning absolutely declined to do so, the Tories in England being bitterly opposed to the spread of republican principles. Moreover, the joint declaration that neither nation would ever acquire territory on the southern continent was a good deal more of a self-denying ordinance for us than for England. Cuba was then lying almost derelict just off the tip of our newly won Florida, and how could the United States, pacific as it might be, pledge itself in perpetuity never to advance beyond the boundaries it then had into adjacent territory in what was unquestionably its sphere of influence? Adams clearly saw the trap, and, combined with other events then happening to the north of us, he decided the time had come for a clear pronouncement of our national policy.

The Russians had been gradually extending their power across Siberia, and had finally crossed Behring Strait. Fur trading posts had been built by them on the west coast of North America as far south as the bay of San Francisco, California then being, of course, a Spanish or Mexican possession. Adams received word that the Czar had ordered all non-Russian vessels not to approach within a hundred Italian miles of the coast of what he called Russian America, and also that he would never recognize the new South American republics.

Adams watched the whole situation develop from different quarters. Following the establishment of our independence and the proof that republican government on a hitherto undreamed of scale could be successful, and also, in Europe, the excesses of the French Revolution, there had been everywhere a great wave of reactionary sentiment in the governments across the sea. Everywhere efforts were being made to stamp out liberalism.

On our own side of the world, the independence of South America was being threatened not only by the restored Bourbons of Spain but by the Bourbons in France. England wished us to guarantee her markets against French aggression but without acknowledging the republics and at the expense of our agreeing never to extend our boundaries southward. To the northwest, even into the Oregon country which we claimed, the most reactionary European power, Russia, was colonizing and warning all other nations to keep out. Liberal institutions were threatened, the United States was running the risk of being hemmed in, with freedom of action denied to her, and both American continents were becoming in danger of being colonized again and exploited by the least enlightened and liberal of European monarchies.

It was to meet and counter these particular conditions of the moment that Adams and Monroe, in consultation with others, prepared and promulgated the declaration of our principles which has ever since been known as the Monroe Doctrine.

The occasion chosen was the message sent by the President to Congress at the begining of its winter session, December 2, 1823. In the course of reviewing the international situation, the President laid down certain general principles. The United States had, he said, always made it its policy not to interfere in the internal affairs of Europe or with existing colonies of European powers, and would not do so. It was our policy to recognize *de facto* governments as legitimate. The two American continents, having become independent of Europe, should not be considered as any longer open to new attempts at colonization by European powers, and we should consider any effort of such powers, which had a political system essentially different from the American, to extend their system to any part of our hemisphere "as dangerous to our peace and safety."

Adams, who was chiefly responsible for the enunciation of the doctrine, although it was in part shaped and considerably tempered in tone by Monroe, would have liked somewhat sharper protests to have been made. The European situation, however, was already shifting, and any immediate danger from that direction was over. The Czar caught the meaning of the message, and in 1824 negotiated a treaty, agreeing that the southern boundary of Russia in America should be the parallel of 54° 40′ instead of 51° as he had earlier claimed.

Americans had not generally been aware of all the diplomatic fencing which had made the declaration of policy needful, but its enunciation was well received and, although arising from conditions of the moment, it was to prove so strong a bulwark and so adapted to meet successive situations and dangers that in the course of more than a century it has now acquired a prestige, as well, we may add, as a haziness of content in the public mind, that it may be considered the chief corner-stone of both our practical and emotional attitude toward foreign policy.

The following year, at the request of Congress, Lafayette visited the United States and was presented with a grant of land and $200,000. If ever an enthusiastic adventure of a young man brought golden rewards, his had. Meanwhile Jefferson was being left to struggle without aid against poverty and old age, Congress having haggled over even the price it was to pay him for the choicest library in America, which his needs compelled him to sell. The Monroe Doctrine had served notice on the Old World that the New was to remain forever free. There was a certain irony in paying with such absurd generosity a debt of grateful memory to Europe just as we locked the doors of the two continents with a warning of "no trespassing" to future Europeans, and declined to assist in his poverty and old age the writer of the Declaration of Independence.

The panic of 1819 was followed by slow recovery, and although the West had suffered the worst, the manufacturing interests, having had a taste of special governmental favors in the protection of their particular industries, clamored for more. Monroe had approached the subject warily in his messages of 1822 and 1823, and in 1824 Congress undertook the framing of a new Tariff Act.

The sectional alignment proved still to be much as on the Tariff of 1816, New England on the whole, led by Daniel Webster, preferring shipping and free trade to manufactures and protection. The Middle States insisted upon protection as did the West, the latter counting upon an industrial population to consume its grain and corn. The South believed, as henceforth it was to continue to do with ever more firm conviction, that it would gain nothing in sales of cotton and would lose on cost of manufactured articles.

In the long Congressional debates, the question of the constitutional right to protect one class or section in its peculiar industry as against others was clearly raised for the first time. Finally passed, the Act was the earliest of the distinctly protective tariffs, as opposed to one for revenue chiefly, which have continued to be enacted ever since. Sectional feeling was beginning to be inflamed but it was not until the "tariff of abominations" four years later, when New England swung into the Protectionist camp and Daniel Webster turned a political somersault, that North and South were to stand solidly opposed to one another, and the fire of controversy was to break into open flame.

Meanwhile, Monroe's presidency and the long reign of the Virginia Dynasty were rapidly drawing to a close. Having served two terms it was well understood that he would not be renominated. On the other hand, the Federalist Party had completely collapsed and took no part in the campaign, which was to be fought on personalities instead of principles. The Republican Party, in its long reign, had begun to disintegrate into factions, and four of these placed candidates in the field, so that America was treated to the peculiar spectacle of a campaign with only one party but with four candidates. John Quincy Adams was much the ablest and was nominated by most of the legislatures of the New England States early in 1824, but his austerity prevented him from ever becoming popular, and his high ideal of public office did not permit him to stoop to the usual political means of assisting his own candidacy.

Of the other candidates, Henry Clay was the most brilliant and his great gifts had made him an outstanding figure in the American life of the day. Although a Westerner, he had a dangerous rival in the immensely popular Andrew Jackson, who as a swashbuckling fighter had become endeared to the West from the days of New Orleans and his Florida and Creek adventures. In him the West found a leader more to its taste and in its own image than it did in the intellectual Clay. The fourth candidate, William H. Crawford of Georgia, suffered a paralytic stroke before the end of the struggle and was thus automatically put out of the race. By the time election day came in 1824, however, the sixteen or seventeen candidates who had been jockeying for position ever since 1822 had been reduced to these four.

The convention system of nominating candidates had not yet come into existence and the former method of nomination in a Congressional caucus of party leaders was not used after 1820, so in 1824 the fight which is now carried on within the walls of the Convention was carried on in the open. Jackson had been first nominated by the lower house of the Tennessee legislature and later received the nomination also at the hands of many local conventions; Adams was nominated by most of the New England legislatures; and Calhoun and Crawford by those of South Carolina and Virginia respectively. However, this new experiment on the part of the people in attempting to develop a system of Presidential nomination more consonant with its democratic taste than the one provided for in the Constitution was destined to last but a brief time.

Of the four men who were to contest the election by an appeal to the suffrages of the people at large, any one could have stood for the principles of the others. On that score there was nothing to choose between them. When the Electoral votes were counted it was found that Jackson had 99, Adams 84, Crawford 41, and Clay 37. Adams had carried all of New England solidly, received 26 out of the 32 Electoral votes of New York, and had a few scattering ones elsewhere. Jackson had won Pennsylvania, New Jersey, Maryland, North and South Carolina, all of the Gulf States and Tennessee, Indiana, and Illinois, the votes of Louisiana and Illinois being split, but in his favor. Crawford had only Virginia and his own State of Georgia, while Clay had only Kentucky, Ohio, and Missouri, although each received a few scattered votes elsewhere. No candidate having received a majority, the election was thrown into the House of Representatives where, Crawford having become incapacitated, it at once became evident that the contest would be between Jackson and Adams with Clay's following as the deciding factor between the chief two contestants.

As between them, Clay honestly believed that Adams was the fitter man for the presidency. Adams had entered diplomacy as secretary to the American Minister to Russia when only a boy; had been our Minister to Prussia and England; one of the Commissioners to negotiate peace at Ghent; and for eight years had made such a notable success as Secretary of State as to have won, a century later, the highest place in the long line of able men who have occupied that office. Contrasting Adams with Jackson, the latter as yet known chiefly for his military exploits, his duelling adventures, and the sort of character which gave him his popularity among the rough elements of the frontier West, Clay did not hesitate.

The story, industriously spread by the Jacksonites, with the exception of Senator Benton of Missouri, to the effect that Clay would throw his influence to Adams in return for a pledge that he would be made Secretary of State had no foundation whatever, as Benton said he could prove. Clay would have done exactly as he did whether he were to become Secretary or not, and as he was the natural candidate for that post Adams would have made him Secretary, as he did later, in any case. That, in spite of the story, both men did as they did is not evidence of blunted consciences but of clean ones.

In the House, Adams was elected on the first ballot by 87 to Jackson's 71, in accordance with the method laid down in the Constitution. The Jacksonites' absurd claim that because their candidate had received the greatest number of Electoral votes the House should therefore have elected him so as not to thwart the will of the people was obviously absurd, and like the Clay-Adams story was merely used to stir up popular resentment and feeling. Had it been the intention of those who framed the Constitution that the House, in a contested election when no candidate had received a majority of the votes in the Electoral College vote, was merely to vote for the one who had received the highest number, there would have been no sense in providing the machinery of an election by the House at all. The Constitution would have provided that the candidate receiving the highest number of Electoral votes would, without further proceedings, have become President.

The false view was in particular upheld by Senator Benton, who had started as a Clay man, gone over to Crawford, and then become a Jacksonian, illustrating the confusion of thought of the times, as he did also in claiming that in the provision for the election of a President by the House in certain cases there was a conflict between "the theory of the Constitution and the democratic principle," or as he usually called it in a horrible barbarism, the "principle *demos krateo.*" Although the first man to shake President Adams by the hand after his inauguration was Jackson, whom Adams had consistently befriended, sometimes alone, during the past eight years when Jackson's impulsive conduct had not seldom been the subject of Cabinet debate, the General was to open war upon the President almost immediately. The bitter campaign of 1828 began even before Adams had become President in March, 1825.

Not only had most of the heroes of that earlier period gone to their rest but the Virginia dynasty which had so long ruled the affairs of the nation had also passed. The Presidents who had thus far served their country had been a remarkable line of men. At their head, in every sense, had first stood Washington. One of the greatest characters of all the ages in all lands, his integrity, his patriotism untainted by thought of self or ambition, his common and uncommon sense, his sound judgment and broad views, his even-handed justice meted out to all men, friend or foe, his self-control in spite of the violent passion in his nature, his physical courage in the face of danger and his moral courage in the face of years of discouragement and adversity,—all had marked him out as the one man who could safely lead the struggling young nation through the perils of revolution and perhaps the yet greater perils of the ensuing years of jealousies, bickerings and weakness.

John Adams offered a great contrast to his predecessor. Short and fat,—nicknamed "his Rotundity,"—he must scarce have measured up to the shoulder of Washington's superb figure. Pompous and fussy instead of like Washington calm and dignified, he had minor traits which rather unjustly obscured for many of his contemporaries the real strength of the man. If he did not possess, as indeed no other American has, a character as rounded and perfectly balanced as that of his former chief, he nevertheless brought to his high office a mind and heart devoted to the service of the country, ability of the first rank, and an independence of thought and action, a freedom from weighing any question with the slightest idea of its influence upon his own personal fortunes, which have been rare in the career of any statesman, among us or other peoples.

Jefferson was more complex. An aristocrat by nature, a democrat in theory and by generous impulse, he also had a far wider range of intellectual and æsthetic interests than either Washington or Adams. Like the teachings of great moral leaders, his teaching of democracy and faith in man has been difficult of application in the world as it has been and perhaps as it always may be, but it is the leaven of his teaching which has done much to keep alive in the hearts of Americans that hope of a better and richer existence for the lowly as well as the great which has been the very essence of what we call our Americanism. Philosopher, architect, musician, farmer, statesman, he touched life at many points in his years abroad and at home. Successful founder of a political party as well as apostle of a political gospel of freedom and opportunity for all, he himself cared but little for the struggle of politics and ignored the terms of his Presidency when he directed that there should be carved on his tombstone only "Here was buried Thomas Jefferson, Author of the Declaration of Independence, Of the Statute of Virginia for Religious Freedom, and Father of the University of Virginia; because by these as testimonials that I have lived I wish most to be remembered."

Jefferson's successor, Madison, was a scholar and when his fellow delegate to the Constitutional Convention, William Pierce, described him as a "profound politician" the word was used in the sense of statesman or student of the art of governing. Modest and shy, short in stature, slight in figure, his presence was not distinguished, but no other man has come to the Presidency with a wider knowledge of all that concerned the United States combined with so deep an insight and understanding of that Constitution of which he has properly been called the "father." He had less ability in the management of practical politics than had either Jefferson or Madison's own successor in office, James Monroe, but he far exceeded the latter in brilliancy and solidity of intellect. Monroe, the last of the Virginia dynasty, which had been broken only by the one term of John Adams, was in many ways a mediocre man, but, like many other such, had made a most useful President, reaching his own judgments deliberately and shouldering responsibility while displaying a fair-minded generosity toward all men and a magnanimity and tolerance which his Secretary of State, John Quincy Adams, felt that he carried to the extent of weakness. He was, however, a worthy successor of the preceding Virginians, and the dynasty ended undimmed when the Presidency once more went to a New Englander.

Old John Adams, the former President, had lived to see his son elected to the same office, but was, rather happily for himself, not to live through the administration. On the Fourth of July, 1826, as he lay dying in Massachusetts, his thoughts turned to the stirring days of '76, and he murmured, "Jefferson yet lives." By a strange coincidence, however, Jefferson did not live but had died on the same day, a few hours before Adams. They were the last of the committee which had framed the Declaration of Independence, and both passed away on the anniversary of the day which that Declaration had made famous. Scarcely a notable living link now remained with the days of revolution.

The four years of Adams's presidency were years of martyrdom. His strong nationalism, his belief that one of the functions of government should be to improve the moral and intellectual condition of the people, his creed that a democracy to succeed must be an

educated and morally sound body of electors, carried no conviction either to a South which feared strong nationalism, or to a West
which had little use for education. The South stood for States' Rights
and a minimum of Federal control, while the West stood for Jacksonian hero-worship. The only President who thus far had failed of
re-election had been Adams's father, and it was a bitter thought that
he himself would be the second. He watched for four years the
furious political struggles of those who hoped to inherit his position,
but declined to lift a finger to assist himself by use of patronage or
promises. His followers, and he had many, despaired of such a man
in practical politics.

Adams was beaten before he began, and his influence on Congress
and in political life was that of a beaten man, a man who declined
to build a machine and who would not have to be reckoned with
beyond the one term. Little that was striking occurred during his
administration, although much was happening under the surface.
Of the increased momentum of the democracy, and of the Tariff
of 1828, made not only for increased protection but to influence the
presidential campaign of that year, we shall speak in the next
chapter.

Our foreign affairs under Adams were peaceful, marked only by
Canning's efforts to increase the prestige of England and to lower
our own among the new South American governments, in which he
was more or less successful. We had use at home for far more capital
than we possessed, and were not particularly interested in the South
American trade, nor did we desire any political control or leadership
at that time in the southern continent. On the other hand, British
capital and trade were both seeking new channels and outlets, and
Canning saw to it that diplomacy backed them up. Especially did
he play a winning hand in the affairs of our nearest neighbor,
Mexico, where our own minister got himself so foolishly embroiled
in factions that he had to be recalled, whereas the British got on the
friendliest terms with the Mexican President. Just before Adams was
inaugurated, we had been invited, together with England, to send
representatives to a conference of the South American republics to be
held at Panama, and Adams had accepted the invitation. After much
delay and wrangling, the Senate finally appointed two representatives, one of whom promptly died and the other reached Panama too

late for the Conference which we allowed to be held without outside participation except by the English.

As for our domestic politics and affairs President Roosevelt truly said in his *Life of Benton,* that there never was a time "when there was more rabid, objectless, and unscrupulous partisanship" than in Adams's administration.

Embittered by factious opposition and powerless to carry out the policies which he believed essential for the welfare of the country, the President lived on and endured. One of the strongest and ablest men we have ever had in public life, his one term of presidential office was singularly ineffective. Happily, his great years and the greatest of his public services lay yet ahead of him.

CHAPTER XIII

THE JACKSONIAN PERIOD

As we have seen in the preceding chapter, the long era of "good feeling" had broken down party lines, and the election of 1824 had been dominated by personalities and not by principles. Of the former, the leading one which had emerged from the struggle was clearly that of the doughty frontiersman and military hero, Andrew Jackson, who, disappointed of the presidency, at once set to work to prepare for the next contest in 1828. He had not been ambitious for the office at first but, having been defeated, his fighting blood and powerful will demanded that he should vindicate himself by victory.

In October, 1825, he resigned his seat in the United States Senate, where he represented Tennessee, and announced that he was a candidate for President in the next election. The history of the Adams administration thus really resolved itself into a mere jockeying for political positions in the race of 1828. Later on, after he had become President, Jackson developed bold policies which he fitted into a philosophy and principles adapted to justify them, but the four years of Adams's term were the incubating period for the new parties which were to arise, and in the absence as yet of clear-cut differences the Jacksonian following had to move warily in order to consolidate as many factions as possible.

By 1826 Martin Van Buren, the political leader of New York State, who had been for Crawford in 1824, decided to cast in his lot with Jackson, and gradually the partisan wing of the Republican Party which formed around the westerner developed its machinery under the name of the Democratic Party. Without distinct principles of its own at first, this new party contented itself in trying to solidify its strength by merely opposing on every occasion the policies of the administration. Thus the wrecking of our participation in the Panama Conference was merely one of the episodes in the four years' partisan battle against Adams.

The difficult position of the Democrats, made up of incongruous elements, and united only by hopes of defeating Adams and installing Jackson in his place, came out clearly in the tariff plot of 1828 at the very end of Adams's term. As has always happened, protected interests were not satisfied with the special privileges they were receiving and clamored for more. The New England manufacturers, having tasted the sweets of the protective pudding of 1824, were bent on another and more ample helping.

Adams himself was in favor of protection but the Jacksonians were in a quandary. They wished to alienate as little as might be of any possible support in New England, and moreover the Middle States and the upper western ones wished protection on their particular manufactures. In addition, western sheep raisers wished to foster the woolen industry and shut out foreign wool, while the growers of grains, largely excluded from the British market by the Corn Laws, desired an increase in the domestic American one. Various elements in the West and East were thus ready to join hands in protectionist legislation. On the other hand, the whole South had by this time definitely decided that a tariff on manufactures was inimical to the interests of that section. The Southerners, in fact, had reversed their earlier position and had become bitterly hostile to protection.

Facing the presidential campaign, the Jacksonites plotted a shrewd move. Jackson knew himself to be very strong in the South, whose support was necessary to him, but, on the other hand, so also was that of such manufacturing States as New York, Pennsylvania, and Ohio. Whatever action on the tariff the Democrats, who controlled the Committee on Manufactures in the House, might take would have to be satisfactory to these conflicting interests.

What, in this difficult situation, they planned to do, as Calhoun explained some years later, was to lay before the House a tariff bill which would have a high range of duties but in which the raw materials especially needed by New England would be so heavily taxed that the New Englanders would not be able to swallow the measure. It was expected that the disgruntled New Englanders voting against it, as would the solid South, would prevent its passage and that the bill would fail. The trick could be explained in the South, and in New York, Pennsylvania, and Ohio the onus for defeat could be laid on the New Englanders.

When the votes in the House and Senate were finally taken, all went as planned except for New England. The South voted practically solidly against the bill and the Middle States and manufacturing West for it. In the House although twenty-three New Englanders voted against it, sixteen voted in favor, and to the discomfiture of the Jacksonians, the bill was passed. In the Senate five New Englanders voted against it but six, under the last minute lead of Daniel Webster, voted in favor, and there also the bill was passed, to receive the signature of President Adams.

Webster had taken the ground, in debating the previous tariffs, that it was unconstitutional to levy duties for the protection of any particular group in industry, and had argued brilliantly for free trade not merely as economically expedient but as constitutionally the only legal course to take. Since 1824, however, he had become more allied to the rich manufacturers of his State, and he was evidently also alive to the political aspects, or as he called them "other paramount considerations," of the necessity of circumventing the Jacksonites. Thus was passed what has ever since been known as the "tariff of abominations," so bad were its economic features. The South voiced the truth about it when John Randolph said that the only manufacture it was really concerned with was "the manufacture of a President," and in South Carolina the question was immediately raised as to whether it were worth while to remain in a Union in which one section could thus oppress another.

In 1814 Webster, denouncing conscription in the war, had declared that in opposing it "it will be the solemn duty of the State Governments to protect their own authority over their own militia, and to interpose between their citizens and arbitrary power. These are among the objects for which the State Governments exist; and their highest obligations bind them to the preservation of their own rights and the liberties of their people." Later the legislature of Massachusetts was formally to annul the Fugitive Slave Act by making it a penal offence for any State official to enforce it. Nullification or secession, indeed, has frequently been threatened when any State or section has felt itself to be especially aggrieved by Federal legislation.

Now, in 1828, the doctrine raised its head in South Carolina as a result of the tariff, and the legislature approved what was called the

"South Carolina Exposition," later known to have been written by Calhoun. This document developed the theory that the Constitution being a compact between sovereign States, each State retained the right to pass on the constitutionality of the Acts of the Federal government. Therefore, if any State should determine adversely to any Act it had the right to nullify it by preventing its enforcement, within the limits of the protesting State.

Meanwhile, the election of 1828 remained to be fought. Presidential elections are not events of which we as Americans have reason to be proud. Their appeals to passion and prejudice, their buncombe and whispered slanders, are not pleasant reading, but of all disgraceful campaigns that of 1828 perhaps was the most hideous. Different as the two candidates, Adams and Jackson, were in most particulars they were alike in that both men were honest according to their own codes in their private lives. The Puritanical Adams of Massachusetts, accustomed to the most polished and intellectual society of Europe, was of an utterly different type from the duelling popular hero of the people from Tennessee, but both, the Puritan and the frontiersman, had the highest code of honor where a woman was concerned. Yet both were bitterly attacked in the press on that score with a scurrility that seems, happily, almost incredible.

Owing to a mistake, easily accounted for under the conditions of the early frontier, Jackson had married the woman to whom his devotion was life-long, under the impression they both had that a divorce from a cruel and worthless husband had been granted earlier in Virginia, Kentucky, where she was living, being then a part of that State. Two years later it developed that only the preliminary proceedings had been gone through with and that Mrs. Jackson had not been free to marry. There was no question of the utter good faith of both Jackson and his wife, and the first husband having won a divorce on the technical ground of adultery, Jackson immediately had another ceremony performed. The episode had been unfortunate but had not reflected in the slightest on the moral integrity of either husband or wife.

In the campaign, however, this thirty-eight year old misfortune was dragged back into light and made the basis for the most slanderous accusations against Mrs. Jackson in the effort to influence popular sentiment against her husband, who shielded her from all knowledge of what the press was alleging, until after the election when, by accident, she discovered it for herself. An invalid, completely devoted to her husband and his welfare, the shock was too great and in less than two weeks she had died. The hounding of the innocent woman in order to make political capital against her husband, with its tragic result, is one of the most pathetic and scandalous in the none too savory history of American journalism.

On the other hand Adams, whose integrity was above reproach, was accused in the press of having sold, while minister to Russia, a beautiful American girl to a Russian nobleman to satisfy his passion. Jackson believed that Adams could have kept the story about Mrs. Jackson out of the administration papers had he chosen to do so, and denounced him as "the basest, meanest scoundrel that ever disgraced the image of his god." It was in this storm of recrimination and counter-charges that the American people elected their President.

That people now numbered nearly 13,000,000, of whom about 9,000,000 lived east of the Appalachian Mountains and the balance to the west of them, so rapidly had the West grown since we glanced at it last. Of the total population, about 7,000,000 lived in the free States and 5,500,000 in the slave. Of the 5,500,000 however, less than 3,500,000 were free whites. New York City, which in 1790 had been only double the size of Charleston, South Carolina, now numbered 242,000 inhabitants as against 30,000 in the leading southern seaboard city. The figures show clearly the rapidity with which the Slave South was being outnumbered by the Free North, and also the importance of the West as holding the balance of power between the two eastern sections, growing more and more opposed to one another in sentiment and economic structure.

By 1828, manhood suffrage had become practically almost universal among the free population, and the old mode of election of Presidential Electors by the legislatures, which had been gradually altering to election by the people, was retained in only two States, Delaware and South Carolina. To a far greater extent than ever before the people at large had the opportunity of expressing their will or emotion at the polls. Democracy was seating itself in the saddle and in 1828 it rode hard.

Adams's stern morality and unbending rectitude,—which would not allow him to stoop to disturb a single office-holder with a view to his own advantage,—his formal manners, his intellectual eminence, and his forbidding personality made no appeal to the ordinary man. Jackson, on the other hand, seemed the embodiment of everyday humanity, a man of the people whom they could understand and who they therefore believed would understand them and their needs. The South, rabid against New England on the tariff question, the democratic West and the poorer classes in the East who found democracy incarnated in "Old Hickory," voted solidly for Jackson. It is surprising that under the circumstances Adams succeeded in polling forty-four per cent of the popular vote, which gives him a much better showing than the 83 votes he received in the Electoral College against Jackson's 178. With the exception of New England, New Jersey, Delaware, and Maryland (the last by a vote of 6 to 5 for Adams), Jackson carried the Electoral vote of every State in the Union, all of them unanimously except New York and Georgia, which were divided but in his favor.

The "revolution" of 1828 had been far more a genuine upheaval of the democratic elements among the people than had been that of 1800 which had swept Jefferson into the White House. Jefferson himself, although a democrat in theory, had been essentially the cultivated, intellectual aristocrat by nature and training. The people had at last declared itself tired of such, and had elected a man in its own image. One has only to contrast the background, character and mental equipment of Jackson with the line of previous Presidents— Washington, Adams, Jefferson, Madison, Monroe, and the second Adams,—to realize that the democracy had made a complete break with the traditions of the past. In spite of the absolutely solid vote Jackson had received in the West, it had really been the South, combining with Pennsylvania and New York, which had elected him. Should the division between North and South in the East become completely defined, it would evidently be the rapidly growing West which would hold the balance of power, and from this point onward we find both eastern sections making bids for the support of the section over the mountains. Something more had happened than that a man of "the Western Waters" was for the first time seated in the White House.

If the common people of the nation had elected Jackson because he was one of themselves, he was no ordinary man whom they had chosen. The old picture of Jackson as an illiterate radical has long since passed from history. Although his knowledge of books was slight he was far from illiterate, and his judgment was firm and quick. He possessed not only courage and strength but, on the whole, sound judgment, tenacity of purpose, and inflexible honesty, together with what was to prove a surprising independence of opinion and character. Completely sincere, he believed in democracy to an extent that no other President had yet done with the exception of Jefferson, and even Jefferson had had mental reservations on the subject denied to Jackson.

The times and circumstances had made the latter the leader of the rising democracy of the nation, and it would be difficult, if not impossible, to point to any other man of his day who could have carried out the task with greater ability or success. The people had chosen him much as they were later to choose Roosevelt, not on account of his military or other glamor, but because they believed he would give them a "square deal" in national administration which they considered to have fallen too much into the hands of the rich and conservative classes.

Such classes were frightened at Jackson as they always are when their complete control of power is threatened, but in point of fact, the new President was far more of a conservative than a radical, and the nation was to owe much to his single-hearted devotion to the people as a whole before he left the White House at the end of eight years, poorer than when he had entered it.

His first task was to choose a Cabinet, and in this he was disappointingly unsuccessful. In the rough draft of his Inaugural Address he had spoken of the need of filling public office with men "uniting as far as possible the qualifications of the head and heart," but, on the whole, in his Cabinet those of the head, at least, were markedly lacking. Martin Van Buren as Secretary of State proved a good choice, but the membership of the rest of the Cabinet was far below mediocrity, and the appointment of Senator Eaton, a staunch friend of the new President who was made Secretary of War, was to make trouble of a most unexpected sort.

As it turned out most of them, because of quiet times, were to make respectable officials, but the President consulted his advisers less than has been done by any other holding the office, and preferred the advice of old and tried friends, such as Amos Kendall, Major William B. Lewis, Isaac Hull, and Francis P. Blair, who formed the group which came to be known as the "Kitchen Cabinet," a term which carries, as it was intended to, a rather unfair impression. Calhoun, the Vice-President, was influential in the choice of some of the regular Cabinet, and the dominating influence of Virginia had at last reached an end, not only in the White House but in its official advisers.

On the day of the inauguration it seemed to the conservatives as though their worst fears had come true. Jackson was followed from the Capitol to the White House by a motley mob, black and white, of all sorts, who pressed into the Mansion to see the new President of the people. They clambered upon the satin furniture with their muddy boots for a better view, and became such a jam as more and more poured in that their hero had to be rescued by a side window. Only after disgraceful scenes in the parlors, in which even women got bloody noses, and several thousand dollars' worth of damage was done, was the situation relieved by the device of setting tubs of punch on the lawn to lure the new "democracy" out of the house.

The scramble for drink and a view of the President, however, was nothing compared with the scramble for office which immediately began. In the Senate, William L. Marcy of New York enunciated the now famous doctrine that "to the victor belong the spoils"; and what has become known as the "spoils system," in its more complete form, at least, dates from the election of the first great tribune of the people. The situation in Jefferson's day had been unique, and there was reasonable excuse for the comparatively moderate changes which he made in the personnel of the civil service. On the whole, that service had been maintained on a high level of permanency of tenure by every successive President, with the thought of service to the people rather than of spoils for the party in power.

Now, however, all was to be changed, and a new era opened in American practical politics. Hereafter distribution of public offices as rewards for campaign services was to become one of the means of building up party machines. Even so staunch a Jacksonian as Senator Thomas H. Benton, of Missouri, saw the mischief that the new system was to bring into our public life and had protested violently against it, but the pressure was overwhelming, and Jackson, with his belief that any honest man could perform any public duties, made no effort to control the situation.

The actual number of changes in proportion to the total number of places has often been exaggerated, something more than one third of the presidential officers being changed and less than ten per cent of the postmasters, but the main point was the change in ideal and system, and the substitution of Marcy's war cry for the old belief in permanent tenure regardless of political affiliations. The spoils system had long been practiced in many of the States locally, and strong pressure had been brought on Adams to introduce it into national politics, though he had not budged an inch in his opposition to it. Indeed, his high stand on the question had been one of the contributing causes of his defeat. With the election of Jackson the dam had burst, and thereafter to an ever increasing extent the "practical" politicians were to be free to debauch our public life.

The new President had scarce taken office when a storm suddenly broke upon him from an unexpected quarter, nearly wrecking his administration before it was fairly started, and completely disrupting the newly formed Cabinet. Major Eaton, the Secretary of War, had married in January a certain Peggy O'Neill who was the daughter of the keeper of the inn where the bachelor Eaton had lodged for some years. Scandal, whether justly or not has never been known, had long played around the reputation of the lady, who had been married to a dissipated naval officer who finally committed suicide in 1828. Eaton's name, among others, had been linked with hers and his marriage was taken as a confirmation of rumor. Whatever the facts may have been, the ladies of Washington society, especially the wives of the other Cabinet officers, would have nothing to do with her, and the social complications became unbearable. Even Mrs. Donelson, the wife of the President's private secretary (a nephew of the late Mrs. Jackson), who was acting as mistress of the White House, was extremely chilly toward the unhappy woman whom the President was defending, and at one time actually left the White House rather than carry out his wishes in the matter.

Jackson's unassailable loyalty to a friend, his naïve chivalry toward all women, and his own personal experience in having the good name of his own wife unjustly attacked, made him inflexibly determined to stand by Eaton and his unfortunate Peggy. Van Buren,

THE "CELESTÉ-AL" CABINET

Jimmy O'Neal, the doorkeeper, introducing Peggy Eaton (Celesté) to the Cabinet. Butler (the second on left) is saying, "She is well enough but I have conscientious scruples on these matters." Van Buren (last on right) answers: "Pooh, pooh, Butler, this is not the age for scruples of any kind. She is of my school. She has popularity and must command votes. Invite her to my ball tonight."

From the Library of Congress

CLEVELAND, FROM CORNER OF BANK AND ST. CLAIR STREETS, 1833

Left to right: Cleveland Academy, Trinity Church (first church erected in Cleveland), First
Presbyterian Church, and the Court House.

From the engraving by Whelpley in the Stokes Collection, New York Public Library.

GRAND RAPIDS IN 1831

whose wife was dead and who thus had no domestic complications to follow his social acceptance of Mrs. Eaton, was the only one in the Cabinet to stand fast with Jackson. The affair had its ridiculous side in that the fate of an administration appeared to be hanging not on the Cabinet but on the Cabinet's wives. Political capital was quickly made of the situation and "the Eaton malaria," as it was called, threatened to upset the new party.

Van Buren and Calhoun had been the chief contesting influences in the formation of the Cabinet, and in seeking to control the President. The rise of Van Buren and the downfall of Calhoun both received important impetus from their contrasting attitudes toward Peggy. When the President was told that a hundred congressmen demanded Eaton's removal, he replied characteristically, "Let them come—let the whole hundred come on—I would resign the presidency or lose my life sooner than I would desert my friend Eaton or be forced to do an act that my conscience may disapprove." When some of the clergy officiously took a hand in the affair, Jackson told one of them that "I did not come here to make a Cabinet for the ladies of this place but for the nation." For a year, however, the "malaria" continued to eat into the health of the administration, until cured, as we shall see later.

Like most of the public men of his day, Calhoun was a massive egotist and consumed with ambition. One of the best speakers of the time, he had been in public life for twenty years, in Congress, as Secretary of State, and twice as Vice-President. Starting as a nationalist and then swinging round to a narrow sectionalism, he had become the most extreme advocate of States' Rights and the interests, as he saw them, of the South. Coldly intellectual but vigorous and courageous, he was not widely popular though politically powerful, and had joined his Southern strength to Jackson's Western one with the expectation that he would succeed that popular idol in the presidency.

Unquestionably the leader of Southern political thought, we have noted how in opposition to the tariff of 1828 Calhoun had begun to lead his State of South Carolina on the road to nullification which was later to end in secession a generation later, although at the time of which we are now writing the question of slavery was not prominent and was entirely overshadowed by the sectional one of the tariff. On the other hand, the types of economic structure and civilization in the North and South were becoming so different that two facts must have been at the bottom of the thinking of Southern politicians. One was that the structure of the South was irretrievably based on slavery, and the other was the waning power of that section as evidenced by population and other statistics.

Since the South Carolina legislature had published and distributed Calhoun's "Exposition" as an official document, nullification had been a topic of more and more heated discussion. It had reached into Congress itself. Calhoun, as presiding officer of the Senate, was unable to voice his own doctrine, but Senator Robert Y. Hayne of Calhoun's State became the spokesman of the nullifiers. A debate on the disposition of western lands in the beginning of 1830 had brought out much sectional feeling, Senator Benton of Missouri claiming that the Northeastern States had always been "selfish and unprincipled" in their attitude toward the West, while Hayne suggested that the West and South form an alliance against the North on the question of the tariff. Finally, at the end of January, Hayne made a long speech, lasting part of two days, in which he not only attacked Webster's stand on the tariff but went on to advocate Calhoun's doctrine of nullification as a proper remedy against Northern despotism.

On the 26th of that month, Webster began his famous reply, the greatest speech of his whole career and by many considered one of the greatest of the nineteenth century. The first day, speaking for three hours without a pause, he confined himself to defending himself and his section against Hayne's charges, and to the question of the tariff. The following day, however, he launched into a magnificent denunciation of the nullification doctrine, interpreting the Constitution as he had when he had appeared as counsel in the cases of *McCulloch vs. Maryland* and others in which he had expounded his views of that instrument.

There was much to be said for the historical rightness of the belief of Calhoun and many others that the Constitution had originally been a compact between sovereign States. Webster may well have stressed too greatly the other point of view from the standpoint of what may have been but probably was not in the minds of the original framers, when they wrote that "we, the people," instead of "we, the States," were to form a more perfect Union. However, in the forty and more years that had elapsed since, under Marshall's decisions, and the course of national expansion and development, the more or less academic question as to what the framers may have meant had been shifted to what the people had come to believe and desire, and there was no doubt that in the minds of most citizens the Union had come to signify something far more binding than it had in the minds of the necessarily compromising Fathers.

"It is to that Union," thundered Webster in the peroration to his speech, "we owe our safety at home, and our consideration and dignity abroad. It is to that Union that we are chiefly indebted for whatever makes us most proud of our country. . . . Every year of its duration has teemed with fresh proofs of its utility and its blessings; and although our territory has stretched out wider and wider, and our population spread farther and farther, they have not outrun its protection or its benefits. . . . I have not allowed myself, Sir, to looked beyond the Union, to see what might lie hidden in the dark recess behind. I have not coolly weighed the chance of preserving liberty when the bonds that unite us together shall be broken asunder.

"I have not accustomed myself to hang over the precipice of disunion, to see whether, with my short sight, I can fathom the depth of the abyss below; nor could I regard him as a safe counsellor in the affairs of this government, whose thoughts should be mainly bent on considering, not how the Union may be best preserved, but how tolerable might be the condition of the people when it should be broken up and destroyed. While the Union lasts we have high, exciting, gratifying prospects spread out before us, for us and our children. Beyond that I seek not to penetrate the veil. God grant that in my day at least that curtain may not rise! God grant that on my vision never may be opened what lies behind! When my eyes shall be turned to behold for the last time the sun in heaven, may I not see him shining on the broken and dishonored fragments of a once glorious Union; on States dissevered, discordant, belligerent, on a land rent with civil feuds, or drenched, it may be, in fraternal blood!

"Let their last feeble and lingering glance rather behold the gorgeous ensign of the republic, now known and honored throughout the earth, still full high advanced, its arms and trophies streaming in their original lustre, not a stripe erased or polluted, not a single star obscured, bearing for its motto, no such miserable interrogatory as 'What is all this worth?' nor those other words of delusion and folly, 'Liberty first and Union afterwards'; but everywhere, spread all over in characters of living light, blazing on all its ample folds as they float over the sea and over the land, and in every wind under the whole heavens, that other sentiment, dear to every true American heart,—Liberty *and* Union, now and forever, one and inseparable!"

The rhetoric today seems somewhat ponderous, as Webster's always was, but it suited perfectly the taste of the people and the time, and the speech gave a living soul to the intellectual concept of Union. It both expressed and developed a passionate devotion in the hearts of multitudes then and since to the belief in union as the paramount good of the nation, making Calhoun's historical hair-splitting seem pale and unreal in comparison.

That statesman, however, and his followers, believed that the President, known to be a strong States' Rights man, would take their side, and some weeks after Webster had electrified the nation in the Senate, they planned a dinner to celebrate Jefferson's birthday, April 13, at which they intended publicly to link the names of the dead and living Presidents to their doctrine of nullification.

After several speeches had been made and toasts proposed, all with the object of showing that nullification was good democratic doctrine, approved by Jefferson and Jackson, it came to the President's turn to propose a toast. To the horror of the plotters he rose, and looking straight at Calhoun proposed "Our Federal Union— it must be preserved!" The toast was drunk, but in silence. Then Calhoun stood up. Hesitating a moment, he proposed "The Union —next to our liberty the most dear," adding, "may we all remember that it can only be preserved by respecting the rights of the States, and by distributing equally the benefits and burdens of the Union."

The President had spoken in a way that could not be mistaken, and the breach between his views and those of the Vice-President was clear. It was about this time that Jackson also discovered for the first time that Calhoun, alone of the Cabinet in Monroe's time, when Jackson had got into hot water in Florida over Arbuthnot and Ambrister, had demanded that the General be arrested and tried, and although Calhoun had subsequently posed as Jackson's defender on that occasion, the real defender had been John Quincy Adams. The facts having been brought to Jackson's attention he frankly demanded an explanation from Calhoun, who replied insincerely in such a way as to destroy Jackson's confidence in him completely.

Almost coincident with this came the culmination of the troubles in the Cabinet, the "Eaton malaria" having at last reached its crisis. By adroit manipulation, Van Buren, who offered his resignation, jockeyed Eaton into offering his also, although it was some days before Jackson would accept either. The President then demanded the resignation of the others, and completely reorganized the Cabinet, placing Edward Livingston of New York in the State Department, Lewis Cass of Michigan in that for War, Levi Woodbury of New Hampshire in the Navy, and making Roger B. Taney of Maryland Attorney-General. Van Buren, now confident of being the heir-apparent to the presidency after Jackson, was given the post of Minister to England, and Calhoun and the South were wholly excluded.

For nearly two years after these events, Calhoun and the nullifiers remained quiet, but the storm broke in 1832 when Congress passed a new tariff, which was more equitable than the old but a compromise which suited no section of the country completely. In November a State convention was assembled in South Carolina which passed an Ordinance declaring the Tariff Act to be null and void within the State after February 1, 1833. Following this, the State legislature also passed various Acts providing for the purchase of arms, and the raising of a military force to protect the people against the enforcement of the tariff by the Federal authorities. The Convention had declared that if the Federal Government employed force the State would be absolved from all obligations to the Union and would secede.

Meanwhile Jackson had just been triumphantly re-elected, with Van Buren replacing Clay as Vice-President. The ticket, which for the first time in American national elections had been nominated in a National Convention, won every State from Clay and Sergeant except Massachusetts, Rhode Island, Connecticut, Delaware, Maryland, and Kentucky, the electoral vote being 219 to 49. South Carolina, then in the throes of the Nullification controversy, deliberately threw away its electoral vote on John Floyd of Virginia, who did not run in any other State. Of the campaign in relation to its chief issue, that of Jackson's antagonism to the Bank of the United

A CARTOON COMPARING CONDITIONS UNDER FREE TRADE AND
PROTECTIVE TARIFF

From "The United States Weekly Telegram," November 5, 1832.

States, we shall speak later, and have here to note only, with regard to nullification, that the President had carried every Southern State except South Carolina. The rest of the South, indeed, showed no wish to follow that fiery Commonwealth along the path it was now treading, and which was eventually to lead to the greatest tragedy in the history of the nation.

Jackson had countered the threats of the South Carolina Convention and legislature by sending General Winfield Scott, a warship and several revenue cutters to Charleston, and posting troops conveniently near but sufficiently far off not to precipitate an immediate clash. In December the President issued a Proclamation to the people of South Carolina (where he had himself been born), pointing out that armed resistance to the Federal government was treason, and that as President he would have to perform his duty to put down rebellion. In January he asked Congress to pass an Act giving him the power to use the army and navy to enforce the tariff law.

Coincident with the passage of this "Force Act," as it was called, Congress also passed hastily a new tariff measure which conceded some of the Carolinians' demands.

South Carolina, receiving no support from her sister States, decided to be content with what she called her victory, and the crisis passed. There had been a somewhat general demand in the country for a lowering of the tariff but it may be questioned whether by passing the Act in seeming compromise with Nullification, the way was not made easier for the far more serious recrudescence of the doctrine in 1860. Jackson himself declared that he believed the tariff was only an excuse, that South Carolina really aimed at a new Southern Confederacy, and that the question would be raised again with the negro as the pretext next time.

Although the President had shown himself a thoroughgoing nationalist, he had been nurtured in the West, and, as we have earlier noted, the West had had its disillusioning experiences with banks in the panic of 1819. Already there had become deep-seated in that section a mistrust of banking and in particular of the "money power" as concentrated in the East.

In 1816 the second Bank of the United States had received its charter as a national institution, and although the charter was not to expire until 1836 Jackson had expressed his hostility toward it in his first inaugural. There was nothing to be done about the matter for the time being, but the President's increasing dislike of the institution was well known. The president of the bank, Nicholas Biddle, preferred to leave the question of securing a recharter open until near the date of the expiration of the old one but various politicians, among them Clay and Webster, urged him to apply for a renewal before the end of Jackson's first term. Biddle, unfortunately, allowed himself to be convinced of the spurious political wisdom of the move. Although a bill for rechartering passed in Congress, Jackson promptly vetoed it, and the fight on the bank was on in earnest.

On the whole, the bank had been managed honestly and had performed useful service. It was interwoven, however, at many points with politics, and in its attempt to circumvent an effort of Congress to preserve the issue of local bank-notes against too great competition by the Bank of the United States, it had made itself vulnerable by the issue of branch bank drafts, which became a circulating medium and decreased State bank profits. On the other hand, its friends were powerful. The period was not one of much delicacy of feeling as to the relation of public office to private profit, and such a man as Daniel Webster, always rather normally obtuse, saw no incompatibility with being at the same time Senator from Massachusetts and a director, counsel, and debtor to the bank, although in his capacity as senator he would have to judge the question of rechartering it dispassionately as a representative of the people. Congressmen and other officials, as well as leading newspaper editors, were favored with loans, and there is little doubt that the bank was buying influence.

In his veto Jackson expressed views on the Constitution which were not only absurd but dangerous. He claimed, for example, that there was no one branch or officer of the government which had the right to pronounce definitely on the constitutionality of any Act. He denied completely that the Supreme Court had any such power and asserted that every official had to interpret the Constitution for himself. Such a naïve theory would lead straight to anarchy, but there was enough of truth in the message to stir public opinion, and to the surprise of the bank and its supporters, Congress sustained the veto.

The party which had been formed in opposition to the President, and which called itself the National Republican (and later the Whig) Party, decided, in the absence of any other issue, to make that of the bank the one on which it should go to the polls in the election of 1832, following the veto. The idea, which was Clay's, was a most unfortunate one, and, as we have seen, Jackson won an overwhelming victory. In whatever way the fight between the bank and the President might otherwise have terminated, the latter now had a clear mandate from the people, as the result of the election, to destroy the hated institution.

There was no longer any hope of securing a new charter, but Jackson, having been stung by the opposition, did not wish to wait even for the natural dissolution of the bank in 1836. In 1833, soon after his second term began, he ordered the removal of the government deposits,—about $10,000,000,—and when the Secretary of the Treasury, Louis McLane, refused to sign the order, Jackson dismissed him and replaced him by William Duane. When he also declined, after some hesitation, Jackson again changed his Secretary and installed Roger B. Taney, who proved more amenable. Leading senators, in opposition, like Clay, Webster, and Calhoun, were furious at what proved a fatal blow to their institution, and, although the House approved the move, they succeeded in securing the passage in the Senate of a resolution of censure on the President for having assumed an authority which they claimed he did not constitutionally possess. It was not until 1837, in response to the constant and insistent demands of Senator Benton, that the President and his followers succeeded in having the obnoxious resolution expunged.

Meanwhile, under unwise laws and the absence of such restraint as the bank had exercised, the currency became inflated by excessive issues of State bank notes. There had been in any case great prosperity, marked by speculative excesses. In 1835 the national debt had been completely paid off, and a surplus of $28,000,000 had accumulated by 1836. Under Clay's leadership an Act was passed in Congress distributing this among the several States, much to the advantage of local politicians but little to that of the people. Shortly before the end of his last year of office, Jackson attempted to stem the tide of speculation and inflation by ordering that only specie could be accepted in payment of public lands bought from the government, but the full effects of the financial situation that developed were to be felt by his successors.

Unwise as Jackson's policy was against the bank, it was undoubtedly popular and embodied the fear of the ordinary American citizen of monopoly and special privilege, in itself an extremely healthy sentiment. In his diplomacy with France, the President also gave expression to another emotion of the now rapidly growing nation, our pride in our increasing strength. America, like other nations, had spoliation claims against France for destruction of the property of its citizens by Napoleon, but although France paid those of other countries, she declined to pay ours, which we properly considered as an insult.

The matter dragged along, and it was not until France had haggled for sixteen years that an agreement was reached in 1832 when, for certain concessions and counter-claims, the French Government finally consented to pay us 25,000,000 francs, in six annual instalments. Even yet, however, France haggled again, and declined to pay the draft for the first instalment, imposing on us $170,000 in charges for its protest. In June, 1833, having got tired of French methods, Jackson ordered our fleet to be in readiness for service, and in a message to Congress recommended that if France did not pay its acknowledged and over-due debt, we should seize enough French property to pay ourselves.

France now claimed that we had insulted her, though it is difficult to see how, and refused to pay until we had apologized, which we properly declined to do. In November, 1836, our minister asked for his passports and left Paris. Neither nation really desired war, and both were glad of the mediation of England to bring matters to a peaceful settlement, which was accomplished by the payment by France of four instalments due at the time. The payments were not made, however, until the old soldier in the White House had notified Congress that "the honor of my country shall never be stained by an apology from me for the statement of truth and the performance of duty."

In 1836 Jackson was a worn man in his seventieth year, and apart from the now well-established tradition of two terms only for a President, it was natural to look for some one else to lead the Democrats in the campaign. Jackson's triumph over all his enemies was completed by the election of his favorite Van Buren, whose nomination he had dictated, the Whigs having nominated William H. Harrison, the old frontier hero of Tippecanoe. It was a thorough beating, Van Buren receiving 170 electoral votes to Harrison's 73. South Carolina, still sulking, threw away her entire vote on Willie P. Mangum of neighboring North Carolina.

Massachusetts gave hers, as a compliment, to Daniel Webster, who was never to achieve the high office which his ambition had craved for years. The more one studies that oratorical statesman, the more

THE DOWNFALL OF MOTHER BANK

Clay's plea as he falls in the ruins is: "Help me up, Webster! or I shall lose my stakes"—to which Webster replies: "There is a tide in the affairs of men, as Shakespeare says! so my dear Clay, look out for yourself."

From the Library of Congress.

HARD TIMES IN 1837

From the Library of Congress.

one has to come to the conclusion that he was a man who had great abilities and performed great service but who was himself essentially not great. Other leading men in public life at that time were also vain, pompous, and theatrical, but with Webster, in spite of his genius as a public speaker and the debt we owe him for his influence on our concept of national Union, we become conscious of a certain fundamental flabbiness of fibre in his character. The people flocked to hear him speak but even if he had secured the nomination for the presidency instead of quadrennial disappointments, he would never have been a popular choice, though he might have been elected. All chance of that was now gone, however.

In one respect the election of 1836 had been unique in that no candidate for Vice-President received the necessary majority of the total votes, and for the only time in our history the choice had to devolve on the Senate, which chose Richard M. Johnson of Kentucky, who had been given the largest vote in the Electoral College.

The new President, Van Buren, was more or less of an enigma to his contemporaries, who called him the "little Magician," and who considered him rather as the slyest of political foxes than as a man of any outstanding ability. A popular bit of doggerel which went the rounds proclaimed that—

> "With his depths and his shallows, his good and his evil,
> All in all he's a riddle must puzzle the devil."

There could be no greater contrast than between him and the swaggering, blustering but open and frank-minded "Old Hickory," now gone to end his days at his beloved "Hermitage" in Tennessee. The short, plump, and dapper little politician from New York, suave and silken in manner and manœuvre, has come to rank rather higher for ability in our day than he did in his own, but his one term of office was to be chiefly marked by one of the great economic catastrophes which America has periodically suffered.

We had been going through one of our speculative debauches in Jackson's term, heavily discounting the future development of the country, plunging ourselves in debt to do so, to an extent, not less, it is estimated, than $500,000,000, of which a great part was tied up in lands and owing to the North by the South and West. The sale of public lands, which amounted to 4,658,000 acres in 1834, was 12,564,-

000 in 1835 and 20,074,000 in 1836. It is quite evident that such an increase did not mean substantial development but wild speculation. The rage seized every one. New York City real estate rose from a valuation of $250,000,000 in 1830 to over $400,000,000 five years later. Farm lands on Long Island were boomed like bubbles to bursting, and in Maine waste tracts of timber were sold in some cases at 1000 per cent of their ordinary value.

In June, 1836, the distribution of the national surplus among the States caused a heavy shifting of deposits, and in July the Specie Circular, making only gold and silver receivable for public land sales, had tended quickly to drain much specie from the East to the small localities in the West. Nervousness grew among business men, and failures began, steadily increasing in the early part of 1837. Two New York banks failed, and on May 9 over $650,000 in coin was withdrawn from the financial institutions of that city. The next day its banks suspended specie payment, soon to be followed by those throughout the whole country, including the former Bank of the United States, in Philadelphia, which had accepted a charter as a State bank when refused a renewal by the Federal Government. New York became almost like a dead city, with building operations stopped and ships and barges lying idle at their docks. What was true of that centre was true of the others, and it was said that the great merchants of New Orleans could not pay five cents on the dollar of their debts to New York.

With many of the banks in which the government had been depositing its money failing, it became a problem what to do with the national funds, which Van Buren could hardly place in the Bank of the United States. The President proposed a plan for an independent Treasury to care for government monies, but this was so bitterly opposed by the Whigs that it did not come into operation until 1840. Meanwhile, the Bank of the United States itself had crashed in 1839, and brought on the second stage of the crisis. Up to that time, the West had fared rather better than the other sections but after that event it felt the full force of the financial storm.

In the East the streets had been filled with men and women of all sorts out of work. Nine tenths of the factories closed in New England, shipping and whaling were largely suspended. The "white-collar" class of the day felt the catastrophe almost as heavily, and it was estimated that one half to two thirds of all clerks and sales-men in Philadelphia had been discharged. Defalcations by bank officers became notable in frequency, and, owing to counterfeiting, confidence was all but destroyed in the currency, it being said that at one time there were nearly 1400 different forms of counterfeit and worthless notes in circulation

It was estimated that between 1836 and 1840 there were 33,000 commercial failures, involving a loss of $440,000,000, in addition to the far huger but incalculable losses in the values of lands, merchan-dise, and other forms of property. The winter of 1838 was unusu-ally severe, and the number of unemployed was so great that even in New York the means of carrying them through were insuffi-cient. In spite of private charity, and overflowing poor-houses, not a few of the destitute died of starvation or were frozen to death. The condition of labor did not reach its lowest point until 1841, after which the general situation began to improve.

While the helpless President in the White House and the people at large were suffering this long agony, events of considerable sig-nificance were happening on our Southwestern border. For some reason, the Emperor of Mexico had early encouraged settlement within the empire by Americans, and had offered far better terms to settlers than our own government did for the taking up of lands. Under the leadership of Stephen F. Austin, several hundred Amer-ican families had settled in one of the best parts of the Mexican province of Texas, and by 1834 there may have been 20,000 Ameri-cans there of whom 2000 were negro slaves. Austin and his first followers had intended to become loyal Mexican subjects, and had believed that they were emigrating from the United States for good.

By the beginning of the third decade of the century, however, the situation had become complex. On the one hand, the government in Mexico had been overthrown, and there seemed little prospect of established order. Slavery, which had been illegal but tolerated, might be in danger, and the settlers had no wish not only to lose their property in slaves but to be reduced to tilling their own soil in the absence of any other form of labor. On the other hand, a different type of settler had of late been emigrating into Texas, slave-smugglers like the Bowies, adventurers of the frontier sort, or restless and ambitious spirits like Sam Houston.

In 1835 Santa Anna, the new ruler of Mexico, proclaimed a Constitution which swept away the local rights of the Texans, and an uprising occurred On March 5, 1836, Santa Anna, with 2000 troops, attacked about 200 Texans shut up in the Alamo in San Antonio, and captured it only after every one of its defenders had been killed or wounded, murdering the wounded after the surrender. Revenge was near at hand, and on April 21 a Texan force completely routed Santa Anna and drove the Mexicans out of the province, the leaders in which then drafted a Constitution legalizing slavery, and proclaimed Texas to be a sovereign and independent State. We had allowed many Americans to join the Texan army, and it can scarcely be said that we had remained neutral in the struggle. On the last day of his term, Jackson had recognized the new republic.

This, however, did not satisfy the Texans, who clamored for annexation to the United States, and Van Buren inherited the problem, as he had the financial panic, from his predecessor. It was far from being a mere diplomatic question with Mexico, which had refused to acknowledge the independence of her revolted province. The more serious aspect of the problem was domestic for us, and involved the whole dangerous subject of slavery. The South had begun to realize that the Missouri Compromise of 1820 was working badly for her. Her steadily decreasing weight in numbers, influence, and wealth, as contrasted with the more rapidly growing North and West, seemed to call for additional territory in a zone where slavery would be profitable in order to redress the balance.

Texas was large enough to be cut up into possibly eight or nine States of approximately the average size of the old ones. There is no need of considering that the situation as it developed had in any way been the result of a Southern plot, although many Northerners began to claim that it had been. The drift into Texas had been as natural as the drift to any other attractive frontier, and the subsequent course of events had also been natural, if violent. The demand of Texas to be admitted to the Union, however, at once changed the aspect of affairs, and the ensuing debate was completely occupied with the question of the extension of slavery within our own borders.

Although the South was as strongly in favor of annexation as the North was opposed to it, and a resolution was introduced into Congress in 1838 for the purpose of annexing the southern Republic, Van Buren, who had no wish to have the slavery question come to sharp issue, was able to keep annexation from more than simmering during his term. As we shall see in the next chapter, however, slavery as an issue had distinctly come to the front, and the reopening of the controversy in more serious form than ever before was to be one of the two distinguishing features of the administration of the unfortunate "little Magician," whose term was dogged by ill-luck from start to finish. We were to recuperate promptly from the panic which was coincident with his four years of office, but the darker issue of slavery was to permit of no such normal and peaceful recovery. Its shadow was now beginning to darken the whole land, and the wisest of statesmen could indulge only in sad foreboding.

CHAPTER XIV

THE NATION IN MID-CENTURY

THE financial storm of 1837 had blown itself out by 1841, and, as has always happened in America, the business activity of the country leaped forward to a higher plane of volume and prosperity than before. In the decades following, a new America was beginning to emerge. Comparatively simple as the nation of 1860 appears to us today, nevertheless a distinct change of phase had occurred, comparable only to that succeeding the panic of 1893, and fundamentally more complete. Confused as the changes and the voices of the period may seem, they were in fact singularly harmonious with one another, as we shall note at the end of this chapter.

One of the noteworthy alterations in the living conditions of a considerable part of the population was in the shift from making goods in the homes to buying those made in factories. Between 1825 and 1855, for example, the number of yards of textiles per person made in the home declined in New York from almost nine yards to only a trifle over a quarter of one yard, and what happened in that State, where we have better statistics than elsewhere, was happening in the nation at large. The other side of the picture was the great rise in the textile manufacturing, which had its centre in New England.

Moreover, what was occurring in the weaving of materials for clothing was occurring in other goods also. For example, many of the farmers formerly had spent their winter evenings making nails and tacks by hand on little forges set up in their kitchens, a good man turning out sometimes 2000 tacks in a day. With the invention of machinery, this handicraft, like so many others, became centralized in factories, Massachusetts supplying about one third of the total product used in the country. By the 1830's the boot-and-shoe industry was also becoming largely localized in that State and in particular places, such as Lynn, which built forty-two new streets between 1831 and 1840. Shoes for slaves were shipped even to the far South, one Boston wholesale house shipping lots of $20,000 and $30,000 at a time to Savannah.

These are but indications of a process which was revolutionizing the life of the people, and in 1851 Horace Bushnell in Connecticut predicted that "the transition from mother-and daughter-power, to water-power and steam-power" was "greater by far than many have yet begun to conceive." Clothes, hats, tools, all sorts of things that had been made in the household by expenditure of time instead of money were beginning to be bought in stores. By the end of the period, 1860, in spite of the panic of 1857, the number of wage earners in manufacturing had risen to 1,311,000 and the value of the product to $1,886,000,000.

Such a huge development would not have been possible except for a purchasing power on the part of the people and such improved means of transportation as would permit of a circulation of goods at freight rates less prohibitive than those called for by the old system. A series of remarkable harvests, combined with an increased demand for produce not only from our own growing urban population but from an increasingly industrialized Europe, provided the capital; and canals, to be followed by railroads, provided the transportation. The opening of the Erie Canal, which we noted, in 1825, had caused an immediate drop in freight rates between Buffalo and New York from $100 per ton of merchandise to less than $8, making possible a heavy interchange of manufactured products of the East for farm produce of the West, and giving New York an incomparable advantage over every other Atlantic seaport.

Other canals were also built farther south but none carried anything like the tonnage of the Erie, which even survived the railroad competition soon to come. In 1830 this competition was negligible as there were only 23 miles of railway in the entire United States, but by 1860 there were over 30,600, chiefly in the North and West. Steamboats had also come on the great rivers, and as early as 1830 Cincinnati and Pittsburgh factories were beginning to supply the Southwest with machinery, furniture, and other factory goods at less than had been the cost of such goods in New York or Philadelphia a decade earlier. One of the marked features of the period was this decreased cost, with consequent widening of markets, due to both machinery and an almost ninety per cent reduction in transportation charges.

All the factors acted and reacted on each other, so that there was not only an enormous increase in business activity but a steady differentiation of occupations. The farmer or plantation owner at the beginning of the century had been a Jack-of-all-trades who had literally *manufactured,* that is made by hand, almost everything used in daily life as well as in raising his crops. He was, however, rapidly giving place to the agriculturist on the one hand and the industrialist on the other.

Moreover, with the growth of manufacturing and of trading centres, town and country were becoming more sharply differentiated in manners, thought, and modes of life. By the end of the period the urban population, that is the number of people living in towns of more than 8000 inhabitants, was increasing almost three times as fast as the total. By 1860 New York, including the now Borough of Brooklyn, had reached a population of about 1,175,000, being double that of its nearest competitor, Philadelphia, which nevertheless had added 200,000 in a decade. Abnormally rapid growth, according to all previous standards, was indeed, in this period, the characteristic of American towns and cities, except, for the most part, of those in the South. Great cities were rising all through the changing West, such as St. Louis, which multiplied its population tenfold, from 16,000 to 160,000, between 1840 and 1860.

The opportunities of the New World attracted foreign immigration in rapidly increasing hordes after 1820, and the famine in Ireland in 1846 and the political troubles in Germany in 1848 made enormous increases in the numbers who came from those two countries. In the decade ending December 31, 1840, 600,000 came to us, mostly from Europe as always; in the next decade 1,713,000, and in the next 2,600,000. Of the last group, those arriving between 1850 and 1860, over 950,000 were Germans, 914,000 Irish, 385,000 English, and 154,000 from Canada. The vast south European immigration of later years had as yet begun only as a trickling stream.

By 1860 there were nearly 4,140,000 foreign born living in the United States, of whom nine tenths were in the free States, settled for the most part in the larger urban centres of the East and in the farm States of the Middle and Northwest, the Irish preferring the

PITTSBURGH AND ALLEGHENY FROM COAL HILL, 1849

From a color lithograph by B. F. Smith in the Stokes Collection, New York Public Library.

FRONT STREET, FROM MAIN TO BROADWAY, CINCINNATI, 1835

From a water-color in the Historical and Philosophical Society of Ohio.

FOURTH STREET, ST. LOUIS, 1840

At the right is the First Presbyterian Church.

From a lithograph by Wild. Courtesy of The Mabel Brady Garvan Institute of American Arts and Crafts, Yale University.

East, and the Germans and Scandinavians the West. Coming to us in abject poverty and with a low standard of living, the Irish were utilized by the factory owners and other employers of labor to reduce wages, and after about 1840 there was a distinct decline both in the character of the New England operatives themselves and in the conditions of their work.

Although in 1828 a political "Workingman's Party" was formed, labor soon turned to the system of trades unions to attain its aims and reforms, chiefly limited to hours of work and better social and educational status. So long as our present form of government lasts a "Labor" as contrasted with a "Socialist" Party is not likely to be successful. The reason for this is that the Federal Government has not sufficient Constitutional powers to enact legislation beneficial to the laboring class, these powers belonging mainly to the States. But a political party limited to a State only is of no influence under the workings of our political system, so that labor, to a very great extent, has necessarily to apply its pressure by other methods.

Some progress was made in the period under review by strikes and other exercises of the power of trades unions, chiefly in securing a more universal ten-hour day instead of one of from twelve to thirteen. One of the early leaders, George H. Evans, published a labor organ in New York, *The Working Man's Advocate,* but the union movement, which had enlisted some 300,000 men by 1836, suffered severely in the terrible years following the crash of 1837 and it was not until the Civil War came with its tremendous effects on laboring conditions that the more characteristic features of the American labor movement were to become notable. In so far as the influx of foreign labor influenced politics in the earlier period it was mainly by greatly enlarging the ranks of the Democratic Party and, in the case of the herded town and city workers, of increasing the power of the local bosses and political machines.

When we turn from city to country we find considerable changes from the beginning of the century. The condition of the New England farmer had in some ways retrograded. Apart from the nature of the soil, the broken character of the land has for the most part always made large-scale agricultural operations in that section difficult or impossible. The small farmer of the old days, having almost no need for cash, had been able to make by family production all he used. It was quite a different problem, however, so to increase the salable products of the small one-man farm as to keep pace with the new and incessant demands for cash with which to pay for the new factory-made goods and tools. This was especially emphasized by the opening of the Erie Canal when the competition of the richer and more easily worked lands of the Mohawk Valley and the West began to be felt severely. In spite of some increase in cash markets afforded by the growth of near-by manufacturing centres, there was a steady flow of New Englanders to the West. To some extent this was due to the pressure of the Irish, who both reduced wages and made certain kinds of work seem beneath the dignity of the native New Englander, who at that period was almost as class-conscious where the Irish were concerned as was the white in the South with regard to the negroes.

To a great extent the soils of Maryland and Virginia had become exhausted for large-scale production of the single staple crop of tobacco, and those States were reverting to the small-farm system, much like New England, a system also found in the uplands of the Carolinas and Georgia. The large plantation-slave economy still held sway, chiefly in the great "Cotton Belt" stretching westward from Alabama to Texas, which took all the native born slaves which could be bought, and all who could be smuggled into the country from Africa.

In the Northwest, the period saw the beginning of wheat growing on the scale which was to make that section the "wheat empire" as the far South was the "cotton kingdom." The invention of farm machinery, such as the McCormick reaper, of which 75,000 were in use by 1867, the Marsh harvester, threshing and other machines, made possible the raising of huge quantities of grain, and when, after an export trade had begun, the price rose in Europe from thirty cents to a dollar and seventy during the Crimean War in 1854, the Western farmers thought their fortunes made. Three years later we exported over $55,000,000 worth of bread stuffs alone as against $48,000,000 of manufactures. The South, however, with an export of $192,000,000 worth of cotton, mostly to feed the looms of England, could well deceive itself into believing that cotton was king.

The fabulous increases in American population by European standards, the building of railroads, the huge development of an export market for our agricultural surplus, the rapid growth of our cities,—all these and other factors tended to foster the spirit of speculation which we shall note in the next chapter, and to nurse that optimism which from now on was to become an American characteristic. Everywhere America was reaching out for new markets and possible profits. In the Southwest, in 1821, a party which,

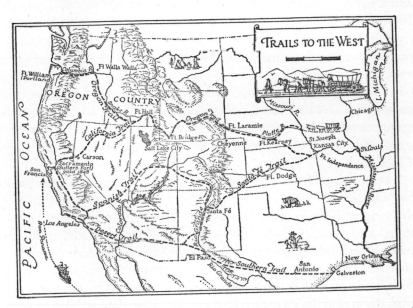

under Captain William Becknell, had left the then remote settlement of Franklin, Missouri, to barter with the Indians for furs, had reached Santa Fé overland, and there found the beginning of a new and profitable trade. One girl at home who had put $60 into the venture netted $900 as her share of the profits. Three years later another party brought back $190,000, mostly in gold and silver, as a sixfold profit on their venture. As a result of this trade, the "Santa Fé Trail" was established, leading southwestward from Independence, Missouri, as the "Oregon Trail" led thence northwestward. Along the latter, by 1845, long trains of the "covered wagons" were passing carrying their hundreds of settlers out to the northwest coast.

While wagons and "prairie schooners" were thus rumbling over the western plains and through the mountain passes, ships from eastern seaports were establishing a temporary maritime supremacy for us on the seas. The picturesque China trade had largely changed since the War of 1812 and by 1840 over eighty per cent of our imports from that country consisted of tea, which we also began to carry to England after that nation repealed her Navigation Acts in 1849.

We had long been building vessels which outsailed the British and it has been said that when the *Oriental,* owned by A. A. Low and Brother of New York, first reached London in 1850 with her cargo from the Far East, she created almost as much excitement in that port as the tea ships had when they arrived in Boston Harbor in 1773. Just as we had adapted old types of wagons to the needs of our long western hauls and produced the "prairie schooner," so our shipbuilders had developed the old type of vessels into what was unquestionably the most perfect sailing ships the world has ever seen, and probably the most beautiful things ever produced in America.

The opening of the Erie Canal had not only given an impetus to our over-seas trade but had gradually resulted in concentrating shipping at New York rather than at Boston, though the old-established and wealthy Boston firms continued in the trade, using the port at the Hudson instead of that on Massachusetts Bay. Speed was an essential advantage, and for this the "clipper" ship was specially designed. Small at first, and not running much over 100 tons until 1840, they rapidly increased in size after that date until the *Great Republic,* built in 1853, attained a tonnage of 4555. Speed rather than size, however, was always aimed at. Some of the older-type vessels, in charge of what was then as fine a breed of sea captains as have ever commanded for any nation, could make remarkable voyages. The *Houqua,* for example, owned by the Lows and commanded by Captain McKenzie, made, among other record-breaking runs, that from Shanghai to New York in eighty-eight days in 1850, but the clipper, first invented and designed by John W. Griffeths of New York in 1841, considerably exceeded in speed the record holders of the older sort.

The first clipper, the *Rainbow,* built for Howland & Aspinwall in 1843, was only 750 tons but the fastest vessel then afloat, though soon to be outsailed by the *Sea Witch.* Her low black hull, her gilded dragon as a figurehead, her rakish masts and cloud of can-

SOUTH STREET WATERFRONT, NEW YORK, 1855
From the model by Dwight Franklin in the Museum of the City of New York.

THE *JAMES BAINES*
Built in 1854 by Donald McKay for James Baines and Company of Liverpool. On June 17, 1856, she made twenty-one knots with main skysail set, the highest rate of speed ever made by a sailing vessel.

THE YANKEE CLIPPER

From a drawing by W. J. Aylward.

vas, made her the handsomest ship then sailing from America, as she was unquestionably the swiftest in the world. In her best twenty-four-hours' run, 358 miles, she could even beat any steamship of her time. These and other clipper ships had completely taken away the prize from Great Britain for shipbuilding, and when the *Oriental* arrived in London, only ninety-seven days out from Hong-Kong, she was the finest ship that had ever been moored at the docks of that port. *The London Times* warned the English ship-owners that they would need all their skill and "dogged determination" to meet the competition, and the Admiralty asked permission to take the lines of the *Oriental* as she lay at dock.

With the opening of the California trade and the gold rush, a fleet of superb clippers under different owners was put into that service, and made some unsurpassed records for speed. The *Flying Cloud* and the *Andrew Jackson* both made the voyage from New York to San Francisco in eighty-nine days, battling their way under vast spreads of sail around Cape Horn, and such other ships as the *Sword Fish,* the *Flying Fish,* the *Great Republic,* and the *John Gilpin* made their records in but a few days longer. There was also the Australian fleet, which included such magnificent clippers as the *Donald McKay* and the *Flying Scud,* while the trans-Atlantic ships cut the time from Boston to Liverpool down to less than fourteen days.

The glorious era of the clipper ship, however, came to an end in the late 1850's. English and American steamship lines had been in business for a couple of decades but had used only side-wheelers, which left the advantage to the swift sailing packets, until the Inman Line began to run fast screw steamships in 1857. The improvement in the steam vessels, the turning from wood to iron for the hulls of ships, our Civil War, and other factors all doomed the old clippers and our merchant marine as a whole, and our supremacy passed to the English. The epoch, however, had been magnificent while it lasted, and had greatly helped to give the Americans that self-confidence and optimistic belief in themselves and their future which was one of the most marked characteristics of the period, together with the abounding energy which, not content with the colossal task of developing the territory we possessed, was reaching out across the plains and seas.

This optimistic spirit was also emphasized by the extraordinary way in which our every effort to develop the resources of the vast and rich public domain was seconded by a scientific discovery which seemed always to come just in the nick of time. For centuries mankind had progressed slowly and it had been only in the more recent centuries that new inventions, such as movable type, the mariner's compass, and so on, had begun to be made at moderate intervals. But almost at the moment when more than half a continent offered its opportunity of exploitation to us, the marvellous changes of the modern age also began.

As Jefferson and Adams had predicted, it might have taken centuries for us to fill up and make habitable our western possessions had the transportation problem not been solved by steam on land and water. From the beginning of history man had to rely upon animal transport on land and sail on sea as the fastest and most efficient means known, each of which, nevertheless, was comparatively useless for the physical tasks which confronted us in subduing our huge portion of an empty continent to the needs of man.

But it was not only steamboat and railroads that seemed to open a new era of boundless expansion and accumulation of wealth and increased population to us. Inventions, literally by the thousand, were being made. Before 1840 a few hundred patents a year only had been taken out; after 1850 the annual number steadily rose above 1000 until, in 1860, 4778 were issued. Many of these were worthless, but great numbers were not. We have already mentioned the enormous importance of the cotton gin. In 1835 came the Colt revolver, and in the next decade the farm machinery of all sorts, the sewing machine in 1846, matches, and furnaces for heating houses in 1850, while the electric telegraph, first used in 1844, covered the whole country with a network of instantaneous communication soon after the founding of the Western Union Company a dozen years later. Although, perhaps fortunately, as we shall see in the next volume, the submarine cable which cut the time of transmission of news between America and England from two or three weeks to a few seconds, was not to be laid until 1866, attempts had been made to lay one since 1850, and success was merely a question of time.

The new political theories of the latter part of the eighteenth century, involving as they necessarily did the natural goodness and the perfectibility of man, had gradually transformed the texture of the ordinary thought of the nineteenth. There had been time for these doctrines to "sink in," as we say, and the change from the older beliefs in the essential sinfulness and vileness of man caused a tremendous outburst of optimism and hope, which often found expression in fantastic ways and in the many "isms" of the period. They were, however, also at the bottom of much of the humanitarian striving and of the many movements for the emancipation of man's spirit and the amelioration of his condition.

Among the more or less fantastic movements were those which led to the formation of communities to carry out various forms of life, mostly communistic in principle, based on the ideas of reformers, such as that of Robert Owen, who had founded New Harmony in Indiana in 1824. More than forty communities of all sorts were established in the decade from 1840 to 1850, of which that at Brook Farm was one of the most famous, including at times among its members such men as George William Curtis, George Ripley, Charles A. Dana, and Nathaniel Hawthorne, and among its visitors Bronson Alcott, Margaret Fuller, Emerson, and others equally distinguished.

Following the teachings of the French philosopher Fourier, many communistic associations, called "Phalanxes," were formed and spread over New Jersey, Indiana, Illinois, Wisconsin, and other States. Some of the communities founded were distinctly religious, and others, like that of Oneida established by the "Perfectionist" John Humphrey Noyes, combined sexual with communistic experiments, in his theory of "complex marriage," a system between ordinary marriage and polygamy. The latter was openly advocated and practised by the followers of the new religion of Mormonism which we shall note below.

Especially in New England and the frontier from New York westwards, the break-down of the old religion to some extent, and the narrowness of emotionally starved lives, provided a hotbed for the rapid spread of new religious ideas no matter how crude. About 1833 William Miller of western New York had begun to preach the immediate second coming of Christ, and gathered communities which finally spread from Maine to Wisconsin. Miller was but one of scores of self-appointed prophets who preached doctrines to the sort of minds impervious to the new teachings of Unitarianism which under the leadership of such men as William Ellery Channing were appealing to thousands of the more intellectual New Englanders and transforming the religious atmosphere of the old Puritan colonies.

In 1823 an otherwise unsuccessful youth of seventeen, Joseph Smith of Wayne County, New York, claimed that he had been visited by an angel from God, who returned four years later and delivered to Smith a holy book written on plates of gold, which Smith translated as "the Book of Mormon." On the basis of the doctrines of this pretended revelation he began to gather disciples, organizing them under the title of "the Church of the Latter Day Saints," Smith himself acting as its "Prophet." A community was formed at Kirtland, Ohio, and the doctrine of polygamy, which had already been practised by Smith and some of the other leaders, was declared to have been received in a written revelation from God, which disconcerting revelation the original Mrs. Smith is said to have put in the fire with considerable display of personal feeling.

Forced from Kirtland by the hostility of their neighbors, the community moved to Missouri, where after a time they were barbarously treated by the Missourians and driven from the State, settling again at Nauvoo, Illinois, where their community grew faster than even the rising city of Chicago. Polygamy evidently had its attractions. When Smith was murdered at Nauvoo, Brigham Young succeeded him, and as a result of a missionary visit to England, brought over 4000 converts, mostly from Liverpool.

Illinois after some years became too hot for the community, and in 1846, Young, who was an excedingly able man and a genuine empire-builder, led the 12,000 Mormons across the plains, spending the winter near Council Bluffs, while Young himself with a chosen group of followers went on to the valley of the Great Salt Lake in Utah. Although many refused to go so far, 5000 followed in the spring and the great Mormon State had been founded. Under the iron, and it may be said, the very efficient and on the whole wise, rule of Young, the new community prospered. The waste country was made to bloom by irrigation and "the busy bees of Deseret," as they later called themselves, grew in numbers and in wealth. Hard

IN THE WOODS AT BROOK FARM

RALPH WALDO EMERSON
From a photograph by J. J. Hawes.

HENRY D. THOREAU
From a crayon drawing by Rowse.

A CAMP MEETING AT SING SING, NEW YORK

From a drawing in "Harper's Weekly," September 10, 1859.

work, shrewd business sense, and the fruits of polygamy quickly developed a commonwealth, in which, however, there was no system of irrigation planned for the mind.

The movements of the time, however, were far from being limited to these aberrations. There were strong crusades against both capital and unusual punishments. It was a time when the hangings of criminals were still too frequently conducted in public, and were sometimes made festive holidays on the theory that the sight would act as a deterrent. In some States, lashings with whips, branding on the face, and other relics of barbarism were legal punishments, and these were fought, and to a considerable extent abolished, by the reformers of this period. The treatment of the insane was unbelievably cruel, and their cause was pleaded in State after State by Dorothea Dix, one of the most modest, noble, and competently efficient and successful women our country has known. In eight years she travelled over 60,000 miles, visiting all the States but three, and in many of them secured great reforms by simply presenting the picture of conditions as she had found them.

The eighteenth century had been notably one of hard drinking, both in England and America, and even in the period of which we are writing not only drinking but drunkenness was common among classes and in situations where public opinion would not tolerate it today, nor for a long time past. Not only was whiskey considered a necessity for workmen and laborers at their work but clergymen drank heavily at their meetings and not seldom fortified themselves with a good stiff drink before they began to preach. Lawyers of national reputation were sometimes drunk when pleading cases in court, as were leading senators of the United States in the Senate chamber. Poor grades of whiskey were so cheap that it was said that a man could get drunk twice for sixpence, and the evil was serious and widespread, especially among the working classes.

Temperance societies had been formed in many places and much missionary work by temperance lecturers had been done for several decades. The great attack, however, came with the rest of the humanitarian movements toward the middle of the century. In 1830 the State of Ohio passed laws providing for partial prohibition, and in 1846 Neal Dow, of Maine, secured the passage of the first complete prohibition law in any of the States, partially modified five years later. Before 1857, thirteen States, all in the North and West, had enacted legislation regulating drinking and the liquor traffic more or less completely. Nevertheless, on the whole, the aim was temperance and not enforced abstinence, the leading organization, the Washington Society, being opposed strongly to any prohibitory laws, and the movement as a whole was based, like the others of the day, on the belief in the essential moral goodness of the individual. As has been well said by Gilbert Seldes, the student of all the "isms" of this period, in the middle of the last century the word "reformer" meant one who was striving to give liberty to others, whereas today it connotes too much one who is seeking to take liberty away.

Drink had been closely linked, too much so probably, in the minds of many with the poverty of the periods following the War of 1812 and the panics of 1819 and 1837, and the condition of the poor was also attacked from another direction. Before the 1830's, sporadic efforts had been made to abolish imprisonment for debt but after 1835 State after State took action as a result of the propaganda against the barbarous custom. Indiana forbade the imprisonment of women debtors, Maine that of any one for sums owing of less than $10, and in varying forms similar restrictions or total abolition were passed by Ohio, Vermont, Connecticut, Louisiana, Delaware, and other States.

In many of the numerous humanitarian reforms, the women of the country had taken great interest as they had a direct stake in the results, but finding that their co-operation was often made difficult, if not impossible, on account of the prejudice against their sex taking part in public affairs, leaders among them began what has become known in all its various aspects as the "woman's movement." One of the starting points had been the refusal to allow eight American women delegates to a World Anti-Slavery Convention in London to take their seats, merely because they were women.

Such leaders as Lucretia Mott, Elizabeth Cady Stanton, and Margaret Fuller, became ardent in the effort to secure fuller civil rights, and in a dozen years following 1839 succeeded in getting laws passed in seven States giving them control, even when married, over their own property. They also began to insist upon their right to attend colleges, and in 1848 the first Woman's Rights Convention of the world was held at Seneca Falls, at which resolutions were passed demanding equality with men in suffrage, before the law and in all opportunities for education and earning a living. Annual conventions were thereafter held, in spite of almost universal condemnation, until the movement, like many others, was temporarily interrupted by the larger exigencies of the Civil War.

Reform, as we have said, was almost wholly directed toward securing a greater liberty for the individual and opportunity for expansion of all his powers and capacities against the pressure of legislation and

HEADING OF *THE LIBERATOR*, GARRISON'S ANTI-SLAVERY PAPER, APRIL 23, 1831
From the original in the New York Public Library.

society instead of securing hobby "reforms" of single groups by the imposition of pressure. There was, of course, much of the crank influence in what was in reality a great surge of public feeling for humanitarianism, but on the whole the goal in each case, that of a better and enlarged life for the individual, was kept clearly in the forefront. Obviously in a movement which was nation wide and which seemed to impinge on every side of our natures and on all classes, the problem of slavery was bound to be considered.

There had long been a certain amount of agitation against it, and the Quaker, Benjamin Lundy, had published from 1812 to 1836, his journal called *The Genius of Universal Emancipation*. This, however, was too conservative for the fiery and unbalanced temper of one of his assistants, William Lloyd Garrison, who in 1831 started a paper of his own in Boston, the famous *Liberator*. In the first copy he struck the keynote which was to be that of the Abolitionists' thought and crusade until war finally came. "I shall strenuously contend," he wrote, "for the immediate enfranchisement of our slave population. . . . On this subject I do not wish to write, or speak, or think, with moderation. No! No! Tell a man whose house is on fire, to give a moderate alarm; tell him to moderately rescue his wife from the hands of the ravisher; tell the mother to gradually extricate her babe from the fire into which it has fallen; but urge me not to moderation in a cause like the present. I am in earnest—I will not equivocate—I will not excuse—I will not retreat a single inch—and I *will be heard.*"

The Abolitionists became so involved with our national political history that their movement more properly belongs in the next chapter, and we need note here only that in 1832 the New England Anti-Slavery Society was formed in Boston with the objects of the abolition of slavery and the immediate emancipation of all slaves, followed the next year by the organization of the American Anti-Slavery Society. The Abolitionist Crusade was greatly influenced by the currents of thought in Europe, as were our Communities, the crusade against drink, that for woman's rights, and other movements. Like all of them, again, Abolitionism exemplified the increasing organization of the people into societies and the admittance of all to a share in the struggle for any object of widespread interest. Just as the old "caucus" in politics, where candidates had been chosen by a few leaders in secret, had given place in 1837 to the political convention, so was the use of the convention becoming universal in other departments of our life, as a result of the democratic spirit of the age.

We were, indeed, on the threshold of the mass-age, notable in many ways, but which was also leading to what has been called the "hysteria system." The gathering together of herds of people in cities, the spread of the press and the greater ease and swiftness of communication of all kinds, were beginning to give us the mob spirit on a larger scale than anything we had yet known. It was a period of passion and strong contagious emotions of all sorts, too little balanced by thought and individuality. The mass-emotion was to be felt in political conventions and presidential elections, in the rapid spread and the emotional appeal of all the humanitarian movements, and in the great mass meetings of the religious revivalists.

Men like Charles G. Finney, "the brigadier-general of Jesus Christ," and a little later Henry Ward Beecher, swept audiences of

KISS ME QUICK.

Children: this is the third time within an hour that I have placed your hats properly upon your heads.—There !!

STOLEN KISSES IN THE FIFTIES
The subtitle of this Currier and Ives print reads: "Children, this is the third time within an hour that I have placed your hats properly upon your heads—there!!"

THE AGE OF BRASS.

A CURRIER AND IVES PRINT REFLECTING ONE PHASE OF THE PUBLIC'S ATTITUDE TOWARD WOMEN'S RIGHTS

From the Library of Congress.

men and women with pure emotionalism, while swarms of lesser itinerant preachers relied solely upon excitement to produce temporarily in their hearers the sense of salvation and of release. The fuller and better life which all craved, and of which humanitarianism was a sound social manifestation, was, in the religious sphere, all too-much debased to the level of mere intoxication, and tended to increase the sense of nervous tension in which the nation was to live, politically and otherwise, during this period.

The great mass of our people in all sections were interested neither in things of the mind nor in healthy sports. There were few diversions either for those crowded into cities or living on l o n e l y farms or clearings. The village w a s unutterably dull. We were emotionally starved, and in many sections the camp meeting revival, with its gatherings of thousands who all let themselves go in common emotions, even sexual orgies, offered alone that release from a life of inhibitions which the normal human being craves. We have to take into consideration this starved life and the ease with which any issue appealing to the emotions would spread like fire, to understand the decades leading to the war.

LOOK AT THIS!

GENTLEMEN.—I have for Sale, at Mr. Batre's former Livery Stable, Two Horses, the one called Josephus, and the other Dick.
Josephus and Dick, can't well agree,
As Dick is ill humored, being a Cherokee;
Dick cries out sell me quickly,
Or in Mobile I'll soon get sickly,
And also observes, he is fond of pacing,
But dislikes the idea of carrying specie.
But as Mobile Bank Bills I can't obtain,
Tombeckbe will do for poor Eugene.
For first cost I'll sell, to the first applicant,
As little Dick is getting so very eloquent.
Then, Messrs. Editors, as the times are dull without exertion,
Give the following equation, one insertion:—
Let X. the cost of Josephus, and Y. that of Dicks, explain,
Hence by a quadratic, you their cost may gain.
When the Cube Root of X. is to the Square Root of Y.
As four times X, is to twelve and a half times Y,
may 19, 47

A SALE OF HORSES ANNOUNCED IN VERSE FORM

From "The Mobile Commercial Register," May 19, 1823. By courtesy of the Mobile City Library.

To leave this life of the new and seething Jacksonian democracy and turn to the unexpected flowering of our literature in the same period is almost to pass into another world. After drifting to the Middle and even Southern States a few generations earlier, the intellectual activity of the nation in the decades before the Civil War had unquestionably returned to the neighborhood of Boston. The

South seemed to be more and more cut off from the main streams of thought that were influencing the rest of the world. Its very type of life, founded upon slavery, was becoming an anachronism in the modern age, and it seemed as though having to entrench itself in this respect against the forces which were sweeping the rest of civilized mankind, resulted in closing its mind for the most part to the newer intellectual currents. It was as though unconsciously it were felt, as by the later religious Fundamentalists, that if the new streams of thought were allowed to invade life at one point, they would end in altering all, and so should be resisted at any point where they might enter.

Whatever the cause, the South in this period may be almost disregarded. It gave to the nation no great religious thinkers nor scientists, and when we compare the names of its chief literati with those of New England the difference is too obvious to need comment. Its most notable writer, William Gilmore Simms of South Carolina, left behind him eighty-seven volumes, mostly of novels now almost wholly forgotten. He has been compared to Cooper but there was far more virility in Simms' robust realism than in Cooper's often absurd idealizing of the frontier, and although the popularity of the *Leather Stocking Tales* much outlasted that of *The Partisan, The Forayers* or *Woodcraft,* the author of the latter novels was perhaps really the stronger mind and the better artist. When, however, we have noted Simms, the now forgotten Paul Hayne, and the minor poet Henry Timrod, both also of South Carolina, we have sufficiently exhausted the contribution of the South to pass northward.

In doing so we may point to one odd fact. The life of the South was becoming more and more unreal, a romanticism, a refusal to look at facts, an insistence upon holding to the past, yet it produced in Simms probably the greatest realist in letters of the period, whereas the North, which was from the Southern point of view all too practical and materialistic, produced almost no realism, and its literature in great part was romantic or transcendental. Pausing in Maryland we meet at Baltimore the lonely figure of Edgar Allan Poe, the most individualistic as well as possibly the greatest of the American romantics, the greatest artist in pure verbal sound whom we have produced, and who in his tales and poems of an utterly unreal world wrought more miraculously in evocation of strange emotions than any other American.

In New York there was an odd assemblage of talent which was much more diversified and variegated than that which blossomed from the grave of Puritanism in Boston. Bryant, whom we noted as just beginning his career in the period before this, was to live on until 1878, serving for fifty years as editor of *The New York Evening Post*. None of his later work, however, reached the height of the slender volume of poems which he published in 1821 and which included "Thanatopsis" and "The Water Fowl." It was more or less symptomatic of the times and of American interests that the young poet ended as editor, as the far less distinguished poet, Fitz-Greene Halleck of the same city, ended as a clerk of John Jacob Astor.

In fiction, James Fenimore Cooper's long list of novels is now in process of being almost as forgotten and little read as Simms, and the once so popular Nathaniel P. Willis has left little except the wonder of how small an amount of genuine merit it may take to establish a great contemporary reputation. Washington Irving, who died in 1859, eight years after Cooper, has lasted better, and parts of his *Sketch Book* and *Bracebridge Hall,* chiefly owing to their delicate charm, have become American classics, and will probably continue a living part of our literature. With no profundity of either thought or emotion, Irving can lay no claim to greatness, but his work will long outlast most of that of the rest of his fellow New York men of letters with the exception of Herman Melville and Walt Whitman.

The former, quite misunderstood and largely ignored in his day, has at last come into his own, and his finest work, *Moby Dick,* is now recognized as one of the masterpieces of American literature. Among all the men of the period, Melville alone had a profound sense of evil, not as human sin as portrayed by Hawthorne, but as something far more than that and inherent in the very structure of the universe. With the most passionate nature of any of his contemporaries in letters, he reacted more deeply than did any of them against the conditions of American life as well as against the terms imposed on man by the cosmos itself. Pouring himself into his books, notably *Moby Dick,* he cloaked his thoughts in a romanticism to which most of his contemporaries found no key.

Whitman spans both this period and the next but had published

331

two editions of his *Leaves of Grass* by 1856. A rebel against the emotional inhibitions and emptiness of American life, he was also the most profound believer in its democracy and in the added riches that might come to human life by the "plowing up in earnest of the interminable average fallows of humanity." Choosing as his medium a form of verse which lacked stanzas, rhyme, and sometimes even regular metre, and was too frequently wanting in taste, he had, like Melville, to wait his time for recognition, but no one, especially in his later work, has given better expression to the gusto and faith of tumultuous democracy.

In passing to New England we may help ourselves a little to understand the transition perhaps by glancing at what a later and very typical New England professor of literature has to say of the New York group, Barrett Wendell in his *History of Literature in America*. In Whitman's style he finds a "decadent eccentricity," and claims that the democracy which led him to ignore values because of his "dogma of equality" was "the least native which has ever found voice in this country," where democracy has tacitly recognized "that excellence is admirable." Noting that Whitman was born in Brooklyn, Professor Wendell says that it was "close to the largest and most corrupt centre of population on his native continent. In Wendell's volume quoted, Herman Melville is not even mentioned.

It would be invidious to note these commissions and omissions unless they were going to help us to understand the New England point of view. The flowering of the mind of that section which after a century and a half of almost complete sterilization occurred in this period, was remarkable, though it is rather absurd to call it a "Renaissance." If one swallow does not make a summer, neither does the appearance of a few authors repeat that wonderful reopening of the human mind to the possibilities of life in all its aspects which distinguished the new era after the Middle Ages in Italy. It must not be forgotten that when Edward Everett placed a statue of the Apollo Belvedere in his Boston home he felt compelled to have it draped.

There were, indeed, marked limitations to the New England "renaissance." The re-opening of the classical literature to the Italy of the real Renaissance had brought about a desire, or was coincident with it, of living a rounded human life far more abundantly than it had been lived for a thousand years, and the leaders were essentially men of their own time. Life was humanized as it had not been for centuries. The America of the period following Jackson was a boisterous country bursting with energy, and in so far may have resembled the Italy of the fifteenth and sixteenth centuries, but to compare Professor Longfellow, Professor and Ambassador Lowell, and Mr. Emerson and the other New England leaders with the leaders of the Italian Renaissance is to note a vast difference.

Perhaps chief among the points we have to observe is the effort to escape from the frowsy, common, vast America of which the Boston and Concord groups declined to be a part, and their refusal to acknowledge or share in the unpleasant or ungenteel aspects of America or the universe. The other point is their desire, for the most part, to look anywhere for the goods of life except in the America outside of the sacred precincts of New England. Both these will come to light as we run down the catalogue of men who did most to enrich our literature in this period, outside of Melville and Whitman.

Although in New York, Irving had published *A Chronicle of the Conquest of Granada,* and lives of Columbus, Goldsmith, and Washington, he was not a scholar, and for two generations or so New England was to produce almost all the scholarly work in history and biography of the entire country. It was a distinguished group which arose in Boston,—Ticknor, Prescott, Motley, Palfrey, Parkman, Hildreth, and Bancroft. It is odd, however, how little they were concerned for the most part with American history outside of their own provincial section, and, because they provided almost all the history to be read and all had an unconquerable New England bias and limitation of interest, they set our history for long after in the New England mould of thought and of actual narrative.

Palfrey, with all his useful research, was not even New England but strictly Massachusetts Bay Puritan, and his *History of New England* was an *apologia* for his Puritan ancestors in which even the other New England colonies, such as Rhode Island, came off very badly whenever it was needful for the author to defend his idolized Masssachusetts against them. Ticknor left the American scene entirely, his chief contribution being a *History of Spanish Literature,* while Prescott wrote gorgeously of the histories of the conquests of

Mexico and Peru, or the lives of Ferdinand and Isabella, and of Philip II. Motley also turned toward Europe with his *Rise of the Dutch Republic, History of the United Netherlands* and *John of Barneveld*.

Bancroft, indeed, planned and largely finished a comprehensive *History of the United States,* written, however, largely around New England, which brought forth, in rejoinder, the more balanced work of Hildreth, with the same title. Although Bancroft was politically a Democrat and the earlier volumes of his History, as has been said, "voted for Jackson," he was rather a parlor democrat. "I love to observe the bustle of the world," he wrote in an early letter, "but I detest mixing in it. I like to watch the shouts of the multitude, but had rather not scream with them."

Greatest of all was Parkman, who did actually get out into our West himself, but whose magnificent series of volumes, among the most delightful of all American histories to read and even yet not superseded in the scholarship devoted to their period, dealt almost solely with the duel between England and France for the continent.

When we leave the historians, we get a yet greater sense of a certain aloofness of the New England mind to the turmoil of the real America of the mid-century decades. Lowell, in spite of lip service to democracy, can hardly be said ever to have understood it, and like Bancroft most assuredly did not like to mix with the crowd. Knowing his London far better than any American city outside Boston, in his seven volumes of literary essays he discusses only two American authors, his own neighbors Emerson and Thoreau. Hating the South, when his poetry dealt with national topics it was for the most part in the most bitter and hostile of sectional strains. Whittier was even more local in inspiration, no bad fault in a poet, but in the four volumes of his poems, though there are poems of Italy, his voice was scarcely ever raised on an American subject outside New England except in the sectional conflict over slavery. Holmes as well might have considered the charming Boston in which he lived as severed from the rest of the United States for all that found its way concerning them into his work. The most popular of the poets, Longfellow, when not dealing with New England themes, found his escape in European letters and legends. Hawthorne in his novels looked less to Europe than to the Massachusetts past and in his classic *Scarlet Letter* struggled with the problem of sin in the setting of the Puritan colony.

Hawthorne, like many of the other New England leaders in letters, seemed not to glimpse at all the unity or the possible greatness of the nation of which New England was merely a province. At the beginning of the Civil War he was to write to a friend: "Whatever happens next, I must say that I rejoice that the old Union is smashed. We never were one people, and never really had a country since the Constitution was formed." In perfection of style and form his *Scarlet Letter* probably surpasses any other "classic" in the brief line which may be thus considered in our literature, but in that book, as in most of his work, his thought derives from the old Massachusetts Puritan conception of personal *guilt* rather than from the deeper and more universal conception of *evil*. Far more of an artist than his one-time friend Melville, the reach and universality of his thought were far more circumscribed. Yet, so far as the limitations of the seventeenth-century Puritan mind of Massachusetts might ever permit of a burgeoning in the field of pure art, Hawthorne was its perfect flower.

The optimism of the period could not be escaped, except by the brooding Hawthorne, but it is also notable that the new religious development which sprouted from it in New England was opposed to the general religious development of the nation. Under the leadership of a group of cultured and saintly men, of whom perhaps the chief was William Ellery Channing, the old Calvinistic theology, with its stress on the essential vileness of man, gave way to an agreeable belief in his goodness, and by the mid-century the Calvinism of the Bostonian churches had been transformed into Unitarianism, which became the religion, not of the masses, but of Boston society. While the people at large were demanding a religion which would satisfy more deeply their emotional nature, New England shifted, when it did, to one that was gradually vaporized into good manners, comely living, and a sense that all was well.

In Concord, Thoreau, whose career extended far into the next period, but who had published his possibly best known volume, *Walden,* in 1854, preceded by some years by his *Week on the Concord and Merrimack Rivers,* was also seeking, in his own peculiar way, escape from the America of his time in solitary living, a rebel against tax-paying and modern society, in his hut on the shore of Walden Pond.

Near him lived Emerson, the greatest figure of all the New England "renaissance." Beginning as a clergyman but feeling too heavily the trammels of authoritative beliefs and ceremonies, he had resigned his pastorate to become a lecturer. A wide-ranging reader but not a scholar, disdaining any organized philosophical system, he was for several generations to remain the stimulating preacher for high-minded youth. Through him passed in full measure the optimism, much of it unthinking, of his period. Almost untroubled by any suspicion of evil in the universe, he preached in scintillating phrases and metaphors that thrilled the heart, the highest idealism which has been the heritage of Puritan New England.

Stressing both the worth and the unlimited possibilities of the humble individual, his was a trumpet voice calling to each to raise himself to the plane of the noblest. American in his optimism, his disregard of evil, and the worth of the individual, he was also American in his reliance upon intuition and his disregard of the hard road to high achievement. Like the Bible, one can find in his writings, texts for almost any attitude toward life, but the mass of his writing, as also innumerable sentences, stir the young reader to an extraordinary self-reliant endeavor after the nobler things of life. In his refusal to be troubled by the deeper problems of the universe, and in his belief that all can attain by effort, he expressed some popular aspects of Americanism more authentically than any other writer of his time. Essentially New England, he became also universal.

New England was thus undoubtedly contributing more to the intellectual needs of the time than any other section. Yet the lasting balance may not be so much in its favor as is often assumed. It produced no such consummate literary artist as Poe of Maryland, no one who so understood democracy as Whitman, and no thinker who sensed the problem of evil in the universe as did Melville of New York. But the influence and reputation of all three of these men were almost negligible in their own time, and Boston, as we have said, was then the intellectual centre of the country.

It is for that reason we have emphasized the fact, important in the next chapter, that on the whole it was an intellectual centre which took little interest, as it derived little sustenance, from our nation considered as a whole. New England, always markedly provincial in outlook, had drifted farther and farther from the main streams of American life, intellectually as well as economically, from the date of the opening of the Erie Canal. For the most part its literature was one which looked from Boston to Europe rather than from

A MISSISSIPPI RIVER SHOWBOAT: SPALDING & ROGER'S FLOATING
CIRCUS PALACE

From the Theatre Collection, Harvard College Library.

Boston over the United States. The flowering of the mind was one of which the nation might be proud, yet it was mainly the flowering of New England, and when the poets who should make the songs of a nation looked beyond their own section in any direction but Europe it was only to be oblivious of the West and scathingly to denounce the South.

New England was thinking wistfully of romantic Europe or of its own fading past. The South, fighting the time spirit, was trying to keep from any alteration in its static civilization which might produce the first crack in the system of slavery. It feared both the future and the main currents of the day. Only in the Middle States and the West were men living intensely in the moment but looking joyously forward and allowing themselves to float, for better or worse, on the full flood of American life.

Education made distinct advances in the period, though to a considerable extent, as always with us, it was in quantity rather than in quality. Some eighty small denominational colleges were founded between 1830 and 1850, and there was also some progress in professional schools of law and medicine. The notable contribution of these decades, however, was to the theory of free education for the masses of the people. This was largely brought about by pressure from the working-class groups and against much opposition by the tax-payers. There was a violent contest in Pennsylvania about 1834, won by those who demanded free schools, and the victory in that State was followed by a gradual adoption of the system elsewhere, already in operation in New York and New England. Whatever the laws might require, however, the schooling, as well as the school buildings, in most States, including the Northeastern, were deplorable for the most part, and it was chiefly in the 1840's and under the lead of Horace Mann of Boston that an improvement was begun which was to prove lasting.

In the arts, literature was the only one which was flourishing in these decades, and, in spite of the founding of the National Academy of Design in New York in 1828, painting, which had seemed to be in its May-time in America just after the middle of the eighteenth century, had slipped back to a dreary March. Even portrait painting had greatly degenerated, and the invention of the daugerreotype gave a blow to the feeble successors of Peale, Copley, and Stuart. Both painters and sculptors tended more and more to escape to Europe, and the cult of Italy and Germany began. Not a single sculptural work of importance was produced in this period, which was mainly concerned with practical matters far remote from the arts. Even in letters, as we have seen, the best men were to a considerable extent neglected, and poets had to appeal to innocuous sentimentalism, like Longfellow, or become advocates of social or political causes, like Whittier and Lowell, to secure wide audiences.

The home of Horace Greeley, who is shown in the foreground.

PRINTS BY CURRIER AND IVES OF A NORTHERN AND SOUTHERN HOME
BEFORE THE WAR
From the Library of Congress.

THE WHITE HOUSE IN 1840
From a contemporary engraving in the Library of Congress.

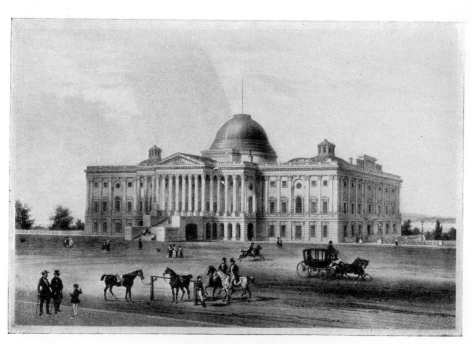

THE CAPITOL IN 1848
From a lithograph by Deroy after a drawing by Köllner.

The sentimental also found expression in music in which there was little interest, although an Academy of Music had been established in Boston in 1832 where Lowell Mason was doing more than any one else to elevate the American taste. The only music which found its way to the hearts of the people was the accompaniment to songs, and the words were even then the greater attraction. It has been said that the largest income derived by any artist in our country in this period was that which poured in on Stephen C. Foster following the publication in 1850 of his "Old Folks at Home," and

The dying words of Little Katy
OR
WILL HE COME.
Written by Solon Robinson.
MUSIC BY
Horace Waters
(Author of the Mothers vow &c.)
arranged by
THOMAS BAKER

VOICE.

Andante Semplice.

PIANO.

8.
Will he come? will he come?— weak hands are feeling!
He has come? he has come.— I see him kneeling—
One kiss— the light— how dim 'tis growing—
I thank— 'tis dark— good bye— I'm going—
     Hot corn— no more shall cry— hot corn!!!

9.
Drop a tear, drop a tear, for she's departed,
Drop a tear, drop a tear, poor broken hearted;
A pledge— a pledge—the world is crying,
Take warning— warning— by Katy's dying.
     Hot corn, who'll buy my nice hot corn.

A BALLAD OF 1853
Part of the original in the J. Clarence Davies Collection in the Museum of the City of New York.

it is to him that we owe also "My Old Kentucky Home," and other negro melodies. Grand opera was organized in New York a little before that date but was mainly, as it has always to a great extent remained, a merely high-priced adjunct to society instead of filling the needs of a genuinely music-loving people.

In the theatre there had been no advance, and perhaps a retrograde movement, so far as repertories were concerned, in the century since 1750, and the stage was mainly supplied by actors from abroad,

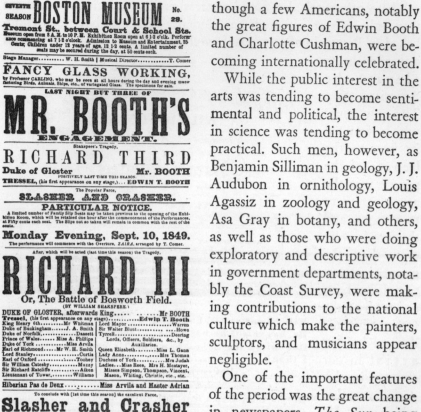

though a few Americans, notably the great figures of Edwin Booth and Charlotte Cushman, were becoming internationally celebrated.

While the public interest in the arts was tending to become sentimental and political, the interest in science was tending to become practical. Such men, however, as Benjamin Silliman in geology, J. J. Audubon in ornithology, Louis Agassiz in zoology and geology, Asa Gray in botany, and others, as well as those who were doing exploratory and descriptive work in government departments, notably the Coast Survey, were making contributions to the national culture which make the painters, sculptors, and musicians appear negligible.

One of the important features of the period was the great change in newspapers, *The Sun* being founded in New York in 1833, and sold for a cent, as was *The Herald,* established by James Gordon Bennett two years later. In 1841 came *The Tribune,* owned by Horace Greeley and edited for a while by Charles A. Dana, who later went to *The Sun. The New York Times,* then comparatively unimportant as contrasted with its position today, began a decade later,

FACSIMILE OF PROGRAMME OF EDWIN BOOTH'S FIRST APPEARANCE ON THE STAGE AT THE BOSTON MUSEUM, SEPTEMBER 10, 1849

From the Shaw Collection in the Widener Library, Harvard.

in 1851. The new press, with its methods, considered extraordinarily sensational and enterprising for the period, with greatly increased circulation, and edited by men who were national figures, soon

FIRST APPEARANCE OF JENNY LIND IN AMERICA, AT CASTLE GARDEN,
SEPTEMBER 11, 1850

From a Currier lithograph in the Museum of the City of New York.

SONTAG, SALVI, AND BADIALI IN "LUCIA DI LAMMERMOOR," AT CASTLE
GARDEN, NEW YORK

From the J. Clarence Davies Collection in the Museum of the City of New York.

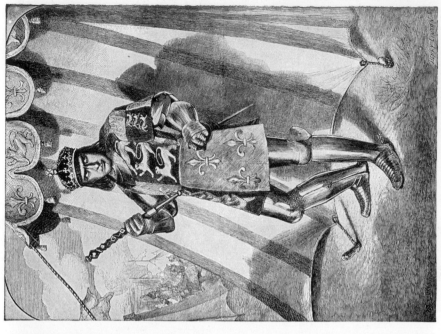

EDWIN BOOTH AS RICHARD III

CHARLOTTE AND SUSAN CUSHMAN AS ROMEO AND
JULIET

From the Theatre Collection, Harvard College Library.

acquired greatly increased prestige and influence. Throughout the country men asked eagerly, not what does the *Sun* or *Tribune* say, but what does Greeley or Dana think? The editorial was a political factor of much weight, and while news-gathering was immensely improved, fabulous sums according to contemporary standards being sometimes paid for reporting of special events, the leading function of the greater papers was still that of organs of opinion.

We have been able in brief space to single out only a few topics for comment, from the seething life of the period, but they all point to four leading forces as becoming dominant,—democracy, humanitarianism, expansion, and sectionalism. All of these were closely intertwined and acted and reacted on each other. We have already seen, for example, how the frontier had contributed greatly to democratic doctrine, and as, instead of standing still and becoming settled and old, it kept receding to ever farther frontiers in the West, its influence increased instead of diminishing. The democratic doctrine, and the riches of the unlimited field for expansion, helped to breed the spirit of optimism, and optimism and democracy both helped to feed the sentiment of humanitarianism,

FACSIMILE OF A GRAND-OPERA PROGRAMME
OF 1847

From the original in the Theatre Collection of the Museum of the City of New York.

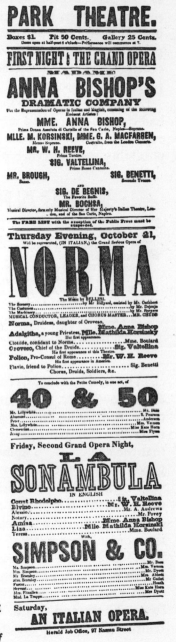

as they also affected the religious shift from the old Calvinistic pessimism. If, from the religious standpoint, men were innately good instead of bad, and if, from the optimistic standpoint, they were capable of indefinite improvement in nature and opportunity, the incentive was enormously increased to improve their position and opportunities in society.

Linked up with these factors were many of the economic ones. It had been the improved means of transport which was making rapid expansion possible, and was increasing at once the desire for, and possibility and influence of, such expansion. It is easy to trace the

MORNING HERALD.

VOL. 1.—NO. 34.   NEW YORK, WEDNESDAY, JUNE 17, 1835.   PRICE ONE CENT.

PUBLISHED DAILY, BY
JAMES GORDON BENNETT, & CO.
Office No. 20 Wall street, basement story.
And 34 Ann-st. (third story.)
TERMS FOR ADVERTISING.

1 square a year, $30 00	1 square 2 weeks, $2 25
do 3 months, 8 00	do 1 week, 1 75
do 2 months, 6 00	do 3 days, 1 00
do 1 month, 3 00	do 1 insertion, 50

Sixteen lines make a square.

HEADING AND PUBLISHERS' NOTICE OF *THE HERALD* OF JUNE 17, 1835

changes in the economic base in other directions. The improvement of the newspaper, for example, was made possible by the new inventions in printing-presses, and the dissemination and gathering of news by other new inventions. From another angle, we may note that the change from home manufacture to the purchase of factory goods released the woman from much of the incessant drudgery to which she had devoted her time, and with additional leisure came the questions of how to occupy it, and of wider opportunities and careers. Combined with democracy, optimism, and humanitarianism, the woman's movement thus sprang inevitably out of the conditions. Economic factors, once more, were making, as we shall note more at length in the later chapters, for sectionalism, especially with regard to slavery. Economic sectionalism was becoming very marked between North and South, tending to intellectual sectionalism, and reinforced by the humanitarian currents, to an increasing spiritual sectionalism.

All of these forces,—democracy, humanitarianism, expansion, and sectionalism,—were of high intensity. They would either have to be lowered in that intensity or else, if they encountered any obstacle, a catastrophe would inevitably follow.

CHAPTER XV

A DECADE OF EXPANSION, 1840–1850

THE catastrophe suggested at the end of the preceding chapter was not to arrive in the form of secession and a threatened break-up of the Union, irrevocably until 1860, but from 1840 the situation grew almost steadily more menacing. Between that year and 1850 the national boundaries were vastly extended. The circumstances and conditions of this increase in the national domain raised questions which brought to men's minds a possible splitting-up of the United States into at least two separate nations. By 1849 the situation seemed desperate, when by a fortunate compromise the evil day was luckily put off for another decade; a fateful delay which gave time for certain forces to come into operation in such a way as eventually to save the Union in spite of civil war.

The election of 1840 was fought out in the shadow of the panic of 1837 and the hard times following it. Van Buren, intending, when elected in 1836, to carry out the popular Jacksonian policies, had been caught in the economic back-wash which those policies had in part caused, though a business crisis would probably have come in his administration in any case. The opposing party, the Whigs, when they met in convention at Harrisburg in September, 1839, to nominate candidates and formulate a platform, were able to agree on the former but not the latter, and had in fact no policies to propose to the country. It was, indeed, a nondescript party, made up of all sorts of contradictory elements united chiefly by their fear of democracy and their desire to secure tariff or other favors from the government. It consisted for the most part of the wealthy and conservative of the several sections, and its ultra-conservativism had to be glossed over if the votes of the masses were to be secured. Especially was this the case if the West were to be lured into its camp. The old perennial Whig aspirants for the presidency, Webster and

Clay, were again passed over, and the western military hero of earlier days, the victor over the Indians at Tippecanoe, General William Henry Harrison, was nominated, with John Tyler, a Virginian politician of small calibre, as his running mate.

The Democrats, when they met in their convention at Baltimore on the 4th of the following May, reasserted the principles of Jefferson and Jackson in clear and unmistakable terms, and renominated Van Buren, although, an amusing and unique episode in our political history, they were unable to agree upon a candidate for Vice-President. Several States had nominated candidates for that office, and the Convention decided not to choose between them but to leave the decision, if necessary, to the Senate. For this they were jeered at by the Whigs, but they gaily flung back the retort that if they could not agree upon men at least they could do so on principles.

The nominations and campaign marked a change brought about by democracy and a widely extended suffrage in a vast country with conflicting local interests in different sections. The advance toward complete manhood suffrage had been steadily going on, and one State after another, Delaware 1831, Mississippi 1832, Georgia 1833, Tennessee 1834, had been abolishing even the small property qualifications for voting which had yet remained. In a widely extended democracy, an outstanding figure in public life, with a career of accomplishment behind him, is bound to have made powerful enemies in groups, classes or sections, and the plan adopted by the Whigs in 1840 of selecting as candidate a known man but one who had a minimum of enemies because he had a minimum of political accomplishment, was henceforth to become the accepted rule of playing safe in the fights for the presidency. The result has been that for some generations, except for unexpected developments of character —like Lincoln's or accidents like McKinley's assassination which brought in Roosevelt,—our statesmen of great ability or strong character have been more likely to be found in the House and Senate than in the presidential chair.

The campagn of 1840 made not the slightest pretence of appealing to the intelligence of the electorate. It was not marred like that of 1828 by bitter attacks on the morality of the candidates but was a prolonged spree of bunkum, torch-light processions, songs and nonsense. To catch the ordinary voter of the poorer classes, East and

West, old General Harrison, who, though sometimes pinched for ready cash, was moderately well-to-do and lived an easy and hospitable life in his large house in Ohio, was shown carrying an axe and wearing a coonskin cap in front of his "log cabin." On the other hand, Van Buren was accused of using gold spoons in the White House, and many a procession marched to the beating rhythm of "Van, Van, is a used-up man."

Coon Banner of 1840.

6¼ CTS. A DAY AND SHEEPS PLUCK to the LABOURER UNDER VAN BUREN

2 DOLLARS A DAY AND GOOD ROAST BEEF under GEN: HARRISON

Coon Promises in 1840.

"The fact of his (Gen Harrison's) election alone, without reference to the measures of his administration. will powerfully contribute to the security and happiness of the people.   It will bring assurance of the cessation of that long series of disastrous experiments which have so greatly afflicted the people.   *Confidence wi'l immediately revive—credit be restored*—ACTIVE BUSINESS WILL RETURN, and the PRICES OF PRODUCE WILL RISE!"—[See Clay's speech delivered at Hanover, Va., June 27, 1840, and published in the Madisonian of July 18.]

AN 1840 CAMPAIGN PROMISE WHICH WAS RECALLED IN THE 1844 CAMPAIGN

From "The Ohio Coon Catcher," published at Columbus, Ohio, October 5, 1844.   In the Library of Congress.

The "log cabin and hard cider" campaign, so notable in our annals, was, indeed, extraordinary in showing how lightly a democracy can decide who shall be its leader in a grave crisis. The Whigs had gauged the electorate accurately, and "Tippecanoe and Tyler, too" rode easily into victory, receiving 234 electoral votes against Van Buren's 60, though, indeed, the votes of the people themselves made a much more favorable showing for the latter, who received 1,129,000 to Harrison's 1,275,000. Increasing interest in politics, as well as our expanding population and perhaps better means of communication, were indicated by the fact that over a million more votes were cast in 1840 than in 1836.

Harrison and Van Buren had not been the only candidates in the field, and although the third party polled scarcely 7000 votes in the whole nation its participation demands more consideration than these figures would indicate. From the day nearly a decade earlier, when Garrison had set up his standard of Abolitionism in Boston, that movement had been carried forward with increasing bitterness, and by 1840 it has been estimated that the several hundred Abolition Societies in the Northern States numbered over 150,000 members. The violence of their views and the absurdity of their programme is shown in Garrison's denunciation (1843) of the Constitution, and his statement "that the compact which exists between the North and the South is 'a covenant with death and an agreement with hell'—involving both parties in atrocious criminality, and should be immediately annulled."

Like all fanatics, of whom we have had rather more than our share in America, the Abolitionists were ready to place their own particular cause above all others, irrespective of a sane sense of values. Slavery was a great evil, which civilized mankind was gradually growing away from, but unless the Abolitionists could have it ended immediately and in the particular way they insisted upon, they were willing to sacrifice the Union and all other national considerations. In fact, so utterly fanatical had they become that when they were demanding the dissolution of the Union by the withdrawal of the Northern States because slavery was not being immediately abolished on their demand they seem to have had no realization of what in truth they were trying to bring about. Like many other fanatics, they were thinking in terms of themselves and their own success rather than in terms of those whom they claimed to be considering, for a dissolution of the Union as they proposed, so far from freeing the slave would simply have fastened the shackles on him more firmly and long postponed the day of emancipation.

Indignation had run high in the South, caught between what seemed the inevitable crash of its economic system and type of life if slavery was destroyed, and the march of modern ideas evidenced by the abolition of slavery in the British Empire and the agitation in our own North. Southerners threatened Abolitionists with personal violence and even death if they should dare to enter Southern States, and demanded that Congress should pass laws forbidding the passage through the mails of incendiary Abolition journals and pamphlets.

On the other hand, there was also almost as violent feeling against Garrison and his followers in the North. Northerners had an intense dislike for the negro, who was frequently less kindly treated in New England and other northern sections than in the South itself. Connecticut was disgraced by the violent methods used against a white woman, Prudence Crandall, who, in spite of public opinion, dared to start a school for negro girls, and Abolitionists were threatened and attacked by mobs. In 1837 Elijah P. Lovejoy, a clergyman who edited an Abolitionist journal at Alton, Illinois, was killed and his printing plant destroyed. Garrison himself was assailed by a mob in Boston, and had to be rescued and placed in jail for safety.

Although Garrison was the most noted of the Abolitionists, and the most fiery in his denunciations of slavery and his demands for immediate and uncompensated emancipation, the Northerners opposed to slavery had many other leaders, and it was some of these who decided to run a third party in the election of 1840 on a platform of emancipation. At a convention held at Warsaw, New York, the group nominated James G. Birney for the presidency. For the most part, the move was bitterly contested by most of the Abolitionist Societies, which in many cases were split by the problem of what policy to pursue. Moreover, we Americans rarely like to throw away votes on third parties which cannot win, and as the hard cider campaign of 1840 got more and more uproarious not one perhaps in fifty of the members of the Abolitionist Societies voted for Birney.

As a result of ten years' agitation, however, a strong anti-slavery party had grown up in the North, intense feeling had been aroused on both sides of Mason and Dixon's line, and the dispute about slavery was more and more coloring our thoughts and entering into political problems which might seem more or less remote from it. Nevertheless, it yet remained a much debated question whether the Abolitionists really did anything to hasten the day of freedom for the slave.

To a great extent, conservative people, both North and South, wished, as far as possible, to let sleeping dogs lie. Both the close business ties between Southern producers of cotton and Northern manufacturers, and a genuine love for the Union untainted by money interest, made them desire to put off what might be the fatal day of decision. Slavery, quite as much as Northern factories and mills

GENERAL HARRISON'S LOG CABIN MARCH AND QUICK STEP

A cartoon in the "Log Cabin and Hard Cider" Campaign.

From the Library of Congress.

A "BARN BURNER" CARTOON IN THE 1848 CAMPAIGN

(See page 374.)   From the Library of Congress.

and bank accounts, was protected by the Constitution. Some day, the conservatives argued, the problem might be capable of solution, without force or injustice. Changed economic conditions had fastened slavery on the South, and another shift sometime might make it possible for the section to get rid of it.

England had done so in the Empire in honest and statesmanlike fashion by spreading emancipation over a number of years and compensating the slave owners. In America all that can be said is that the Abolitionists aroused passion and focussed attention in such a way as to make the question of slavery a burning one, without possessing the intellectual ability to offer any solution. At any rate, the country was under the dark shadow of sectional feeling of the most rabid sort, when the people so light-heartedly marched and sang their way through a contest between a party without principles and one without a Vice-Presidential candidate.

Vice-Presidents had not, indeed, been very important so far in our history. The health of Presidents had been good; no assassin's hand had reached them; and presiding over the Senate was a dull job. Suddenly, however, our people were to discover that a Vice-President might hold a most disconcerting importance for them. Harrison, who had been born in 1773, before the American Revolution, died before he had been a month in office. The country had elected old Tippecanoe but it was going to have Tyler for President for practically the whole four years.

No one, possibly least of all Tyler, knew what he would do. The Whigs, when they had nominated him, had never dreamed of his becoming President, and the nomination had come about only from peculiar political conditions. For most of his career Tyler had been a Democrat, albeit a strong anti-Jacksonian one, and was anti-banks, anti-Federalism and anti much else which the Whigs stood for, so far as they stood for anything. The man himself is yet unknown, and although historians have taken strong positions for or against him, we have not got, in fairness, much beyond the appraisal of one of the most careful and competent of them. As Channing wrote, "We know so little of his inner life that one cannot say whether he was a high-minded man of principle or a weak-minded Virginian who broke his word for the hope of election to the presidency in 1844." Whatever he may have been, his course was almost at once to involve him in hopeless opposition to the party which had placed him in the White House.

Henry Clay considered himself the leader of that party, and had expected to control the administration even with Harrison as President. With Tyler in his place Clay scarce took the trouble even to be courteous. Congress had been called in special session and promptly passed a bill for a national bank, which Tyler as promptly vetoed. The President was strongly opposed to a bank but after a consultation with him, the details of which are obscure, the leaders left with the impression that he would sign a bill if certain minor changes were made, largely in verbiage and eliminating the name of "bank."

When this was passed, Tyler again vetoed it, and Clay and the other leaders claimed that he had treated them falsely. Within two days the whole of Harrison's Cabinet, which Tyler had taken over without change, resigned with the exception of Daniel Webster, who as Secretary of State felt that in the midst of certain negotiations with England, which we shall note later, he should remain temporarily. Not only did the party chiefs thus humiliatingly express their disapproval of the man whom they themselves had given to the nation as President, but in a caucus they solemnly pronounced that "all political connection between them and John Tyler was at an end," not even giving him the title of President. That they thus stultified themselves by proclaiming that they had not been able to estimate the already well-known man whom they had advised the nation to place in its second highest office, did not penetrate through their emotions to their minds.

As the Whigs had a majority in Congress, though not enough to pass measures over vetoes, and as the President had been rejected by them, there was no prospect for accomplishing much by legislation until the cards were shuffled again. Unimpressive as Tyler's administration was, nevertheless many things happened during it, some of which were of prime importance. The meager legislation of his four years included the Pre-emption Act of 1841, fathered by Clay, which finally adjusted some of the worst evils of the land situation in the West and did much to hasten settlement and to relieve the pioneer of his most serious grievance. As far as political matters are concerned, however, the chief claims to remembrance of the Tyler presidency were in the domain of foreign affairs, which throughout the entire decade from 1840 to 1850 were to loom large.

On Tyler's accession to office, relations with England were already delicate at several points, and within the next year or two were to become dangerously involved. In the South, the new nation of Texas, whose independence had never been acknowledged by its parent State, Mexico, had been endeavoring to have itself annexed to the United States. Thus far, this had been prevented mainly by the fact that if Texas came into the Union it would have to be as a slave State, and many of the Northerners were already beginning to frame up the story that the whole Texan revolution and subsequent request for annexation had been merely a plot on the part of the South to extend the slave section of the country. There was no truth in this but with the increasing tension between North and South the question of annexation was inextricably involved with that of slavery and the balance of power between free and slave sections.

On the other hand, some of the European nations, notably England, had, like ourselves, recognized the independence of the Lone Star Republic, and early in Tyler's administration suspicions were aroused that England was trying to gain a stronger hold over our new neighbor than we could sanction. It would obviously have been to England's advantage to have a great cotton producing country independent of us which she could to some extent play off against the considerable monopoly of our South. England, however, was pledged to human freedom, and it was rumored by 1843 that she was negotiating with Texas to make a sufficient loan to her to indemnify the slave owners if the slaves should be freed, and to influence Mexico to acknowledge her independence.

England had not gone as far as rumor credited her with having gone, but there were clearly dangers in having any European nation gain such a control over the policies of so vast a State on our Southwestern border. The mounting American optimism of the times, our irresistible desire for expansion, and the growing belief in the future greatness of the nation, all made it impossible that we should look with equanimity on the permanent blocking of our road to the Pacific, directly westward from any part of our domain. The sectional forces for the time being were preventing annexation, but the expansive forces equally prevented our permitting the development of a European influence in Texas which might become predominant. The problem was not to be resolved until the very last month of Tyler's term, but during all of it, it formed part of the background of our relations with England.

In that background were such other facts as the heavy losses of English investors in our panic of 1837, some of the enterprises in which they had been led to invest by American prospectuses having been of a very unsavory sort. In some of the cases the American saw only a temporary set-back to the development in the future in which he still believed, whereas the Englishman quite naturally saw mere common fraud. In two instances our States actually repudiated bonds which had been legally issued, and largely sold in England. Whatever may be said for the later repudiations by some of the Southern States for debts incurred in the Reconstruction period after the war, there was no excuse whatever for a permanent repudiation of their promises to pay by Mississippi and Michigan and the then Territory of Florida, in the earlier period, unrectified acts of bad faith which even a century later are yet held against us in England. As the States declined to pay, and as they could not be coerced by the Federal Government, Tyler was helpless in adjusting this particular source of friction.

Another, also involving the peculiar Federal relations of our sovereign States, a relation which Europe has always, and not without reason, found hard to understand and to reconcile with the ordinary theory of international responsibilities and obligations, nearly involved us in war with England in Tyler's first year.

During the revolt in Canada in 1837, its leader, Mackenzie, had won recruits and received aid from Americans across the New York border, just as Texas had on a larger scale when rebelling against Mexico, and as Cuba did on several occasions. There was no doubt that we were lax in enforcing neutrality and in preventing our citizens from embroiling us in situations with which we had nothing to do. Late on December 29, 1837, under cover of the night, a force of loyal Canadians crossed the Niagara River in a rowboat, and burned a small vessel, the *Caroline,* which was used by the Americans to ferry supplies and aid across to the rebels.

The question at once arose as to whether these Canadians had been merely private persons or had been acting under official orders of the British or Canadian governments. Unfortunately, Lord Palmerston, an extremely difficult Englishman to deal with, was head of the Foreign Office, and we had made no progress in our diplomatic negotiations over the incident when it was suddenly complicated by a drunken fool in New York. In 1840, a Canadian named McLeod, who had been drinking heavily in a saloon in New York City, boasted that he had been one of the party which had burned the *Caroline,* and that he had himself killed one of her crew. McLeod was arrested on a charge of murder, whereupon Palmerston at once admitted that the party had been acting under official orders when the *Caroline* was destroyed, and, in his usual blustering fashion, stated that if McLeod were found guilty and hanged, the execution would be followed by immediate war with England. Tyler and Webster tried to adjust the matter with Governor Seward of New York, who, as touchy and assertive as Palmerston himself, declined to allow the course of justice in his State to be dictated by a British Foreign Minister. Fortunately McLeod, who appears to have been only boastfully lying when drunk, was acquitted on trial, and peace was preserved between the two nations.

There was yet more, however, in the background of our relations, which it was high time was cleared up. Just as our South and North, because each was the best customer of the other, wished to avoid controversy, so in spite of American rebel sympathizers and English blusterers, the two nations were too heavily dependent upon each other in trade to let diplomatic difficulties push them too far on the road to conflict. In the Far West, the Oregon boundary was still unsettled but both parties were willing to allow that question to lie a bit longer. The boundary between Maine and Canada was also unsettled, and a much more serious source of danger, owing to clashes between those living in or near the disputed strip. It was a rough country and its inhabitants may have rather enjoyed their occasional fights, but diplomatically they were firebrands which might ignite a conflagration.

In 1841 the cactus-like Palmerston had been succeeded, on a change of ministry, by Lord Aberdeen who was anxious to adjust matters in dispute. Lord Ashburton was despatched to Washington to negotiate with Webster, and both sides proving conciliatory, a compromise line was agreed upon. Neither the State of Maine, however, nor the

Senate in Washington was in a mood to compromise with the British, and, on the other hand, Parliament had no desire to give up territory to the Americans.

By one of the most curious and happy coincidences in diplomatic history, two maps came to light, one in each country, both of which had the Maine boundary drawn in red and both of which were presumed by their respective finders to have been the one so described that was used at the treaty negotiations in 1783. The one which turned up in America gave so much more territory to the British than they had claimed, that Maine and the Senate were glad to get off with what the new Treaty negotiated by Ashburton gave us; and the one which appeared from the British Museum, not known to Ashburton when negotiating nor to the public until 1896, so supported our original claim that Parliament was similarly silenced. With McLeod safely out of jail and with our northern boundary definitely settled as far west as the Lake of the Woods, the two nations could breathe easily again, although Texas and Oregon yet remained.

Meanwhile the ferment in America continued. We tried to show in the last chapter something of the swirling currents in the mental life of the period, and we have to note now that much of the passion and prejudice developed by new ideas and conditions found vent in mob action and a general reign of violence. Nor was this by any means confined to the dispute over slavery and Abolition. The mobbing mania which attended that problem was merely a symptom of a far wider unsettlement in a society changing so rapidly that the forces of law and order were outrun by those making for new adjustments.

The great increase in the number of foreigners arriving as immigrants was raising religious, economic, political, and social questions which were met in too many cases in the spirit of the mob. Although the Germans also suffered in places, the Irish were the special target for violence. There were anti-Catholic riots in numerous villages and cities, one of the worst being the burning of the Ursuline Convent at Charlestown, Massachusetts, by a mob of nearly 4000 in 1834. Catholic churches were burned and priests maltreated in many States, and almost invariably sufferers could get neither redress nor protection. In the anti-Irish and Catholic riots in

Philadelphia in 1844, for example, which lasted several days, the troops, who had been ordered out, did nothing while buildings were burned and sacked.

The Irish, who settled largely in the more populous centres of the East, and who underbid the older Americans in the labor market, were often roughly handled by mobs throughout the whole period, and in the Forties a new political party, the "Native American," was formed solely to combat the influence in various fields of the new immigrants. Demands were made for repeal of the naturalization laws or for a limit of twenty-one years before a foreigner could become a citizen, and for the permanent disability of all but native born to hold office. In New York some Democrats withdrew from Tammany Hall when a few Irish were put on minor committees, but gradually the politicians saw the advantage of attaching the new-comers to their party organizations, and the activities of the Native American Party redounded to the benefit of the Democrats who began to play the rôle of protector of the downtrodden immigrants as they had been of the poorer class of Americans themselves.

In 1842 the effort to settle a question by means of violence almost precipitated civil war in Rhode Island, which had been backward in abolishing the freehold qualifications for the franchise. In this particular eddy of the national life, economic conditions, democracy, the negro, and the foreigner all played a part. Both the franchise and representation of the towns were antiquated in that State, which was yet being governed under its old colonial charter. In the early days, the freehold qualifications had not been onerous when almost every one was a farmer and could own a few acres. The economic change from agriculture to shipping, and especially to manufacturing, had produced a considerable class of citizens who were no longer freeholders, but who, in the democratic atmosphere of the age, considered that they had the right to vote. The conservatives in control were stubbornly opposed to an enlargement of the electorate, but the malcontents found a leader in Thomas W. Dorr, the son of a wealthy manufacturer and a graduate of Phillips Exeter Academy and of Harvard College.

When the new "People's Party," as it was called, was rebuffed by the legislature, which declined to consider their grievances, a convention was assembled at which a new constitution for the State was drawn up and submitted to the people at large. Nearly 14,000 votes were cast in favor of it, the number including a majority of the qualified voters of the State. Technically neither the convention nor the new constitution had any legal status, but an election was held and Dorr was elected governor.

Meanwhile, the legislature had at last been stung into action, and had prepared a new constitution also, which, however, was defeated at the polls. There were now two governments in the State, and both appealed to President Tyler for aid. This he declined to give to either. The Dorrites next attempted to seize the arsenal, but the legal government of the "Landholders," as they called themselves, broke the rebellion, and Dorr had to escape from the State. The Landholders had sought to make political capital by claiming that the Dorrites were trying to enfranchise "the low Irish and the niggers," but in the end they overreached themselves, and by the passage of laws of extreme severity against the rebels, known as the "Algerine Laws," and by the condemnation of Dorr to life imprisonment, they lost almost all popular support.

Before the end of 1842 they were forced to submit a new constitution to the people, which gave the franchise to all male citizens over twenty-one without regard to color, provided they paid a tax of not less than one dollar a year. Three years later Dorr was liberated from prison, and his civil rights were restored in 1851. The "Dorr War" was thus successful though the armed revolt itself had been suppressed.

Meanwhile, the slavery agitation was continuing as an ominous undertone in the national life. Almost every question before Congress became tinged with it, and many men who were far from being Abolitionists were dragged into it.

John Quincy Adams, disastrously defeated for re-election to the presidency in 1828, had accepted election to Congress in 1831, and from then until his death on the floor of the House in 1848 he fought gloriously and without support for the right of every issue, as he saw it, which arose during his long period of office. In doing so he displayed a fearlessness, a singleness of purpose and a disregard of political consequences to himself which at last won the admiration of even his foes.

Early in this new phase of his career, petitions against slavery began to be presented to Congress by societies and groups of individuals, which continually wrought on the sensitiveness of the South and increased the swelling flood of anger which the Abolitionist literature was producing. Adams, although opposed to slavery, was not an Abolitionist, but owing to his independence and his refusal to be intimidated, the petitions came more and more to be presented to the House through him as a channel.

At the end of 1836, the House finally passed a rule that thereafter all such petitions should be laid on the table without being read or printed, a rule which not only prevented the exercise of free speech in Congress but unconstitutionally deprived the citizen of the right of petition. For eight years after this, at every session of Congress, Adams continued to fight for constitutional freedom and for the rescinding of the "gag rule," winning his cause at last, by pertinacity and strength of will, at the December session of 1844.

How slavery was beginning to affect all aspects of our civilization was indicated in that same year by the split in the Methodist Church. From 1816 the rule of the church had been that no clergyman of its order should own slaves in a State in which they could be legally emancipated, but the larger and Northern part of the church had meanwhile fallen under the influence of the Abolitionists. In 1832 a Georgian, the Reverend James O. Andrew, had been elected a bishop, one of the recommendations being that he was not a slave-owner, though a Southerner. In January, 1844, he married a woman who did own slaves, whereupon the church took action, and in the General Conference it was resolved that he should not perform the duties of his office so long as "the impediment remains." As a result of the discussion, the Church was divided into Northern and Southern sections, and the following year the Baptist Church followed the Methodists in scission, actions which Clay rightly feared might serve as examples both "perilous and alarming."

In some ways, slavery had had to be considered ever since the Missouri Compromise of 1820, and in 1836 when Michigan and Arkansas had been admitted to the Union, the old balance of one free State for one slave had been maintained. Slavery, however, was beginning to color all questions, and that of the annexation of Texas, with an area capable of being divided into many States, all of which would be slave, was becoming serious.

In 1843 Tyler and his Secretary of State, Abel P. Upshur, both Virginians, were disturbed by the more definite rumors that both England and France were flirting with Texas, and Tyler suggested to Sam Houston, then President of the Texan Republic, that it might be well to discuss possible annexation again. This suggestion Houston, then negotiating with England, treated coolly. Tyler pressed the point, and finally Houston agreed to treat with the United States, the negotiations continuing with Calhoun who had succeeded Upshur on the accidental death of the latter. On April 12, the two Republics signed a treaty by which the United States agreed to annex Texas and to assume her public debt up to the amount of $10,000,000, the Federal Government becoming owner of all the public lands of the annexed State.

When the treaty was submitted to the Senate, the North was furious, claiming that the South was trying to extend slavery and to overturn the balance between the sections. On the other hand, the South claimed in turn, that the North, from mere prejudice, was attempting to prevent the natural and necessary expansion of the whole nation. In the Senate, from a combination of very varied motives on the part of senators, neither party wishing to assume responsibility for ratification on the eve of a Presidential election, the North won, and the treaty was defeated, embittering the campaign then just opening.

Northwestward as well as southwestward expansion was to enter into the campaign, however, and the Oregon question now again came to the fore. The title to the Oregon country, disputed between England and ourselves, was an uncertain one when it came to delimiting it by specific boundaries, and although the question had several times been raised between the two powers since the ten-year agreement of joint occupancy had been made in 1818 (renewed with somewhat different terms in 1827), no boundary, mutually satisfactory, coud be determined upon.

The line as far west as the Rockies had been set at the 49th parallel of latitude, and we had offered to accept this out to the coast, but England had declined any settlement which did not give her the north bank of the Columbia River. Until 1834 the only

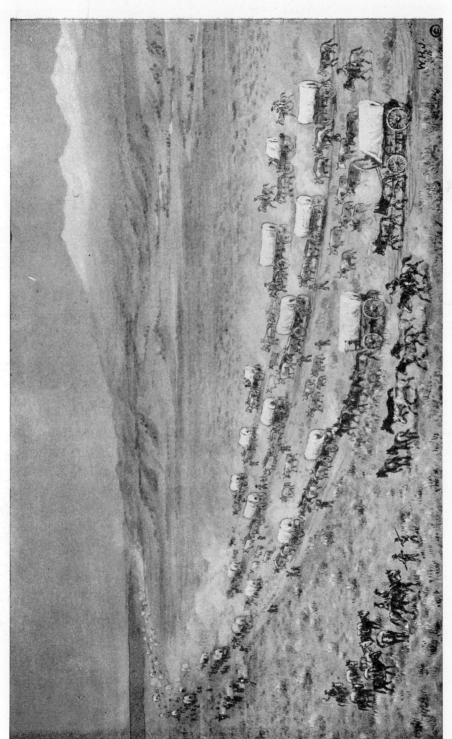

THE OREGON TRAIL IN SOUTH PASS, 1852.

From a painting copyright by the Oregon Trail Association.

PEND D'OREILLE, A JESUIT MISSION IN THE ROCKIES, 1862

A lithograph included by Captain Mullen in his report on the construction of a military road from Fort Walla Walla to Fort Benton. This road was constructed to obtain data on the character of the country between the Mississippi and the Pacific with future railroads in mind.

THE WHITMAN MISSION, "WAIILATPU," NEAR WALLA WALLA, IN 1843
Courtesy of the Oregon Historical Society, Portland, Oregon.

Americans in the district had been hunters, trappers, and fur traders, and comparatively little interest had been excited, but in that year Methodist missionaries went out with a few permanent settlers, followed the next year by some Presbyterians. In 1836, Doctor Marcus Whitman took a wagon across the Rockies and set up a mission at the junction of the Snake and Columbia Rivers. By 1842 there may have been 500 Americans permanently located in the country, and from that time on the "Oregon Trail," from Independence, Missouri, up the Platte and over the mountains, was to see thousands pour into the new frontier, all bitten by the "Oregon fever."

In 1843 the settlers formed a government of their own and asked Congress to erect them into a territory. Although the Treaty of 1827 could be denounced on a year's notice, Congress was not yet ready to act, but it was clear that the Oregon question was entering upon a new and far more dangerous phase. A rapidly growing agricultural population with farms and villages was very different from a few hunters for furs when it came to the settlement of boundaries.

Such was the situation as the campaign of 1844 drew near. In the possible occupation of Oregon, the South saw a chance to placate the North for the annexation of Texas, and the Oregonians themselves, anxious to establish their own position, and to add the territory to the Union, began to clamor for the annexation of all of the disputed northern country, raising the war cry of "Fifty-four Forty or Fight" regardless alike of our own several offers to accept the Forty-ninth parallel and of England's valid claims.

The election of 1844 was chiefly influenced by two of the strongest forces of the time, those of expansion and of sectionalism. Tyler had become a man without a party, for although elected by the Whigs he had gone over to the Democrats, and he was out of the running as far as either major party was concerned. At the beginning of the year it seemed certain that the Democrats would nominate Martin Van Buren and the Whigs Henry Clay.

On being asked to take their stand on the burning question of Texas, however, both candidates met embarrassing situations. So far had sectionalism already entered into politics that Van Buren, "little Magician" as he was, could not oppose annexation without alienating the important Democracy of the South, nor favor it without losing the North. He chose to oppose it, although offering to submit the question to Congress if Mexico should threaten Texas in such a way as to involve our interests. At once the South was politically in arms, and Van Buren's candidacy became impossible. On the other hand Clay, like his opponent, had expressed himself in a letter also, the "Raleigh letter" as it came to be called, in much the same terms as to Texas, and although most of the Whig strength was in the North and West, the famous "compromiser" was forced to hedge in such a way as to leave complete doubt as to where he did in reality stand.

"Times ain't now as they used to was."

Coon of 1840.

Coon of 1844.

Sic transit gloria coonery!
Well, and truly has the poet said,
"That 'coon is the leanest of all the lean squad,
And totters a furlong while marching a rod."

*From "The Ohio Coon Catcher" of October 5, 1844.
In the Library of Congress.*

Both party conventions were held in Baltimore in May, and, although the Whigs unanimously nominated Clay, the Democrats were in a quandary. After taking many ballots, in which Van Buren steadily declined in strength, and his rival, Cass of Michigan, gained up to a certain point, it became evident that there was a deadlock. As a result of consultation during the night, the first "dark horse" of American national politics was suddenly brought forward in the morning, and James K. Polk, of Tennessee, after one ballot, was unanimously chosen as the Democratic candidate. The country, bewildered, at once asked "Who is Polk?" He was, indeed, not entirely unknown. He had been a Speaker of the House for a time and had received one electoral vote for Vice-President in 1840, but he had made no mark in public life, and the nation was ignorant as to what opinions he might hold, if any. The opinions, however, were provided by the Democratic Party platform which grandiloquently proclaimed, with little regard for facts, that "our title to the whole territory of Oregon is clear and unquestionable; that no portion of the same ought to be ceded to England or any other power; and that the re-occupation of Oregon and the re-annexation of Texas at the earliest practicable

The Whig State Central Committee of Ohio at the wake of "that same old Coon."

AFTER POLK'S ELECTION

From "The Ohio Coon Catcher" of November 16, 1844. In the Library of Congress.

period are great American measures, which this convention recommends to the cordial support of the Democracy of the Union."

Of course, this was sheer bunkum, although it may have been good politics. We had never officially claimed farther north in Oregon than 49°, and England unquestionably had a good claim to part of the disputed territory. As for "re-annexing Texas," that phrase was based upon the absolutely invalid assumption that we had ever

361

held title to it, which we never had. It was hoped that the South could be won by the promise of Texas, and that the North would be placated by getting Oregon while its sensibilities might be eased as to Texas by the suggestion that we were merely taking back what we had once owned.

Tyler, who had hoped for the Democratic nomination, was nominated by a separate party, but the movement was dead from the start and the candidate withdrew from the contest in August. Clay's vacillation on the Texas question, however, had serious results in the appearance of a third party at the polls, the so-called "Liberty Party," which again nominated James G. Birney who had run in 1840. Backed by the Abolitionists who refused to vote for Clay because of his stand, or lack of it, on Texas, the Liberty Party polled over 62,000 votes and held the balance of power. As Polk received 1,337,-243 and Clay 1,299,062, had the Abolitionists voted for Clay he would have received not only the greater number of popular votes but they would have been so placed that instead of being defeated by Polk in the Electoral College by 170 to 105 he would have won by 146 against 129. Thus by their ill-considered action, from the standpoint of their own objective, the Abolitionists had made practically certain a huge addition to slave territory.

That the election indicated the certain absorption of Texas was understood by Tyler, who at once proceeded to recommend to Congress in December immediate annexation by means of a joint resolution of the two houses instead of a treaty, the former method requiring only a majority vote whereas the ratification of a treaty would require the consent of two thirds of the Senate. The resolution, which passed at once, provided that Texas should be made a State of the Union as soon as she had presented an acceptable constitution, and that the President could complete the process of annexation by negotiating with Texas or Mexico as he should deem fit.

The vote in the Senate had been close, 27 to 25, and some of the Senators had been induced to vote in favor only, as was claimed, by assurance from Polk that Mexico would be honorably treated. Tyler, however, paid no attention to what may or may not have been a promise by his successor, and immediately sent a messenger to close the transaction with Texas. A few months after Polk became President, Texas, on December 29, 1845, was admitted as a State. Meanwhile, our annexation of a Mexican province, whose independence had never been acknowledged, was embroiling us with our southern neighbor.

Practically since her winning of freedom from Spain, Mexico had been in a most unstable condition, politically and economically. The country with which we were soon to go to war had a white population of only about one million, or less than twice as many as there were in our city of New York. The remainder of her 7,000,000 were

THE FIRST CAPITOL BUILT BY THE REPUBLIC OF TEXAS

made up of 4,000,000 Indians and perhaps 2,000,000 half-breeds. Her territory at the time of gaining her independence included all of the present Mexico, and our present States of Texas, New Mexico, Arizona, Utah, Nevada, and California.

The problem of governing such a vast domain with such a population would have been extremely difficult in any case, but in addition the people, after winning their independence from Spain, were not at all ready for self-government. The result was a succession of revolutions. Foreign investors, however, insisted upon holding Mexico to the same standard of accountability as they would have the United States or England. The consequence was the piling up of the usual "claims" under such conditions.

In 1838 France had collected some of these for her citizens by force of arms but England had refrained. In 1839 after long negotiations, a treaty was signed providing that the claims of American citizens should be arbitrated, and, when the award was made, Mexico paid three instalments and then stopped.

Although Justin H. Smith, one of the few American historians who uncompromisingly defends our war with Mexico, points to this default as a breach of faith, we may note that it occurred in the very year in which English bondholders were making bitter protests to our own Secretary of State, regarding the defaulted payments of Pennsylvania, Arkansas, Illinois, Michigan, Maryland, Indiana, and Florida. At that time our minister to Mexico, Wilson Shannon, was a blustering, blow-hard fourth-rate political stump speaker, while his predecessor, Anthony Butler, is described by Smith as a "national disgrace," "shamefully careless about Legation affairs . . . a bully and a swashbuckler . . . wholly unprincipled . . . and openly scandalous in his conduct."

Under such circumstances our relations with the Mexicans, who were proud and touchy, naturally went from bad to worse. There were plenty of grievances on both sides, but our own skirts had been far from clear in the Texan revolt, and when we annexed that State there was bound to be further trouble. In the summer of 1845 General Zachary Taylor was ordered to the Rio Grande with troops and orders were sent to Commodore Sloat in the Pacific to seize California as soon as war might come.

Meanwhile, hoping to get what he wanted without war, Polk sent John Slidell to Mexico with an offer of $25,000,000 for California, $5,000,000 for what was then called New Mexico, and our agreement to assume the claims of our own citizens. The envoy was also to try to have the Texas boundary settled as reaching to the Rio Grande, which under both Spanish and Mexican rule had never gone south of the Nueces River, though Texas had claimed the farther line. Slidell arrived in Mexico City at a moment of government crisis, and the attempted negotiations came to nothing. Polk then made up his mind to war.

He had been elected, however, on a platform which had demanded not only Texas but Oregon, and preparatory to the conflict, which he now felt was certain if we were to have Texas and California, he began negotiations with England to settle the northern question. Congress denounced the Joint Occupation Treaty, and

FUNERAL OBSEQUIES OF FREE-TRADE.

This unfortunate youth died of Home Consumption and was buried in 1846. He was carried to the grave by Polk, Dallas, Buchanan, and Marcy. Sixteen States have already contributed to his Cenotaph which is to be erected by the Whigs.

From the original in the Library of Congress.

The subtitle on the cartoon is: This unfortunate youth died of Home Consumption and was buried in 1846. He was carried to the grave by Polk, Dallas, Buchanan, and Marcy. Sixteen States have already contributed to his Cenotaph which is to be erected by the Whigs some months later England offered a new one setting the Oregon boundary at the Forty-ninth Parallel, which, in spite of the campaign nonsense, Polk accepted and the Senate confirmed. The northern boundary was thus settled from the Atlantic to the Pacific, the Treaty with England having been signed June 15, 1846. In that same year a new tariff Act was passed by Congress and signed by Polk which has sometimes been said to have marked a return to Free Trade principles but which rather merely diminished the extreme protectionism of the preceding Acts. The main interest of Polk's term, however, was not to be domestic but to continue to centre in our foreign relations. Oregon out of the way, Polk was free to deal with Mexico.

Meanwhile General Taylor had taken up his position at Corpus Christi, on Mexican soil, as it was south of the Nueces, but when it was known that Slidell had failed, the troops were ordered on to the Rio Grande. The Mexicans had thus far remained on the south bank of that river, but when Taylor appeared, he was requested to fall back to the Nueces, and as he refused to do so, the Mexicans, under General Ampudia, crossed the stream on April 24, 1846, and captured a party of the Americans. Polk then proclaimed that our patience was exhausted, that the Mexicans had invaded the United States, and asked Congress for war. On May 12 bills were passed appropriating $10,000,000 for war expenses and ordering the enlistment of 50,000 additional troops, the votes being 174 to 14 in the House and 40 to 2 in the Senate.

Mexico, not believing we would fight, took no formal action at this time, and in August Polk tried to have a measure passed in Congress authorizing him again to try to buy from Mexico what we intended to take. This action, which came to nothing, is chiefly interesting from the first appearance, in connection with it, of the "Wilmot Proviso," which was constantly to make trouble between North and South for many years after. While the bill was being considered, a Pennsylvanian, David Wilmot, tried to have an amendment attached to it providing that no territory acquired by the purchase or war should ever be open for slavery. This would have deprived the South of all its anticipated advantages and made the slave States almost negligible politically. Although defeated, it served to increase yet further the sectional tension.

Meanwhile, military operations had already begun. Marching from Fort Leavenworth to Santa Fé, Colonel S. W. Kearney captured that town without bloodshed, and at once issued a proclamation declaring all of New Mexico (including the present Arizona, Nevada, and Utah) to be part of the United States. He then set out for the further march to California, but that was already ours, as he was informed by Kit Carson when only a short distance on his way.

There had been some American settlers on the Pacific coast, and the great Province of California, so remote from Mexico City, was bound to it by the slenderest of ties. There had been talk of French or English occupation of the Province, separated as it had been from the United States by mountain ranges and wide stretches of foreign territory. In October, 1845, Polk had sent instructions to our consul at Monterey, saying that the President would make no effort nor use any influence to induce California to join the Union unless the people should desire to do so of themselves, and if it could be done without giving Mexico cause for complaint. What this would mean was clear enough from the history of our steady advance, and the small respect we had for either Indians or Spaniards.

We need not go into detail in relating the somewhat confused events of 1846, one of the first of which was the threatening appearance of Colonel Frémont with armed American forces at Monterey, and subsequently the raising of the American flag over his camp. Although a clash was then avoided, on June 10 a party of American settlers in the Sacramento Valley attacked a party of Mexican troops, who they imagined had been sent to force them from the lands on which they were illegally squatting. Four days later another party captured General Vallejo at Sonoma, and then proceeded to issue a proclamation declaring the independence of the American settlements, hoisting a flag on which were painted a star and bear. It has always remained obscure whether Frémont, who was a son-in-law of Senator Benton, was involved in this insurrection and how far, if at all, it may have had the secret sanction of the Washington authorities.

Meanwhile, Commodore Sloat had sailed for Monterey, reaching that port on July 2, when he immediately had an interview with our consul there. Mexico had not yet declared war, but Larkin, the consul, was the confidential agent of the American Government, and his peculiar instructions had been made yet more enigmatic according to international codes of friendship by the order that he was to "arouse in the bosoms" of the Californians "that love of liberty and independence so natural to the American Continent." Five days later, Sloat landed a force, took possession of Monterey, hoisted the American flag, and declared California to be a part of the United States. By the end of the year we had established ourselves in every part of the province.

While these operations had been in progress on the coast, Taylor and his troops had not been idle across the Texas border in northern Mexico. In May he had defeated the enemy at Palo Alto and Resaca de la Palma. On the 18th he won another victory at Matamoras, forcing the Mexicans back to Monterey, the capital of the province of Nuevo Leon. After a considerable rest and delay in waiting for supplies, Taylor continued to advance, and on September 23 captured the strongly fortified city of Monterey.

These easy successes against an incompetent Mexican general began to make Taylor a possible presidential candidate, by no means to the satisfaction of Polk, who decided to entrust the leadership of operations in future to Major-General Winfield Scott, whom he thought both a better soldier and a less dangerous political rival. Opinions differ as to the real ability of Taylor, who had seen little but Indian frontier fighting on a small scale, and who, in spite of great courage and a personality which inspired his men, had slight knowledge of strategy or the handling of large bodies of troops. On the other hand, he had won victories, and had done so with the scant support of the government, facts which were to count heavily in his favor later and make him at last President, as Polk feared they might.

The new plans, however, called for a direct attack on the city of Mexico by way of Vera Cruz, and Taylor was called upon to despatch half his troops to the Gulf port to join Scott. We had had a blockading squadron there, and through it we had, as a matter of policy, allowed our former and future enemy, Santa Anna, to return to his country from exile in Cuba. He had made us believe he could manipulate the political situation at the capital so as to end hostilities by negotiation, but the pride of the Mexicans and their not unjustified hatred of us precluded the possibility of any peaceful settlement of our dismemberment of their State by the method of bargain and sale. Santa Anna, whatever his original aims or motives may have been, turned round, and put himself at the head of the Mexican forces. All that Polk's attempt at intrigue had succeeded in doing was to present our enemy with their strongest leader.

Having discovered that Taylor's force had been heavily depleted by the troops sent to Scott, Santa Anna decided upon a quick blow. With a good army of 16,000, the largest we had ever been called upon to face since the Battle of Long Island in 1776, he marched northward against Taylor and his 5000. It was expected that Taylor would retire, but he appears to have thought the coming attack less important than it was. Remaining at Saltillo, he posted General Wool with most of the troops in a valley a couple of miles wide on the ranch of Buena Vista, which gave its name to the ensuing battle.

Owing to the rough and broken nature of the terrain, the disparity in numbers was practically overcome completely. Santa Anna had had to march through a dry, desert country, with scarcely any water, but on February 22 he reached the American forces and launched his attack. In spite of his gaining some of the commanding heights, the American position was too strong for him and our artillery mowed down the Mexicans as they tried to force their way up the narrowing valley. There was terrible slaughter but night came without the Mexicans having been able to make good their attack, and during the darkness Santa Anna drew off his forces, to the infinite relief of the Americans, who were in an awkward plight.

As Santa Anna retreated across the San Luis Potosi desert, his men died by hundreds from fatigue and thirst, and, what with the losses from battle and the retreat, he reached Mexico City again with approximately one third of the troops he had led out. Buena Vista was notable not only for being one of the best-fought battles of the whole struggle but also for the men who were engaged in it, among them Bragg, Sherman, and Thomas, all to make their mark in the later Civil War, and, by an odd coincidence, two who were later to become Presidents of the United States and of the Confederate States, General Taylor himself and his son-in-law, Jefferson Davis.

We must now turn to Scott and his troops, who had been sent by boat to Vera Cruz down the Gulf. On March 27, 1847, they captured that city, and began the march to Mexico by the old road which had led thence from the coast long before the first white man had come to disturb the peace of Montezuma. At Cerro Gordo, about 55 miles from the Gulf, Santa Anna had placed a force of about 13,000 men to oppose Scott, who had about 10,000. Occupying strong positions on the heights commanding the road, the obstacle to the advancing Americans was formidable. Scott had among his officers, however, even a more brilliant group than Taylor had had, Robert E. Lee, U. S. Grant, George G. Meade, George B. McClellan and P. G. T. Beauregard. Lee discovered that it might be possible to reach the heights by a trail up which artillery could be dragged and the Mexicans outflanked. In spite of some bungling, the plan was carried out with success, and after a battle on April 18 the enemy fled, abandoning their guns, and leaving about 3000 prisoners.

The march then proceeded to Puebla, where Scott found himself almost without supplies, one tenth of his force in hospital, and many volunteers, whose time had expired, refusing to advance farther. These he sent back to Vera Cruz, called up the garrisons he had left at several points behind him, and with about 10,000 men, to be followed by 2000 reinforcements who had arrived at the coast, he continued his way to the capital. He reached the outskirts early in August and on the 7th and 20th defeated bodies of Mexicans at Contreras and Churubusco, only a few miles outside the city.

There one last attempt was made at negotiation. Scott concluded an armistice with Santa Anna, who it is said received a bribe of $10,000 and the promise of a million if peace were made according to our terms. These were drastic enough. We demanded the Rio Grande as the southern boundary of Texas; California, and the entire expanse of "New Mexico," and a canal route across the Isthmus of Tehuantepec. Polk had placed the negotiations in the hands of the chief clerk of the State Department, an unimportant person by the name of Nicholas P. Trist, who could easily be disavowed.

When the Mexicans came back with proposals to cede no territory except Texas with the Nueces as boundary, and a demand that we pay the entire cost of the war, it was clear that Mr. Trist would not get far, and as Santa Anna broke the terms of the armistice in several particulars, Scott at once moved against the city. On September 8 he made an attack on some factory buildings, called El Molino del Rey (the Royal Mill), which he wished to capture because of the war materials being manufactured there. The effort proved extremely costly, over 700 men of the 8000, which was all Scott then had with him, being killed.

Two causeways which led into the capital were dominated by the hill of Chapultepec, and it was necessary to control the height before the city could be entered. This also proved an expensive undertaking, but the way was at last made clear, and with about 7000 troops the victorious American general entered the capital city. There, governmental affairs were in chaos, and the American commanders began a disgraceful playing of American politics in a series of charges and counter-charges and of courts-martial. Santa Anna resigned the presidency, however, and a new government consented to negotiate a treaty with Trist, who had been ordered back to Washington but had declined to move. The British Minister made it plain to the Mexicans that they could expect nothing from England, and Trist succeeded at last in getting a treaty, signed at Guadaloupe Hidalgo on February 2, 1848, according to the terms of which Mexico was to cede all of New Mexico and California,[1] and acknowledge our possession of Texas with the Rio Grande as boundary in exchange for $15,000,000 and our assumption of the claims of our citizens against Mexico to the extent of $3,250,000.

We thus secured an addition to our territory embracing all of the present States of Texas, Utah, Nevada, and California, and most of New Mexico and Arizona, the small balance of the latter two being added by purchase in 1853 to round out the boundary and give us the best route from Texas to California. For this strip, known as the "Gadsden Purchase" from James Gadsden who negotiated the treaty for us, we were eventually to pay $10,000,000 more.

Trist had been without authority to act but on March 10, 1848, the Senate ratified the results of his negotiations by a vote of thirty-eight to fourteen. Meanwhile on January 24 some gold particles had been found in the millrace on Sutter's ranch in California, and as soon as the news spread there was a rush such as the world had never

[1] I have spoken of "California" rather than "Upper California" because "Upper California" was what we know today as simply California, the peninsula then known as "California" being what is today called "Lower California," still in the possession of Mexico.

known. San Francisco was almost deserted, as were the ships which touched at California ports. When the word reached the East, men of all types and of all grades of life started either across the continent or by way of vessels to Panama, across the isthmus and by vessel again to San Francisco to win a fortune. Almost as soon as we had acquired title to the soil from Mexico, the "Forty-niners" and their successors were building up a populous and turbulent

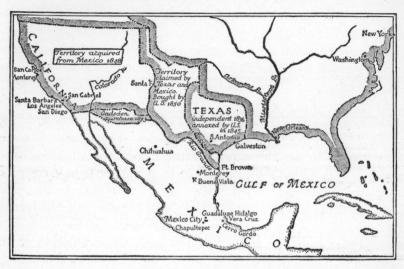

THE DISPUTED TERRITORY AND REGIONS ACQUIRED BY THE UNITED STATES AS A RESULT OF THE MEXICAN WAR

State. By 1850 there were over 92,000 persons, mostly men, and by 1860, 380,000.

The war had been extremely unpopular in the North, especially among the Abolitionists and other strong anti-slavery groups who had seen in the whole Texas question merely a plot of the South to extend slavery. James Russell Lowell, writing in homely Yankee dialect the first series of his widely popular Biglow Papers, voiced the indignation and strong sectionalism of Massachusetts, as did Whittier also. In point of fact, the huge acquisitions of 1846–48 had increased that portion of the Union which must be free by nature far more than it had the slave portion, for slavery was economically impossible in most of what was to become New Mexico, Arizona,

A VIEW OF SAN FRANCISCO

A lithograph by Hanhart after Marryat, interesting in the delineation of miners' costumes and indicating the number of Chinamen in California in 1851.

Courtesy of The Mabel Brady Garvan Institute of American Arts and Crafts, Yale University.

POST-OFFICE AT PIKE AND CLAY STREETS, SAN FRANCISCO, AT THE TIME OF THE GOLD RUSH

From a lithograph by Endicott. Courtesy of The Mabel Brady Garvan Institute of American Arts and Crafts, Yale University.

VIEW OF CHICAGO AS SEEN FROM THE TOP OF ST. MARY'S COLLEGE

Drawn for Rae's Commercial Chart, 1849.

From the lithograph by Köllner in the Stokes Collection, New York Public Library.

California, Colorado, Utah, Oregon, and Washington. The few States which might be, but never were, carved out of Texas itself could not counterbalance in Congress these seven others. This, however, was not foreseen, and the partisan bitterness of the nation had been immensely increased by the war. Expansion had won a colossal victory, but at the cost of an equal colossal increase in the tension of sectionalism.

Even before peace was declared the question of slavery in the new Far West had already agitated the country. The whole of the new western acquisitions was without established forms of government, and Polk wished to organize territories on the basis of the old Missouri Compromise of 1820, that is, to make the parallel of 36° 30′ the dividing line between slave and free.

Calhoun, who had then for some time been the acknowledged leader of the most fiery pro-slavery party in the South, insisted on the other hand that the whole of the new West having become the property of the nation, and slavery being legal under the Constitution, it was legal everywhere in the additions to the national domain. Webster took the ground that the Constitution affected only the States of the Union, and that there never having been slavery in California or the Oregon country, those sections were free as they stood. After heated debates in May, 1848, Oregon was erected into a territory on the basis of the

130   THE BIGLOW PAPERS.

I 've ben a votin' Demmercrat, ez reg'lar ez a clock.

But don't find goin' Taylor gives my narves no gret 'f a
  shock ;

Truth is, the cutest leadin' Wigs, ever sence fust they
  found

Wich side the bread gut buttered on, hev kep' a edgin'
  round ;

They kin' o' slipt the planks frum out th' ole platform
  one by one

An' made it gradooally noo, 'fore folks know'd wut
  wuz done,

Till, fur 'z I know, there aint an inch thet I could lay
  my han' on,

But I, or any Demmercrat, feels comf'table to stan' on.

An' ole Wig doctrines act'lly look, their occ'pants bein'
  gone,

Lonesome ez staddles on a mash without no hay-
  ricks on.

I spose it 's time now I should give my thoughts upon
  the plan,

Thet chipped the shell at Buffalo, o' settin up ole Van.

FACSIMILE (REDUCED) OF THE
BIGLOW PAPERS
*From the first edition in the Lenox Collection (1848)
in the New York Public Library.*

fundamental provisions of the old Northwest Ordinance, that is, as free soil, but Congress could reach no compromise as to California and the rest of the territory included under the title of New Mexico.

Meanwhile, the election of that year was drawing on, to be dominated, as all were now until the Civil War, by the politics of the slavery controversy. Polk was not a great man, although he had shown a doggedness of purpose which had not been anticipated from him. A man of very narrow range of interests, with no personal magnetism, he did not possess the qualities of a great leader, although he had added, oddly enough as a Democratic President, a greater proportional amount of new territory to the United States than any other President except another Democrat, Thomas Jefferson. When elected, he had declared that he would serve but one term, and as a matter of fact he could not have been elected to another.

The Democratic Convention met at Baltimore May 22, 1848, in some confusion owing to the bitter factional fight which had been going on for some time in New York. There the party had become completely split into what were known in the political slang of the time as the "Barn Burners" and the "Hunkers." The first-named were made up from a reform element which included Silas Wright, with the support of Van Buren, and the editor of *The New York Evening Post,* William Cullen Bryant. Considered impractical, they were given their political designation from the story of a dull farmer who burned his barn to get rid of the rats. The other group, under the lead of William L. Marcy, were the practical politicians of the State, and, it is said, derived their title of "Hunkers" from their "hunger" for public office.

Both factions claimed to be the Democratic Party in New York, which thus sent two full delegations to the convention. After much wrangling over which should be seated, both finally declined to vote, the Barn Burners withdrawing entirely from all participation in the proceedings. Although the platform adopted endorsed the administration of Polk and the righteousness of the war, Polk received no votes, and Lewis Cass of Michigan was unanimously nominated for the presidency, with General William O. Butler as running mate. All the candidates suggested for President had been men who were opposed to the principles of the Wilmot Proviso, and it was hoped that the election might be won by enunciating Southern principles and nominating a man personally popular in the West.

The "Hunkers," as practical politicians, agreed to endorse Cass but the "Barn Burners" broke with the party, and at a later convention held at Utica nominated Van Buren on an anti-Southern platform which demanded the enactment of the Wilmot Proviso.

AN AVAILABLE CANDIDATE.
THE ONE QUALIFICATION FOR A WHIG PRESIDENT
For sale at 152 Spruce St. N.Y.

The Whigs at their convention at Philadelphia in June had nominated General Taylor, a Louisiana slave-holder but a war hero who it could be claimed deserved well of his country because he had been neglected by the government. United with him on the ticket was Millard Fillmore of New York.

A CARTOON OF THE CAMPAIGN OF 1848 REPRESENTING TAYLOR'S CANDIDACY AS A RESULT OF HIS MEXICAN WAR CAMPAIGN

From the original in the New York Historical Society.

The already mixed situation was to be made more so by the dissatisfaction of many Northern Democrats, who insisted upon a more definite stand as to slavery, with both the Baltimore and Utica Conventions. As "Free Soilers" they held a convention of their own at Buffalo in August, at which they adopted a platform demanding, among a great variety of other things, the "rescue" of the government from the control of the slave power and the acknowledgment that Congress had no power to permit slavery in any territory beyond the original slave States. Rather inconsistently, Van Buren received the nomination for President on this ticket also, with Charles Francis Adams of Massachusetts as Vice-President, though Van Buren was far from wishing to encumber himself with the platform. Entering the campaign with the slogan, "Free Soil, Free Speech, Free Labor, and Free Men," the sectional character of the party, as well as that of the election as a whole, was manifestly clear.

New York proved the pivotal State, and there Taylor received 218,000 votes against 120,000 for Van Buren, and 114,000 for Cass, carrying the 36 electoral votes, though they would have gone for Cass had Van Buren not been running on the two insurgent tickets. The "Reform" Democrats and the extreme Anti-slavery men had thus given the presidency to a Southern slave-owner, the sort of result that has invariably followed the formation of third parties by disgruntled elements. This was clearly noted by Roosevelt when writing his life of Senator Benton in 1887, though, so great is the influence of egotism and political ambition, Roosevelt himself was to bolt to a third party at the end of his career.

General Taylor, the military hero of two wars, successfully elected by 163 to 127 in the Electoral College, was, as has often been the case, a minority President, receiving only 1,360,000 popular votes as compared with 1,512,000 for his two opponents combined. Moreover, defeated by Cass in such Southern States as Alabama, Arkansas, Georgia, Mississippi, Missouri, Virginia, and Texas, it was evident that the Whigs, even with a Southern platform and a slave-owner and a Southerner at the head of their ticket, could not carry the South against a Democrat.

On the day when Taylor was inaugurated, Congress adjourned after three months of wrangling over the problems of the new territories, and those of slavery. No progress had been made toward establishing governments in New Mexico and California, and only new bitterness had been aroused. The Southerners had freely indulged in threats of secession, and a committee of leading Southern congressmen had issued a manifesto calling upon the South to resist the North and to demand its fair share of the conquered territory. The new President, "Old Rough and Ready," took office under conditions which appeared to presage a downfall of the Union unless some agreement and compromise could be reached between the sections, both of which were becoming steadily more virulent in their recriminations and threats against one another.

CHAPTER XVI

THE INEVITABLE CONFLICT

THE intensity of the political situation was shown when Congress met in December, 1849. Sixty-three ballots had to be taken before the factions could agree upon the election of a Speaker for the House. In personnel the Senate was one of the most brilliant which had assembled in America since the days of the first Continental Congress and of the Constitutional Convention. Foremost, and almost at the end of their careers and lives, were the great trio of debaters, Webster, Calhoun, and Clay. There, also, were Benton, Cass, Seward, Douglas, and Jefferson Davis.

The five leading questions which they had to discuss, all deeply involved with slavery, were whether the new State of California should be admitted as free, what should be done with slavery in the territories of Utah and New Mexico, how far westward should the Texans be allowed to establish their boundary, what should be done about the growing scandal of publicly selling slaves in the Federal District of Columbia, and what to do about the unenforced Fugitive Slave Law.

As slavery had been forbidden in Mexico, all of the territory we had acquired by the war from that nation had been free according to Mexican law. In defiance of that law, slavery had existed in Texas, and there was no intention of disturbing it there, the tacitly assumed problem being what to do in the remainder of the annexed territory. The politicians, North and South, had been busy with the question, and the Virginia House of Delegates had expressed the Southern view by passing a series of resolutions declaring that the Union would be subverted if the Federal Government should attempt to prevent the citizens of any part of it from carrying their property of "whatever description" into a territory owned by the nation. If such attempt were made Virginia declared she would be called upon to resist at all hazards.

Taylor, with a soldier's contempt for politicians and with a desire to settle the disputes before they could begin to wrangle over them, promptly took the initiative along lines which dismayed his Southern followers. First he sent out to California a representative to stir the Americans there up to framing a constitution and applying for immediate entrance to the Union as a State without first passing through territorial status. Secondly, he warned the Texans that if they should make any move to carry out their desire to extend their boundary far beyond that of the old Spanish province, an extension as threatened which would have added nearly half the present State of New Mexico to the slave State of Texas, he would immediately head the United States Army personally and march to the border to prevent it.

No plan for the settlement of the group of problems seemed possible that would satisfy all sections. The North would have nothing to do with the suggestion that the old line of the Missouri Compromise, 36° 30′, be extended to the Pacific coast. California, of which fully half was south of that line, had adopted Taylor's suggested constitution by the overwhelming majority of 12,061 to 811 votes in December, 1849. It had prohibited slavery, and now by the almost unanimous wish of her citizens was seeking admission as a Free State. Texas was restless, and New Mexico and Utah were suffering from lack of any government at all. The President's suggestion that California be admitted and that then the rest of the questions be taken up met with no favor, and in the South talk of secession was rapidly growing more ominous.

If both North and South insisted in full upon the demands of their more extreme elements, a break-up of the Union appeared inevitable. So serious had the situation become that Clay, who at seventy-three had been out of Congress for some years and had only two more of life, had fought and won an election to the Senate so as to return to public life and secure if possible some compromise which might preserve the nation. In January, 1850, he made his proposals, the last of his great compromising efforts. As concessions to Northern anti-slavery feeling he suggested that California be admitted at once as free soil, and that the slave-trade be forever prohibited in the District of Columbia. To the South he offered the passage of a more stringent Fugitive Slave Law; an agreement not to abolish slavery in the District of Columbia without the consent of Maryland; the payment of the State debt of Texas in return for her abandonment of most of her claim to an extended boundary; an official denial that Congress had any control over the inter-State slave trade; and the erection of New Mexico and Utah into territories without the enactment of the Wilmot Proviso, leaving the question of slavery to be settled by their own citizens.

For parts of two days Clay, ill, hollow-eyed and haggard, almost exhausted, pleaded for his compromise as the only means of saving the Union. Urging tolerance in the North and acquiescence in the South, he warned the former section that a Fugitive Slave Law must be enforced to meet the legitimate constitutional demands of the Southern owners of property; and in turn, he warned the South that secession was not only unconsitutional but could never be effected without a bloody war. It was enough, for one point, that the North and West would never again yield up the mouth of the Mississippi to any nation but their own.

Webster had already practically made up his mind to support Clay, but took no important part in debate until March. On the 4th of that month, Calhoun, who was too ill to speak himself, and who was to die within the month, sat glowering at his opponents while Senator Mason of Virginia read his prepared speech for him. The old defender of slavery had no constructive suggestion to propose but threatened secession, which he was right in claiming was bound to come, unless the North ceased to agitate the slavery question and would acquiesce in his demands for admitting slavery into the lands acquired from Mexico, would honestly enforce the Act for returning fugitive slaves, and give the South its rights and that balance of power which was slipping from her.

Two years earlier he had urged in correspondence that the South force the issue at once while "stronger than we shall be hereafter, politically and morally." Now, in spite of his expressed love of the Union, he pointed out that the cords were fast breaking which bound the sections together. Unless a perfect equilibrium could be maintained between the slave and free portions, the secession of the South was inevitable, and this equilibrium, he explained later, involved the election of two presidents, one from each section and each with a veto on the other! Such a fantastic plan for the absolute

WEBSTER ADDRESSING THE SENATE, MARCH 7, 1850
From the engraving in the Library of Congress.

KEY TO THE ABOVE

1. R. C. Winthrop. 2 J. S. Phelps. 3. E. Risley. 4. H. W. Hilliard. 5. H. H. Sibley. 6. H. A. Haralson. 7. H. Marshall. 8. J. B. Thompson. 9. C. Butler. 10. L. C. Levin. 11. H. D. Gould. 12. G. N. Fitch. 13. A. F. Owen. 14. John McLean. 15. P. H. Sylvester. 16. A. C. Dodge. 17. J. P. Phoenix. 18. A. Felch. 19. Wm. A. Richardson. 20. I. P. Walker. 21. C. S. Morehead. 22. J. J. Crittenden. 23. J. M. H. Beale. 24. Henry Dodge. 25. Pierre Soule. 26. D. S. Dickenson. 27. R. M. T. Hunter. 28. I. D. Bright. 29. J. Clemens. 30. A. P. Butler. 31. M. Norris, Jr. 32. H. L. Turney. 33. Thos. G. Pratt. 34. Solon Borland. 35. D. L. Yulee. 36. W. R. Sebastian. 37. J. W. Bradbury. 38. Jeff. Davis. 39. J. C. Calhoun. 40. James Whitcomb. 41. T. J. Rusk. 42. Lewis Cass. 43. T. H. Fenton. 44. H. Hamlin. 45. S. W. Downs. 46. J. M. Mason. 47. Wm. R. King. 48. H. S. Foote. 49. D. R. Atchison. 50. D. Sturgeon. 51. Millard Fillmore, V.P. 52. T. L. Harris. 53. Andw. Johnson. 54. R. C. Schenck. 55. F. P. Stanton. 56. Andw. Ewing. 57. Saml. Calvin. 58. J. Freedley. 59. Jos. Lane. 60. R. K. Meade. 61. L. Burrows. 62. Wm. M. Meredith. 63. T. L. Clingman. 64. Wm. H. Seward. 65. H. D. Moore. 66. Jas. L. Orr. 67. A. W. Buel. 68. A. H. Stephens. 69. A. G. Brown. 70. A. M. Schermerhorn. 71. J. L. Johnson. 72. R. L. Rose. 73. Asbury Dickens, Sect'y. 74. R. M. McLane. 75. W. A. Gorman. 76. Howell Cobb. 77. Robt. Toombs. 78. Jas. Cooper. 79. Jno. P. Hale. 80. J. Wales. 81. P. Spruance. 82. I. R. Underwood. 83. Henry Clay. 84. Wm. C. Dawson. 85. Jno. McP. Berrien. 86. Wm. L. Dayton. 87. Willie P. Mangum. 88. Wm. Upham. 89. J. W. Miller. 90. Jas. A. Pearce. 91. Sam. Houston. 92. S. P. Chase. 93. Jas. Shields. 94. R. S. Baldwin. 95. J. H. Clarke. 96. Thos. Corwin. 97. John Davis. 98. Daniel Webster. 99. Joseph Hoxie. 100. S. S. Phelps. 101. Jackson Morton. 102. Truman Smith. 103. Geo. W. Jones. 104. John Bell. 105. A. C. Greene. 106. S. A. Douglass.

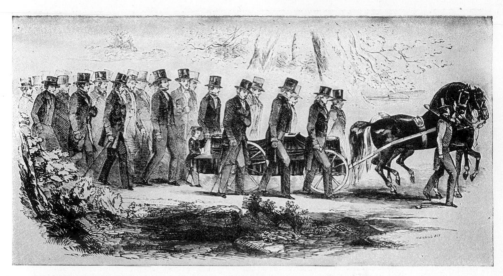

FUNERAL PROCESSION OF DANIEL WEBSTER AT MARSHFIELD, MASSACHUSETTS
From "Gleason's Pictorial," November, 1852.

FUNERAL PROCESSION OF HENRY CLAY IN NEW YORK
From "Gleason's Pictorial," August 14, 1852.

deadlock of the Federal Government could have gained no adherents, but his statement that the South had nothing either to compromise or to concede expressed all too clearly the belief of that section. In the last stages of tuberculosis, he sat, enveloped in flannels, glaring about, as he bade his last defiance to the spirit of the age.

Three days after his own speech, Calhoun, who was doomed to die within the month, tottered like a figure of death into the Senate Chamber to hear his old enemy, Daniel Webster, make his, the famous "Seventh-of-March" speech which was to rank only below his "Reply to Hayne." Webster himself, sixty-eight years old and ill, with but two years of life before him, seemed like a shadow of the national past and of his former self. It was the last great speech that America's most noted orator was to make. "I wish to speak today," he began, "not as a Massachusetts man, nor as a Northern man, but as an American. . . . The imprisoned winds are let loose, the East, the North, and the stormy South, combine to throw the whole sea into commotion, to toss its billows to the skies, and disclose its profoundest depths. . . . I speak today for the preservation of the Union. 'Hear me for my cause.'"

Calmly he discussed the whole history of slavery in the nation, stressed the inviolability of the Missouri Compromise, and pointed out that even without legislation slavery would never gain a foothold in New Mexico and California by reason of the nature of their soils and climate. He asserted that the South was right in demanding that the Fugitive Slave Law should be enforced, like any other law, and that the Abolitionists had done no good and much harm by the violence of their agitation. At the end he pleaded, as at the end of the "Reply to Hayne," for the preservation of the Union above all other considerations, and warned again that there could be no such thing as a peaceable secession.

It was not as great a speech as his former one, nor of such lasting importance as an interpretation of the Constitution, but it made a greater immediate impression. It deeply exasperated the anti-slavery elements in the North, and Webster was denounced in his own State as a Benedict Arnold and a traitor to his followers and to humanity. Sentiment in the North had been peculiarly bitter against the laws for the capture and return of slaves who had escaped from their masters into the Free States, and there had been many instances, which had caused public commotion, of open resistance to the enforcement of such acts. The "Underground Railroad," as it was called, had been organized among the Abolitionists in the North to hide escaping slaves and help them on their journeys, and there was intense dislike on the part of many who were not Abolitionists to seeing men who had escaped from slavery captured and returned to it.

Massachusetts had been the centre of agitation against slavery and that the senator from that State, perhaps the leading statesman of the nation, should urge obedience to a new and more imperative law for reclaiming escaped slaves brought down on Webster such wrath as few statesmen have been called upon to face at the end of such a long

FUGITIVE
SLAVE BILL!

HON. HENRY WILSON

Will address the citizens on

Thursday Evening, April 3,

At the

At 7 o'clock, on the all-engrossing topics of the day—the FUGITIVE SLAVE BILL, the pro-slavery action of the National Government and the general aspect of the Slavery question.

Let every man and woman, without distinction of sect or party, attend the meeting and bear a testimony against the system which fills the prisons of a free republic with men whose only crime is a love of freedom—which strikes down the habeas corpus and trial by jury, and converts the free soil of Massachusetts into hunting ground for the Southern kidnappers.

Ashby, March 29, 1851.

White & Potter's Steam Press....4000 Impressions per hour.,Spring Lane, Boston.

ANNOUNCEMENT OF AN ADDRESS AT ASHBY, MASSACHUSETTS, IN MARCH, 1851, ON THE FUGITIVE SLAVE BILL WHICH "CONVERTS THE FREE SOIL OF MASSACHUSETTS INTO HUNTING GROUND FOR THE SOUTHERN KIDNAPPERS.'

From a broadside in the American Antiquarian Society, Worcester.

and distinguished career. In the Senate, however, it brought heavy support to Clay and his compromise. As the summer went on, it began to appear that Clay might win, and feeling grew more bitter in the South.

In June, a convention of delegates from the Southern States met at Nashville to consider the situation. Although Langdon Cheves of South Carolina, always throughout this long controversy the most disunionist of States, introduced a resolution declaring that secession was the only remedy "from the usurped and unrestrained power of the Federal Government," the resolutions actually adopted did not go quite so far. Certain interesting points, however, were made in an address which was prepared for circulation. It claimed that the North wished not only to destroy Southern property in the form of slaves but to place on Southerners "the brand of inferiority," an inference, of course, from the Northern contention as to the essential immorality of slavery, and accusations against slave-owners. The address also noted the increasing predominance of the North in Congress, and predicted that in fifty years the South would be hopelessly outnumbered. An adjourned meeting of the convention was held in November, by which time the compromise spirit had greatly increased, although South Carolina, largely under the influence of the irreconcilable fire-eater, R. Barnwell Rhett, was as strong for secession as ever.

Meanwhile, the position in Washington had been much altered by the unexpected death of President Taylor on the 9th of July. Millard Fillmore, who now became President, was a friend both to Clay and the Compromise, and in September the latter complete, Fugitive Slave Law and all, in the shape of separate bills, was passed by both houses of Congress and received the President's signature.

Clay and Webster, with their followers, had saved the Union, although no compromise could be lasting. Slavery had become an anachronism among modern civilized races, and if, as was to prove the case, the Union could not continue half slave and half free, even less, in time, could it have continued overwhelmingly free and a small part slave. Calhoun had been right when he believed that the South had no time to lose if it were going to settle the question in its own favor for its own type of civilization. Slavery was not merely a local problem, and this the Fugitive Slave Law showed. It was one that permeated the thought of the entire nation, and which would one day have to be settled.

Had the Abolitionists not aroused the South to fury, and sections of the North to frenzy, by their violence, it is possible, though no one can say truly, that in time the problem might have been worked out peaceably and with a minimum of hard feeling. Economic changes, such as have now occurred in the South, might have in-

duced the Southerners to realize and admit the economic wasteful-
ness of slavery as contrasted with free labor, and wrought a willingness to allow emancipation in exchange for compensation, as in the
British West Indies. The South had in reality two problems, one of
which was racial, the presence in its midst of the millions of the
black race, and the other of which was economic, the problem as to
whether a slave or a wage system of labor was the more conducive to
profit by the plantation owners, assuming that they could recover the
capital invested in slave property.

The latter question, however, had ceased to be one of economics,
and had been made one of fear and passion, thanks mostly to the
Abolitionists. The North had both damned and threatened the
"peculiar institution" of the South, and the South could regard every
increase of free territory and of every additional Northern senator
and congressman who helped to overturn the political balance of
power, only as bringing the danger of conflict nearer in defense of
what were deemed the constitutional rights of the Southern States.
There was no question at all but that the right to hold slaves was as
strongly imbedded in the Constitution as any other right which
could be claimed by either North or South.

For the time being, however, the storm which had threatened
destruction had been lulled, and, for various reasons which we shall
note later, when it broke again with even greater violence, the
North had greatly increased its power to preserve the Union by
force as compared with 1850. It was in that sense only that Clay and
Webster had been successful. They had not devised a formula which
was to be permanently workable. They had merely put off the day
of reckoning for another decade. That, however, was of supreme
importance.

Meanwhile, North and South, with the exceptions of the extreme
radicals of both sections, settled down to accept the Compromise as
though it were permanent, an acceptation that was made somewhat
easier by the rapid growth of business and the coming of a boom
which was to become so wild as to bring on the economic debacle
of 1857 as an inevitable sequence. Thanks partly to the Crimean War
in Europe and the discovery of gold in California, the United States
entered upon one of its periodic outbursts of rapid development,
and under the apparent protection of the Compromise men gave

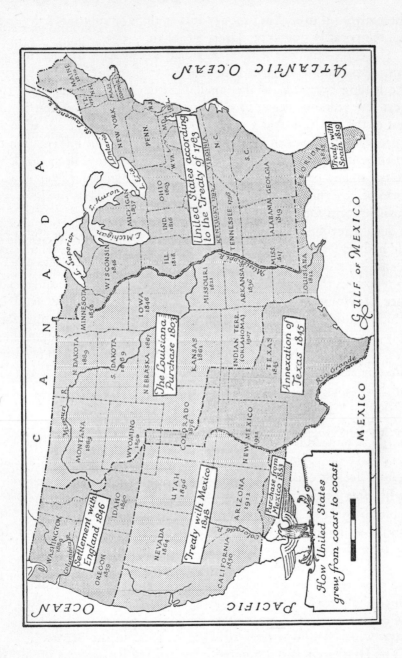

How United States grew from coast to coast

themselves up to making money rather than to splitting hairs over the temporarily quiescent slavery problem.

The end of the war with Mexico had left us with our continental possessions and boundaries rounded out to their present shape, with the trifling exception of the small Gadsden Purchase, and for the next few years we began to take an odd and sudden interest in the rest of the world. It was a period of great revolutionary agitation in Europe, and American sympathy, often with no real information to intelligent appreciation of the conditions, has always been quick to go out to any people fighting for self-determination or a republican form of government, though the latter may sometimes be the worst possible form for the people in question.

Such a revolution was in progress in Hungary in 1849, and Taylor had sent one of that endless stream of "observers," which has been a constant accompaniment of our European diplomatic policy, to report on the situation with a view to recognizing the independence of Hungary from Austria at the first opportunity. Austria, which considered our conduct as unfriendly as it was unquestionably precipitate, made representations to us through its representative, Chevalier Hülseman. A couple of years earlier we had been invited by revolutionaries in Ireland and Sicily to annex those islands but had sanely made no move to comply with such fantastic suggestions.

In 1850, however, Webster had become Secretary of State in Fillmore's new Cabinet, and decided to answer Austria in such a way as to make the eagle scream so loudly that, as he said, any American should "feel sheepish and look silly who should speak of disunion." In his note he described the benefits we had received from our republican form of government, claiming that we had the right to cherish an interest in nations struggling for similar institutions. In the tone of a stump speech he added that "the power of this republic, at the present moment, is spread over a region, one of the richest and most fertile on the globe, and of an extent in comparison with which the possessions of the House of Hapsburg are but a patch on the earth's surface." America was beginning to feel its oats, and the letter, when read, was received with applause in the Senate.

The Hungarian revolution, with the help of Russia, was promptly suppressed by Austria but the following year when its leader, Louis

Kossuth, came to America in December he was received with wild enthusiasm. In spite of public demonstrations, however, he returned empty-handed, except for $100,000 which he had collected, the government wisely declining to interfere in European affairs beyond making the American eagle outscreech the Austrian one.

A far more important bit of European diplomacy was concerned with the respective rights, or perhaps it would be truer to say ambitions, of England and the United States in Central America. For a couple of centuries England had claimed a protectorate over the Mosquito Indians in Nicaragua, and instead of letting go her hold when the Central American States had won their independence from Spain, had considerably extended it. In January, 1848, British warships had seized Greytown on the San Juan River, and in April Polk had reiterated his strong insistence upon maintaining the Monroe Doctrine, "a policy which no European power should cherish the disposition to resist." Apart from our general reasons for having proclaimed that Doctrine which warned all European nations not to establish new colonies in America, we had a peculiar interest in the isthmus of Central America, which, since our acquisition of California, was the shortest route between our East and far West.

There had for long been talk of the possibility of a canal being dug across it, which would permit a continuous water passage between our two coasts, and in any case a railroad there was a simple matter as contrasted with our yet unbuilt transcontinental lines. England, interested in trade above all else, also had a stake in whatever might mean a new trade route for the world at large, and when, in 1849, we secured by treaties with Honduras and Nicaragua the right of transit across their territories, England began to take notice.

At the end of that year a special envoy, Sir Henry Lytton Bulwer, arrived in Washington from that country with the offer to stop quarrelling and to negotiate a treaty that would define the rights of each nation. The negotiations were in the hands of John M. Clayton, then Secretary of State under Taylor, and a treaty, known from the chief two negotiators as the Clayton-Bulwer Treaty, was signed on April 19, 1850, to become of great importance on the eve of our entry into the European War more than threescore years later.

The Treaty, which was ratified on July 5, agreed that both

nations would guarantee the neutrality of any canal built, that neither would fortify it or ever insist upon exclusive control over it, the canal further being stated to be built for the benefit of the world and to be operated on "equal terms for all." No canal was, in fact, built during the century, but the Treaty, in spite of some ambiguous clauses that made trouble in the next few years as to British occupation, undoubtedly cleared the international atmosphere after the more immediate difficulties were got over.

It was well that it should be so cleared for by the mid-century a new factor had entered American politics. As we had previously noted, the Irish had been coming in great numbers, and by 1850 there were nearly a million of them, settled for the most part in the industrial centres of the East. The relations of Ireland to England had always been extremely difficult, and there is no question but that England's handling of them until after the nineteenth century was the chief blot on her record of imperial administrative ability. The Irish who reached America as immigrants came for the most part with intense hatred of England in their hearts. Although they were assuredly not popular among ourselves, partly due to their Catholic religion and partly to economic causes, they developed a marked aptitude for politics, and locating as they did in large masses in important centres like Boston, New York, and Philadelphia, their vote became an important and even at times a determining one.

Politicians were quick to see the need of catering to it, and the simplest way to do that was to play upon hatred of England. There was still enough feeling left from the Revolution and the War of 1812, emphasized in the education of every child by his text-books and "pieces to speak," as to make denunciation of England and a strong anti-British policy almost as welcome to Americans as to the Irish. Our history in 1850 was still brief, and history in those days was almost wholly taken up with politics and wars. Until the Mexican struggle our only two wars as an independent nation had been those against England, and our whole history appeared as one long struggle against that power. "Twisting the lion's tail" thus came to be one of the surest means of winning votes in the absence of domestic issues of overwhelming importance.

For a moment, in 1852, it seemed as though the chief domestic issue, slavery, had been settled, the Free Soil Party alone emphatically denying it; and the election proved that the people as a whole wished to forget. In the platform drawn up by the Democrats at their convention in Baltimore in June, 1852, the Compromise as passed by Congress in 1850 was unqualifiedly approved, and a further plank pledged the party to "resist all attempts at renewing, in Congress or out of it, the agitation of the slavery question, under whatever shape or color the attempt may be made." Certainly nothing could have been more explicit than that, and whoever voted the Democratic ticket knew what he was voting for, an advantage that, in both parties, is all too frequently denied to the voter of today.

The two wings of the party into which it had split in the previous election were willing to unite, and the only difficulty was a candidate. To satisfy the North and South and the two united Democratic factions, it was necessary to choose as colorless and recordless a candidate as could be turned up, but it was not until the forty-ninth ballot that he was found by a stampede to Franklin Pierce, of New Hampshire, who had probably been determined on from the first by the party leaders, who did not. however, bring out his name until the thirty-fifth ballot.

The Whigs in their convention, which also met in Baltimore ten days after the Democrats adjourned, also had their difficulties in settling on a standard bearer. Their greatest statesman, Webster, who had long aspired to the Presidency, had seriously injured himself by his Seventh of March speech, and could not count even upon a united New England to support a favorite son, as Maine had not forgiven his settlement of its boundary question. Although Fillmore was approved by many for re-election, the Whig Party, having no principles and driven also to straddle North and South, finally chose, as did the Democrats, a man of whom the public knew little as to his position.

On the fifty-third ballot the nomination was given to General Scott, the fifth general to run for President in our history of sixty years. The Whigs, however, unlike the Democrats, hedged carefully in their platform, which in the matter of States' Rights and other points of doctrine read curiously like a Jeffersonian declaration of political faith. They merely "deprecated" and agreed to "discountenance" further agitation of the slavery question, and insisted upon maintaining the Acts making up the Compromise "until time and experience shall demonstrate the necessity of further legislation."

The Free Soilers, in their convention at Pittsburgh in August, where John P. Hale of New Hampshire was nominated for President, roundly denounced the Compromise, and collected in their platform the usual incongruous lot of ideals and suggestions that always afflict reform third-party movements.

If we consider the platforms, it is quite evident what the people wanted when we find that of the electoral votes Pierce received 254, Scott 42, and Hale none. The popular vote, though not quite so overwhelming for the Democrats, was unmistakably clear also: Pierce 1,601,000, Scott 1,386,000, Hale 156,000. The Democrats, accepting the Compromise and pledging themselves to avoid any possible controversy over slavery, carried every State in the Union except Kentucky, Massachusetts, Tennessee, and Vermont. In only three States, Ohio, New York, and Massachusetts, did the Free Soilers poll over 10,000 votes. Before the campaign was over Clay and Webster had joined Calhoun in death, both having missed their greatest ambition. Had either of them received the honor he had so long and earnestly desired, the result would have been a problem we have not yet faced, the death of a nominated candidate for the presidency before election. That of 1852 seemed to promise a new era of harmony, and the deaths of the great triumvirate opened the arena for new men.

Although the nation had voted overwhelmingly, both North and South, to let the slavery question lie sleeping, there were many forces at work tending powerfully to keep it awake. In the South the steadily increasing disequilibrium between the two sections could not fail to be watched with alarm as the statistics for both population and economic resources in the Free States drew rapidly ahead of those for the South. As Calhoun had pointed out, the slave-holders would become increasingly outnumbered by their opponents, and unless the latter would develop a tolerance that would enable the two types of civilization to live peacefully side by side in the Union, the contest so far from having been settled would merely become more and more hopeless for the South unless secession might be permitted without recourse to arms. Every decade that passed would see the disparity increased.

In spite of the Democratic platform and the desire of the ordinary business man to forget slavery, there were those in the North who would not allow it to be forgotten. Attempts to enforce the Fugitive Slave Law among a people who were not slave-owners themselves and who, with the rest of the world outside the South, were coming more and more to view slavery as a crying evil, aroused the passion of humanitarianism which was one of the chief emotional currents of the age, and convinced many a man who was far from being a radical or an abolitionist that the system could not be allowed to go on forever.

This humanitarian sentiment was also continually stirred and played upon by the Massachusetts group of authors, then the most distinguished and popular in the nation. Whittier and Lowell in verse and Emerson in trenchant prose from the days of the agitation over the admission of Texas had kept up their propaganda against slavery and its attendant laws and evils. Emerson swore he would not obey the Fugitive Slave Law and advised every one else to break it "on the earliest possible occasion."

In 1852 there appeared, first in magazine form and then in a book, one of the most famous appeals made in the entire history of literature, Harriet Beecher Stowe's *Uncle Tom's Cabin,* considered many years later by Lincoln to have been one of the leading causes of the Civil War. It roused such a storm of emotion and anger as has no other book in the annals of America, and probably in the world. Three hundred thousand copies were sold in the first year and the work was translated into twenty foreign languages. A violent attack on the evils of slavery in the form of a novel, the book had slight literary merit, and was crude both in psychology and style. Its emotionalism was melodramatic and its picture of the sufferings of the slaves very much overdrawn so far as the normal life of the South as a whole was concerned, although each of the incidents which it piled together in one heap might have occurred separately in real life. Like Paine's *Common Sense,* at the time of the American Revolution, the enormous influence of the book lay neither in its style nor its thought but in its tremendously powerful

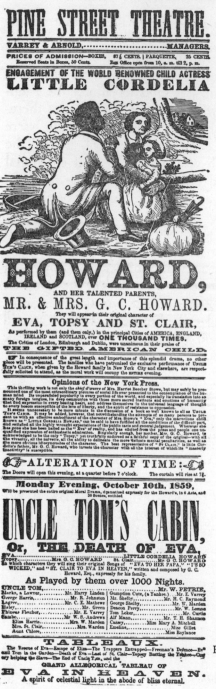

PINE STREET THEATRE.

VARREY & ARNOLD,..............................MANAGERS.

PRICES OF ADMISSION—BOXES, 37½ CENTS. | PARQUETTE, 25 CENTS.
Reserved Seats in Boxes, 50 Cents. Box Office open from 10, a. m. till 2, p. m.

ENGAGEMENT OF THE WORLD RENOWNED CHILD ACTRESS

LITTLE CORDELIA

HOWARD,

AND HER TALENTED PARENTS,

MR. & MRS. G. C. HOWARD.

They will appear in their original character of

EVA, TOPSY AND ST. CLAIR,

As performed by them (and them only,) in the principal Cities of AMERICA, ENGLAND,
IRELAND and SCOTLAND, over **ONE THOUSAND TIMES.**
The Critics of London, Edinburgh and Dublin, were unanimous in their praise of

THE GIFTED AMERICAN CHILD.

☞ In consequence of the great length and importance of this splendid drama, no other
piece will be presented. The families who have patronized the exclusive performance of UNCLE
TOM'S CABIN, when given by the Howard family in New York City and elsewhere, are respectfully solicited to attend, as the moral work will occupy the ENTIRE evening.

Opinions of the New York Press.

This thrilling work is not only the *chef d'œuvre* of Mrs. Harriet Beecher Stowe, but may safely be pronounced one of the most extraordinary pictures of social life ever presented to the contemplation of the human mind. Its unparalleled popularity in every portion of the world, and especially its translation into so
many foreign tongues, its deep communion with those more sacred instincts and emotions of humanity
that find expression in every beating heart, and address themselves in the universal language of thought
to every bosom susceptible of the love of liberty, and the spirit of resistance to oppression.
It seems unnecessary to be more minute in the discussion of a book so well known to all as UNCLE
TOM'S CABIN. It may be added, however, that notwithstanding the attempts of so many persons to present us with an offensive embodiment of the character of Mrs. Stowe's "Eva," only the marvelous child
known as "LITTLE CORDELIA HOWARD," can be said to have fulfilled all the conditions of the difficult part,
and satisfied all the highly wrought expectations of the public taste and general judgement. Wherever she
has gone she has been hailed as the "Eva" of reality, and has elicited from the press and people one un-
qualified expression of enthusiastic admiration. Singularly enough, her mother, Mrs. G. C. Howard, is
acknowledged to be the only "Topsy," not truthfully endorsed as a faithful copy of the original—with all
the vivacity, all the naïveté, all the subtle, the more delicate mental peculiarities, as well as
the more obvious idiosyncrasies of the character. The best representative of "St Clair," is little Cordelia's father, Mr. G. C. Howard, who invests the character with all the interest of which its "masterly
inactivity" is susceptible.

☞ **ALTERATION OF TIME:** ☜

The Doors will open this evening, at a quarter before 7 o'clock.   The curtain will rise at 7½.

Monday Evening, October 10th, 1859,

Will be presented the entire original Moral Drama, dramatized expressly for the Howard's, in 6 Acts, and
30 Scenes, entitled

UNCLE TOM'S CABIN,

Or, THE DEATH OF EVA,

EVA,..............................LITTLE CORDELIA HOWARD
Topsy,.............................Mrs. G. C. HOWARD | St. Clair,......................Mr. G. C. HOWARD

In which characters they will sing their original Songs of "EVA TO HER PAPA," "I'S SO
WICKED," and "ST. CLAIR TO EVA IN HEAVEN," written and composed by G. C.
Howard, Esq., expressly for his family.

As Played by them over 1000 Nights.

UNCLE TOM,................		................Mr. W. PETRIE,	
Marks, a Lawyer,........	Mr. Harry Linden	Gumption Cute, (a Yankee,).	Mr. E. Varrey
George Harris,...........	Mr. R. Johnston	Mr. Shelby,...........	Mr. H. C. Raymond
Legree,..................	Mr. C. E. Mathews	George Shelby,........	Mr. W. Marden
Haley,...................	Mr. Green	Deacon Perry,........	Mr. W. Lomas
Phineas Fletcher,.......	Mr. E. Varrey	Tom Loker,...........	Mr. Curtis
Sambo,...................	Mr. W. S. Andrews	Alf Mann,............	Mr. T. H. Shannon
Eliza Harris,...........	Mrs. W. Marden	Cassy,...............	Miss Mary A. Mitchell
Mrs. St. Clair,.........	Mrs. Warden	Emeline,.............	Miss Gillet
Aunt Chlory,............			Miss Boylance

TABLEAUX

The Rescue of Eva—Escape of Eliza—The Trappers Entrapped—Freeman's Defence—Eva
and Tom in the Garden—Death of Eva—Last of St. Clair—Topsey Butting the Yankee—Ony
cry helping the Slave—The End of Uncle Tom, and the

GRAND ALLEGORICAL TABLEAU OF

EVA IN HEAVEN.

A spirit of celestial light in the abode of bliss eternal.

appeal to some of the most fundamental and generous emotions of the common man.

Especially to women and youth it presented an unforgettable picture of what might happen to human beings under slavery, which, to the rage of the South, was readily translated by assumption into what was happening daily in our own land. One of the most staggering blows ever struck at slavery, it was hailed abroad by such diverse minds as Heine, George Sand, and Macaulay. Continuing to sell in large quantities and dramatized for the stage with phenomenal runs, its influence was cumulative year after year. Its characters became as living in the ordinary Northern household as any in real life, and the events of the next decade must be considered with the book as background. "Uncle Tom" and "Little Eva" worked steadily in the minds of ordinary people against the merchants and statesmen who were doing their best to keep slavery out of the national sight.

FACSIMILE OF A PROGRAMME OF ONE
OF THE BEST-KNOWN TOM SHOWS
By Courtesy of the Yale University Press.

Meanwhile other events were rapidly destroying the new assumed harmony in the Union. A large section of the public domain, lying west of Missouri and Iowa and north of Texas, was as yet unorganized and without even a territorial form of government. It all lay north of the old Missouri Compromise line of 36° 30′, and if organized as Free Soil in accordance with the agreement of 1820 would have further disturbed the balance of power in favor of the North both in the House and Senate. There had been suggestions of organizing it all into one territory under the name of Nebraska, but so strong was the feeling that Senator Atchison of Missouri swore he would see it "sunk in hell' before he would vote for it as free soil.

There were complications, however, which interestingly illustrate the increasing pressure of new economic forces against the slave power. It was a period of rapid railroad construction, the lines fast extending westward. For the most part they were being built by the industrial North which had, and could secure, ample capital for such enterprises as contrasted with the South, whose capital was largely "frozen" in lands and slaves. The Northern capitalists, whether with prescience of the coming sectional struggle or not, preferred to extend their transcontinental projects across free territory, and although the Missourians were slaveholders who sympathized with Atchison they did not wish on the other hand to lose the chance of making St. Louis a railway centre from which to tap the business of the growing West. The senator, therefore, consented to reverse himself to the extent of allowing "Nebraska" to be made a territory, leaving the question of slavery to be determined by its future citizens.

The matter came to a head in the Congress which met in December, 1853, and which confirmed the Gadsden Purchase on the 30th of that month. The preceding Congress had authorized the making of four surveys for railways to the Pacific coast. The most southerly would have to run through the new Purchase, the organized States of Texas and California, and the Territory of New Mexico, whereas the three more northerly ones would cross the unorganized territory in dispute. The Chairman of the Senate Committee on Territories happened to be Stephen A. Douglas of Illinois, who was also heavily interested in railroad extension and western land speculation. Douglas wished the new railroad to follow the route westward from St. Louis for reasons of his own. A great debater and a self-made man who had rapidly risen to a position of national distinction, immensely popular with the Democrats of the North, he

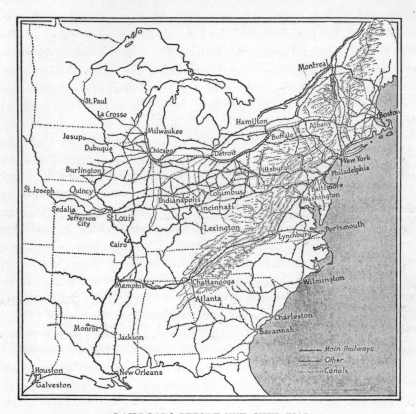

RAILROADS BEFORE THE CIVIL WAR

also had the usual Senatorial ambition to become President, which meant that he must win the South.

When, therefore, a bill to erect "Nebraska" into a Territory, introduced by a senator from Iowa, emerged from Douglas's committee to which it had been referred, it came out with an amendment embodying Atchison's plan of allowing the citizens to decide as to the question of slavery within its borders. Douglas's real-estate holdings and his railroad plans called for a settled government in the

Territory. He seemingly was led to take on the amendment by the two facts that the South might not permit the bill to pass without it and that by aiding it he would at the same time strengthen himself in that section for the presidential nomination.

It was assuredly a question how much of the old Missouri Compromise of 1820 was still left after New Mexico had been made a Territory on the "squatter sovereignty" theory of allowing the citizens to determine for themselves as to slavery, and California had been admitted as a Free State although half of it was south of the old line. Finally, after much opposition, a bill passed Congress in 1854 substantially on the lines proposed by Douglas except that out of the lower portion of the huge "Nebraska" Territory two Territories were to be carved instead of one. The southern part was to be made into what is now the State

NEBRASKA AND KANSAS TERRITORIES

of Kansas and the part immediately north of that into what is now Nebraska. A clause was also inserted in the measure explicitly repealing the Missouri Compromise.

At once a howl of execration went up from the Northern anti-slavery ranks. The South might claim that the Missouri Compromise had really been abrogated when Utah, New Mexico, and California had been admitted on terms not consonant with it, forgetting that in that Compromise of 1850 the South had received especial favors in exchange for what they might be giving up. The explicit repeal of the older Compromise, however, opened the whole of the national domain, not yet organized, to the advance of slavery, and what the South was planning was more than hinted at in an amendment moved by Senator Dixon of Kentucky. This expressly provided that Southerners should be at complete liberty to take and hold their slaves "within any of the Territories of the United States" or the States later to be formed from them.

It is a curious fact that Northern sentiment and fanaticism, which had always been so sympathetic and ardent in favor of the black man, had never been aroused in the slightest by the plight of the red man. When Jackson was President and when Americans thought of the territory now in dispute as merely a desert waste of no value to us, the honor of the United States had been pledged forever to the Indians in a guarantee to them that, having been driven by a succession of broken treaties from every other part of America east of the Rockies, the section over which we were quarrelling in 1854 should be forever theirs, to roam and hunt over as they would. In all the dispute over what should be the rights of the negro in the lands we were now exploiting, only a single voice was raised in defense of the national honor pledged to the red, that of the Southern slave owner, Sam Houston.

Rufus Choate is quoted as having said that *"Uncle Tom's Cabin* would make 2,000,000 Abolitionists," and now Greeley wrote in *The Tribune* that the Kansas-Nebraska Bill would make more of them in three months than Garrison and the Abolitionist orators like Wendell Phillips would make in fifty years. Politically the country was thrown into chaos as far as the old parties were concerned. The Whigs were completely split, every Whig congressman from the North voting against the bill, while all but seven from the South voted in favor of it. The Whig Party had ceased to exist.

On the other hand, Douglas had forced a large section of the Democratic Party out of its ranks. With the two great Compromises of 1820 and 1850 broken, with the parties in confusion, with the old leaders dead, and lesser known and experienced men in command, it was clear that the ship of state was drifting perilously. No longer were there any to stand with the authority of Clay or Webster for Union as the supreme good of the nation. In the White House, the President, although a Northern man, had gone over to the doctrines of the South, and Jefferson Davis, of Mississippi, was his Secretary of War.

An effort was made, largely by side-steppers from the old parties, chiefly Whig, to form a new one, based on Nativism and Protestantism, and in form an odd mixture of a secret society and a political party. All of its members were pledged to follow the dictates of the inner council, and none could join who were not native born and wholly unconnected in any way with Roman Catholicism. The appeals to that love of mystery and ritual which seems to be one of the characteristics of the ordinary American, and to racial and religious prejudice, made the new party grow like a mushroom at first.

From the fact that when asked anything about it, its members were required to answer that they "did not know," it came to be called the "Know Nothing Party," and in 1854 was a formidable power at the polls, accounting for a quarter of the total vote of New York, two fifths of that in Pennsylvania, and two thirds of that in Massachusetts, in which last State it elected the Governor and entire legislature. The next year, after having required an oath from all its members to maintain the national Union, it carried Connecticut, New Hampshire, and Rhode Island, claiming it had a million members enrolled. In preparation for the campaign of 1856 it held a national convention in Philadelphia in June, 1855, calling itself the American Party, but there the Southerners got control of it and ended its career by passing resolutions denying the authority of Congress to legislate on the subject of slavery.

The year before, however, a far more important event had happened in the formation of the present Republican Party, which may be considered to date from a convention held at Jackson, Michigan, on July 6, 1854. Composed of men pledged to resist all encroachments of slavery, it put a State ticket in the field, and invited other States to hold conventions and to do the same. In the general confusion, the crumbling of the American Party added greatly to the strength of the Republicans who were to enter the national contest in 1856.

The administration was giving the anti-slaverites plenty to think about. Pierce in his inaugural address had hinted at the acquisition of Cuba, which island, large, rich, full of slaves, Polk, when in full expansionist career, had offered to buy from Spain for $100,-000,000. Our experience in buying Louisiana seemed to have given us the idea that we could, whenever we wanted, buy territory and its population like any other merchandise, an odd idea for a nation committed to the doctrine that all just government derived its power from the consent of the governed. So far, however, we had found no other nation with the huckstering spirit of the French under Napoleon, and Spain, quite as proudly as Mexico, had declined to part with any portion of its domain in exchange for American dollars.

The rejected offer was followed by filibustering expeditions from the South sent out to the island with the hope of intensifying the perennial disorder there, and bringing about successful revolution and subsequent annexation. These also failed, although in 1854, when the Spanish authorities seized the cargo of an American vessel, the *Black Warrior,* for having disobeyed regulations of the port of Havana, there was for a moment prospect of war. America, fortunately, was much more taken up with Kansas than with Cuba, and the "insult" being apologized for unexpectedly by Spain, the world went on as before.

The chief interest in Cuban affairs, apart from the irritation caused in the North by the reaching out of the South for more slave territory, was due to one of the most asinine episodes in our entire diplomatic history. Pierce had sent as Minister to Spain a Louisianian, Pierre Soulé, who had no qualities for the post but whom his fellow State politicians wanted to get out of the way. In London, we were represented by James Buchanan of Pennsylvania, and in Paris by the unimportant John Y. Mason of Virginia.

Soulé was instructed to confer with both of these when it became evident that he was making no headway in persuading Spain to sell us Cuba against her will. The report drawn up by the three conferees and signed by them on October 18, 1854, has always been called the Ostend Manifesto from the place where they first met, although in fact before they signed it they had moved to Aix-la-Chapelle in Prussia. The only explanation for the extraordinary document which the three diplomats drew up was that the irresponsible Louisianian must have been the "perfect bird-charmer," which Mason called him, and perhaps sang of the White House to Buchanan. Professor H. B. Learned has recently discovered the hitherto unknown fact that our Secretary of State, William L. Marcy, had instructed Soulé to try to get Spain to sell the island for even as much as $130,000,000; and failing that to endeavor "to detach that island from the Spanish dominion," whatever the incautious secretary might have meant by that vague word "detach" to such a representative as Soulé.

The manifesto, as finally completed, recommended the offering to Spain of $120,000,000 for the island, and if that nation "actuated by stubborn pride and a false sense of honor" should decline again to sell it to us, then, after certain intervening events which the diplomats predicted, "by every law, human and divine, we shall be justified in wresting it from Spain if we possess the power," and so long as we "preserve our own conscious rectitude and self-respect . . . we can afford to disregard the censures of the world." Whatever Marcy's intention had been when he sent his instructions for all these extraordinary proceedings, he turned a cold shoulder at once to the manifesto, and for a while we allowed Spain to do as she would with her own.

In the same year when we were trying to "detach" the much-coveted island of Cuba from its owners, we engaged in a more epoch-making adventure with islands on the other side of the world. Japan was practically a closed land to the rest of the nations, the ruling powers there having resisted all attempts to open the empire to a general commerce and intercourse for fear of what the impact of our western and, as they considered it, not wholly without reason, barbarian civilization might be on their own. In 1844 we had made a commercial treaty with China, one with Hawaii in 1849, and another with Borneo in 1850.

Commodore Matthew C. Perry was now despatched to succeed, by show of force, in making one with the tightly sealed Japan. Arriving in July, 1853, he declined to leave, as requested, and insisted upon the letter from the President being sent to the Shogun. This having been agreed to after an examination of the guns on his sloop-of-war, he sailed for China, to give the Japanese time to think it over. When he returned in February of the following year, the Japanese had decided that there was nothing to do but yield to our threats, and receive the gifts which American civilization in the person of our commodore presented them with,—farming machinery, munitions of war, and a large quantity of whiskey. Having thus accepted civilization and been initiated into its blessings, they signed a treaty on March 31 by which thereafter American vessels would be allowed to enter certain Japanese ports for trade.

A less important treaty, which remained in force for only a little over ten years, was that negotiated by Marcy for establishing reciprocity with Canada and settling the vexed question of the fisheries, temporarily at the fore owing to England's having sent armed vessels to keep New England fishermen out of prohibited waters. The treaty, which had not only to run the usual gauntlet of our senators, but that of five Canadian Provincial legislatures, as well as that of the Dominion itself, involved the expenditure of an amount of money in Canada for the influencing of opinion by a confidential agent which shocked the Secretary of State but left President Pierce entirely complacent.

In all these diplomatic matters, the American people were taking comparatively slight interest. Far more exciting events nearer to their lives and thoughts were happening in their own West, where in a real sense the great Civil War, so long threatened in Senatorial rhetoric, was beginning in earnest.

As the Kansas-Nebraska Bill had determined that the question of slavery in those Territories should be settled by their own inhabitants and not by Congress, the North took up the challenge of the South, and both sections poured settlers into Kansas, which as the more southern of the two and adjoining Missouri would be the first scene of the struggle. Hordes crossed from Missouri, carrying their slaves with them, and the North sent men who went, not with the spirit of the usual pioneer but with that of crusaders. When the anti-slavery Northerners organized an "Emigrant Aid Society" to assist financially in peopling the Territory with men pledged to keep it free soil, indignation became even greater in the South. For the most part the slave-owners settled along the Missouri River, at Atchison, Lecompton, and Leavenworth, while the Northerners located along the Kansas at Topeka, Lawrence, and Osawatomie.

Both factions were armed, and constant conflicts took place between them, giving the title of "bleeding Kansas" to the Territory. In March, 1855, an election was held for a Territorial legislature, and bands of Missourians crossed the State border, voted illegally, and promptly returned to their own State. The pro-slavery party having thus won at the polls by the aid of the "border ruffians," the anti-slavery citizens refused to accept the result, and holding a convention at Topeka in October adopted a constitution prohibiting

ONE OF THE SHIPS IN THE PERRY EXPEDITION, MARCH, 1854

COMMODORE MATTHEW C. PERRY

As he appeared to a Japanese artist in 1854.

From contemporary sketches by Japanese artists in the Chadbourne Collection of the Library of Congress.

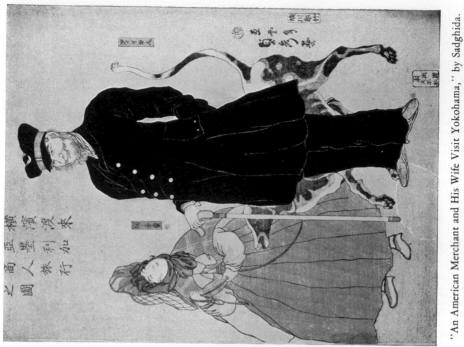

slavery, the pro-slavery men throughout the Territory refusing to vote. The violence steadily increased, and the following May the Northern settler and fanatic John Brown, with seven other men, including four of his sons, killed five pro-slavery settlers in their cabins along Pottawatomie Creek.

At about the same time, the anti-slavery settlers, who had adopted

FREE STATE CONVENTION!

All persons who are favorable to a union of effort, and a permanent organization of all the Free State elements of Kansas Territory, and who wish to secure upon the broadest platform the co-operation of all who agree upon this point, are requested to meet at their several places of holding elections, in their respective districts on the 15th of August, instant, at one o'clock, P. M., and appoint five delegates to each representative to which they were entitled in the Legislative Assembly, who shall meet in general Convention at

Big Springs, Wednesday, Sept. 5th '55,

at 10 o'clock A. M., for the purpose of adopting a Platform upon which all may act harmoniously who prefer Freedom to Slavery.
The nomination of a Delegate to Congress, will also come up before the General Convention.
Let no sectional or party issues distract or prevent the perfect co-operation of Free State men. Union and harmony are absolutely necessary to success. The pro-slavery party are fully and effectually organized. No jars nor minor issues divide them. And to contend against them successfully, we also must be united—Without prudence and harmony of action we are certain to fail. Let every man then do his duty and we are certain of victory.
All Free State men, without distinction, are earnestly requested to take immediate and effective steps to insure a full and correct representation for every District in the Territory. "United we stand; divided we fall."
By order of the Executive Committee of the Free State Party of the Territory of Kansas, as per resolution of the Mass Convention in session at Lawrence, Aug 15th and 16th, 1855.

J. K. GOODIN, Sec'y. **C. ROBINSON, Chairman.**

Herald of Freedom, Print.

CALL FOR DELEGATES TO A FREE STATE CONVENTION AT BIG SPRINGS, KANSAS, 1855
Signed by the chairman and secretary of the Executive Committee of the Free State Party of the Territory of Kansas.
From a broadside in the Kansas State Historical Society, Topeka.

the Topeka constitution, petitioned Congress to admit Kansas as a State and with that constitution. In the course of the debate in the Senate, characterized by bitter feeling and unpardonable invective, Senator Sumner of Massachusetts outdid himself in heaping abuse on Senator Butler of South Carolina, and three days later, Butler's nephew, a member of the lower House, entered the Senate chamber, and approaching Sumner while he was writing at his desk, beat him heavily over the head with a heavy stick until the Massachusetts senator was unconscious and so badly wounded that he was unable to return to the Senate for three years. The almost insane invective of the Northerner and the dastardly act of the Southerner showed all too clearly that the day of violence predicted and feared by Clay and Webster could not long be postponed by paper compromises. In Kansas, the same week, a Northern man had murdered the Southern sheriff of Lawrence while the latter was preparing to make an arrest, and in retaliation, the Southerners marched on the town and burned and sacked its hotel, printing-office, and many of its dwellings.

It was in the midst of such passion and tumult that the political parties held their conventions for the presidential campaign of 1856. The delegates of the American or "Know Nothing" Party had met as early as February, nominating Millard Fillmore for President and rejecting the platform which had been before adopted by the "National Council." The rejecting motion, however, stated that no candidates would be nominated who were not in favor of interdicting slavery by Congressional action north of the old line of 36° 30'. A seceding section of the party later held another convention and nominated Colonel John C. Frémont in place of Fillmore.

The Democrats held their convention at Cincinnati instead of Baltimore, and in spite of all the turbulence in Kansas flatly reiterated their adherence to the Compromise of 1850, the Kansas-Nebraska Act, the impotence of Congress to deal with the question of slavery, and the right of "squatter sovereignty." After seventeen ballots, the American Minister to England, Buchanan, was nominated for the presidency, and John C. Breckenridge of Kentucky was joined with him on the ticket.

On the 17th of June the new Republican Party assembled at Philadelphia with tremendous enthusiasm and nominated Colonel Frémont, who had already secured the backing of the seceding Know-Nothings. In their platform they declared that it was not only the right but the duty of Congress to prohibit slavery in the Territories, denounced the Ostend Manifesto, and demanded the immediate admission of Kansas as a free State. In September the moribund Whigs convened and nominated Fillmore on a rather colorless platform.

The campaign was a spirited one in the North but aroused no excitement in the South, where there was little question which way it would go. Although not absolutely, the election followed almost the line between the two sections, Buchanan carrying the entire

South except Maryland, where Fillmore got his only electoral votes, whereas Frémont carried all of the North and West above 36° 30′ except Pennsylvania, Indiana, Illinois, and California, which last was bisected by the line. Slavery had made the sectional character of our politics manifestly clear, and it was known that the South would not remain in the Union if a Northern man should win. The Union

YE ABOLITIONISTS IN COUNCIL—YE ORATOR OF YE DAY DENOUNCING
YE UNION
From a cartoon in "Harper's Weekly" of May 28, 1859.

would have to bow to slavery, be dissolved, or face a war. The election of 1860 would decide.

The disloyal talk, however, by no means all came from the South. The Abolitionist elements in the North had reached a pitch of fanaticism akin to insanity, as extreme fanaticism always is. At a disunionist convention at Worcester, Massachusetts, in January, 1857, Garrison shrieked for separation from the South and for "No Union with Slaveholders." Wendell Phillips called our Union "accursed of God," "built i' the eclipse, and rigged with curses dark," and declared that we were in reality two nations. The Reverend S. J.

May wanted New England immediately to secede, even if Massachusetts had to do so by herself alone. Clergymen preached to their congregations to "tread under their feet" such parts of the Bible as sanctioned slavery. Both whites and blacks were urged by Parker, Phillips, Garrison, and others to kill without compunction any one attempting to capture a runaway slave.

For such men as these and others like Charles Sumner, all sense of proportion and values had been lost. The dishonor involved in our treatment of the Indian left them cold. They were untouched by the demands for justice from their own factory laborers. For them the universe had narrowed to the slavery of the black and hatred of Southerners. Of the latter, there can be no doubt. It was shown by the indecency of Sumner's language in the Senate, and the foul-mouthed abuse of such men as the Reverend Theodore Parker, who talked of teaching manners to the South, "thriftless, idle, drunken, lewd, shrill-voiced . . . feeble bodied and ugly to look upon." For twenty years that was the sort of thing which Northern Abolitionists had been hurling indiscriminately at an entire section of our people. They were neither statesmen nor genuine humanitarians but madmen bent on burning down the whole national structure in a conflagration of hate in order that their own brand of fanaticism might be made to prevail. It is little wonder that the more radical Southerners returned defiance for defiance and gave back hate for hate.

Buchanan had been in the White House only two days when a decision of the Supreme Court roused a storm, the shock of which jarred the two sections of the nation farther apart. Churches and political parties had been split and now the highest court in the land was to be split by the question of slavery. The case had been leisurely working its way up through State and Federal Courts for ten years. Briefly, it had had its inception in suits brought by a negro named Dred Scott and his wife Harriet for their freedom from their mistress who claimed them as slaves.

Scott had been a slave in Virginia, and having been sold to an army officer had been taken by him as a servant into Illinois and Wisconsin, both free soil. In the North, Scott had married and had two children, all of the family returning with the officer when he was ordered to a post in Missouri. The owner, Emerson, dying, he left the slaves in trust for his wife, who later remarried. There were three fundamental questions involved in the suits, the somewhat complicated nature of which need not detain us. Could Scott claim to be a "citizen" of the United States, with power to sue? What was the effect on his status of his having been taken to a free State and subsequently back to a slave State? Had Congress the right to legislate as to slavery and was the Missouri Compromise, making free the domain north of 36° 30', a valid exercise of power by the legislature?

Of the members of the Supreme Court, five, including the Chief Justice, Roger B. Taney, were Southerners, and four were Northerners, of whom all the Southerners and one Northerner agreed in substance with the decision as handed down by Taney on March 6, 1857. That declared that at the time of the formation of the Constitution negroes had not been considered as forming part of "the people," and that negroes, free or slave, were not and never had been made citizens. It was also stated that Scott's having been free in a free State would not have prevented his return to the status of a slave on his having returned to a slave State, and, in addition, that slaves being property and Congress having no right to deprive citizens of their property without due process of law it had no right to legislate slavery out of the Territories, and consequently the Missouri Compromise had always been unconstitutional.

In a dissenting opinion, Justice Benjamin R. Curtis, from Massachusetts, argued that at the time of the adoption of the Constitution negroes had in point of fact been citizens in several of the States, and moreover that Congress had power to legislate with respect to property in slaves.

Our Constitution, which was adopted and ratified only with great difficulty and as a result of a series of compromises, tacit or expressed, was by no means a clear document in many respects. Much had been left in it for future interpretation should need arise. The varying individuals and States that accepted it did so unquestionably at the time with mental reservations in favor of their own varying interpretations.

In some respects, notably its attitude toward slavery, the South had remained at, and in some parts even retrograded from, the general point of view of 1787, whereas the North, partly from economic conditions and partly from sharing more in the intellectual movements of the world than the South, had advanced to a position very different from that of 1787. There was thus ample room for a genuine divergence of legal opinion, but slavery was no longer a matter to be argued from the supposed intentions of the framers of the Constitution. It had become a burning political issue, rapidly passing from the sphere of law to that of brute force, and the decision of the Court was received in the North as a blow aimed by conspirators against all the progress for freedom which had been made in more than a generation.

One result of the decision was considered to be the legalization of slavery in all the Territories, and consequently in Kansas, where the struggle between the two groups of citizens was still proceeding. The Topeka Constitution having been rejected by Congress, another attempt was made, this time by the pro-slavery element, to have the Territory admitted as a slave State. Drawing up a constitution, so worded that whoever voted for it had to sanction slavery as an institution, they submitted it to the people, and, the anti-slavery men refusing to vote at all, the pro-slavery ones declared it carried, and offered it to Congress, where a sufficient number of members denounced it as a fraud to prevent its acceptance. Kansas had still four years to wait.

Meanwhile one of our periodic panics was sweeping the country. After our recovery from that of 1837 we had, as each generation does, forgotten its lessons, and as the business of the nation rose to new levels we had expanded our operations on credit far beyond what was safe. This expansion had been easily fostered in an unhealthy way by the huge quantity of gold that was coming from California, rising to $55,000,000 in one year. In the nine years from January 1, 1849, we had built 21,000 miles of new railroads, much of them flimsily and with too little regard for immediate traffic. This sudden construction of about seven ninths of the entire mileage of the country had entailed an expenditure of about $700,000,000, a sum far greater than the people could provide. The failure of a great life insurance company which had loaned heavily on the new lines precipitated a crash in April, 1857, and within a short time practically every bank in the United States had had to suspend specie payment.

The nation was prostrate. Property fell in price anywhere from 25 to 75 per cent, business became stagnant, and the suffering among the unemployed, estimated at between 30,000 and 40,000 in New York City alone, was intense. Mobs paraded the streets with cries of "Bread or Death," and Federal forces had to protect the Sub-Treasury in that city. Construction work on the new railroads was stopped, and not only individuals and firms but cities and counties in the West were practically bankrupt. Conditions were worst in the North, the South getting off comparatively lightly, and slaves were selling there at top figures of from $1500 to $2000 each. It was not until 1860 that a real recovery started,

NEW YORK to PHILADELPHIA BANK. "Going to suspend yourself, eh? Is that your Brotherly Love?"

A CARTOON FROM *HARPER'S WEEKLY* OF OCTOBER 17, 1857

and from that point we should undoubtedly have entered upon another period of great national prosperity had it not been that the storm of war, so long gathering, was then at last to break on us.

For a little while the terror of the panic had overshadowed the discussion of slavery. The Dred Scott decision, evidently favored, if not hastened, by President Buchanan, and the abortive attempt to bring in Kansas as a slave State some months later, had made a serious rift between the Northern and Southern elements in the Democratic Party. As the leading Northern Democrat, spoken of by many as the next President, the situation had begun to grow difficult for Senator Douglas of Illinois, the founder of the "squatter sovereignty" theory for the settlement of the slavery question in the Territories, a theory apparently torn to shreds by the Supreme Court. Moreover, Douglas had sacrificed much of his popularity in the South by his opposition to the Lecompton Constitution in Kansas. Political conditions in the mid-term elections of 1858 appeared to give the new Republican Party an unusually good chance to consolidate its forces with a view to 1860, and the campaign in Illinois, where Douglas had to stand for re-election, promised to be lively. In fact, it was to become the most famous State campaign in American history.

The Republicans decided to pit against the great Douglas for the senatorship a man, forty-nine years of age, not nationally known though he had been elected to Congress in 1846 for one term, named Abraham Lincoln. He had made no reputation in Washington, where he had opposed the Mexican War and voted in favor of the Wilmot Proviso five times in his single term. He had, however, taken no great part in the slavery debate until in a political speech at Peoria on October 5, 1854, he had come out clearly with his own sentiments.

Speaking on the Kansas-Nebraska Bill and the repeal of the Missouri Compromise, he declared that the repeal was "Wrong—wrong in its direct effect, letting slavery into Kansas and Nebraska, and wrong in its prospective principle, allowing it to spread to every other part of the wide world where men can be found inclined to take it." Of the slave system he said: "I hate it because of the monstrous injustice of slavery itself. I hate it because it enables the enemies of our free institutions with plausibility to taunt us as hypocrites; causes the real friends of freedom to doubt our sincerity; and especially because it forces so many good men among ourselves into an open war with the very fundamental principles of civil liberty." The holders of slaves, however, Lincoln added, were not to be blamed,—"they are just what we would be in their situation."

He could appreciate all that the South said about the difficulty of ridding itself of the institution. "I surely will not blame them for not doing what I should not know how to do myself. If all earthly power were given to me, I should not know what to do as to the existing institution." If Lincoln was little known in the East and

South, his political activities, and especaly this speech, had made him famous in the Northwest. On the other hand, raw, gaunt, unattractive in personal appearance, poor, a failure in his political career, running on the ticket of a party that had become a national one only two years before, he seemed an unimportant antagonist for the great Democratic leader, Douglas, a man of international repute, popular, a noted speaker, buttressed with powerful friends and influences, one of the outstanding figures in the nation.

Lincoln, however, dared to challenge his opponent to a series of debates through the summer and autumn, to be held at such places throughout the State that practically all the voters might have an opportunity to hear the two candidates thresh out the questions of the campaign. Before they began, Lincoln made a speech at the nominating convention which expressed the heart of its doctrine for the Republican Party in the coming years of its eventful history, though condemned by one of his friends to whom he read it in private before delivery, as "a damned fool utterance." Another friend, Herndon, was nearer the truth when he told Lincoln it would make him President.

In the course of it, the senatorial candidate made what was to become a classic declaration. Pointing out that all attempts at compromise had failed, and that the policy of the Democrats to suppress the agitation of the slavery question had been without effect, he continued, "In my opinion it will not cease until a crisis has been reached and passed. 'A house divided against itself cannot stand.' I believe this government cannot endure permanently half slave and half free. I do not expect the Union to be dissolved—I do not expect the house to fall—but I do expect it will cease to be divided. It will become all one thing, or all the other. Either the opponents of slavery will arrest the further spread of it and place it where the public mind shall rest in the belief that it is in course of ultimate extinction, or its advocates will push it forward, till it shall become alike lawful in all the States, old as well as new—North as well as South. Have we no tendency to the latter condition?"

This speech was taken up by Douglas after the debates began, with the question as to why, after all, a Union of slave and free States could not continue in harmony. In the course of their swing around the circuit, speaking before vast audiences which numbered thousands, every aspect of the slavery question was debated. In view of the situation created by the Kansas-Nebraska Bill, Lincoln asked point-blank of the advocate of squatter sovereignty, "Can the people of a United States Territory, in any lawful way, against the wish of any citizen of the United States, exclude slavery from its limits prior to the formation of a State constitution?"

The only answer, which Lincoln had foreseen, was that the sole manner in which they could do so, but an effective one, would be to refuse to pass laws protecting that form of property,—much the same manœuvre, it may be noted, to which some States have resorted in the more recent fight over Prohibition enforcement. Although Lincoln had destroyed any chance which Douglas might have had for the presidency by forcing him into expressions of opinion that ruined him in the South, Douglas won the senatorial election by 190,000 to 174,000 for candidates to the legislature, which later elected Douglas to the national Senate by 54 to 46. The chief result of the famous campaign was that Lincoln had become a national figure.

Even amid crashing banks and failing firms, the slavery question had once more come to the front. In Wisconsin the legislature threatened to nullify the Fugitive Slave Law in defiance of the Supreme Court, but an act of violence by a Northerner was in a few months to startle the nation and anger the South even as it had not yet been. On October 16, 1859, the fanatic, John Brown, whom we have already found murdering Southerners in Kansas, seized the arsenal at Harper's Ferry, Virginia, and with his party of nineteen, part white and part black, terrorized the town. His plan had been to start a slave insurrection, the nightmare of the South for two centuries, and a movement which, if it had spread, would have entailed on our white men and women unspeakable horrors and atrocities. The party was quickly captured by a small Federal force under Colonel Robert E. Lee, and after a fair trial Brown was condemned and hanged for treason, criminal conspiracy, and murder. His fanatical courage at the end, and the great dignity of his presence, should not blind us to the criminal recklessness of his insensate act. Emerson might claim him as a "new saint" who had made "the gallows glorious like the cross," but soberer Northern opinion properly condemned him. The only effect in the South was to inflame passions yet more and bring one step nearer the "impending crisis."

In 1857 a book with that title, severely criticising the economic value of slavery, had been published by a Southerner, H. R. Helper, and about the time of Brown's raid was republished and spread broadcast by the Republicans, again adding to the resentment of the South, which at that time had reached a high point of prosperity as contrasted with the North, not yet emerged from the panic. Steps, frequently violent, were taken in the South to prevent the circulation of Helper's book, and perhaps nothing shows more clearly how impossible any sane consideration of slavery had become, in either section, than this refusal of the South to permit a book written by one of its own citizens, mainly on the economics of the slave system as contrasted with the wage system, to be read by its people. The approaching election of 1860 was clearly to be the most fateful in the history of our nation.

In a little over two generations the inhabitants of the original thirteen weak and jealous British colonies had achieved not only their independence, but had spread over a continent and had erected a great Federal Union. The world had freely predicted that such a Union could not last. The problem of whether or not that Union was in reality strong and enduring or whether it would be broken in two, gradually perhaps to disintegrate into more numerous smaller units, was now at last to be presented to our people in such a form as to prevent any escape from grappling with it even to death. It has been the rise of the Union with which we have been chiefly concerned in this first volume. In the next and final one, we shall follow the great struggle for its maintenance, and, success having been achieved, watch the evolution of modern, complex, industrial America from the comparatively simple agricultural nation of the days before our Civil War.

INDEX

INDEX

415

INDEX

INDEX

INDEX

INDEX

INDEX

421

INDEX

INDEX

INDEX

INDEX

INDEX

Virginia, 7, 27, 28, 30, 33, 58, 64, 65, 71, 153, 199; the first charter, 10; settlement in, 11; the first Virginians, 12; a Royal Colony, 13; prosperity of, 14; colony of, 15; people in revolt, 36; Germans in, 56; life in, 60; ratifies Constitution, 164; most populous State, 195; design for capitol, 205; dynasty of, 285

Virginia Dare, first English child in America, 11

Virginia Gazettes, 73

Virginia Plan, the, 156

Virginia Resolves, drawn up by George Mason, introduced by George Washington, 86, 94, 193

Votes, Apportionment of, 211

Wages, high, 78; increase of wage earners, 315

Wall Street, 167

War of the Austrian Succession, 46

War of 1812, 237 f.; events leading to, 229; blame for, 245; attitude toward, 246; plans badly executed, 247; luck at sea, 248; campaign, 248; a stalemate, 256; losses of, 260

War on England and Spain declared by France, 178

"War Hawks," 242

"War of Jenkin's Ear," 45

War of Spanish Succession, 44

Warner, Colonel Seth, 126

Warr, Lord de la, bringing food, 12

Warren, Commodore, 46

Warwick, Earl of, 8

Washington, George, brothers of, 46; first command, 47; saving of Braddock's army, 48; delegate, 103; Commander-in-chief of American forces, 109; one of most prominent men in Virginia, 110; condition of army, 111; no efficient War Department, 112; difficulties overcome, 112; efforts at organizing army, 115; takes Boston, 117; marches to New York, 117; protest against independence, 118; masterly retreat across East River, 123; across the Delaware, 123, 124; movement of troops around New York, 123; march to Trenton, 124; at Morristown, 124; interference of Congress, 124; watches Howe, 125; army destitute, 128; overruled by Congress, 131; makes Cornwallis's army his objective, 133; issues order against secret meetings, 137; appearance at Newburg, 137; last leave of officers, 138; return to Mount Vernon, 138; statue of, 138; tribute of English historian, 138; made chairman of Constitutional Convention, 154; influence of, 160; chosen President, 165; ambition to live at Mount Vernon, 166; starts to New York to assume presidency, 166; First Inaugural Address, 168; signs Bank Bill, 175; rift in his Cabinet, 176; unanimously re-elected, 177; faced by problem of French Revolution, 179; adopts Jefferson's view, 179; issues Proclamation of Neutrality, 179; war in his Cabinet, 181; calls out State militia, 185; assailed, 186; declines to be candidate, 186; "Farewell Address," 187; death of, 194; office-holders, 217; leader of Virginia dynasty, 285; characterization, 286; life of, by Irving, 333; quoted, 111, 116, 129, 141, 155, 183, 187, 203

Washington, city of, 201 f.

Wasp, sloop of war, 248

Water Fowl, The, by Bryant, 331

Watertown, town of, 19; tax levied, 23

Wayne, Anthony, protest of, 118, 184

Wealth, of Orient, 47; in New England, 64 f.; in the South, 263

Weaving, changes in, 314

Webster, Daniel, 282, 305, 307, 350, 353, 378, 380; quoted, 292, 301, 302; vote on tariff, 292; famous reply to Hayne, 300; effect of reply to Hayne, 302; views on private profit, 306; character of, 308; views of Constitution, 373; Seventh of March speech, 381; wrath against, 382; Secretary of State, 386; death of, 390

Webster, Pelatiah, attempts to fix prices, 142

Wellington, Duke of, 252

Welshmen, styles of, 59, 64

Wendell, Barrett, quoted, 332

Wesley, John, 70

West, the, opening of, 144; national aspect, 145; contrasted with East, 146; interests distinct from East, 149; problem of lands, 160; development of, 183; religion in, 209; characteristics of, 209; life of settlements, 210; migration to, 263; wealth accumulating in, 267; route to, 265; mistrust of banking, 305

West, Benjamin, President of the Royal Academy in London, 67

West Indies, 16, 26, 47, 67, 81, 178; trade with, 36; new seat of war, 129

West Point, Military Academy at, established, 219

Westchester, manors in, 60

Western Union Company, founded, 322

Westover, 65

Westsylvania, proposed State, 145

Whigs, 168, 310, 350, 359; convention at Harrisburg, 344; convention at Baltimore, 389

Whiskey, 185; tax on, abolished, 218; drinking, 325

White House, the, 202, 213, 227, 295, 297, 298, 311, 350, 396, 398, 404

White Plains, battle of, 123

Whitefield, George, 70

Whitman, Marcus, across Rockies, 359

Whitman, Walt, 331. *See Leaves of Grass*

Whitney's cotton gin, 203

Whittier, John Greenleaf, 334, 372, 391

Wieland, novel by Brown, 201

Wilkinson, General, 227

William and Mary, news of accession, 39

William and Mary College, 68, 69

Williams, Roger, 23, 26, 28

Willis, Nathaniel P., poet, 331

Wilmington, colony of Swedes, 29

Wilmot Proviso, 366, 374

Wilson, Alexander, poet and ornithologist, 201

Wilson, James, 154, 155, 160

Wine Islands, 28

Winslow, John, news from England, 39

Winter of 1778-9, dark for American cause, 128

Winthrop, John, 19, 21, 23; first governor, 18; sails for Massachusetts, 19; death of, 26

Wirt, William, *British Spy*, 204

Wirt, William, of Virginia, attorney general, 260

Witchcraft, in Massachusetts, 61

Wolcott, Oliver, in Adams's Cabinet, 189

Women, Convention for Rights, 326; humanitarian reforms, 326; released from drudgery, 342

Woodbury, Levi, Navy Department, 303

Word of God, interpreters of, 19

Workingman's Party formed, 317

World, the European, 3

World Anti-Slavery Convention, 326

INDEX